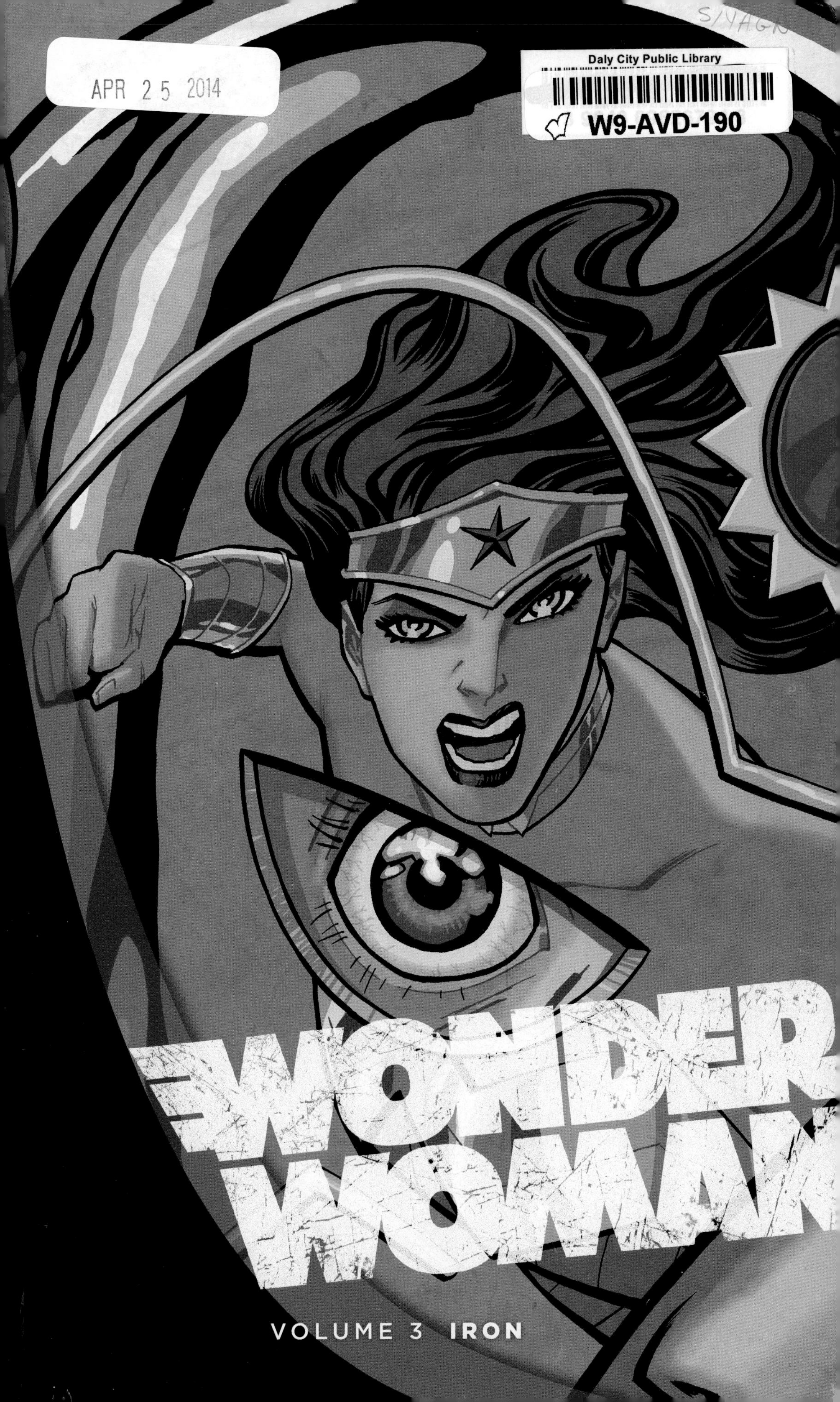
WONDER WOMAN
VOLUME 3 IRON

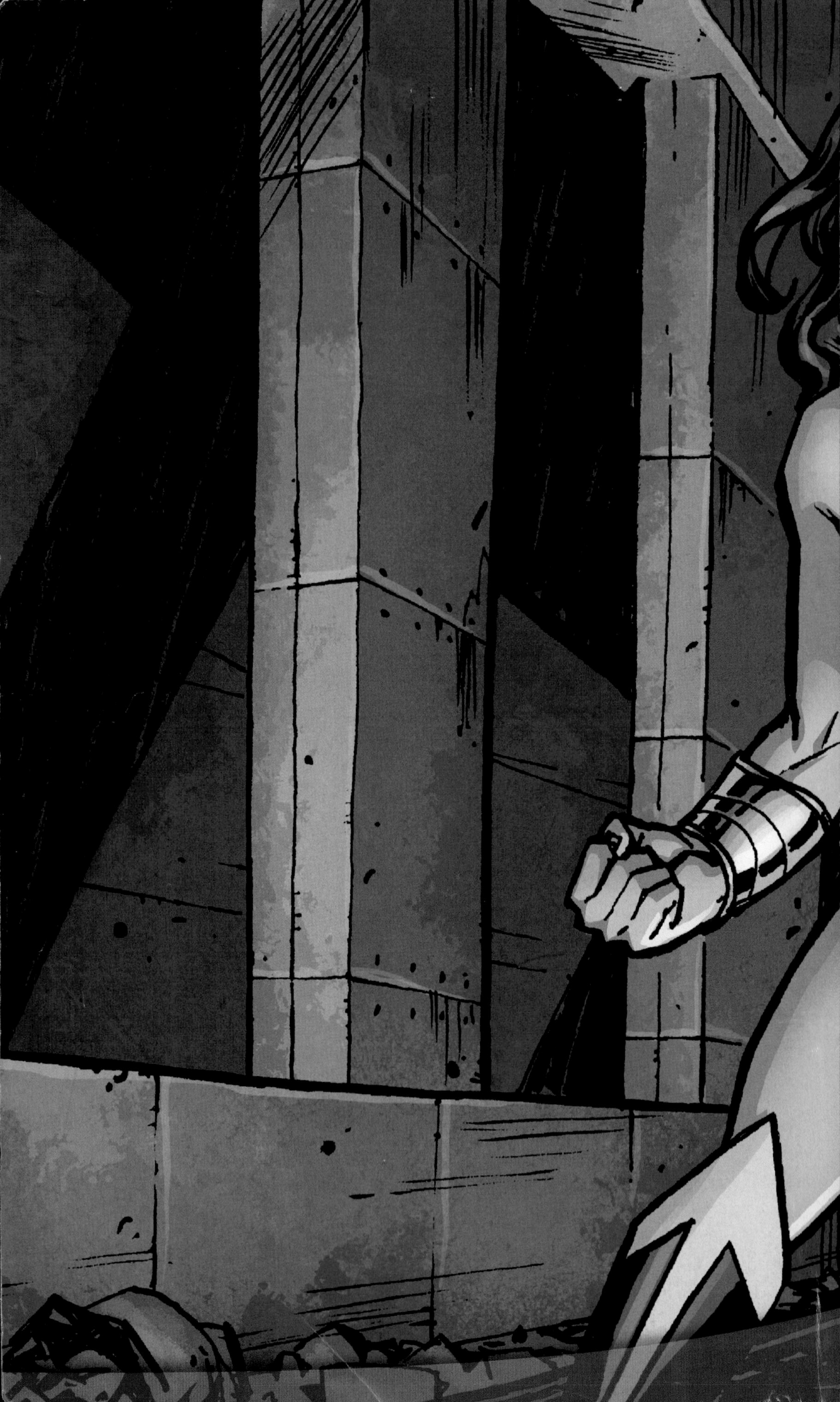

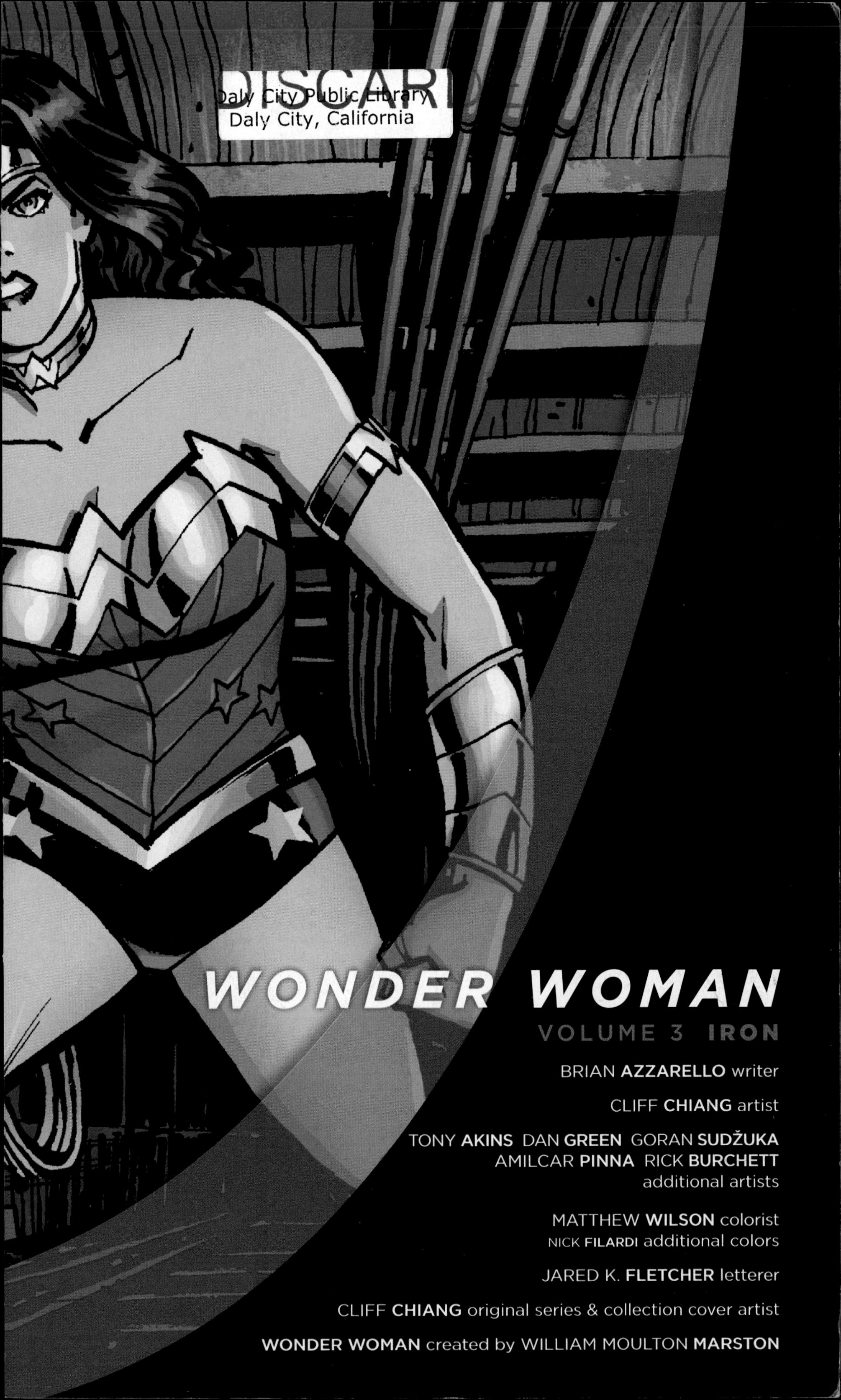

WONDER WOMAN

VOLUME 3 IRON

BRIAN **AZZARELLO** writer

CLIFF **CHIANG** artist

TONY **AKINS** DAN **GREEN** GORAN **SUDŽUKA**
AMILCAR **PINNA** RICK **BURCHETT**
additional artists

MATTHEW **WILSON** colorist
NICK **FILARDI** additional colors

JARED K. **FLETCHER** letterer

CLIFF **CHIANG** original series & collection cover artist

WONDER WOMAN created by WILLIAM MOULTON **MARSTON**

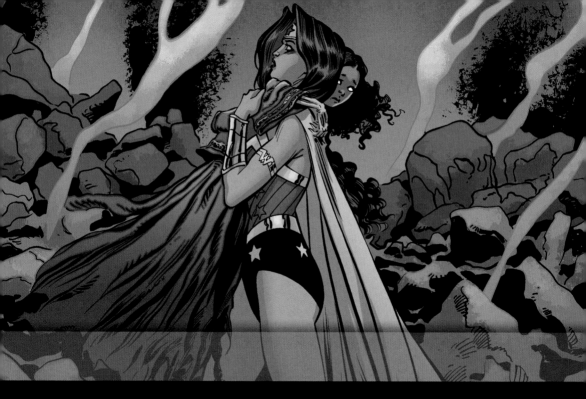

MATT IDELSON Editor - Original Series CHRIS CONROY Associate Editor - Original Series
RACHEL PINNELAS Editor ROBBIN BROSTERMAN Design Director - Books
ROBBIE BIEDERMAN Publication Design

BOB HARRAS Senior VP - Editor-in-Chief, DC Comics

DIANE NELSON President DAN DIDIO and JIM LEE Co-Publishers
GEOFF JOHNS Chief Creative Officer
JOHN ROOD Executive VP - Sales, Marketing and Business Development
AMY GENKINS Senior VP - Business and Legal Affairs NAIRI GARDINER Senior VP - Finance
JEFF BOISON VP - Publishing Planning MARK CHIARELLO VP - Art Direction and Design
JOHN CUNNINGHAM VP - Marketing TERRI CUNNINGHAM VP - Editorial Administration
ALISON GILL Senior VP - Manufacturing and Operations HANK KANALZ Senior VP - Vertigo and Integrated Publishing
JAY KOGAN VP - Business and Legal Affairs, Publishing JACK MAHAN VP - Business Affairs, Talent
NICK NAPOLITANO VP - Manufacturing Administration SUE POHJA VP - Book Sales
COURTNEY SIMMONS Senior VP - Publicity BOB WAYNE Senior VP - Sales

WONDER WOMAN VOLUME 3: IRON

DC Comics, 1700 Broadway, New York, NY 10019
A Warner Bros. Entertainment Company.
Printed by RR Donnelley, Salem, VA, USA. 2/07/14. First Printing.

ISBN: 978-1-4012-4607-5

SUSTAINABLE FORESTRY INITIATIVE
Certified Chain of Custody
At Least 20% Certified Forest Content
www.sfiprogram.org
SFI-01042
APPLIES TO TEXT STOCK ONLY

Library of Congress Cataloging-in-Publication Data

Azzarello, Brian.
Wonder Woman. Volume 3, Iron / Brian Azzarello, Cliff Chiang, Tony Akins.
pages cm
"Originally published in single magazine form in Wonder Woman 13-18."
ISBN 978-1-4012-4261-9
1. Graphic novels. I. Chiang, Cliff. II. Akins, Tony. III. Title. IV. Title: Iron.
PN6728.W6A99 2013
741.5'973—dc23
2013016905

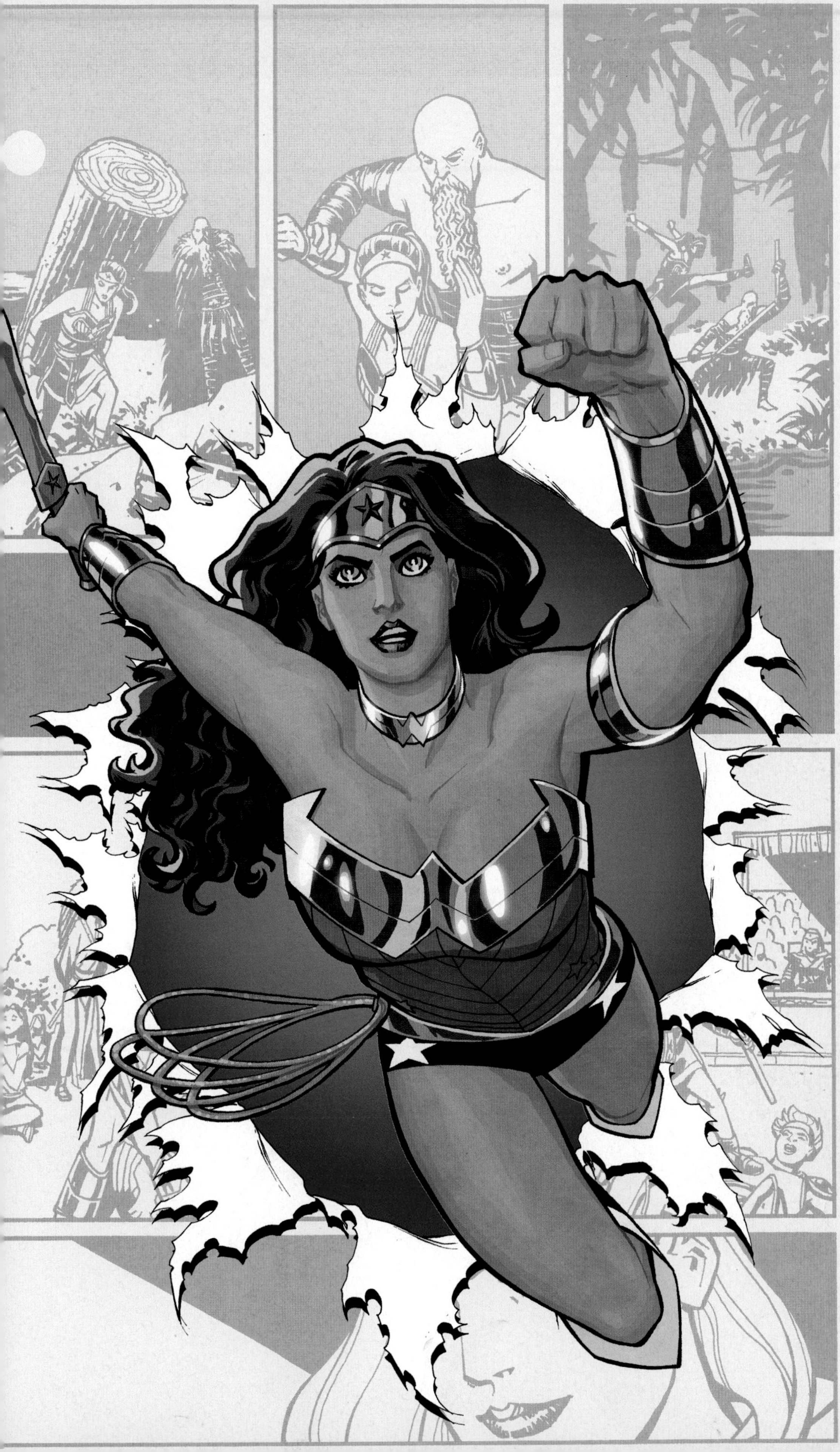

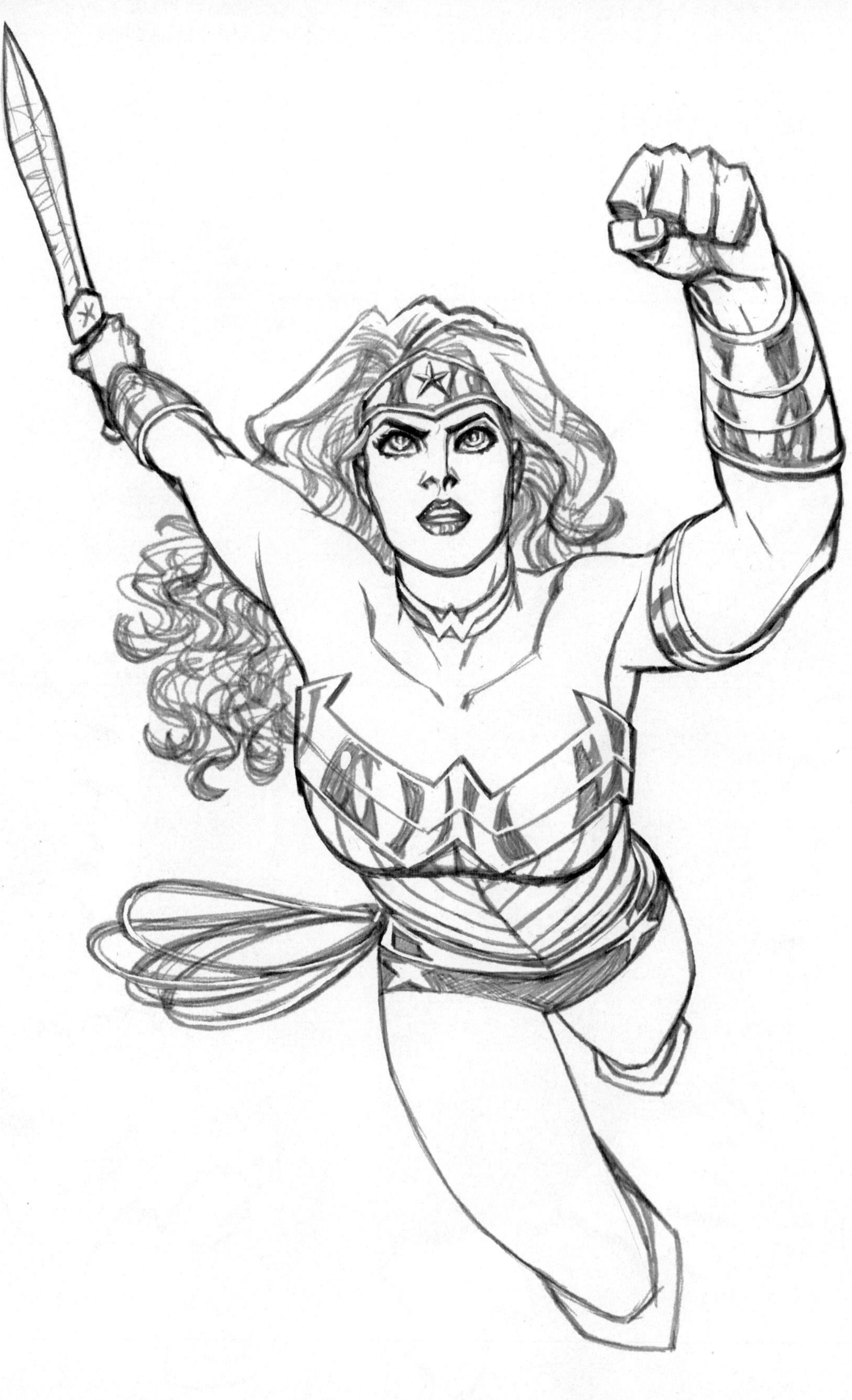

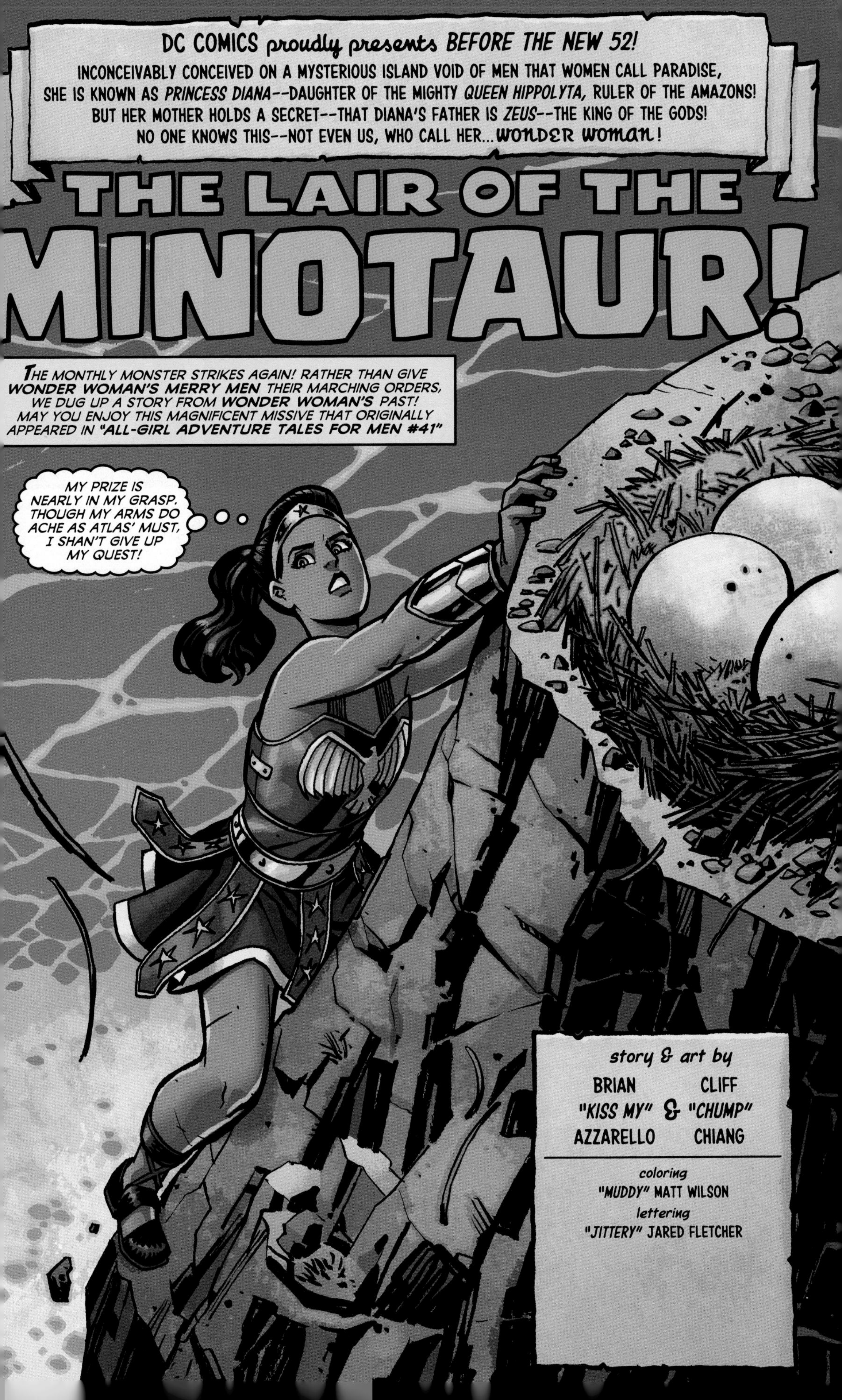
DC COMICS proudly presents BEFORE THE NEW 52!
INCONCEIVABLY CONCEIVED ON A MYSTERIOUS ISLAND VOID OF MEN THAT WOMEN CALL PARADISE, SHE IS KNOWN AS PRINCESS DIANA--DAUGHTER OF THE MIGHTY QUEEN HIPPOLYTA, RULER OF THE AMAZONS! BUT HER MOTHER HOLDS A SECRET--THAT DIANA'S FATHER IS ZEUS--THE KING OF THE GODS! NO ONE KNOWS THIS--NOT EVEN US, WHO CALL HER...WONDER WOMAN!
THE LAIR OF THE MINOTAUR!
THE MONTHLY MONSTER STRIKES AGAIN! RATHER THAN GIVE WONDER WOMAN'S MERRY MEN THEIR MARCHING ORDERS, WE DUG UP A STORY FROM WONDER WOMAN'S PAST! MAY YOU ENJOY THIS MAGNIFICENT MISSIVE THAT ORIGINALLY APPEARED IN "ALL-GIRL ADVENTURE TALES FOR MEN #41"
MY PRIZE IS NEARLY IN MY GRASP. THOUGH MY ARMS DO ACHE AS ATLAS' MUST, I SHAN'T GIVE UP MY QUEST!
story & art by BRIAN "KISS MY" AZZARELLO & CLIFF "CHUMP" CHIANG
coloring "MUDDY" MATT WILSON
lettering "JITTERY" JARED FLETCHER

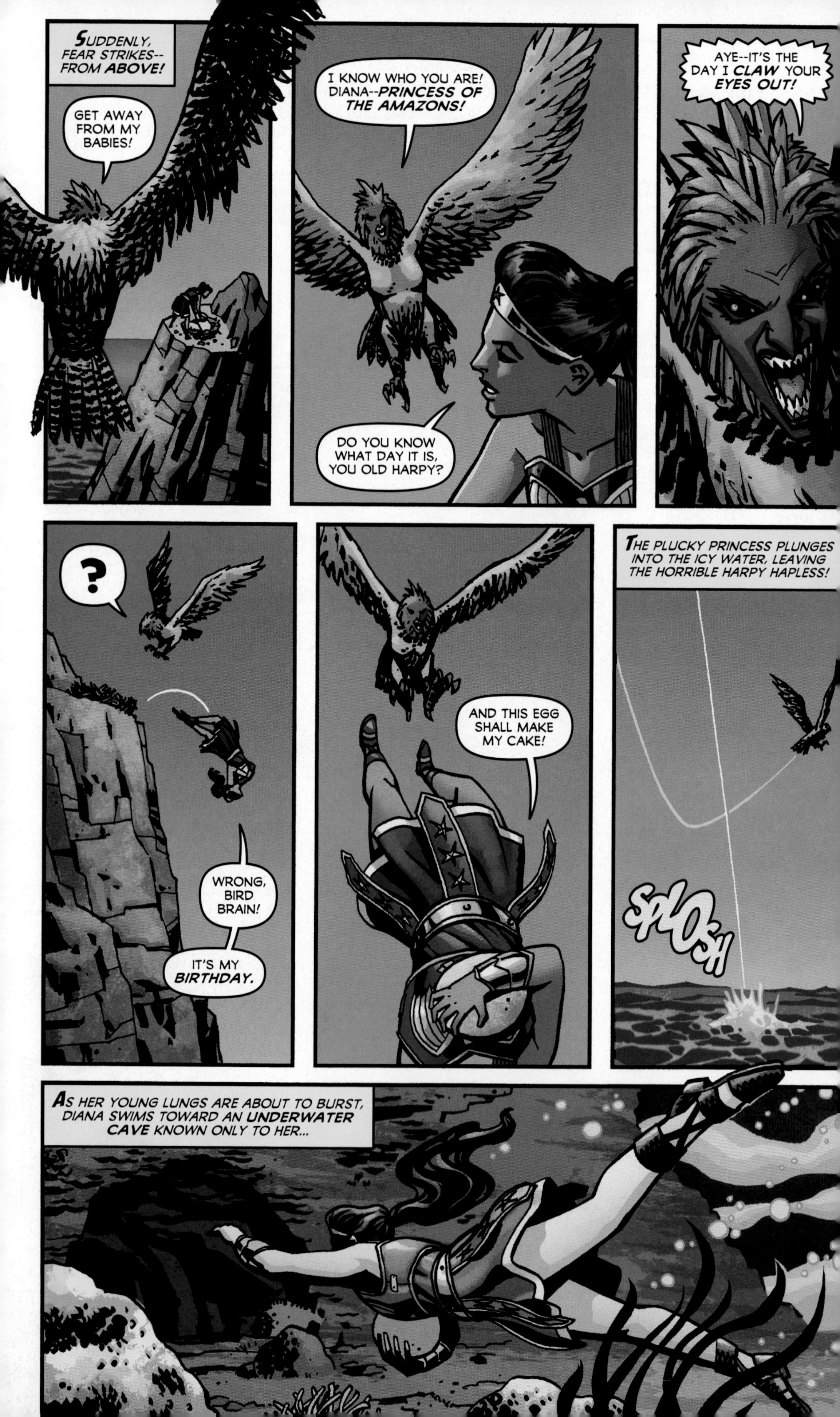
SUDDENLY, FEAR STRIKES-- FROM ABOVE!
GET AWAY FROM MY BABIES!
I KNOW WHO YOU ARE! DIANA--PRINCESS OF THE AMAZONS!
DO YOU KNOW WHAT DAY IT IS, YOU OLD HARPY?
AYE--IT'S THE DAY I CLAW YOUR EYES OUT!
?
WRONG, BIRD BRAIN!
IT'S MY BIRTHDAY.
AND THIS EGG SHALL MAKE MY CAKE!
THE PLUCKY PRINCESS PLUNGES INTO THE ICY WATER, LEAVING THE HORRIBLE HARPY HAPLESS!
SPLOSH
AS HER YOUNG LUNGS ARE ABOUT TO BURST, DIANA SWIMS TOWARD AN UNDERWATER CAVE KNOWN ONLY TO HER...

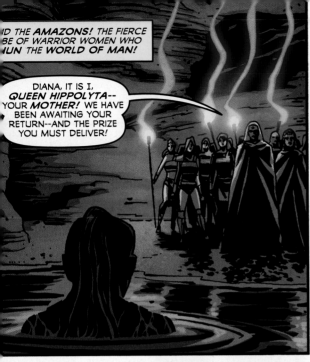

...ND THE **AMAZONS!** THE FIERCE ...BE OF WARRIOR WOMEN WHO ...UN THE **WORLD OF MAN!**

DIANA, IT IS I, *QUEEN HIPPOLYTA--* YOUR **MOTHER!** WE HAVE BEEN AWAITING YOUR RETURN--AND THE PRIZE YOU MUST DELIVER!

QUEEN HIPPOLYTA'S TONE MASKS HER CONCERN...FOR SHE KNOWS THAT MANY YOUNG AMAZONS *FAIL* IN THEIR QUESTS...

TODAY IS YOUR BIRTHDAY...

AS IS OUR CUSTOM, YOU NEED TO PRESENT ME WITH A *SUITABLE PRESENT*, OR THE PASSING OF YOUR YEAR WILL *NOT* BE ACKNOWLEDGED.

MY QUEEN, FORGIVE ME. ALL I COULD FIND...

...IS A *HARPY'S EGG!*

HOORAY FOR PRINCESS DIANA!

...FROM THE SHADOWS AN ...MINOUS FIGURE DRAPED IN VULTURE PLUMES STANDS IN WATCH...

THE GIRL EXHIBITS SKILLS FAR BEYOND HER YOUNG AGE...

PERHAPS *SHE* IS THE ONE...

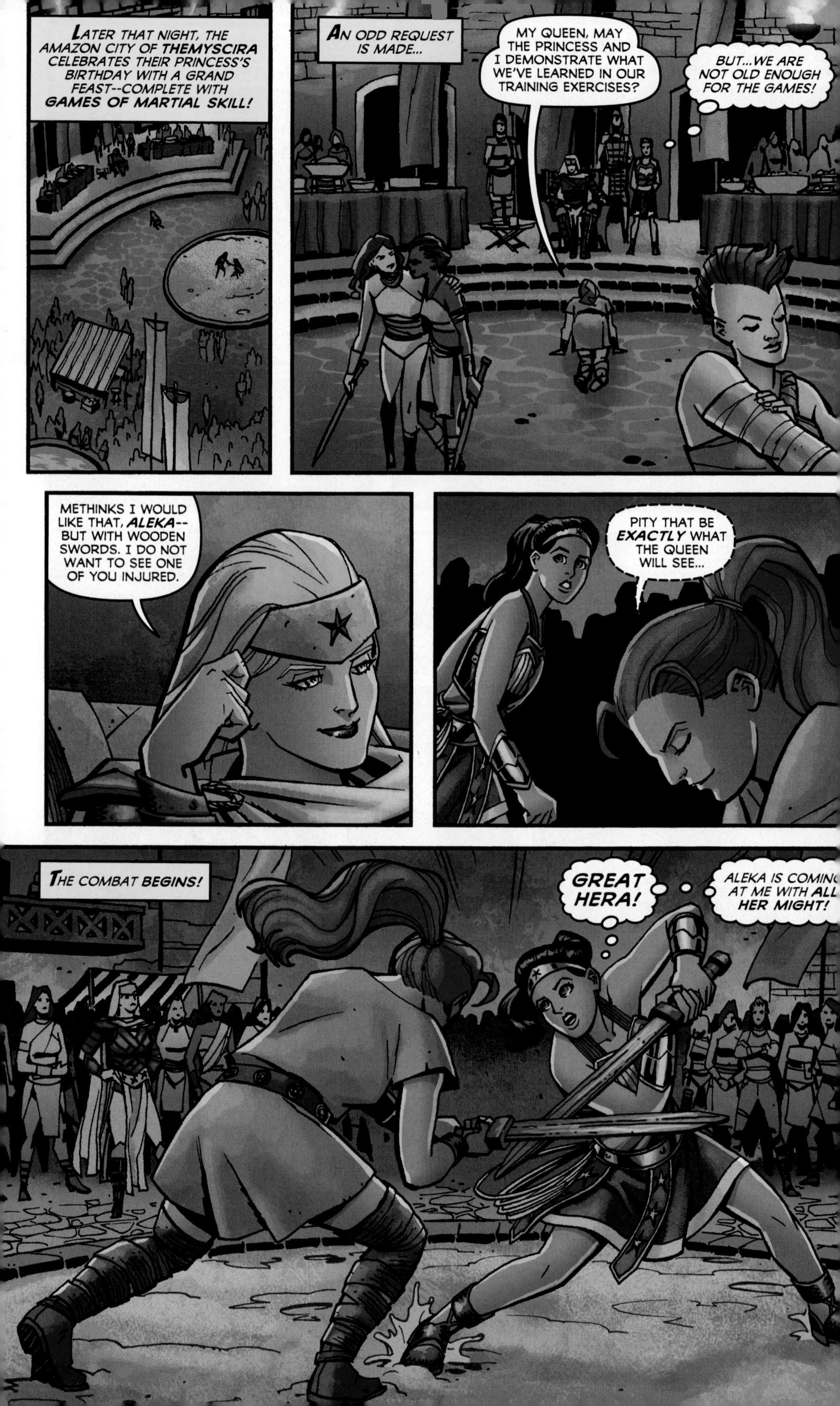
LATER THAT NIGHT, THE AMAZON CITY OF THEMYSCIRA CELEBRATES THEIR PRINCESS'S BIRTHDAY WITH A GRAND FEAST--COMPLETE WITH GAMES OF MARTIAL SKILL!
AN ODD REQUEST IS MADE...
MY QUEEN, MAY THE PRINCESS AND I DEMONSTRATE WHAT WE'VE LEARNED IN OUR TRAINING EXERCISES?
BUT...WE ARE NOT OLD ENOUGH FOR THE GAMES!
METHINKS I WOULD LIKE THAT, ALEKA-- BUT WITH WOODEN SWORDS. I DO NOT WANT TO SEE ONE OF YOU INJURED.
PITY THAT BE EXACTLY WHAT THE QUEEN WILL SEE...
THE COMBAT BEGINS!
GREAT HERA!
ALEKA IS COMIN AT ME WITH ALL HER MIGHT!

ALEKA IS FIGHTING FOR REAL--MEANING I'D BETTER, TOO! I DO NOT WISH TO HURT HER THOUGH, SO PERHAPS IF I...

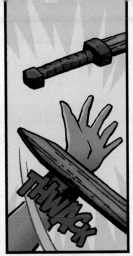

THWACK

YIELD?

NEVER! I AM A TRUE AMAZON WARRIOR!

NOT YET YOU'RE NOT!

WELL, YOU WILL NEVER BE...

CLAY!

THE MUD STINGS, BUT NOT AS MUCH AS ALEKA'S WORDS...

...WORDS THAT SEND THE PRINCESS INTO A RAGE!

TAKE IT BACK!

≷KOFF≷

YIELD!

≷KOFF≷

DAUGHTER, STOP! YOU'RE HURTING HER!

I--

I'M SORRY!

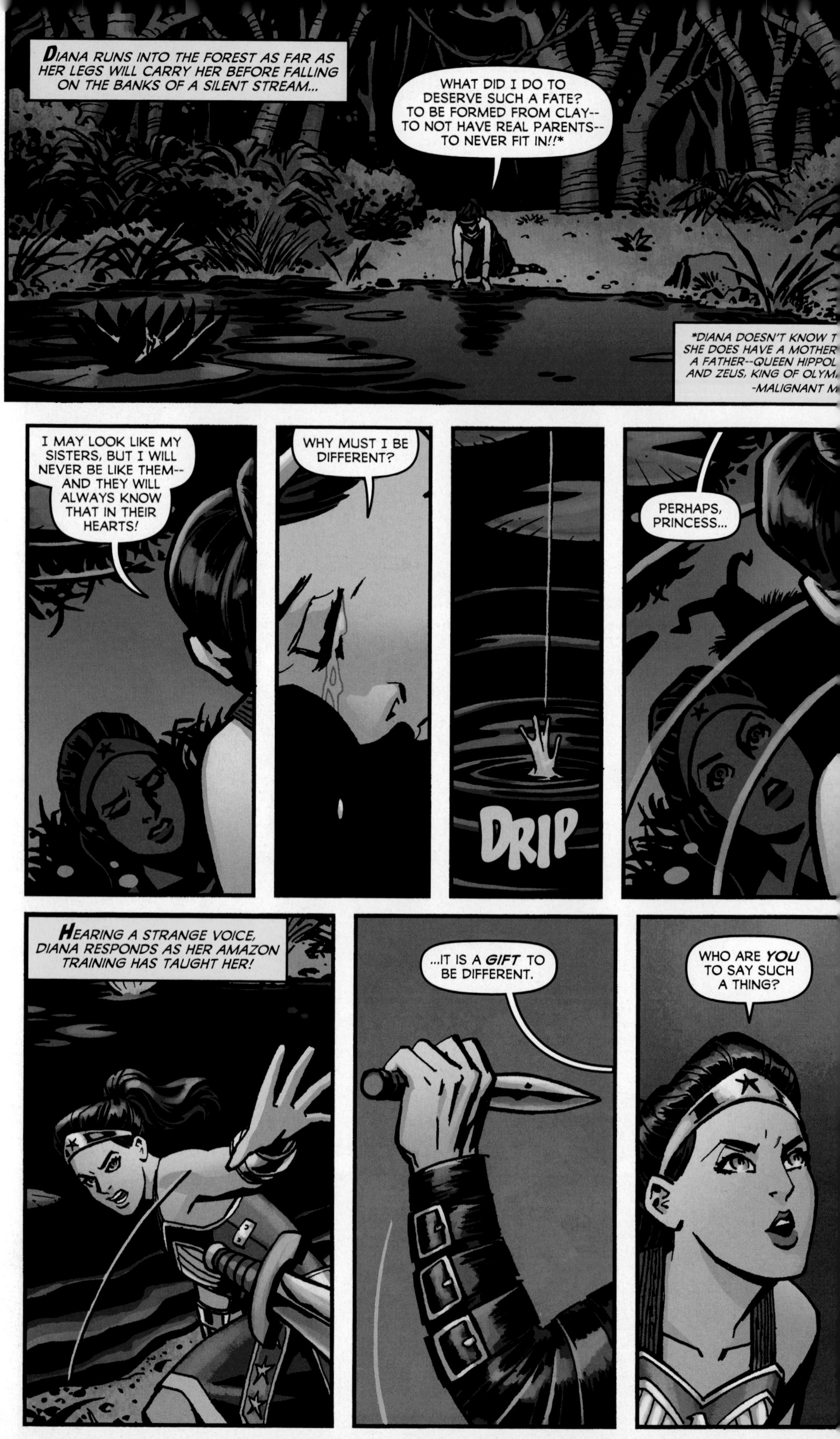
DIANA RUNS INTO THE FOREST AS FAR AS HER LEGS WILL CARRY HER BEFORE FALLING ON THE BANKS OF A SILENT STREAM...
WHAT DID I DO TO DESERVE SUCH A FATE? TO BE FORMED FROM CLAY-- TO NOT HAVE REAL PARENTS-- TO NEVER FIT IN!!*
I MAY LOOK LIKE MY SISTERS, BUT I WILL NEVER BE LIKE THEM-- AND THEY WILL ALWAYS KNOW THAT IN THEIR HEARTS!
WHY MUST I BE DIFFERENT?
DRIP
PERHAPS, PRINCESS...
HEARING A STRANGE VOICE, DIANA RESPONDS AS HER AMAZON TRAINING HAS TAUGHT HER!
...IT IS A GIFT TO BE DIFFERENT.
WHO ARE YOU TO SAY SUCH A THING?

*DIANA DOESN'T KNOW T
SHE DOES HAVE A MOTHER
A FATHER--QUEEN HIPPOL
AND ZEUS, KING OF OLYM
-MALIGNANT M

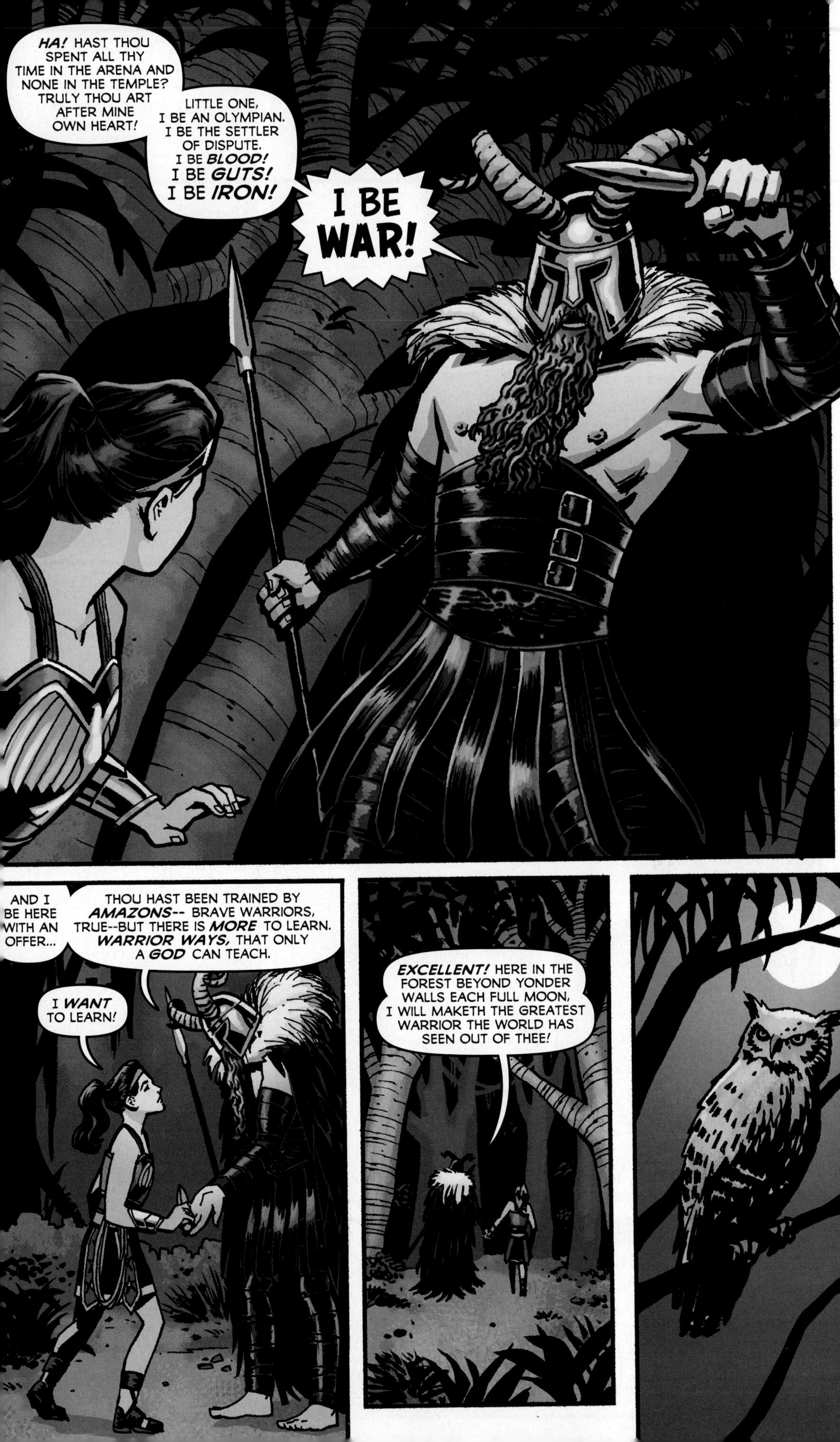

HA! HAST THOU SPENT ALL THY TIME IN THE ARENA AND NONE IN THE TEMPLE? TRULY THOU ART AFTER MINE OWN HEART!
LITTLE ONE, I BE AN OLYMPIAN. I BE THE SETTLER OF DISPUTE. I BE BLOOD! I BE GUTS! I BE IRON!
I BE WAR!
AND I BE HERE WITH AN OFFER...
THOU HAST BEEN TRAINED BY AMAZONS-- BRAVE WARRIORS, TRUE--BUT THERE IS MORE TO LEARN. WARRIOR WAYS, THAT ONLY A GOD CAN TEACH.
I WANT TO LEARN!
EXCELLENT! HERE IN THE FOREST BEYOND YONDER WALLS EACH FULL MOON, I WILL MAKETH THE GREATEST WARRIOR THE WORLD HAS SEEN OUT OF THEE!

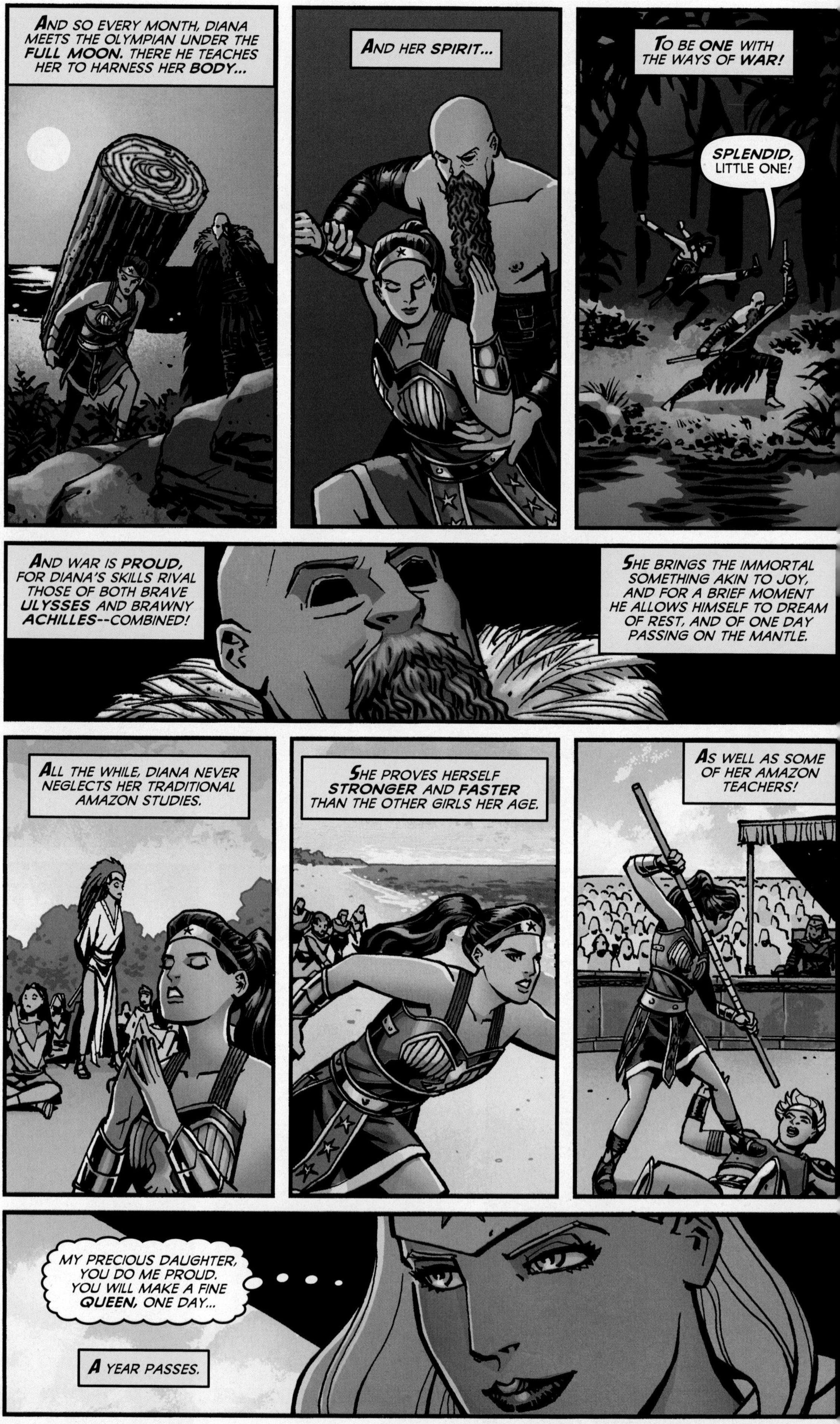
AND SO EVERY MONTH, DIANA MEETS THE OLYMPIAN UNDER THE FULL MOON. THERE HE TEACHES HER TO HARNESS HER BODY...
AND HER SPIRIT...
TO BE ONE WITH THE WAYS OF WAR!
SPLENDID, LITTLE ONE!
AND WAR IS PROUD, FOR DIANA'S SKILLS RIVAL THOSE OF BOTH BRAVE ULYSSES AND BRAWNY ACHILLES--COMBINED!
SHE BRINGS THE IMMORTAL SOMETHING AKIN TO JOY, AND FOR A BRIEF MOMENT HE ALLOWS HIMSELF TO DREAM OF REST, AND OF ONE DAY PASSING ON THE MANTLE.
ALL THE WHILE, DIANA NEVER NEGLECTS HER TRADITIONAL AMAZON STUDIES.
SHE PROVES HERSELF STRONGER AND FASTER THAN THE OTHER GIRLS HER AGE.
AS WELL AS SOME OF HER AMAZON TEACHERS!
MY PRECIOUS DAUGHTER, YOU DO ME PROUD. YOU WILL MAKE A FINE QUEEN, ONE DAY...
A YEAR PASSES.

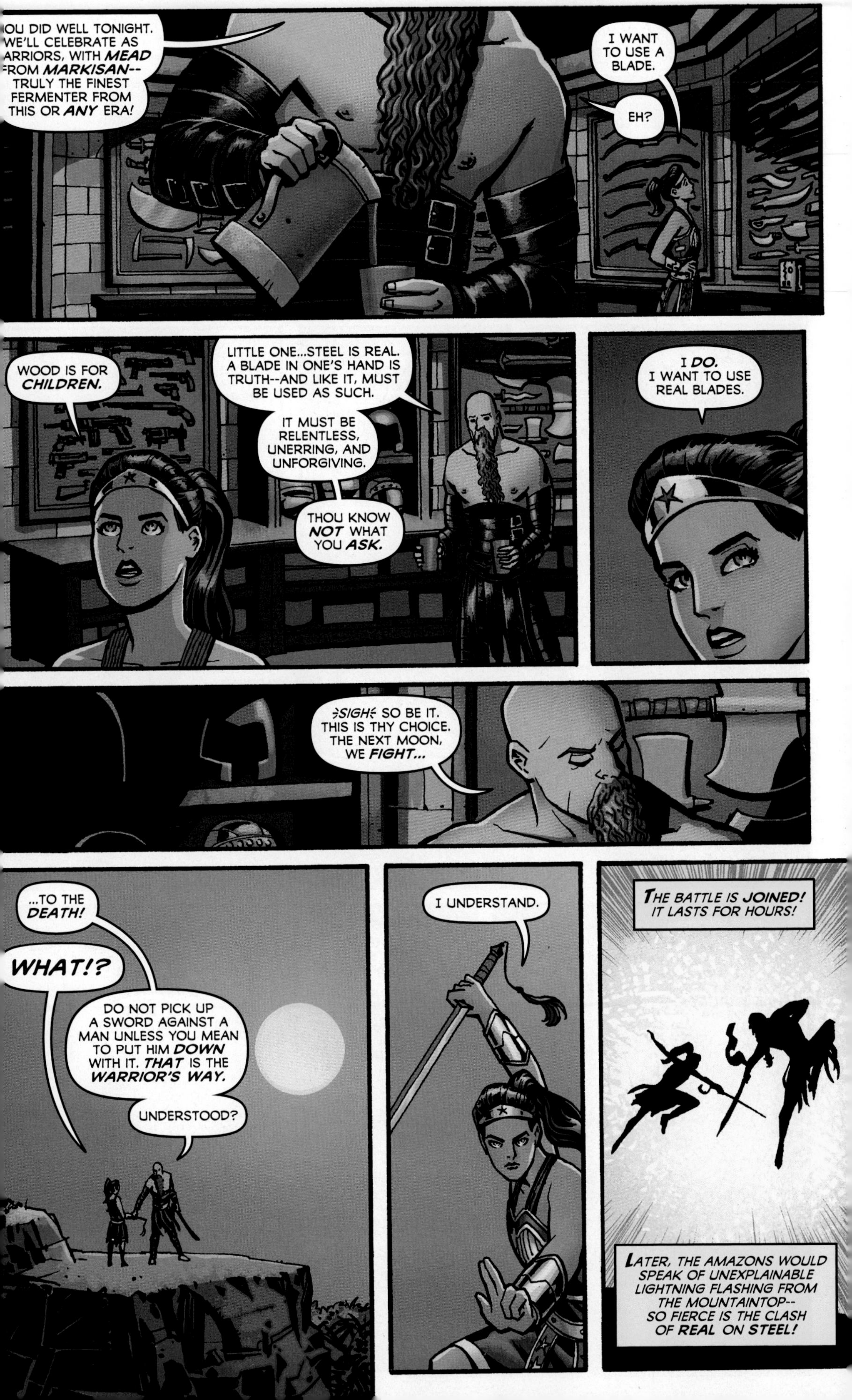

OU DID WELL TONIGHT. WE'LL CELEBRATE AS ARRIORS, WITH *MEAD* FROM *MARKISAN*-- TRULY THE FINEST FERMENTER FROM THIS OR *ANY* ERA!
I WANT TO USE A BLADE.
EH?
WOOD IS FOR *CHILDREN.*
LITTLE ONE...STEEL IS REAL. A BLADE IN ONE'S HAND IS TRUTH--AND LIKE IT, MUST BE USED AS SUCH.
IT MUST BE RELENTLESS, UNERRING, AND UNFORGIVING.
THOU KNOW *NOT* WHAT YOU *ASK.*
I *DO.* I WANT TO USE REAL BLADES.
SIGH SO BE IT. THIS IS THY CHOICE. THE NEXT MOON, WE *FIGHT*...
...TO THE *DEATH!*
WHAT!?
DO NOT PICK UP A SWORD AGAINST A MAN UNLESS YOU MEAN TO PUT HIM *DOWN* WITH IT. *THAT* IS THE *WARRIOR'S WAY.*
UNDERSTOOD?
I UNDERSTAND.
THE BATTLE IS *JOINED!* IT LASTS FOR HOURS!
LATER, THE AMAZONS WOULD SPEAK OF UNEXPLAINABLE LIGHTNING FLASHING FROM THE MOUNTAINTOP-- SO FIERCE IS THE CLASH OF *REAL* ON *STEEL!*

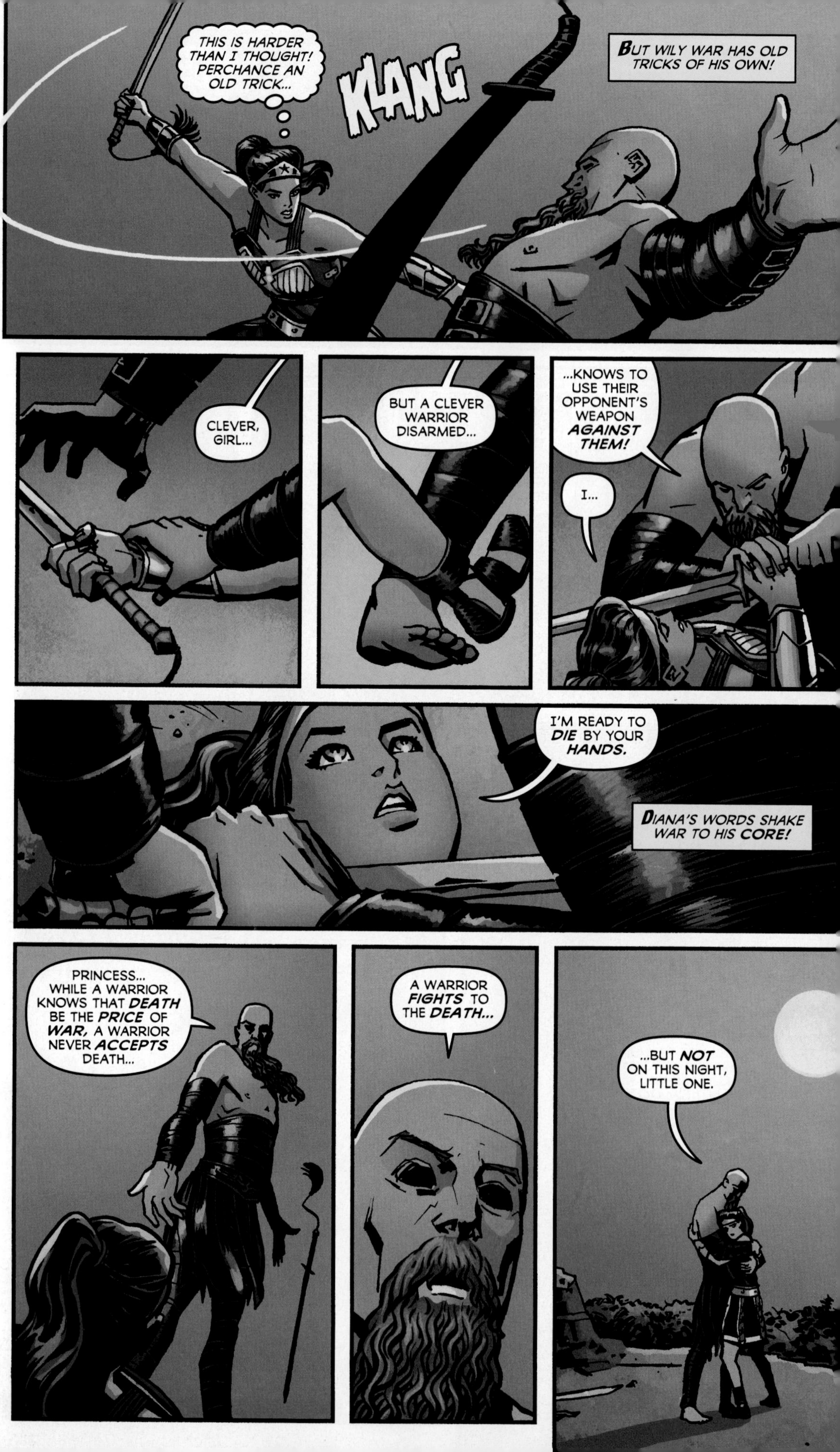
THIS IS HARDER THAN I THOUGHT! PERCHANCE AN OLD TRICK...
KLANG
BUT WILY WAR HAS OLD TRICKS OF HIS OWN!
CLEVER, GIRL...
BUT A CLEVER WARRIOR DISARMED...
...KNOWS TO USE THEIR OPPONENT'S WEAPON AGAINST THEM!
I...
I'M READY TO DIE BY YOUR HANDS.
DIANA'S WORDS SHAKE WAR TO HIS CORE!
PRINCESS... WHILE A WARRIOR KNOWS THAT DEATH BE THE PRICE OF WAR, A WARRIOR NEVER ACCEPTS DEATH...
A WARRIOR FIGHTS TO THE DEATH...
...BUT NOT ON THIS NIGHT, LITTLE ONE.

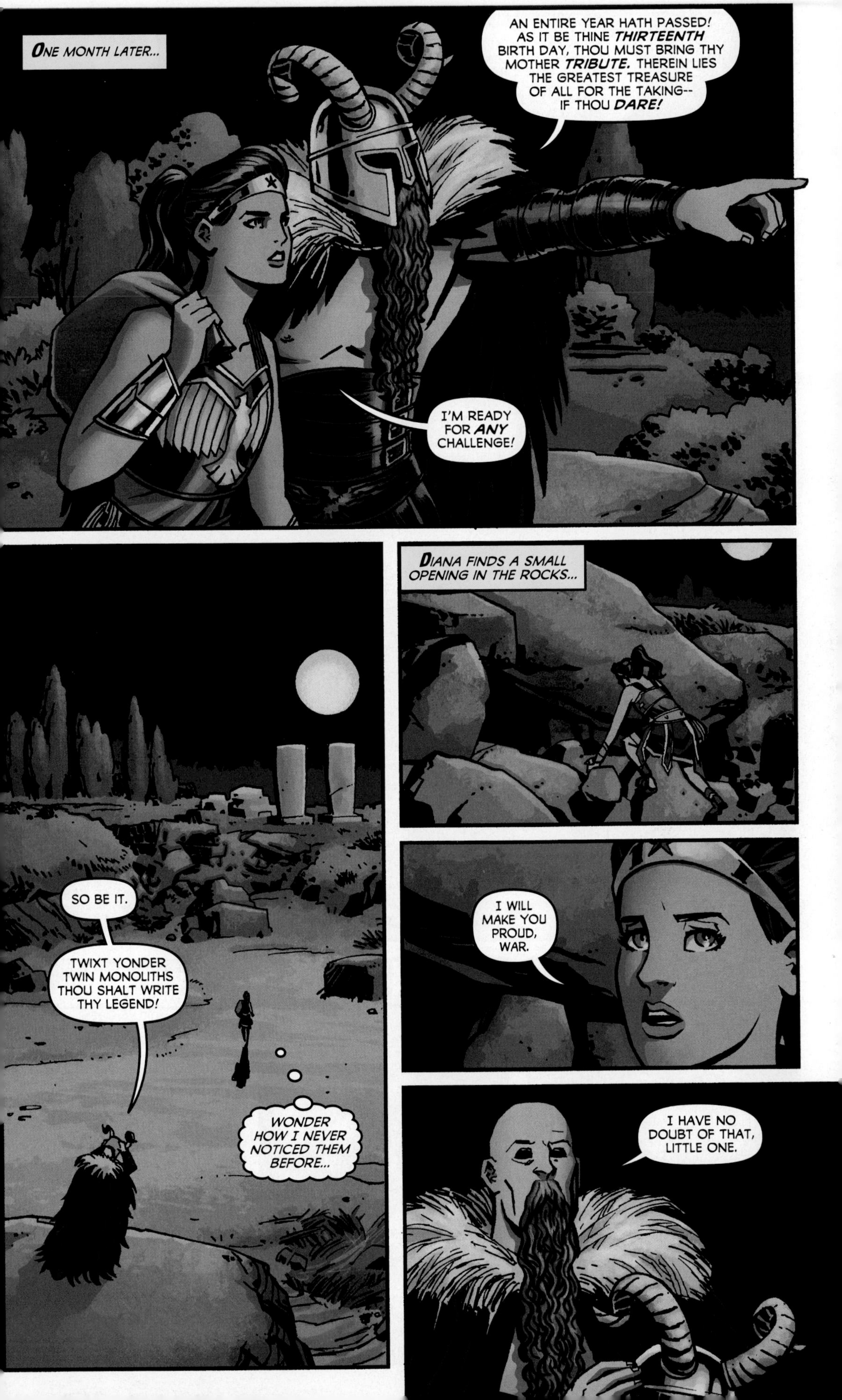
ONE MONTH LATER...
AN ENTIRE YEAR HATH PASSED! AS IT BE THINE THIRTEENTH BIRTH DAY, THOU MUST BRING THY MOTHER TRIBUTE. THEREIN LIES THE GREATEST TREASURE OF ALL FOR THE TAKING-- IF THOU DARE!
I'M READY FOR ANY CHALLENGE!
SO BE IT.
TWIXT YONDER TWIN MONOLITHS THOU SHALT WRITE THY LEGEND!
WONDER HOW I NEVER NOTICED THEM BEFORE...
DIANA FINDS A SMALL OPENING IN THE ROCKS...
I WILL MAKE YOU PROUD, WAR.
I HAVE NO DOUBT OF THAT, LITTLE ONE.

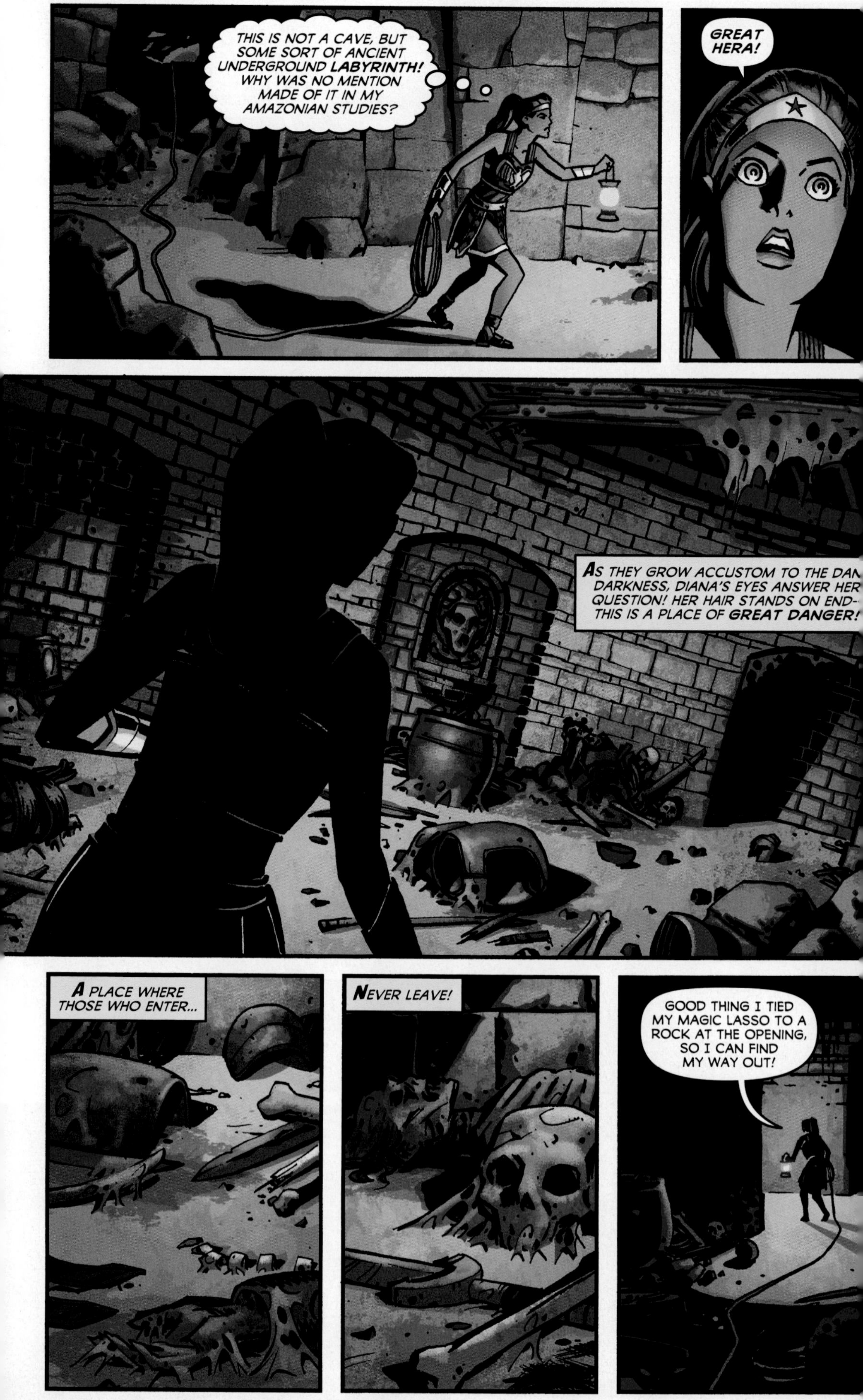

THIS IS NOT A CAVE, BUT SOME SORT OF ANCIENT UNDERGROUND LABYRINTH! WHY WAS NO MENTION MADE OF IT IN MY AMAZONIAN STUDIES?
GREAT HERA!
AS THEY GROW ACCUSTOM TO THE DAN DARKNESS, DIANA'S EYES ANSWER HER QUESTION! HER HAIR STANDS ON END-- THIS IS A PLACE OF GREAT DANGER!
A PLACE WHERE THOSE WHO ENTER...
NEVER LEAVE!
GOOD THING I TIED MY MAGIC LASSO TO A ROCK AT THE OPENING, SO I CAN FIND MY WAY OUT!

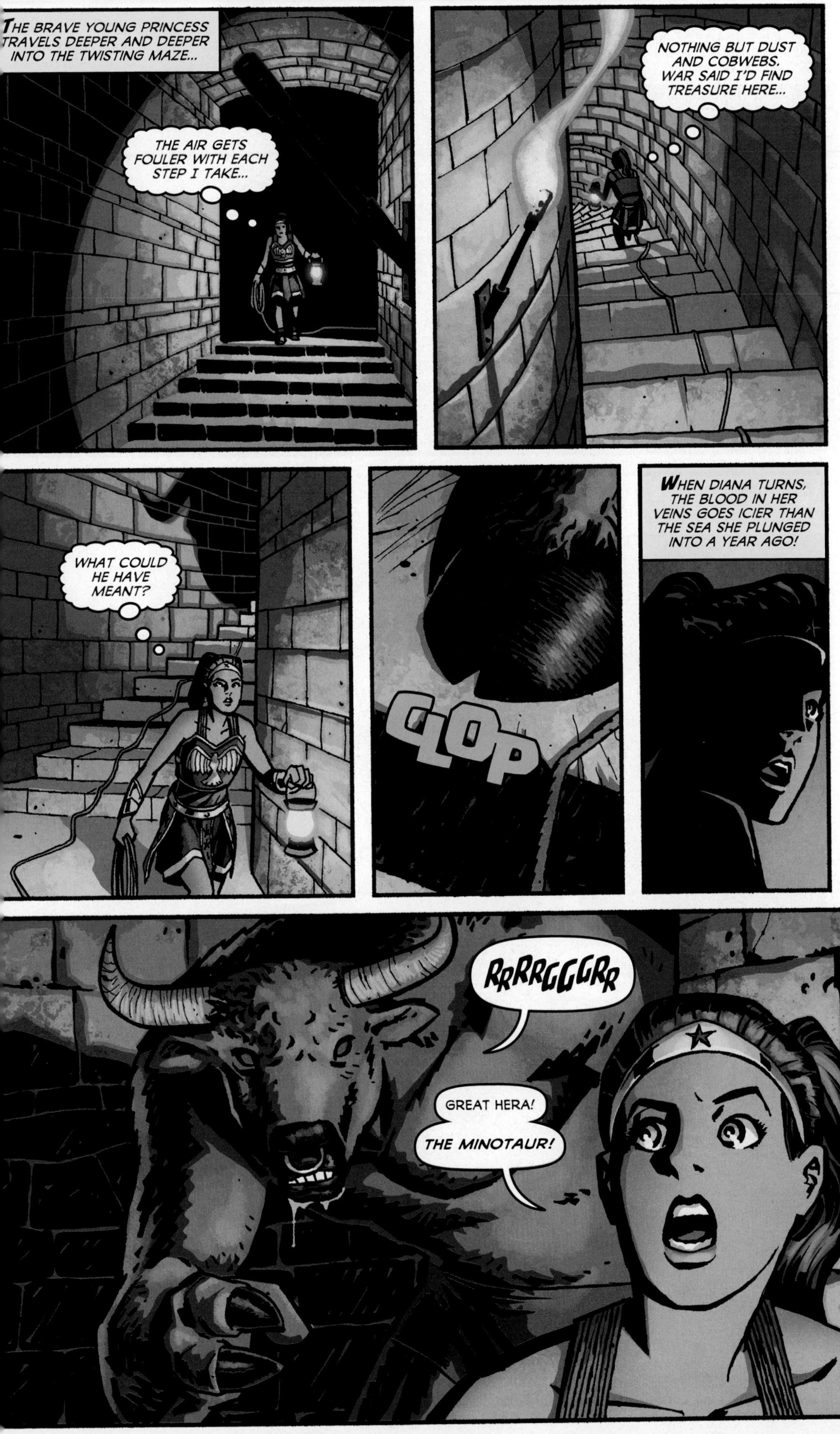
THE BRAVE YOUNG PRINCESS TRAVELS DEEPER AND DEEPER INTO THE TWISTING MAZE...
THE AIR GETS FOULER WITH EACH STEP I TAKE...
NOTHING BUT DUST AND COBWEBS. WAR SAID I'D FIND TREASURE HERE...
WHAT COULD HE HAVE MEANT?
CLOP
WHEN DIANA TURNS, THE BLOOD IN HER VEINS GOES ICIER THAN THE SEA SHE PLUNGED INTO A YEAR AGO!
RRRRGGGRR
GREAT HERA!
THE MINOTAUR!

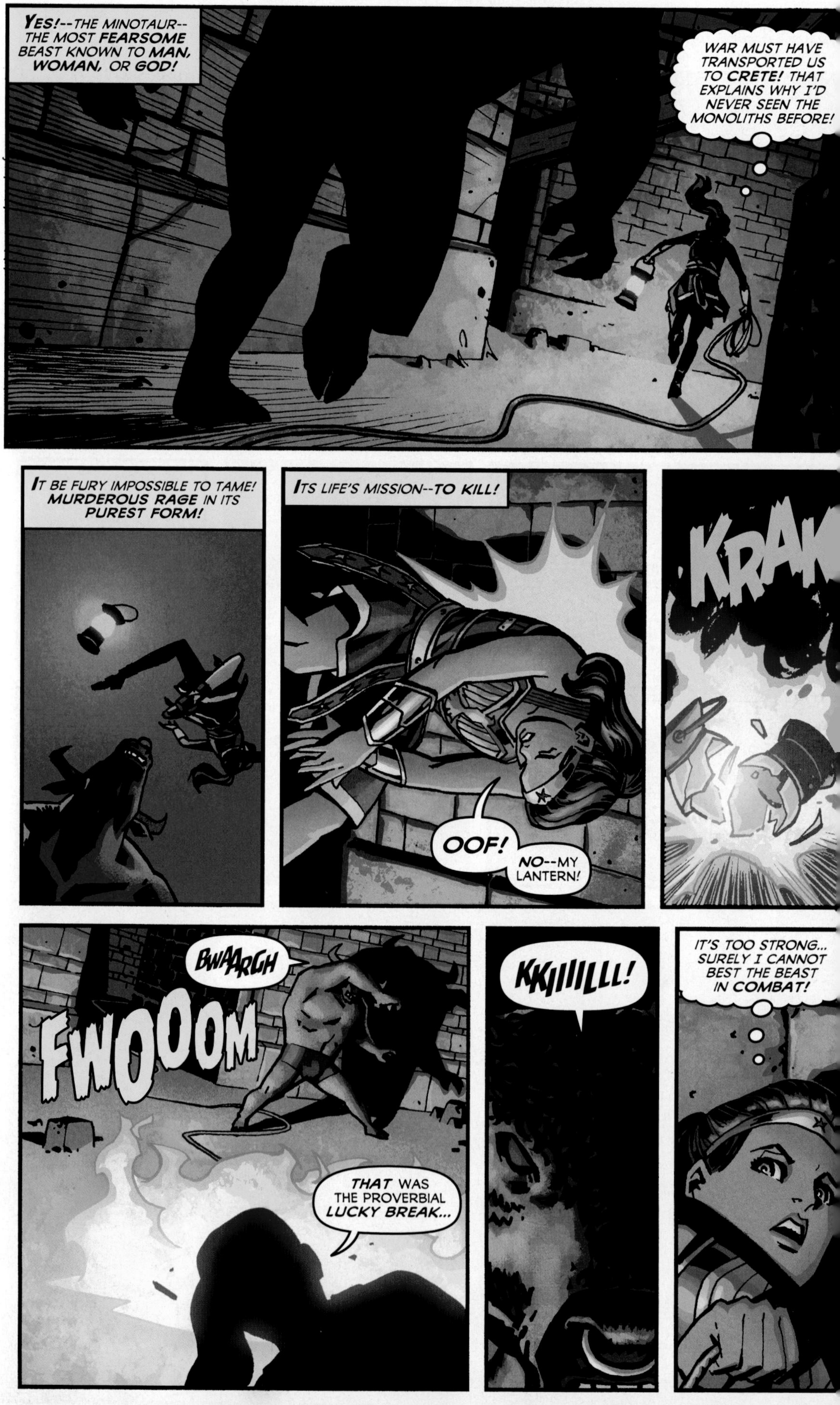
YES!--THE MINOTAUR--THE MOST FEARSOME BEAST KNOWN TO MAN, WOMAN, OR GOD!
WAR MUST HAVE TRANSPORTED US TO CRETE! THAT EXPLAINS WHY I'D NEVER SEEN THE MONOLITHS BEFORE!
IT BE FURY IMPOSSIBLE TO TAME! MURDEROUS RAGE IN ITS PUREST FORM!
ITS LIFE'S MISSION--TO KILL!
OOF!
NO--MY LANTERN!
KRAK
BWAARGH
FWOOOM
THAT WAS THE PROVERBIAL LUCKY BREAK...
KKIIIILLLL!
IT'S TOO STRONG... SURELY I CANNOT BEST THE BEAST IN COMBAT!

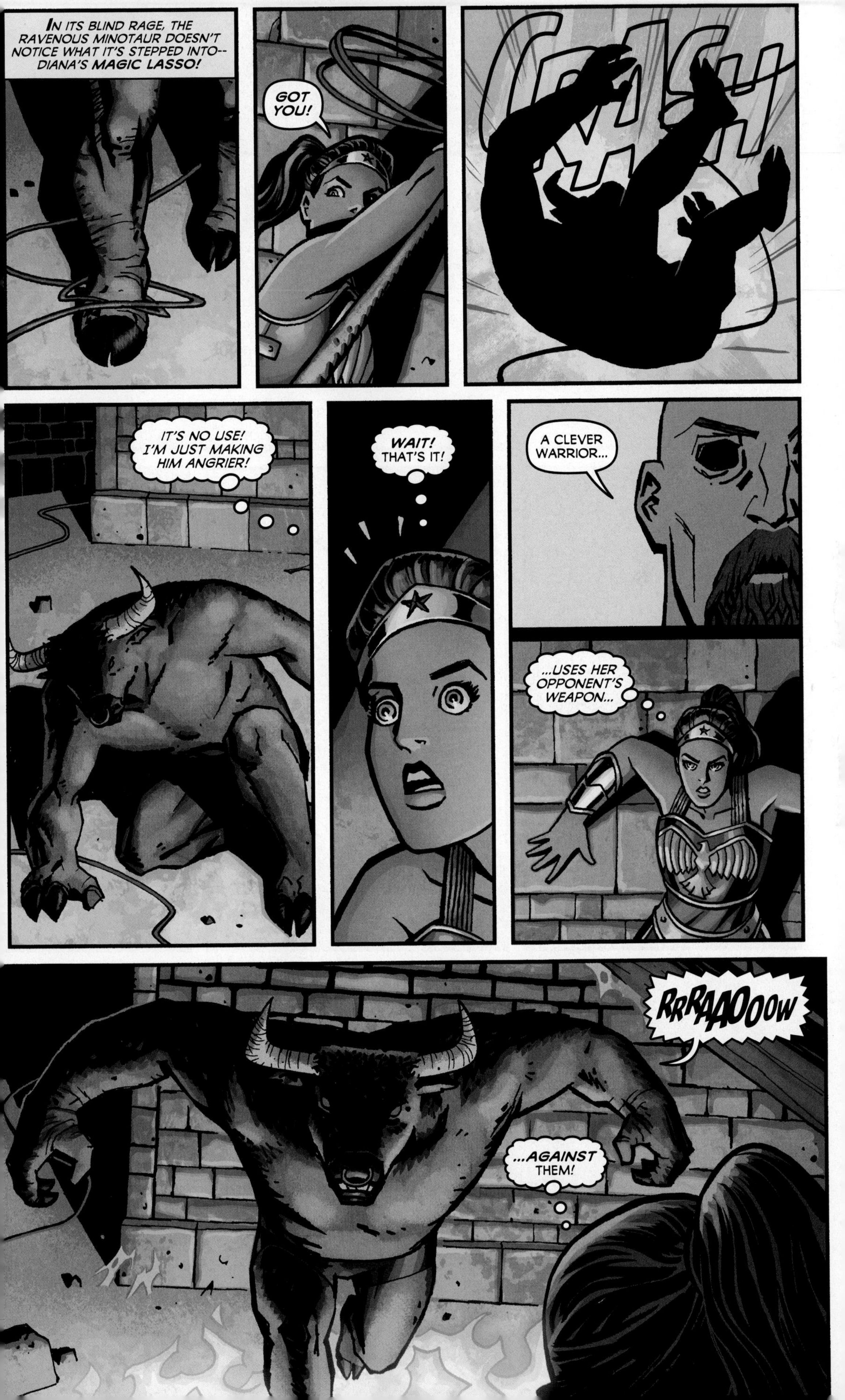
IN ITS BLIND RAGE, THE RAVENOUS MINOTAUR DOESN'T NOTICE WHAT IT'S STEPPED INTO-- DIANA'S MAGIC LASSO!
GOT YOU!
CRASH
IT'S NO USE! I'M JUST MAKING HIM ANGRIER!
WAIT! THAT'S IT!
A CLEVER WARRIOR...
...USES HER OPPONENT'S WEAPON...
RRRAAOOOOW
...AGAINST THEM!

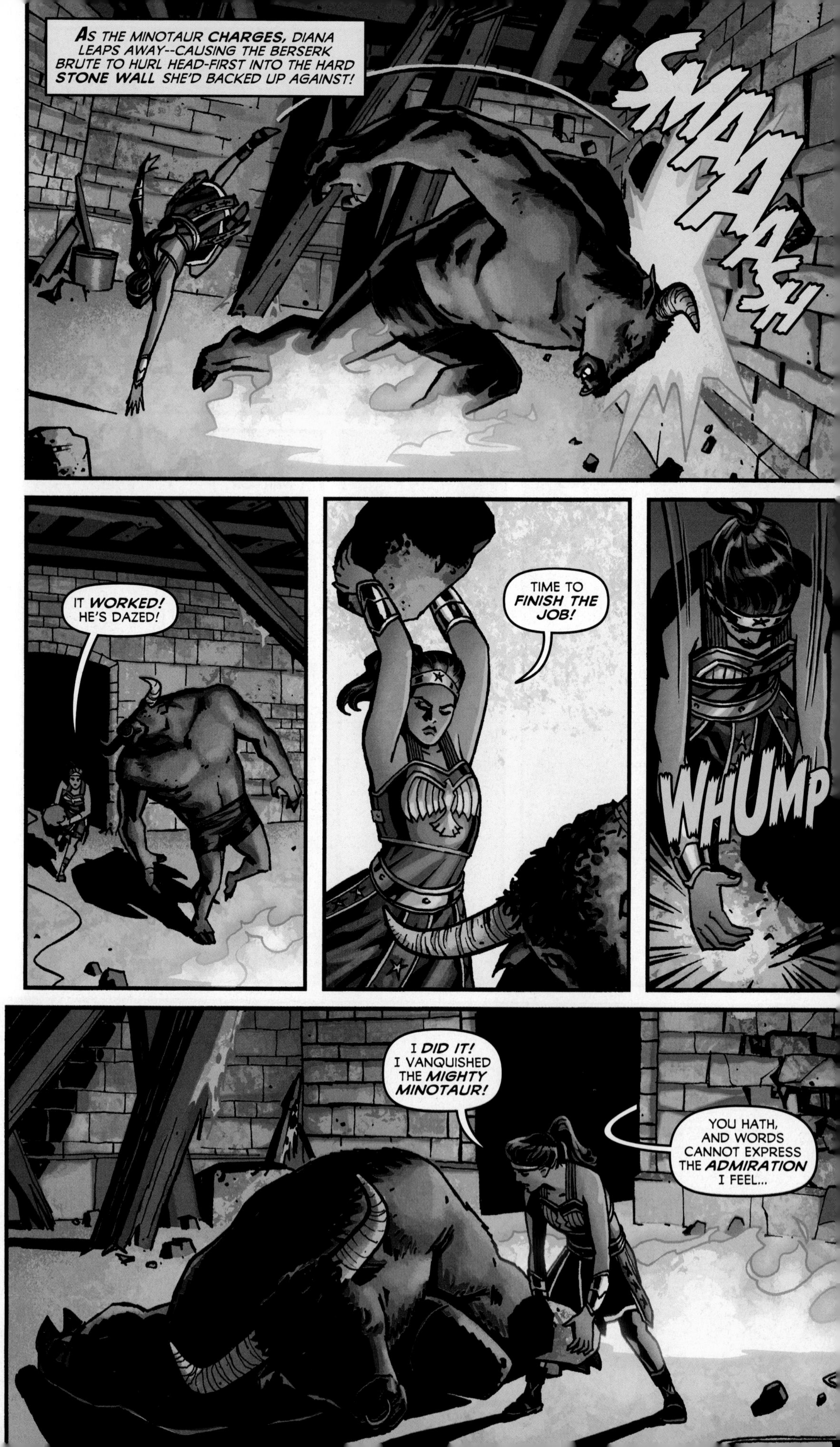
AS THE MINOTAUR CHARGES, DIANA LEAPS AWAY--CAUSING THE BERSERK BRUTE TO HURL HEAD-FIRST INTO THE HARD STONE WALL SHE'D BACKED UP AGAINST!
SMAAAH
IT WORKED! HE'S DAZED!
TIME TO FINISH THE JOB!
WHUMP
I DID IT! I VANQUISHED THE MIGHTY MINOTAUR!
YOU HATH, AND WORDS CANNOT EXPRESS THE ADMIRATION I FEEL...

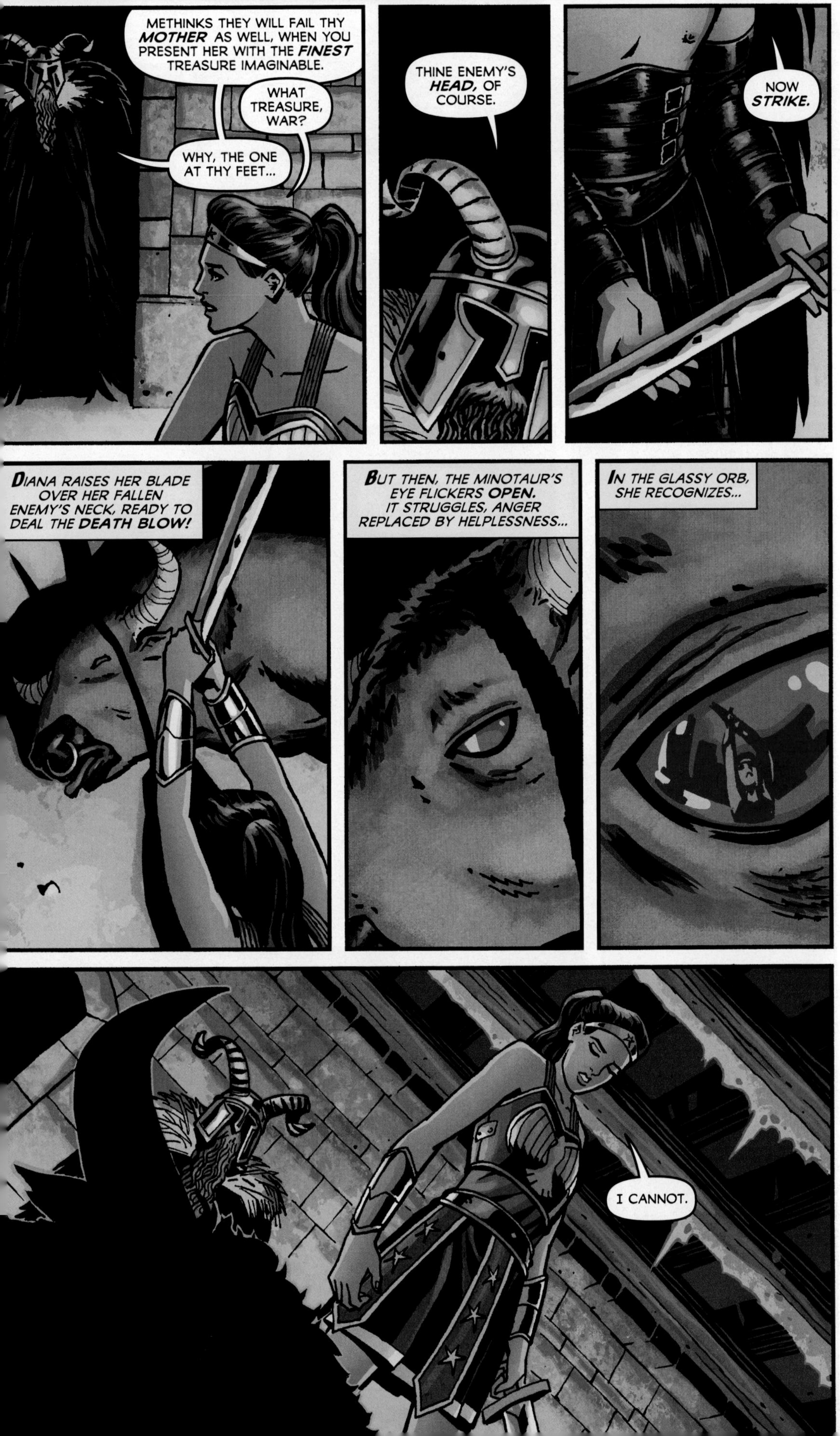
METHINKS THEY WILL FAIL THY MOTHER AS WELL, WHEN YOU PRESENT HER WITH THE FINEST TREASURE IMAGINABLE.
WHAT TREASURE, WAR?
WHY, THE ONE AT THY FEET...
THINE ENEMY'S HEAD, OF COURSE.
NOW STRIKE.
DIANA RAISES HER BLADE OVER HER FALLEN ENEMY'S NECK, READY TO DEAL THE DEATH BLOW!
BUT THEN, THE MINOTAUR'S EYE FLICKERS OPEN. IT STRUGGLES, ANGER REPLACED BY HELPLESSNESS...
IN THE GLASSY ORB, SHE RECOGNIZES...
I CANNOT.

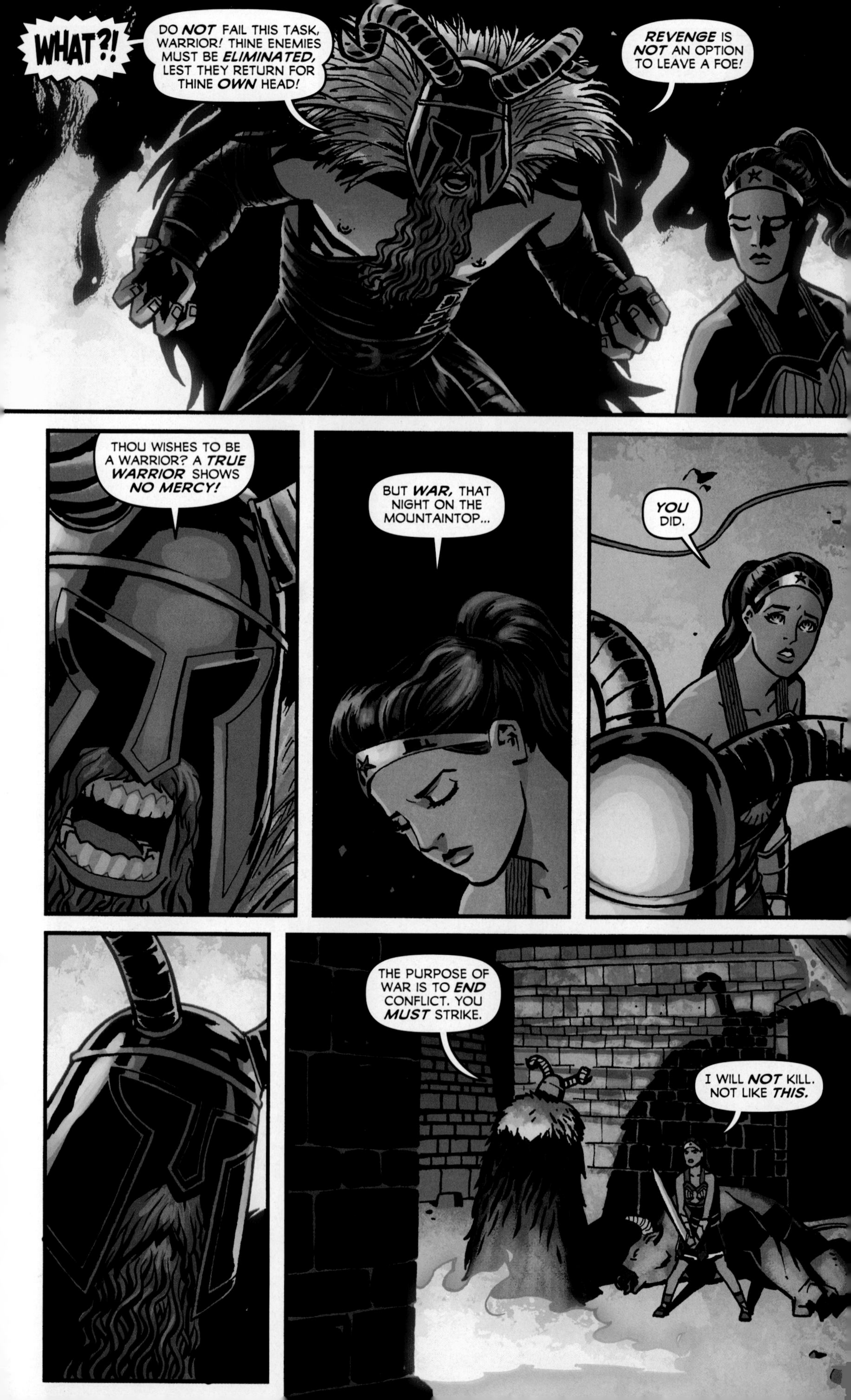
WHAT?!
DO NOT FAIL THIS TASK, WARRIOR! THINE ENEMIES MUST BE ELIMINATED, LEST THEY RETURN FOR THINE OWN HEAD!
REVENGE IS NOT AN OPTION TO LEAVE A FOE!
THOU WISHES TO BE A WARRIOR? A TRUE WARRIOR SHOWS NO MERCY!
BUT WAR, THAT NIGHT ON THE MOUNTAINTOP...
YOU DID.
THE PURPOSE OF WAR IS TO END CONFLICT. YOU MUST STRIKE.
I WILL NOT KILL. NOT LIKE THIS.

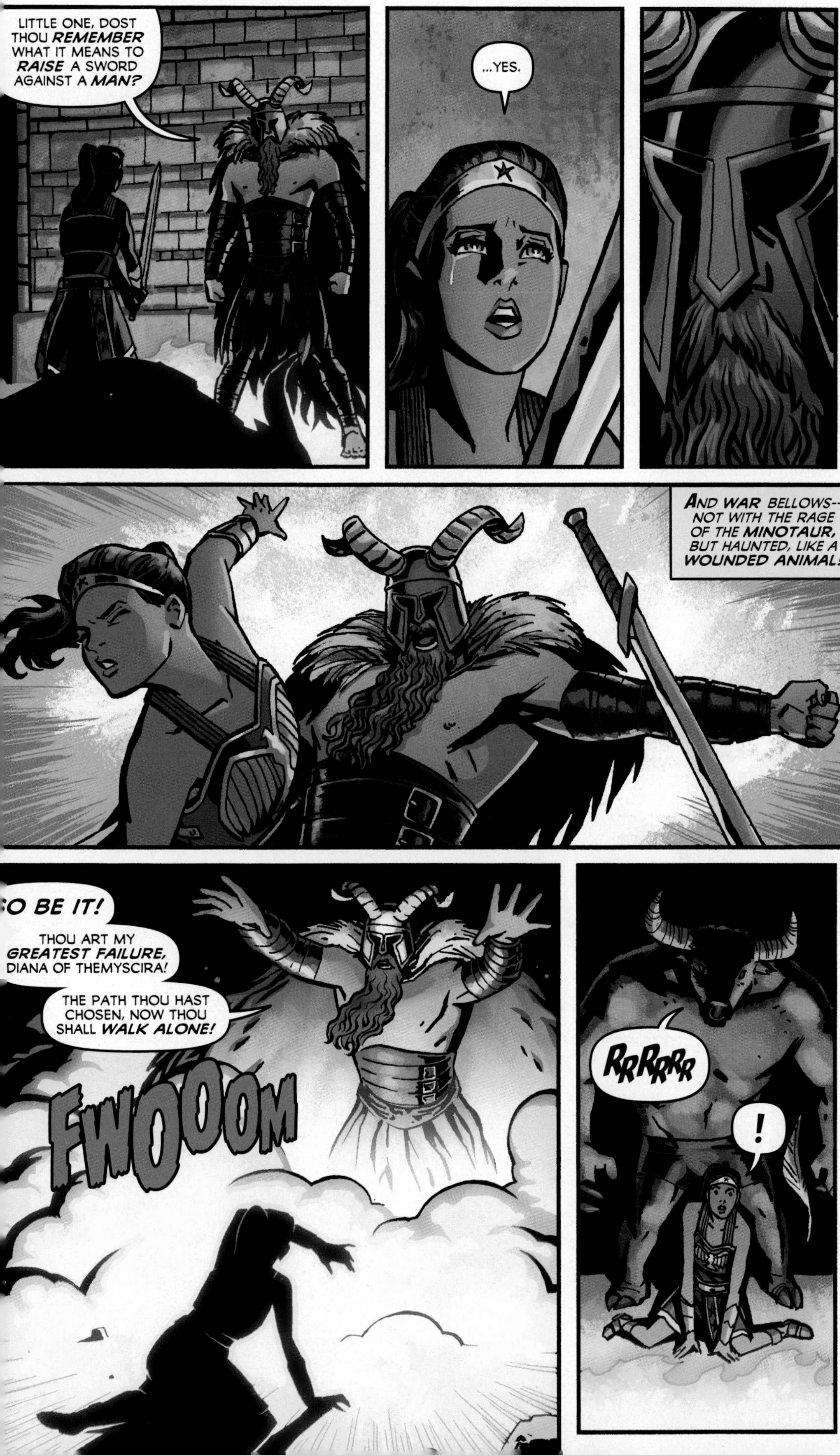
LITTLE ONE, DOST THOU REMEMBER WHAT IT MEANS TO RAISE A SWORD AGAINST A MAN?
...YES.
AND WAR BELLOWS-- NOT WITH THE RAGE OF THE MINOTAUR, BUT HAUNTED, LIKE A WOUNDED ANIMAL!
SO BE IT!
THOU ART MY GREATEST FAILURE, DIANA OF THEMYSCIRA!
THE PATH THOU HAST CHOSEN, NOW THOU SHALL WALK ALONE!
FWOOOM
RRRRRR
!

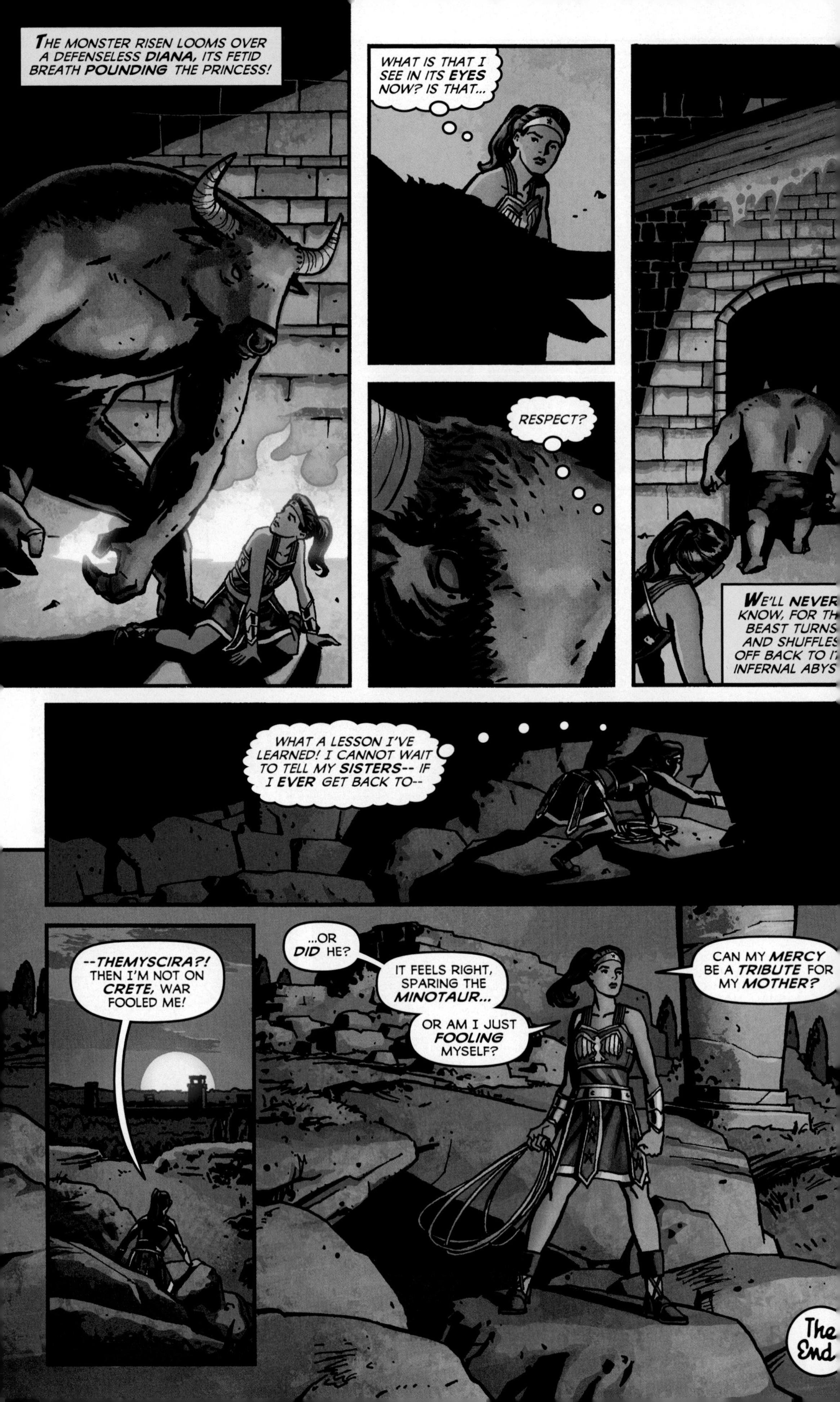
THE MONSTER RISEN LOOMS OVER A DEFENSELESS DIANA, ITS FETID BREATH POUNDING THE PRINCESS!
WHAT IS THAT I SEE IN ITS EYES NOW? IS THAT...
RESPECT?
WE'LL NEVER KNOW, FOR TH BEAST TURNS AND SHUFFLES OFF BACK TO IT INFERNAL ABYS
WHAT A LESSON I'VE LEARNED! I CANNOT WAIT TO TELL MY SISTERS-- IF I EVER GET BACK TO--
--THEMYSCIRA?! THEN I'M NOT ON CRETE, WAR FOOLED ME!
...OR DID HE?
IT FEELS RIGHT, SPARING THE MINOTAUR...
OR AM I JUST FOOLING MYSELF?
CAN MY MERCY BE A TRIBUTE FOR MY MOTHER?
The End

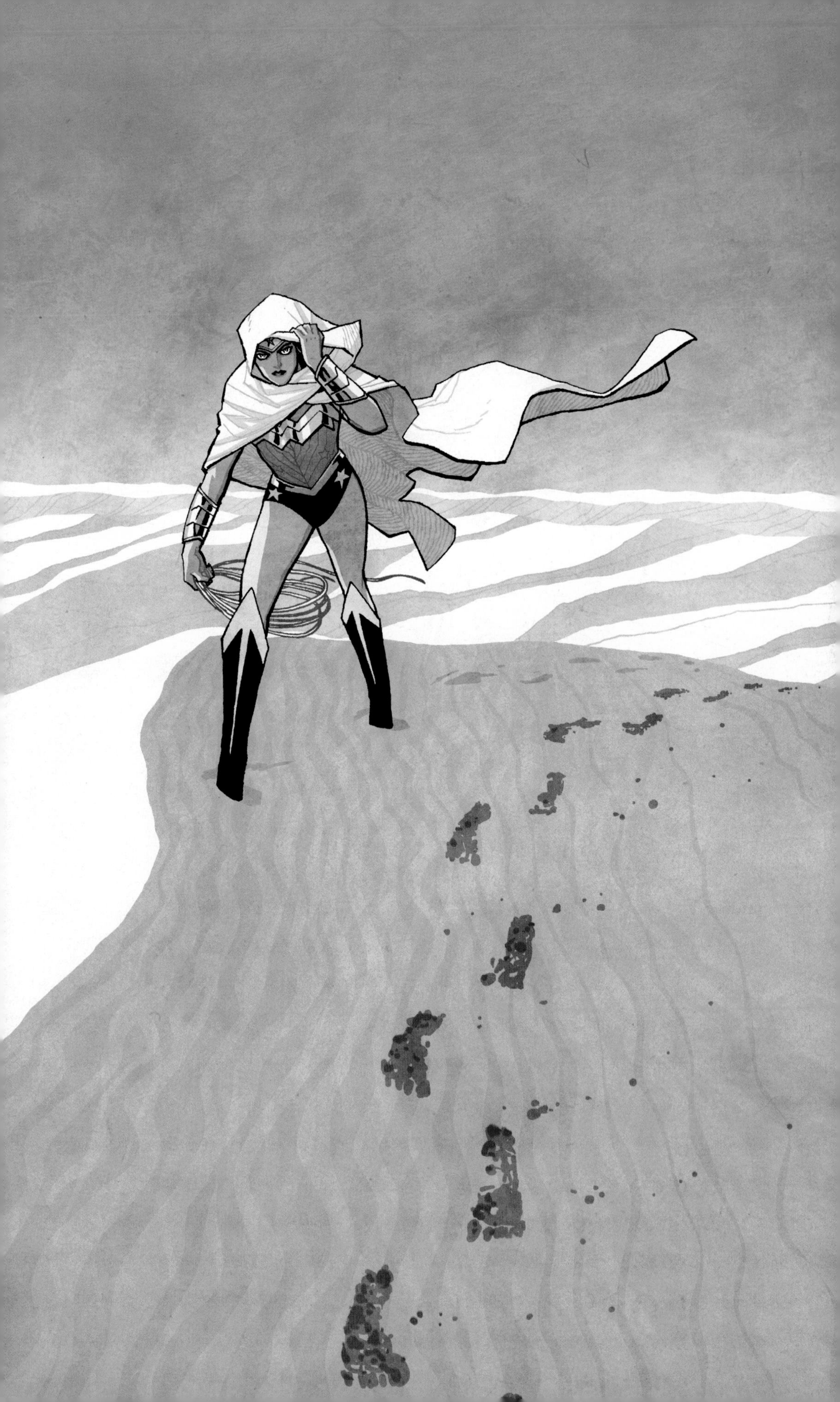

SIN OF THE FATHER

TONY AKINS penciller **DAN GREEN** with **TONY AKINS** inkers

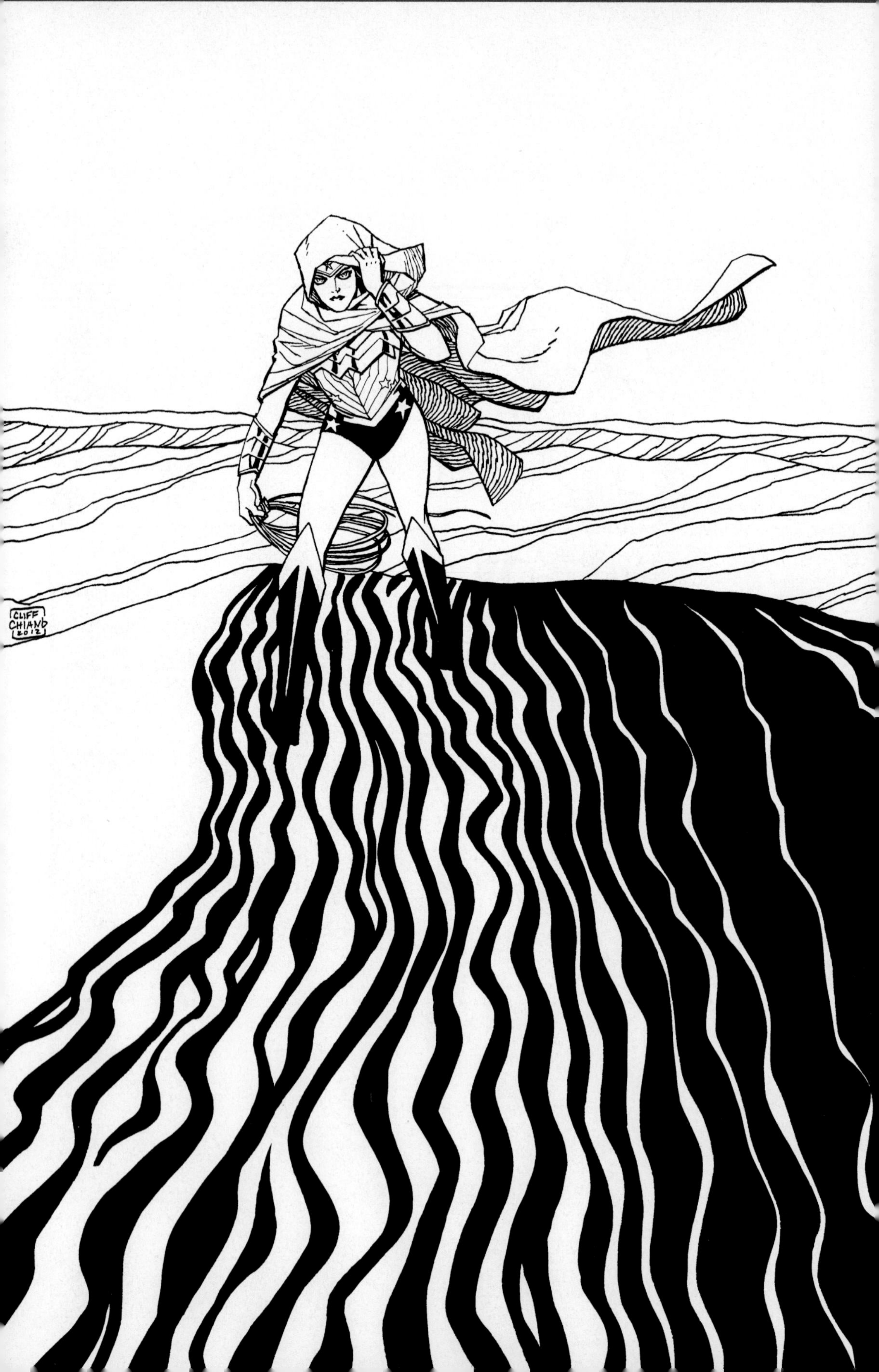
CLIFF CHIANG 2012

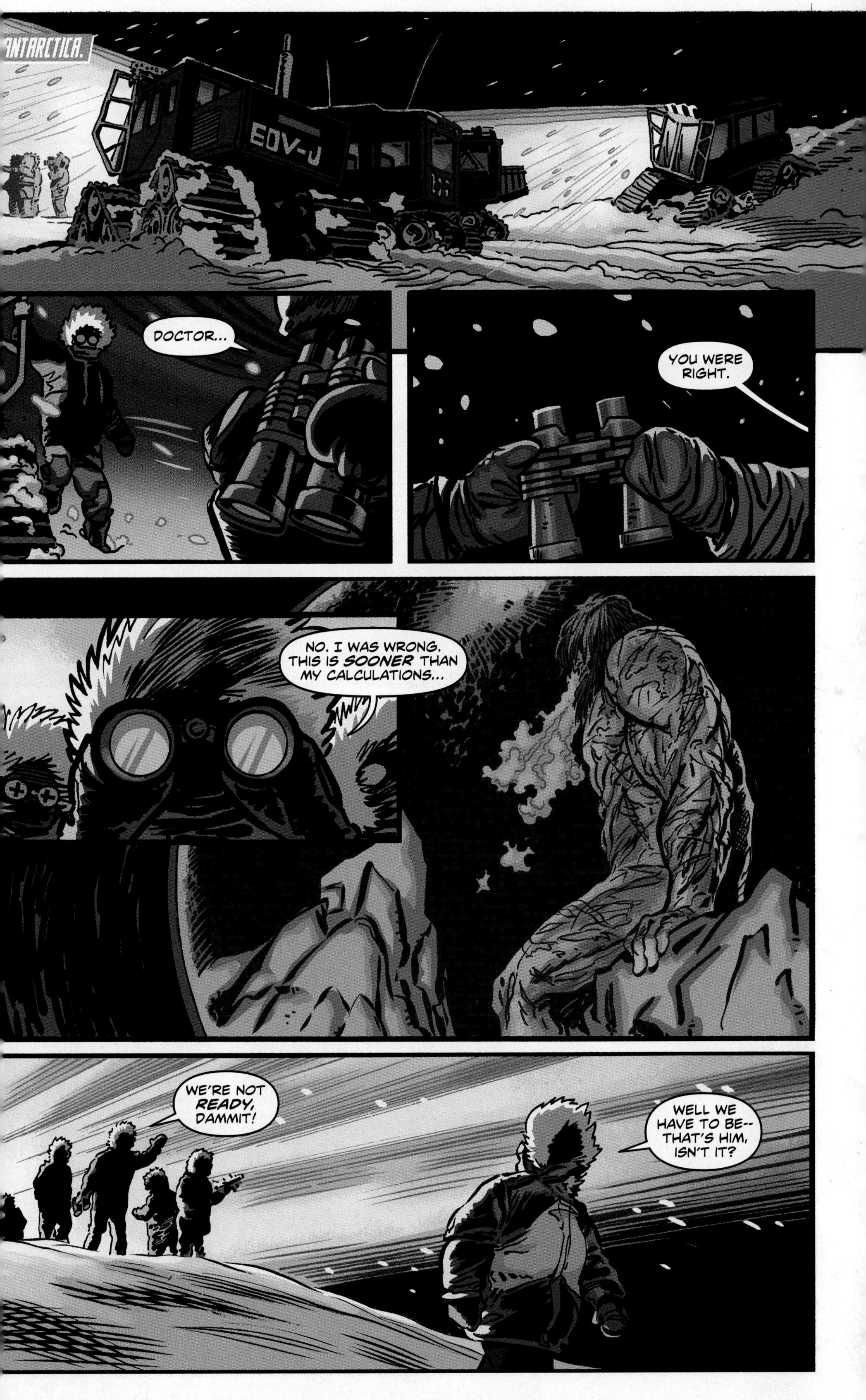
ANTARCTICA.
EDV-J
DOCTOR...
YOU WERE RIGHT.
NO. I WAS WRONG. THIS IS SOONER THAN MY CALCULATIONS...
WE'RE NOT READY, DAMMIT!
WELL WE HAVE TO BE-- THAT'S HIM, ISN'T IT?

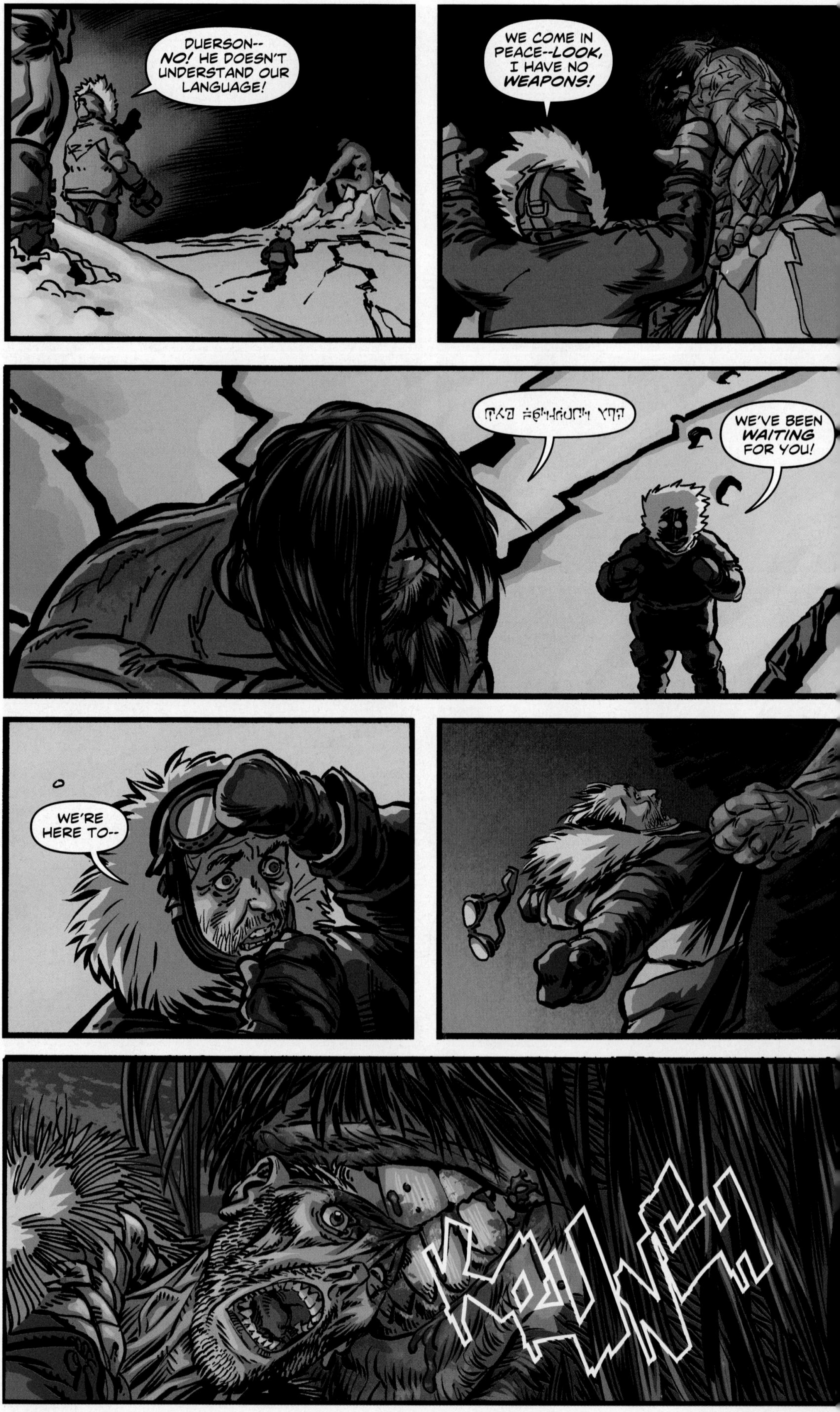
DUERSON--
NO! HE DOESN'T UNDERSTAND OUR LANGUAGE!
WE COME IN PEACE--LOOK, I HAVE NO WEAPONS!
WE'VE BEEN WAITING FOR YOU!
WE'RE HERE TO--

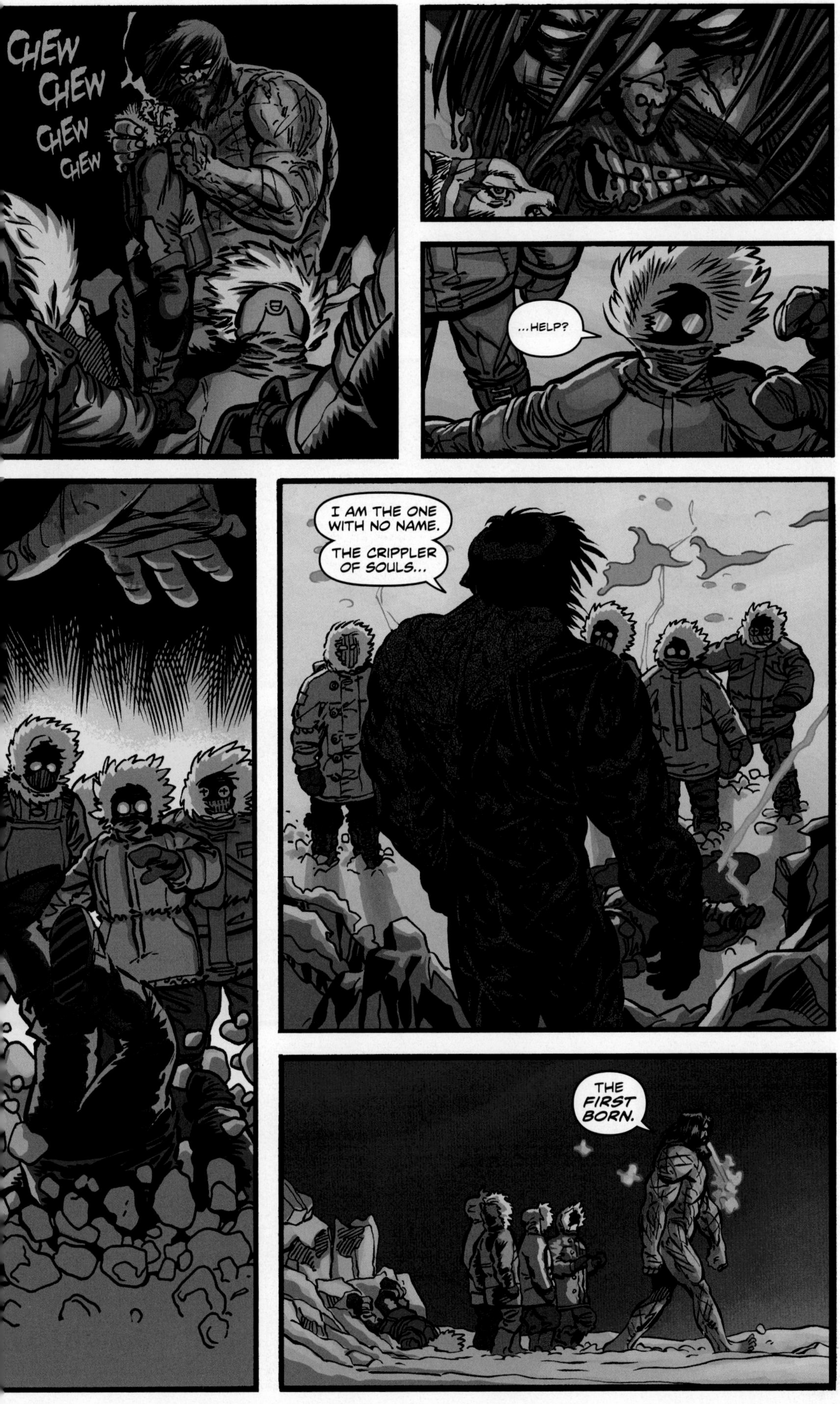
CHEW
CHEW
CHEW
CHEW
...HELP?
I AM THE ONE WITH NO NAME.
THE CRIPPLER OF SOULS...
THE FIRST BORN.

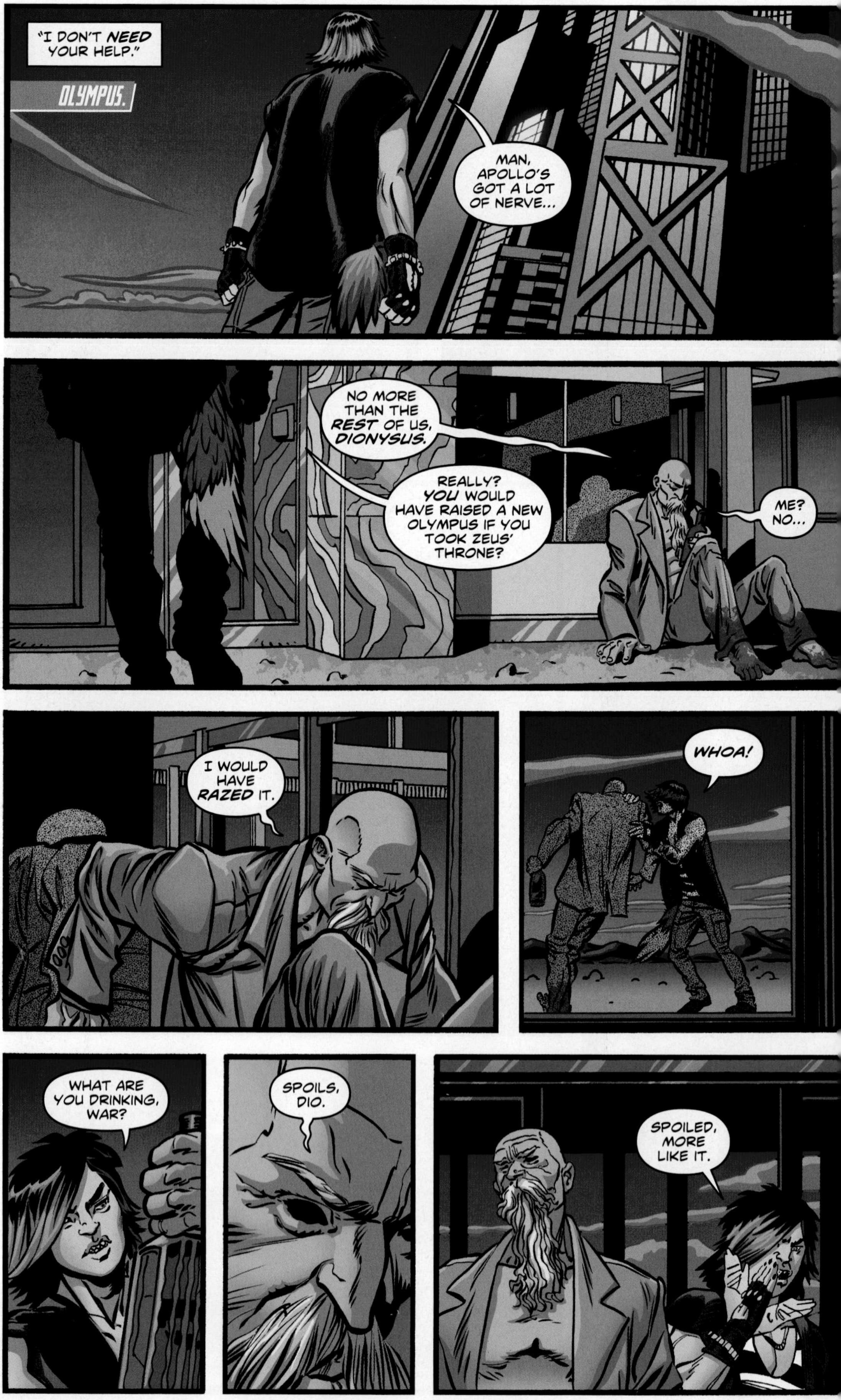
"I DON'T NEED YOUR HELP."
OLYMPUS.
MAN, APOLLO'S GOT A LOT OF NERVE...
NO MORE THAN THE REST OF US, DIONYSUS.
REALLY? YOU WOULD HAVE RAISED A NEW OLYMPUS IF YOU TOOK ZEUS' THRONE?
ME? NO...
I WOULD HAVE RAZED IT.
WHOA!
WHAT ARE YOU DRINKING, WAR?
SPOILS, DIO.
SPOILED, MORE LIKE IT.

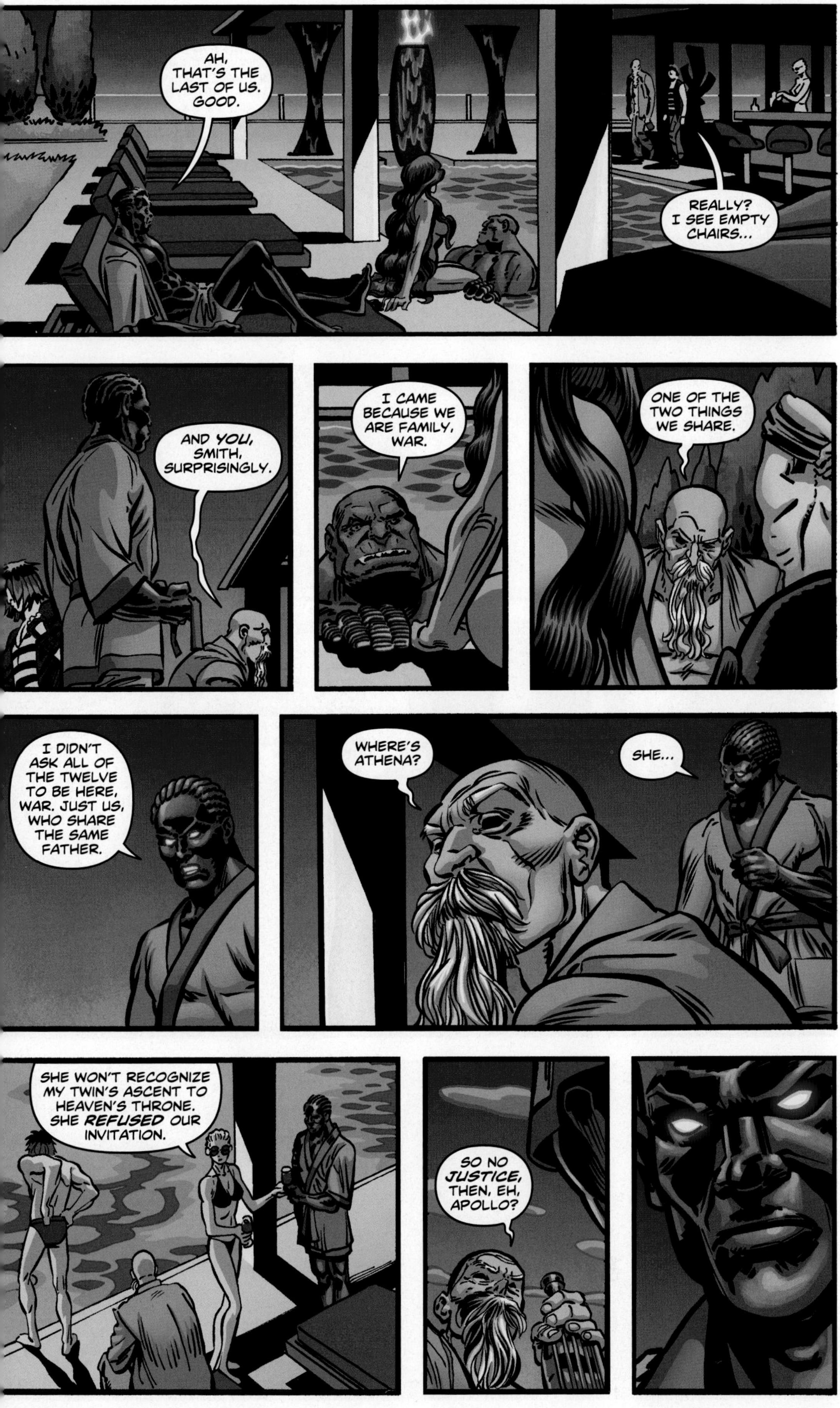
AH, THAT'S THE LAST OF US. GOOD.
REALLY? I SEE EMPTY CHAIRS...
AND YOU, SMITH, SURPRISINGLY.
I CAME BECAUSE WE ARE FAMILY, WAR.
ONE OF THE TWO THINGS WE SHARE.
I DIDN'T ASK ALL OF THE TWELVE TO BE HERE, WAR. JUST US, WHO SHARE THE SAME FATHER.
WHERE'S ATHENA?
SHE...
SHE WON'T RECOGNIZE MY TWIN'S ASCENT TO HEAVEN'S THRONE. SHE REFUSED OUR INVITATION.
SO NO JUSTICE, THEN, EH, APOLLO?

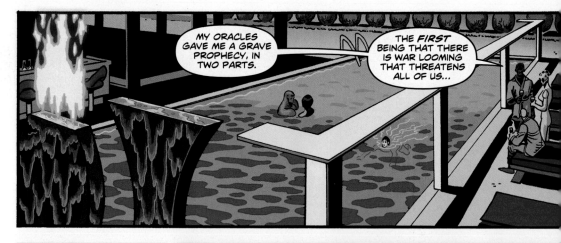

MY ORACLES GAVE ME A GRAVE PROPHECY, IN TWO PARTS.

THE *FIRST* BEING THAT THERE IS WAR LOOMING THAT THREATENS ALL OF US...

AND SECOND, THAT A CHILD OF ZEUS WOULD SLAY ONE OF US, AND TAKE A THRONE FOR THEMSELVES.

WE ARE NOT THE ONLY CHILDREN OF ZEUS.

WE *ARE* THE MOST POWERFUL.

WE ALREADY HAVE *OUR* THRONES, APOLLO. I THINK YOU'RE SAFE.

I WOULD HAVE AGREED, HAD I NOT WITNESSED ANOTHER OF FATHER'S CHILDREN DISPLAY POWER IN A WAY THAT WOULD PUT THE LION TO SHAME.

BROTHER...

MOON'S BRUISES SPEAK LOUDER THAN MY WORDS, NO?

WHO *DID* THAT?

THE LAST *AMAZON.*

DIANA OF THEMYSCIRA...

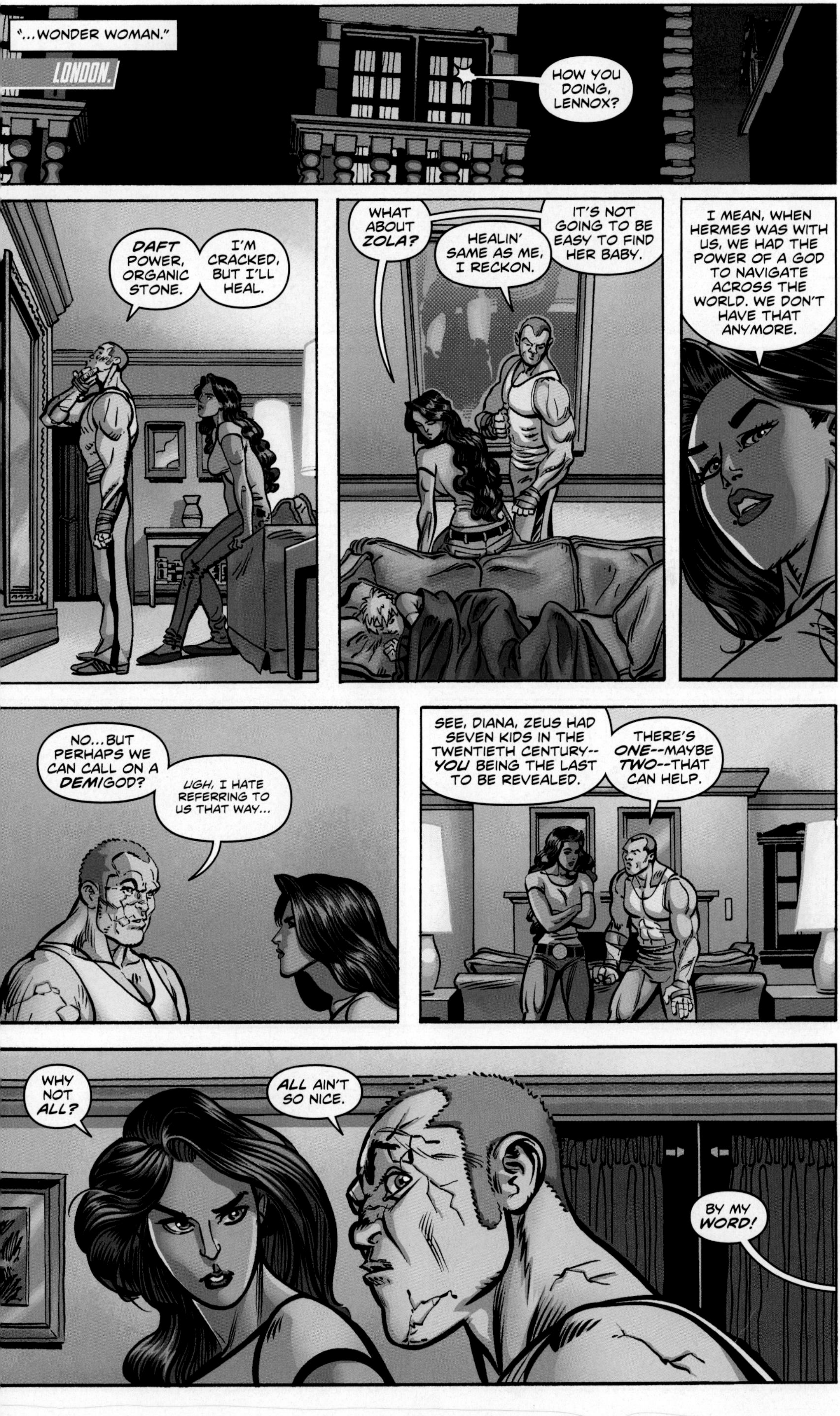
"...WONDER WOMAN."
LONDON.
HOW YOU DOING, LENNOX?
DAFT POWER, ORGANIC STONE.
I'M CRACKED, BUT I'LL HEAL.
WHAT ABOUT ZOLA?
HEALIN' SAME AS ME, I RECKON.
IT'S NOT GOING TO BE EASY TO FIND HER BABY.
I MEAN, WHEN HERMES WAS WITH US, WE HAD THE POWER OF A GOD TO NAVIGATE ACROSS THE WORLD. WE DON'T HAVE THAT ANYMORE.
NO...BUT PERHAPS WE CAN CALL ON A DEMIGOD?
UGH, I HATE REFERRING TO US THAT WAY...
SEE, DIANA, ZEUS HAD SEVEN KIDS IN THE TWENTIETH CENTURY--YOU BEING THE LAST TO BE REVEALED.
THERE'S ONE--MAYBE TWO--THAT CAN HELP.
WHY NOT ALL?
ALL AIN'T SO NICE.
BY MY WORD!

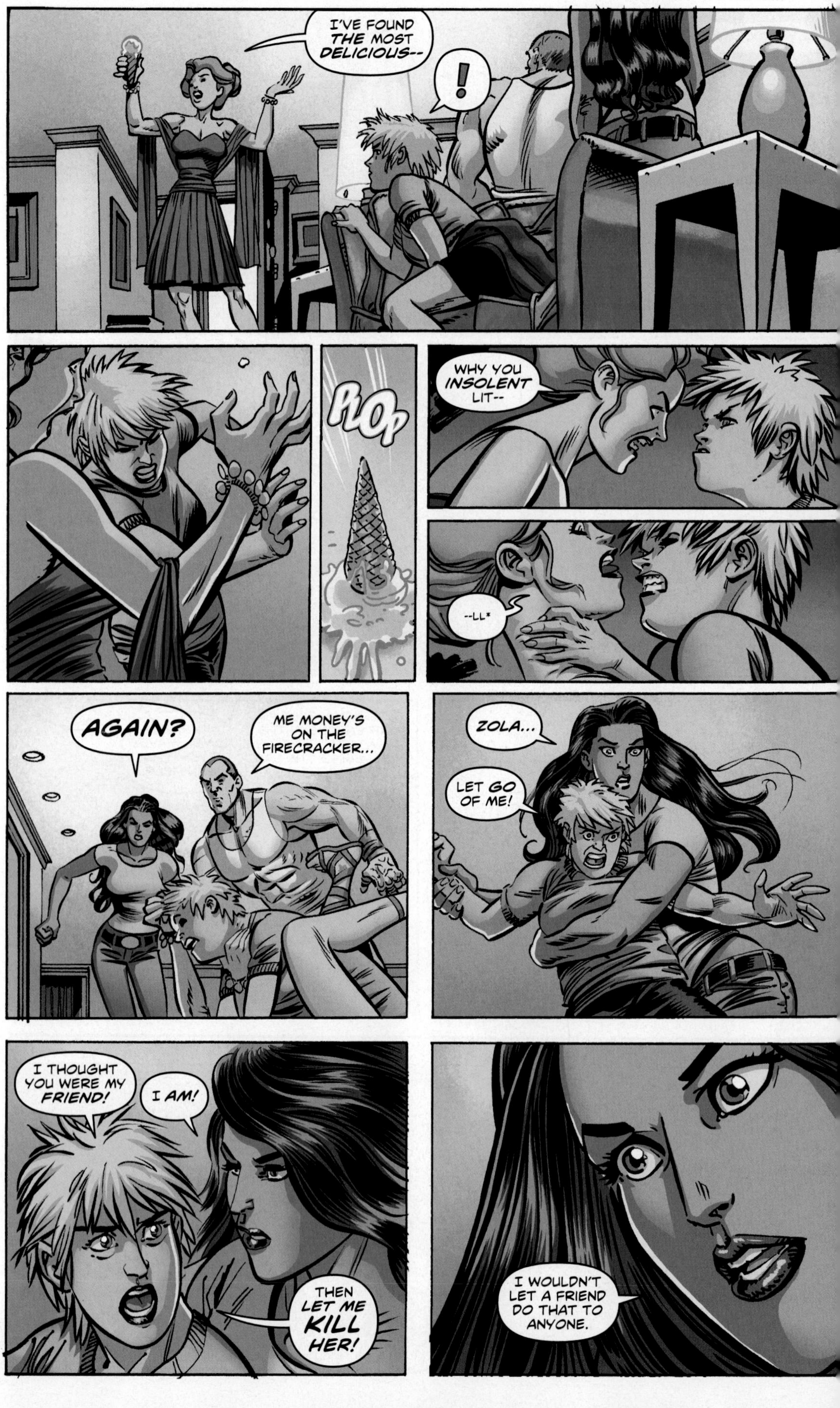

I'VE FOUND THE MOST DELICIOUS--
!
PLOP
WHY YOU INSOLENT LIT--
--LL*
AGAIN?
ME MONEY'S ON THE FIRECRACKER...
ZOLA...
LET GO OF ME!
I THOUGHT YOU WERE MY FRIEND!
I AM!
THEN LET ME KILL HER!
I WOULDN'T LET A FRIEND DO THAT TO ANYONE.

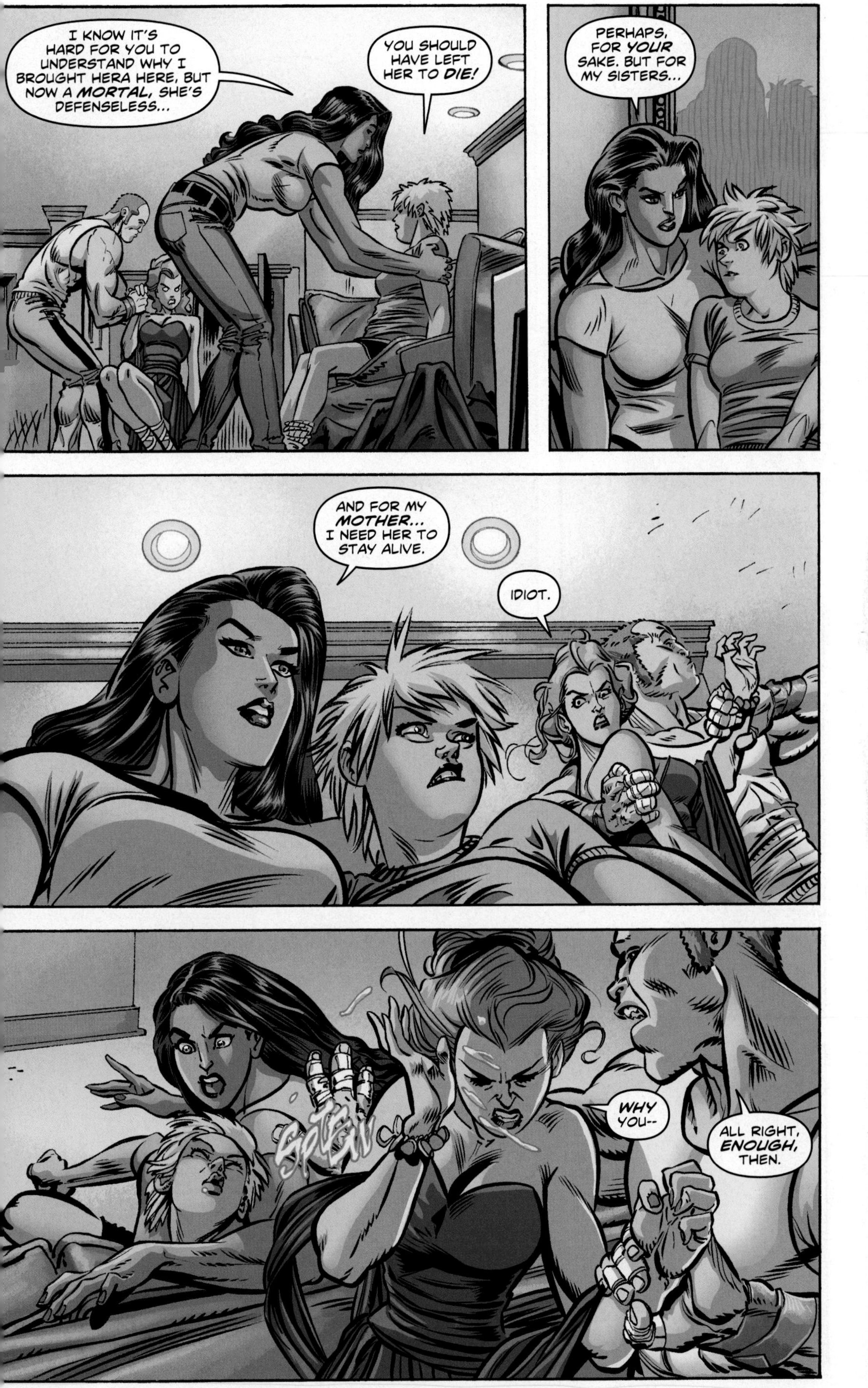

I KNOW IT'S HARD FOR YOU TO UNDERSTAND WHY I BROUGHT HERA HERE, BUT NOW A *MORTAL*, SHE'S DEFENSELESS...
YOU SHOULD HAVE LEFT HER TO *DIE!*
PERHAPS, FOR *YOUR* SAKE. BUT FOR MY SISTERS...
AND FOR MY *MOTHER...* I NEED HER TO STAY ALIVE.
IDIOT.
SPLAT
WHY YOU--
ALL RIGHT, *ENOUGH,* THEN.

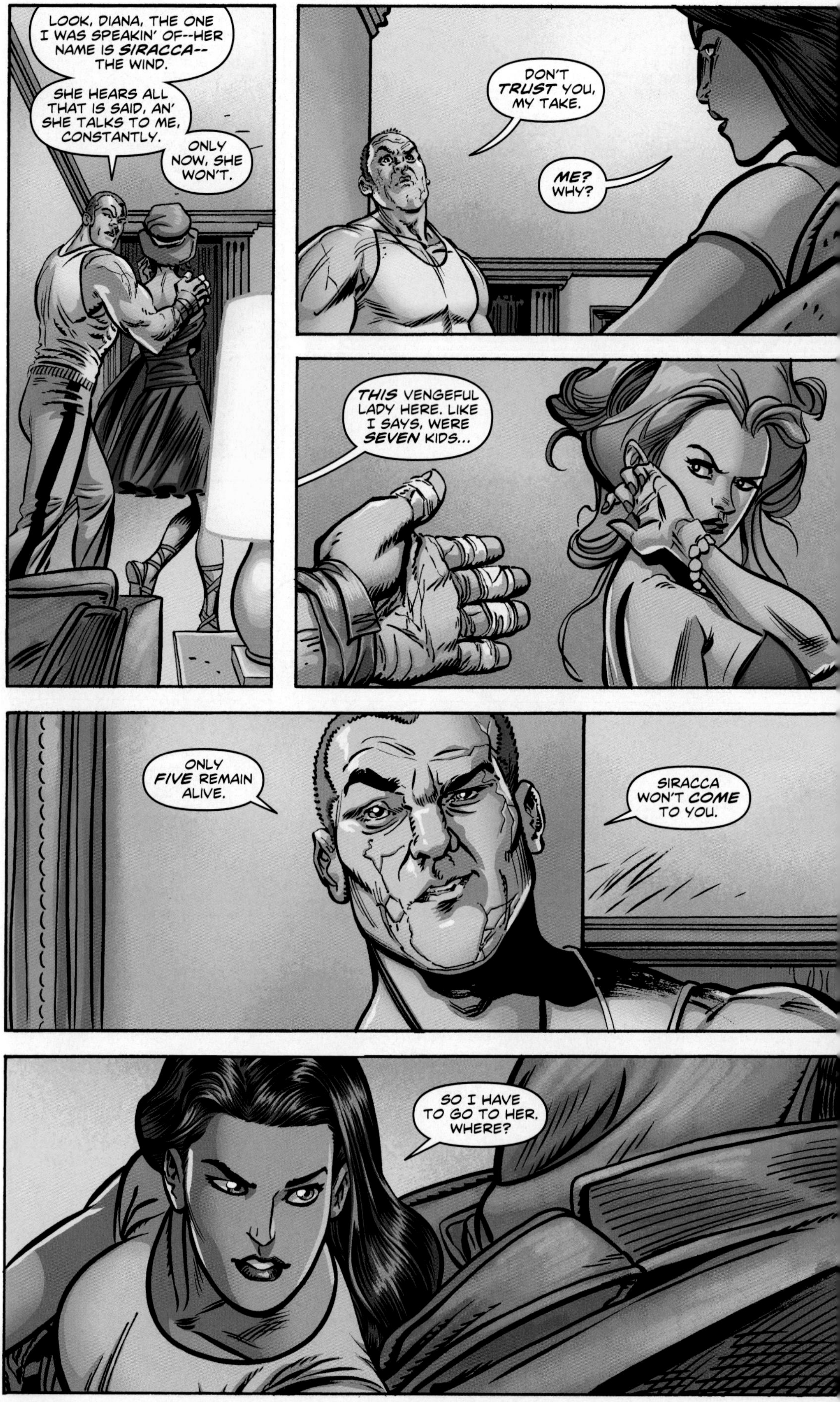
LOOK, DIANA, THE ONE I WAS SPEAKIN' OF--HER NAME IS SIRACCA-- THE WIND.
SHE HEARS ALL THAT IS SAID, AN' SHE TALKS TO ME, CONSTANTLY.
ONLY NOW, SHE WON'T.
DON'T TRUST YOU, MY TAKE.
ME? WHY?
THIS VENGEFUL LADY HERE. LIKE I SAYS, WERE SEVEN KIDS...
ONLY FIVE REMAIN ALIVE.
SIRACCA WON'T COME TO YOU.
SO I HAVE TO GO TO HER. WHERE?

WE'RE SAFE HERE.

YES. WE NOW HAVE PLENTY OF FOOD, WATER... COUPLED WITH THE AMMUNITION...

LET'S CALL IT SAFE.

FOR A CHANGE.

COLONEL--

A WOMAN APPROACHES...

A WOMAN?

WHY, I...

"...WONDER?"

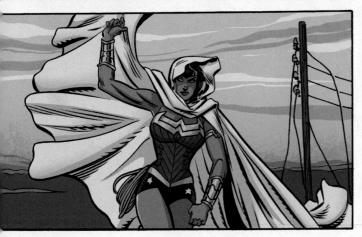

OPEN FIRE!

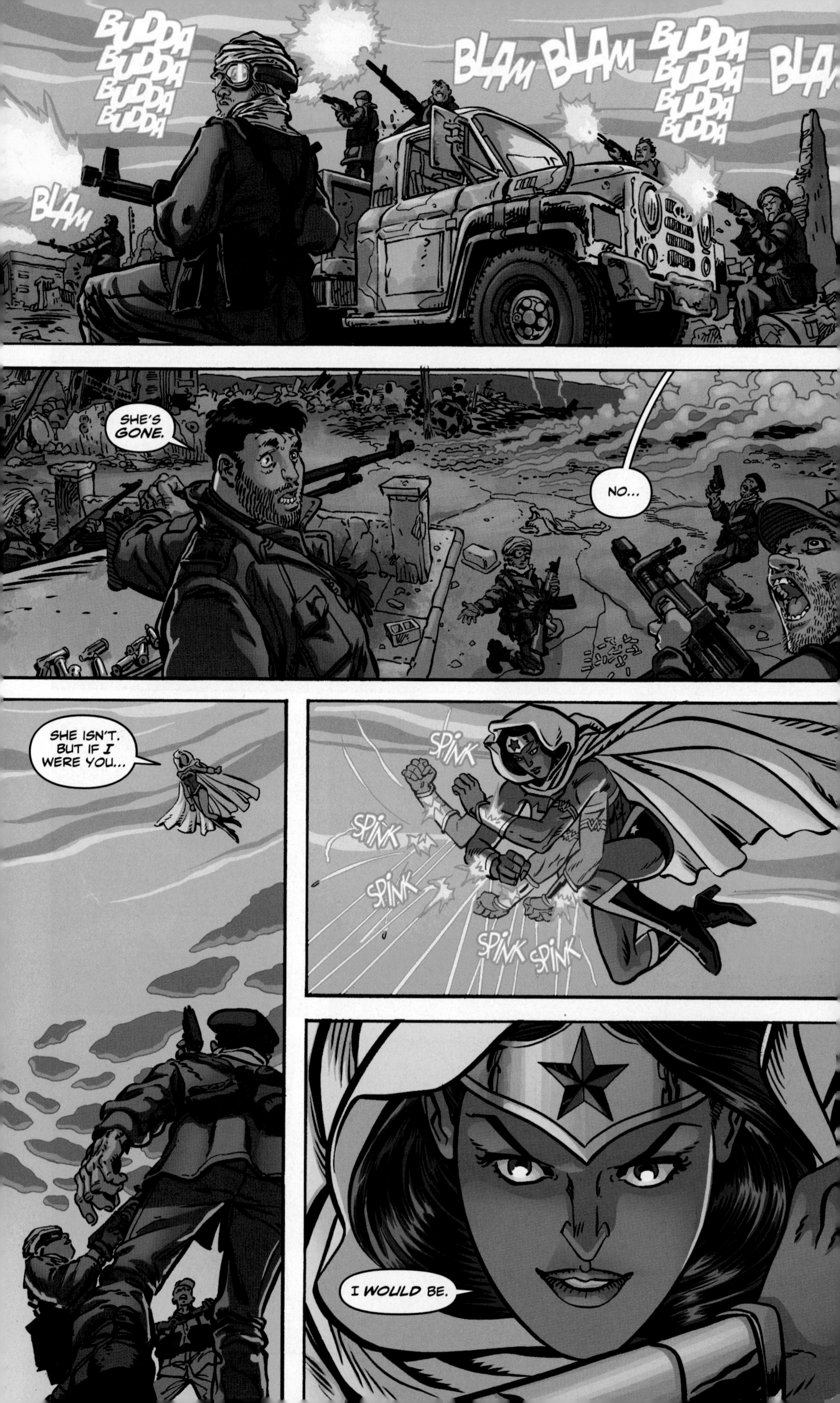
BUDDA BUDDA BUDDA BUDDA
BLAM BLAM BUDDA BUDDA BUDDA BUDDA
BLA
BLAM
SHE'S GONE.
NO...
SHE ISN'T. BUT IF I WERE YOU...
SPINK
SPINK
SPINK
SPINK SPINK
I WOULD BE.

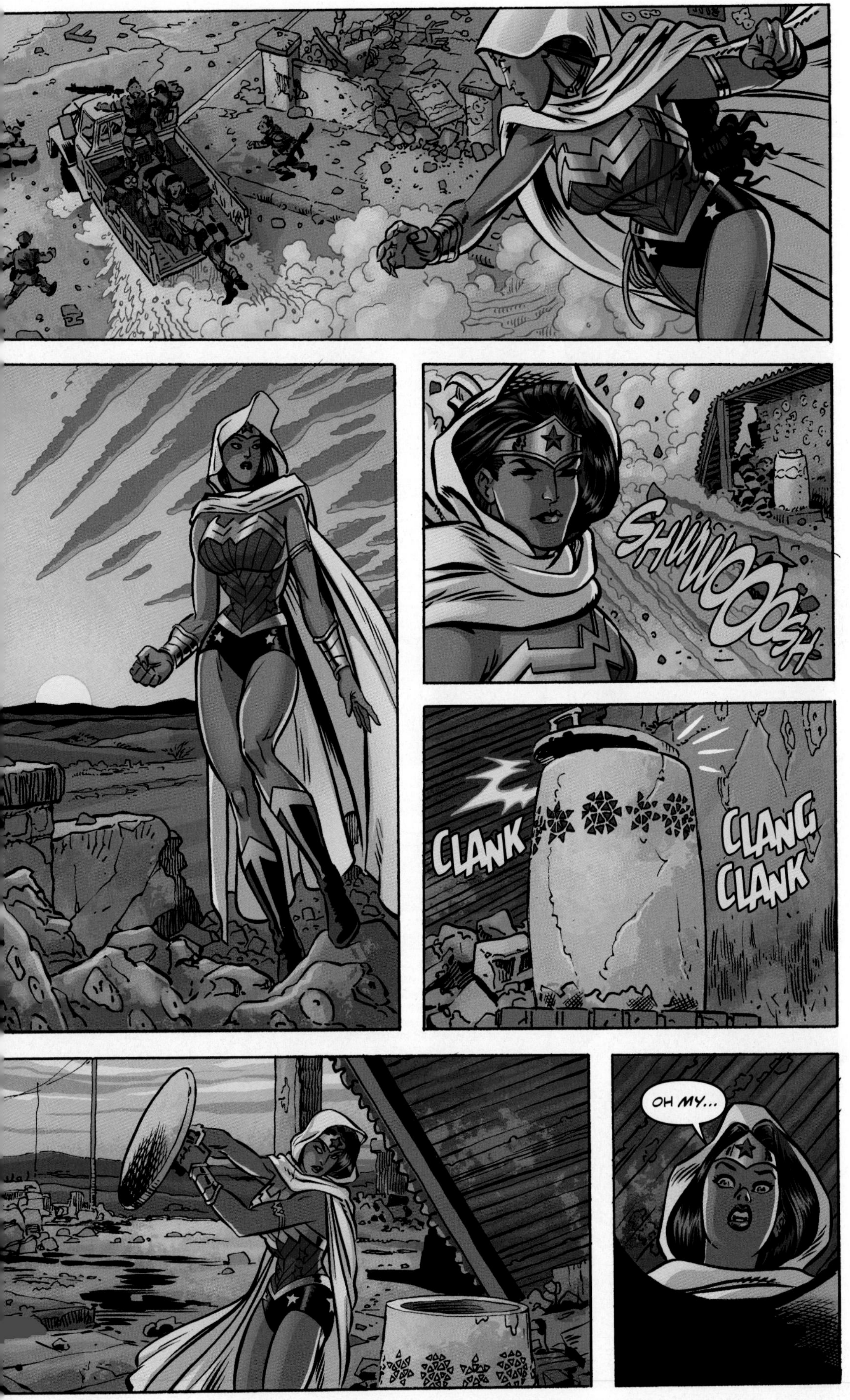
SHWOOOOSH
CLANK
CLANG
CLANK
OH MY...

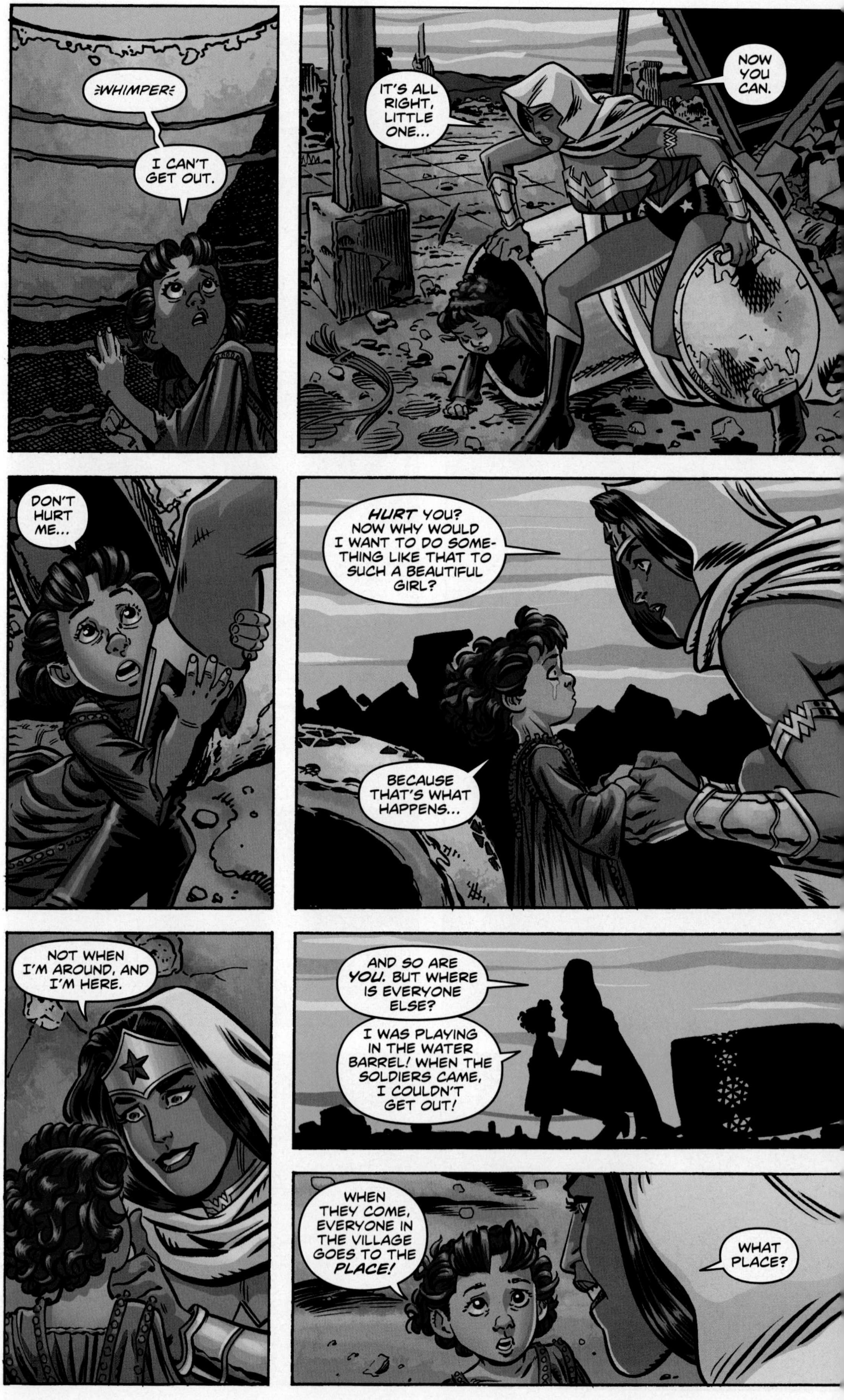
WHIMPER
I CAN'T GET OUT.
IT'S ALL RIGHT, LITTLE ONE...
NOW YOU CAN.
DON'T HURT ME...
HURT YOU? NOW WHY WOULD I WANT TO DO SOME-THING LIKE THAT TO SUCH A BEAUTIFUL GIRL?
BECAUSE THAT'S WHAT HAPPENS...
NOT WHEN I'M AROUND, AND I'M HERE.
AND SO ARE YOU. BUT WHERE IS EVERYONE ELSE?
I WAS PLAYING IN THE WATER BARREL! WHEN THE SOLDIERS CAME, I COULDN'T GET OUT!
WHEN THEY COME, EVERYONE IN THE VILLAGE GOES TO THE PLACE!
WHAT PLACE?

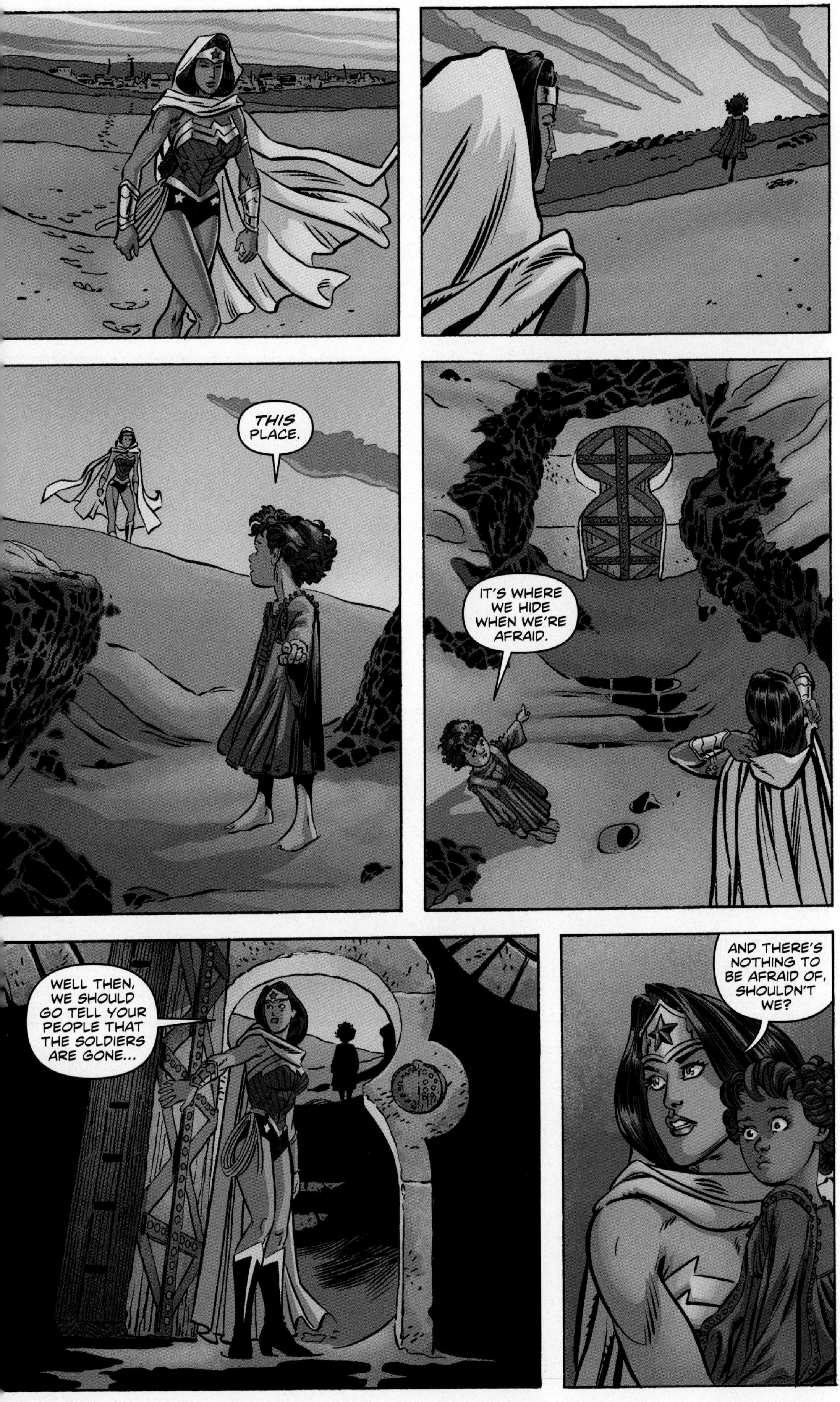
THIS PLACE.
IT'S WHERE WE HIDE WHEN WE'RE AFRAID.
WELL THEN, WE SHOULD GO TELL YOUR PEOPLE THAT THE SOLDIERS ARE GONE...
AND THERE'S NOTHING TO BE AFRAID OF, SHOULDN'T WE?

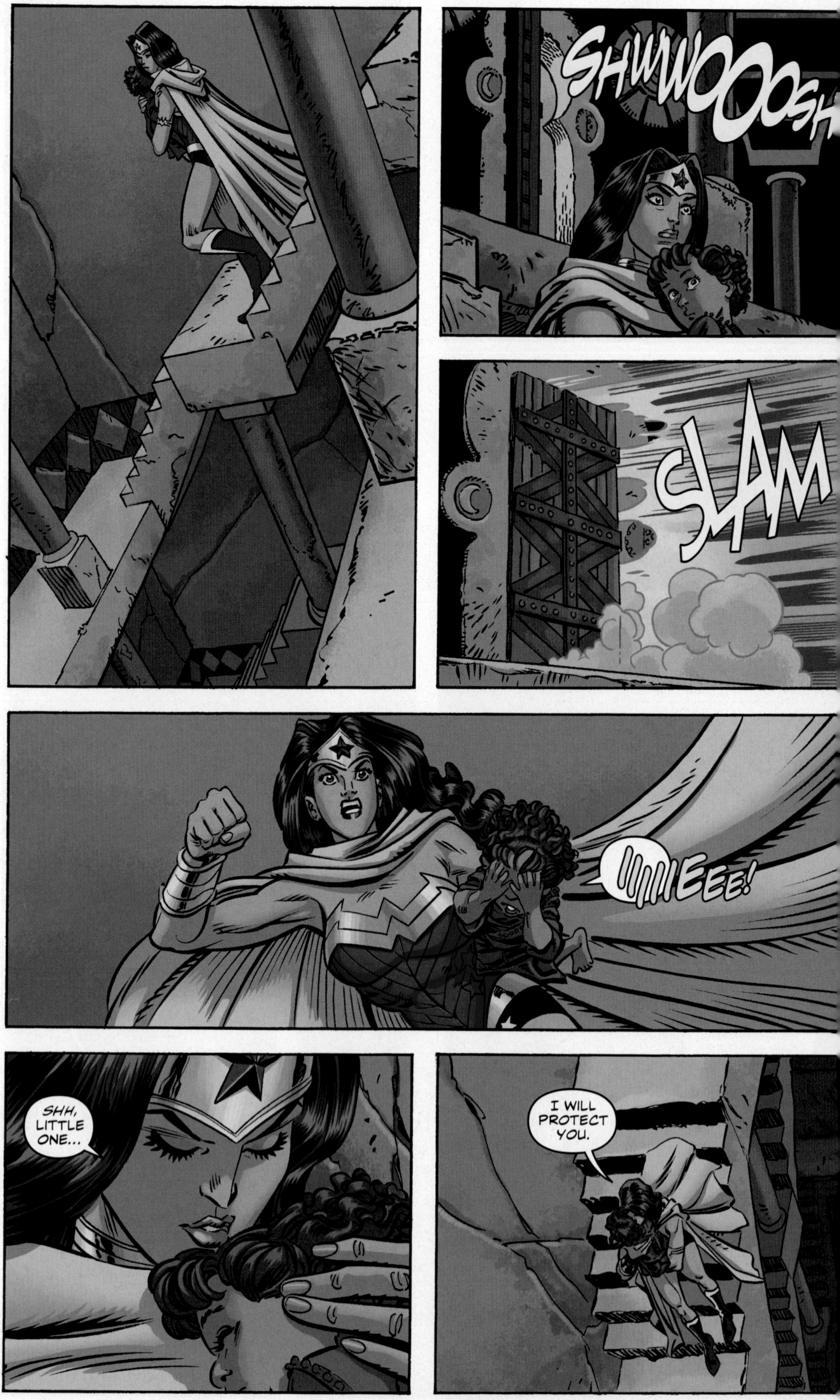
SHWOOOSH
SLAM
IIIIIEEE!
SHH, LITTLE ONE...
I WILL PROTECT YOU.

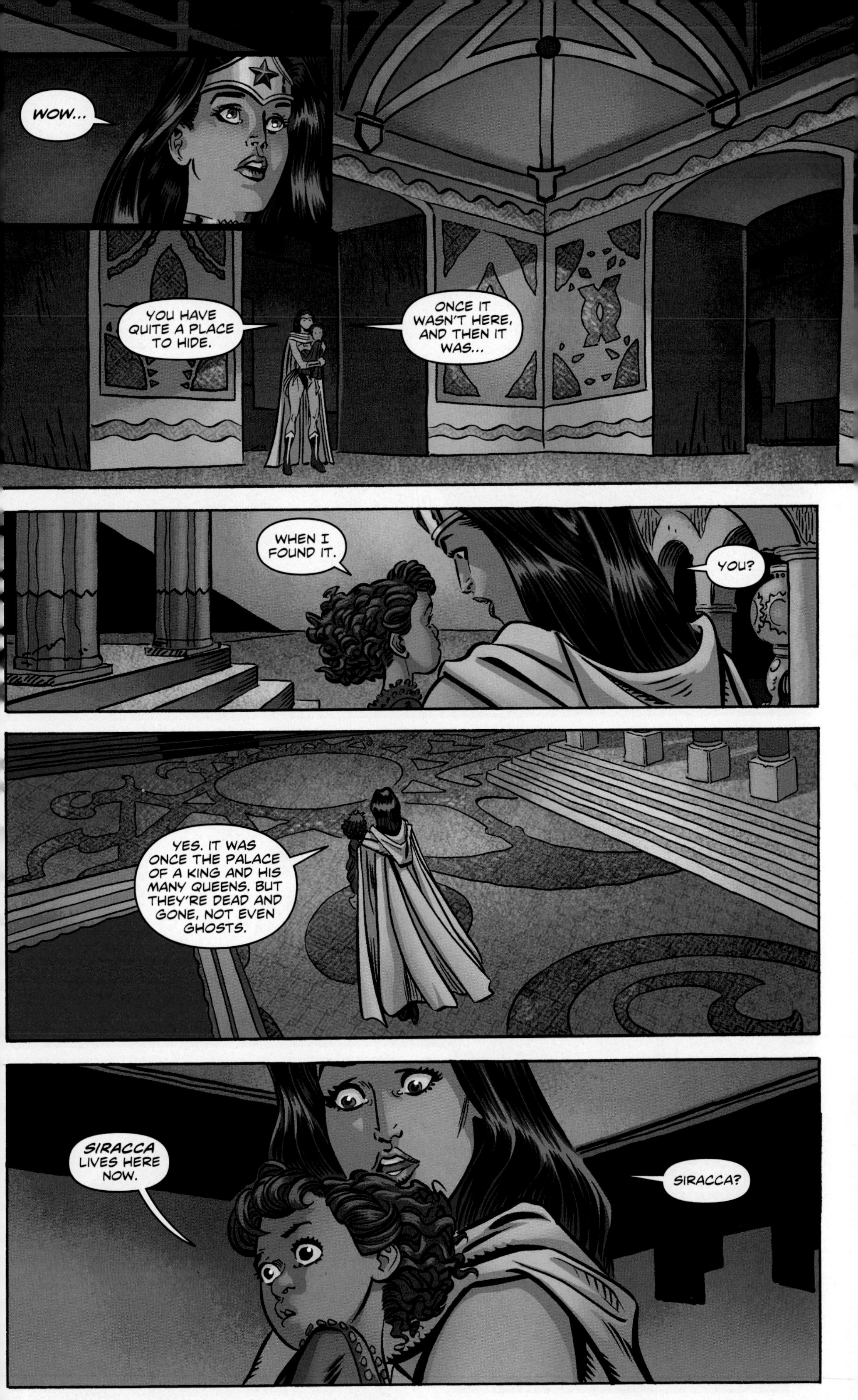
WOW...
YOU HAVE QUITE A PLACE TO HIDE.
ONCE IT WASN'T HERE, AND THEN IT WAS...
WHEN I FOUND IT.
YOU?
YES. IT WAS ONCE THE PALACE OF A KING AND HIS MANY QUEENS. BUT THEY'RE DEAD AND GONE, NOT EVEN GHOSTS.
SIRACCA LIVES HERE NOW.
SIRACCA?

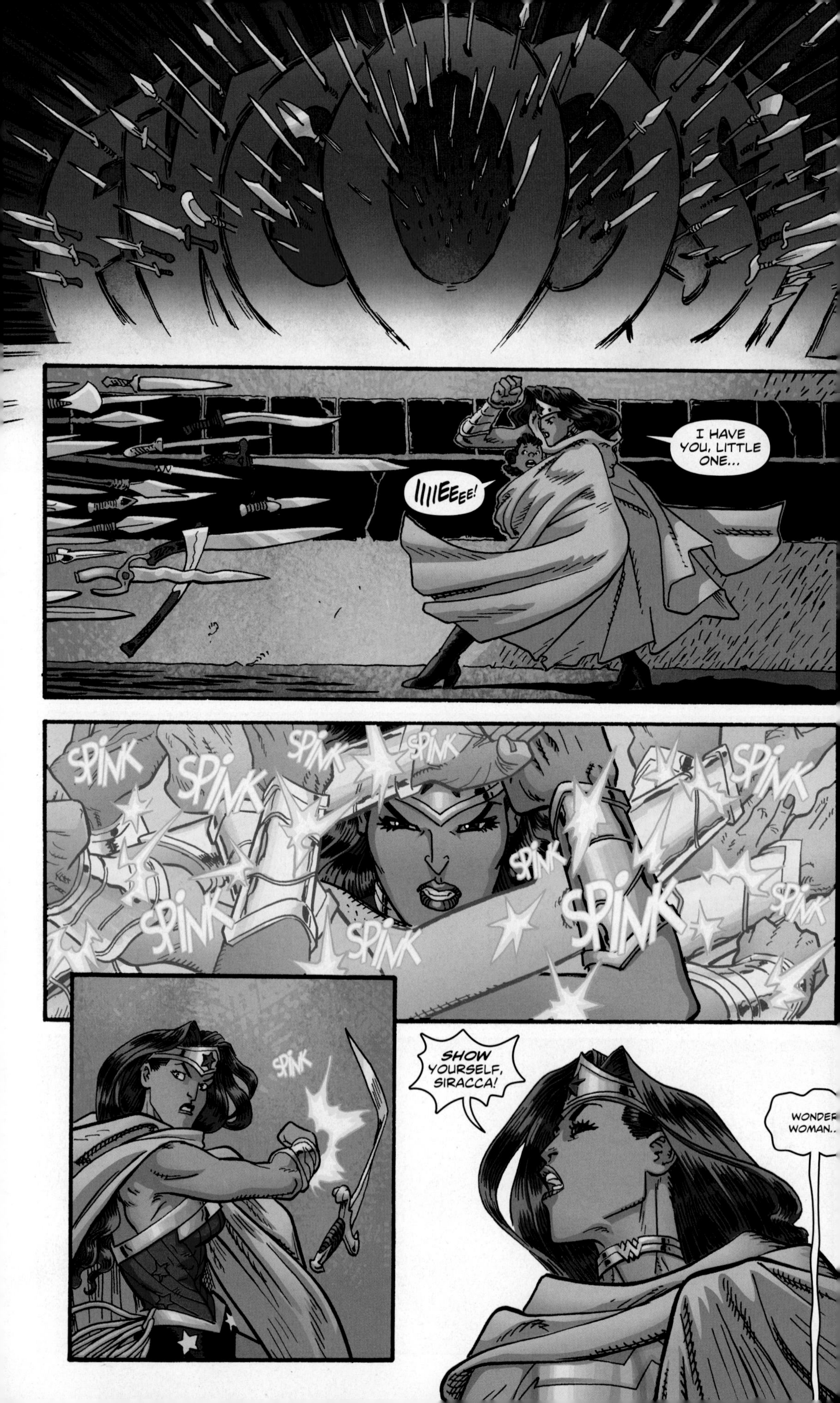

I HAVE YOU, LITTLE ONE...
IIIIEEEE!
SPINK
SPINK
SPINK
SPINK
SPINK
SPINK
SPINK
SPINK
SPINK
SPINK
SPINK
SHOW YOURSELF, SIRACCA!
WONDER WOMAN...

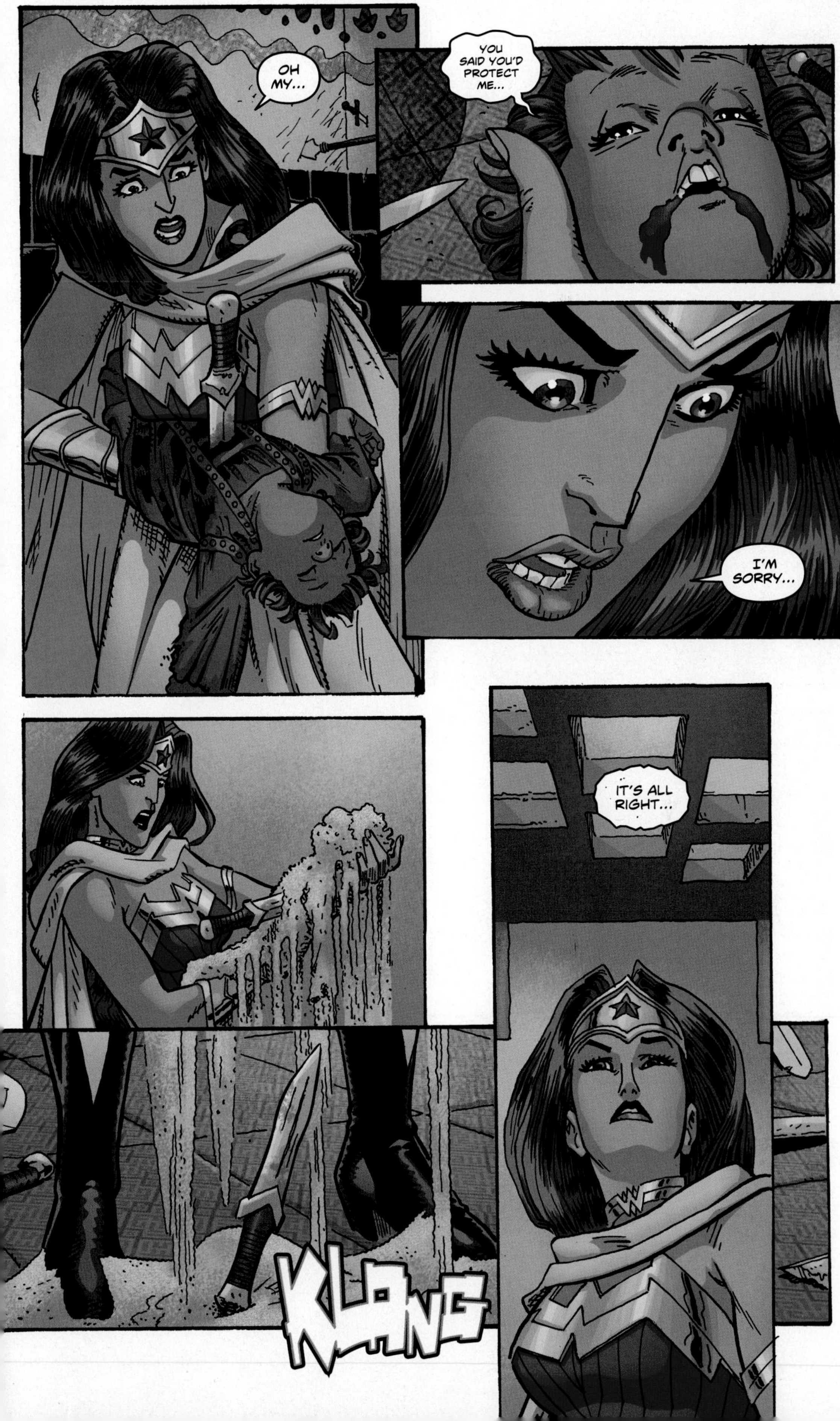
OH MY...
YOU SAID YOU'D PROTECT ME...
I'M SORRY...
IT'S ALL RIGHT...
KLANG

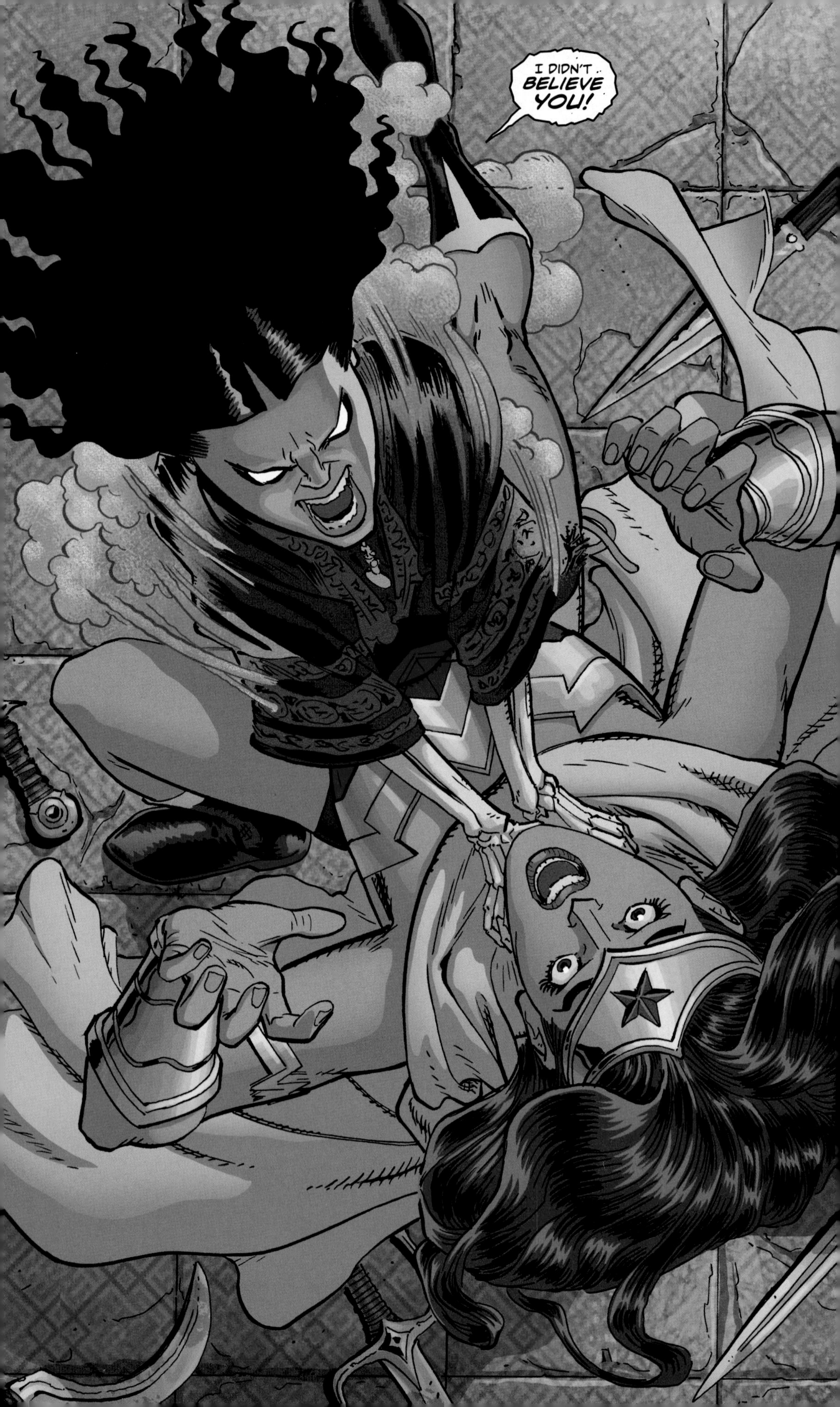
I DIDN'T BELIEVE YOU!

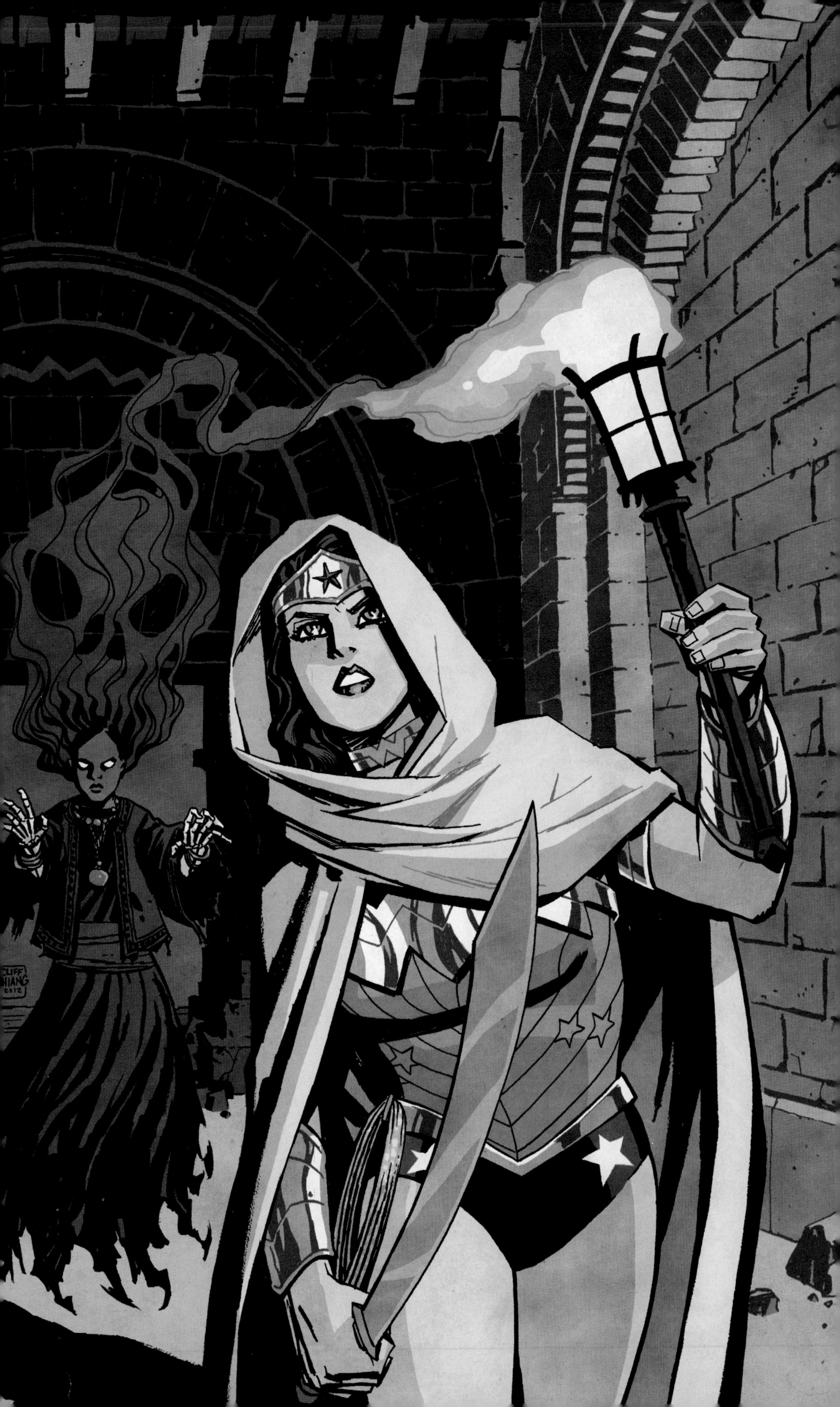
CLIFF CHIANG 2012

JUST DESERTS

TONY AKINS layouts **DAN GREEN (pages 1-7, 10-12)** and **RICK BURCHETT (pages 8-9, 13-20)** finishes

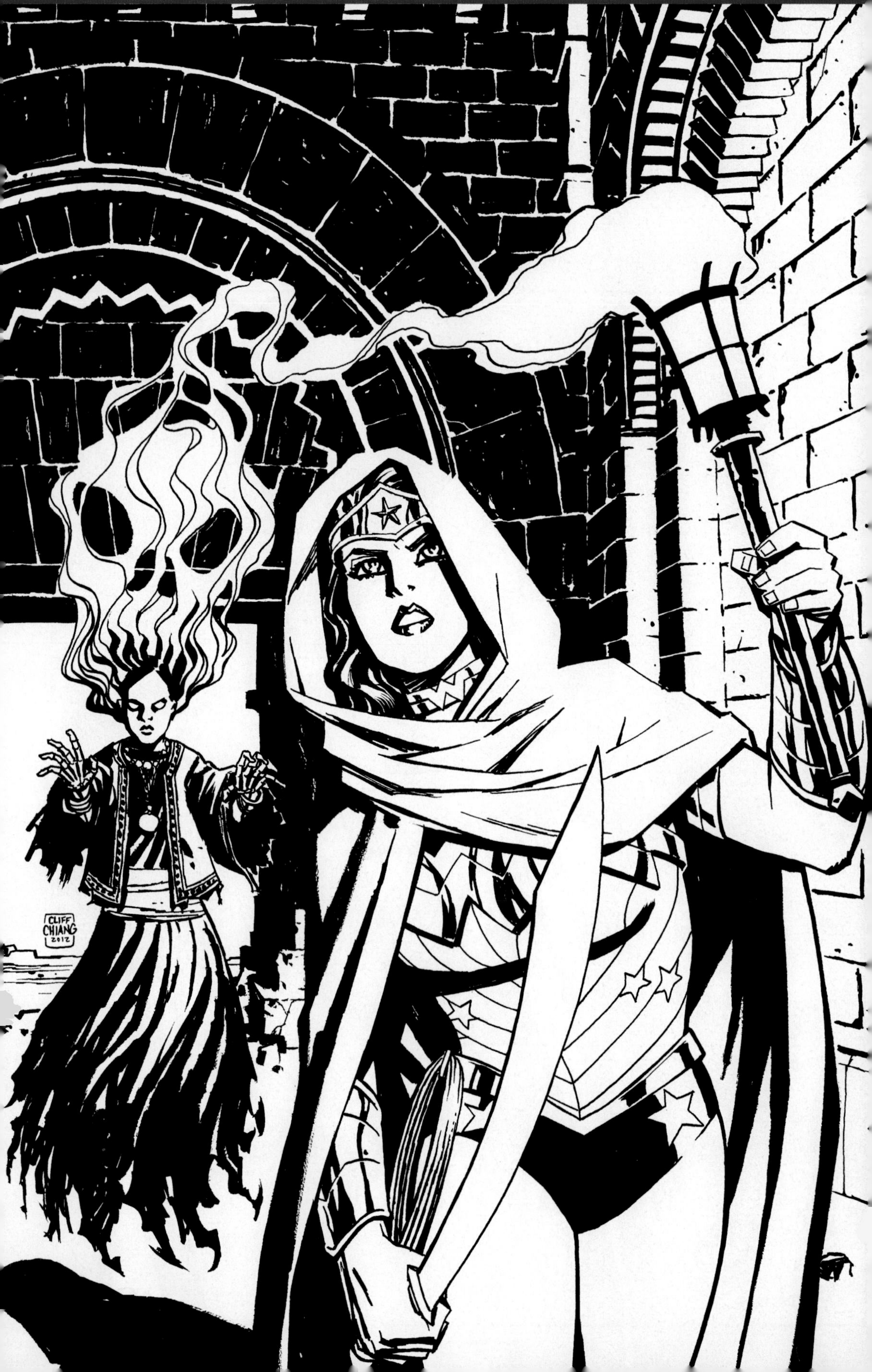
CLIFF CHIANG 2012

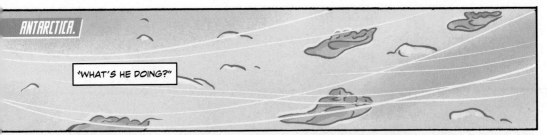

"WHAT'S HE DOING?"

NOTHING. HE HASN'T MOVED IN OVER SIX HOURS.

CASSANDRA... IS IT TRUE THAT HE ATE DOCTOR DUERSON'S BRAIN?

TO LEARN OUR LANGUAGE, MR. BUTLER.

IS THAT POSSIBLE?

IT HAPPENED. HE SAID HE DIDN'T NEED OUR HELP.

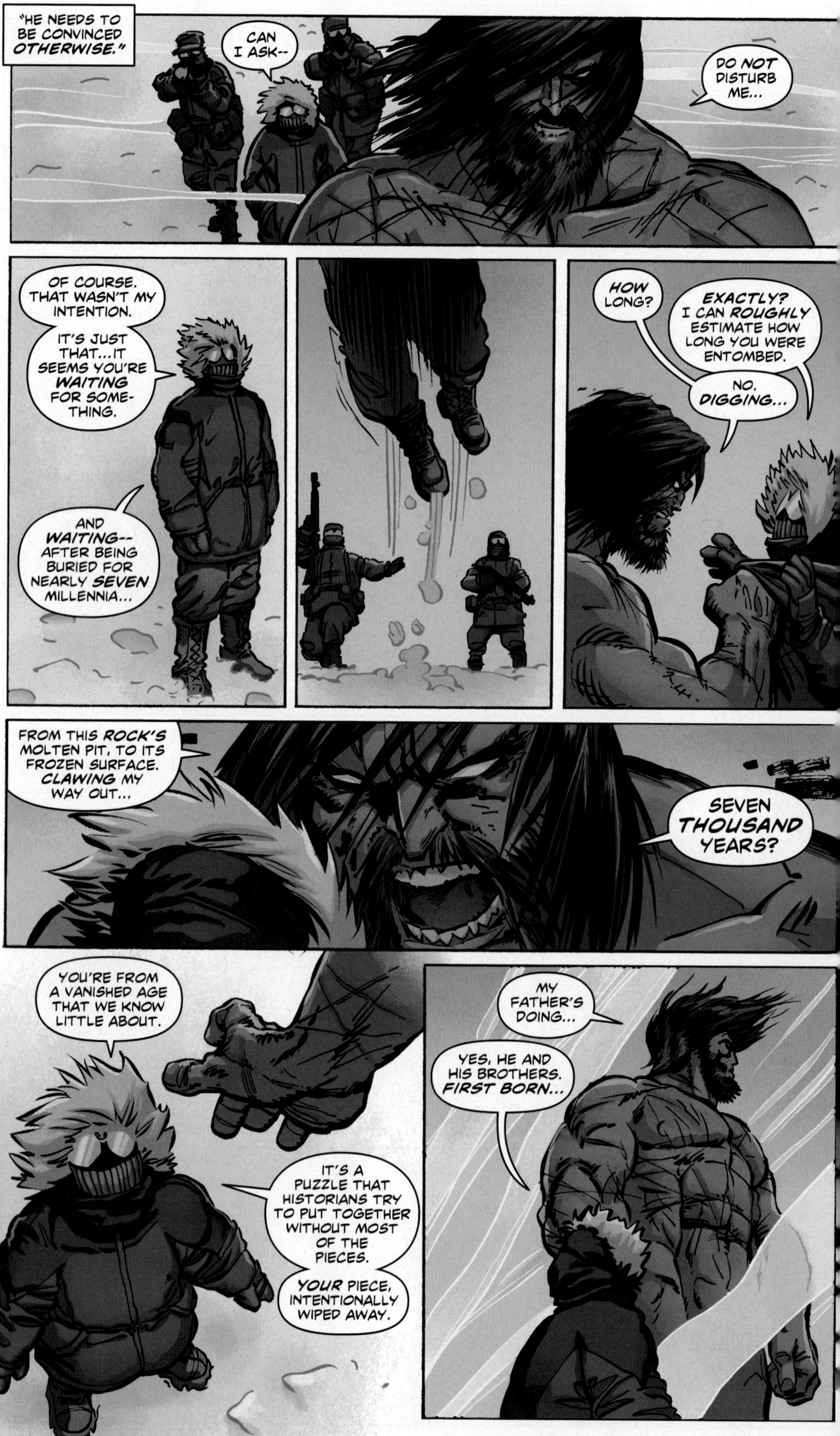
"HE NEEDS TO BE CONVINCED OTHERWISE."
CAN I ASK--
DO NOT DISTURB ME...
OF COURSE. THAT WASN'T MY INTENTION.
IT'S JUST THAT...IT SEEMS YOU'RE WAITING FOR SOME-THING.
AND WAITING--AFTER BEING BURIED FOR NEARLY SEVEN MILLENNIA...
HOW LONG?
EXACTLY? I CAN ROUGHLY ESTIMATE HOW LONG YOU WERE ENTOMBED.
NO. DIGGING...
FROM THIS ROCK'S MOLTEN PIT, TO ITS FROZEN SURFACE. CLAWING MY WAY OUT...
SEVEN THOUSAND YEARS?
YOU'RE FROM A VANISHED AGE THAT WE KNOW LITTLE ABOUT.
IT'S A PUZZLE THAT HISTORIANS TRY TO PUT TOGETHER WITHOUT MOST OF THE PIECES.
YOUR PIECE, INTENTIONALLY WIPED AWAY.
MY FATHER'S DOING...
YES, HE AND HIS BROTHERS. FIRST BORN...

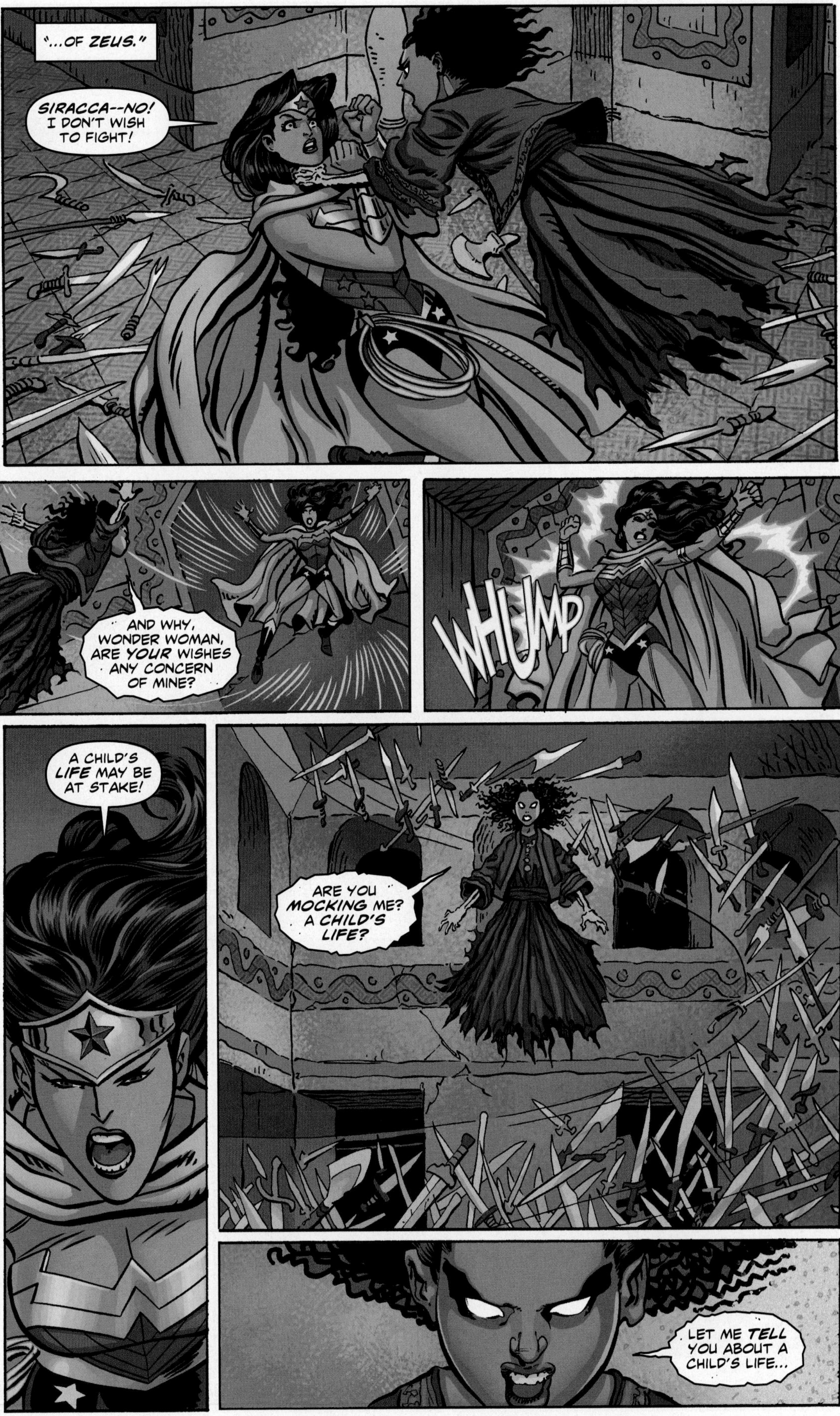
"...OF ZEUS."
SIRACCA--NO! I DON'T WISH TO FIGHT!
AND WHY, WONDER WOMAN, ARE YOUR WISHES ANY CONCERN OF MINE?
WHUMP
A CHILD'S LIFE MAY BE AT STAKE!
ARE YOU MOCKING ME? A CHILD'S LIFE?
LET ME TELL YOU ABOUT A CHILD'S LIFE...

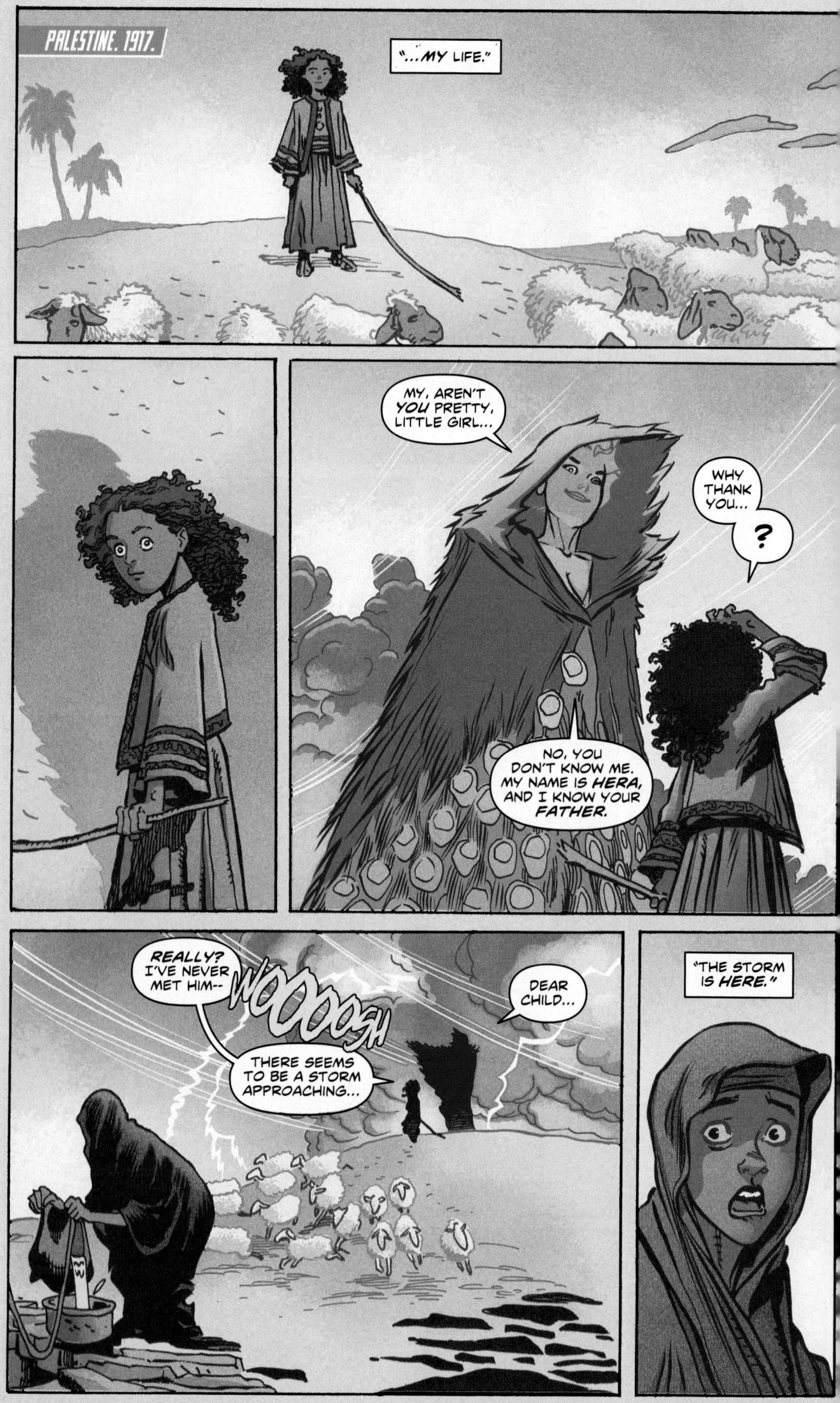
PALESTINE. 1917.
"...MY LIFE."
MY, AREN'T YOU PRETTY, LITTLE GIRL...
WHY THANK YOU...
?
NO, YOU DON'T KNOW ME. MY NAME IS HERA, AND I KNOW YOUR FATHER.
REALLY? I'VE NEVER MET HIM--
WOOOOOSH
THERE SEEMS TO BE A STORM APPROACHING...
DEAR CHILD...
"THE STORM IS HERE."

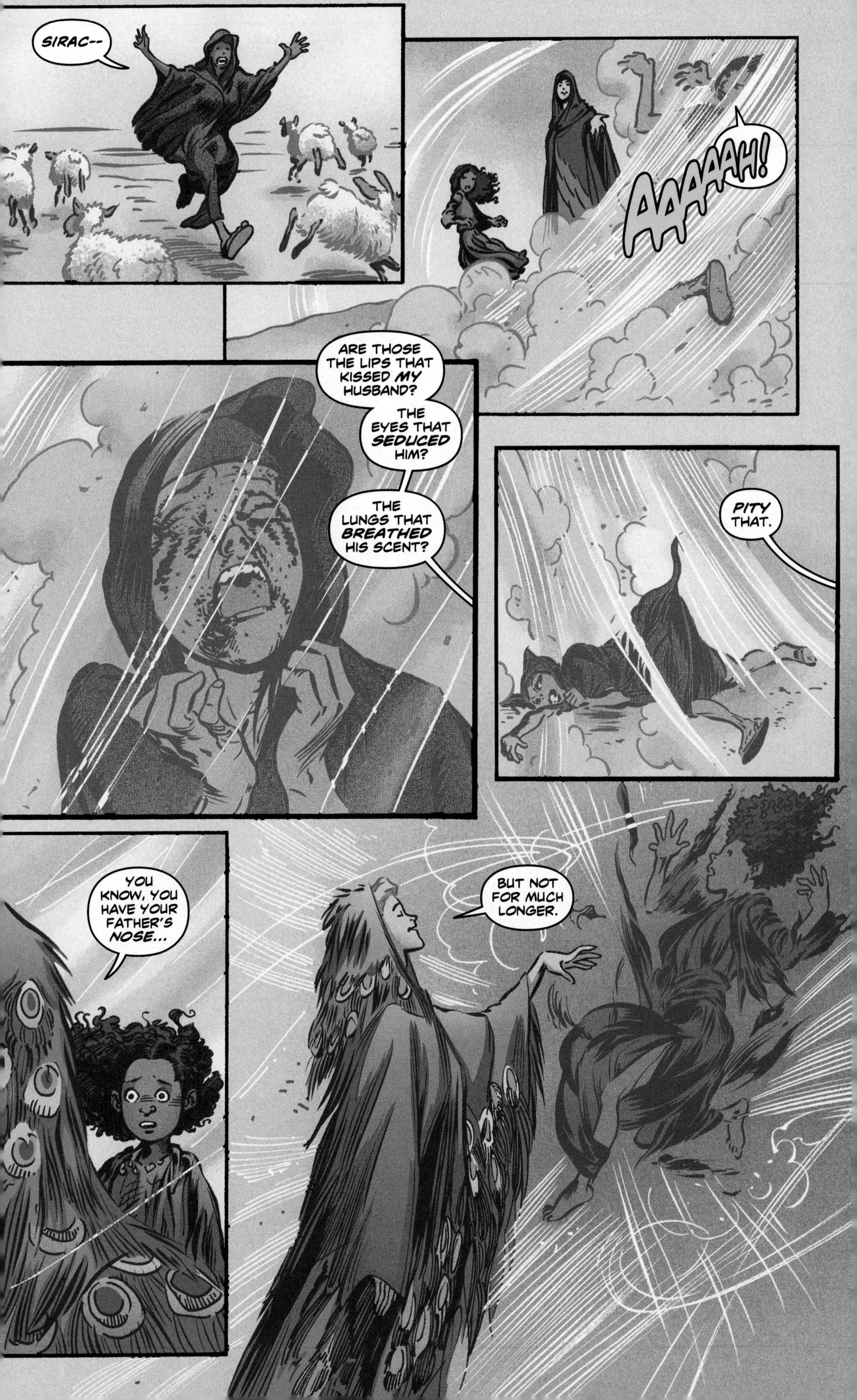
SIRAC--
AAAAAH!
ARE THOSE THE LIPS THAT KISSED MY HUSBAND?
THE EYES THAT SEDUCED HIM?
THE LUNGS THAT BREATHED HIS SCENT?
PITY THAT.
YOU KNOW, YOU HAVE YOUR FATHER'S NOSE...
BUT NOT FOR MUCH LONGER.

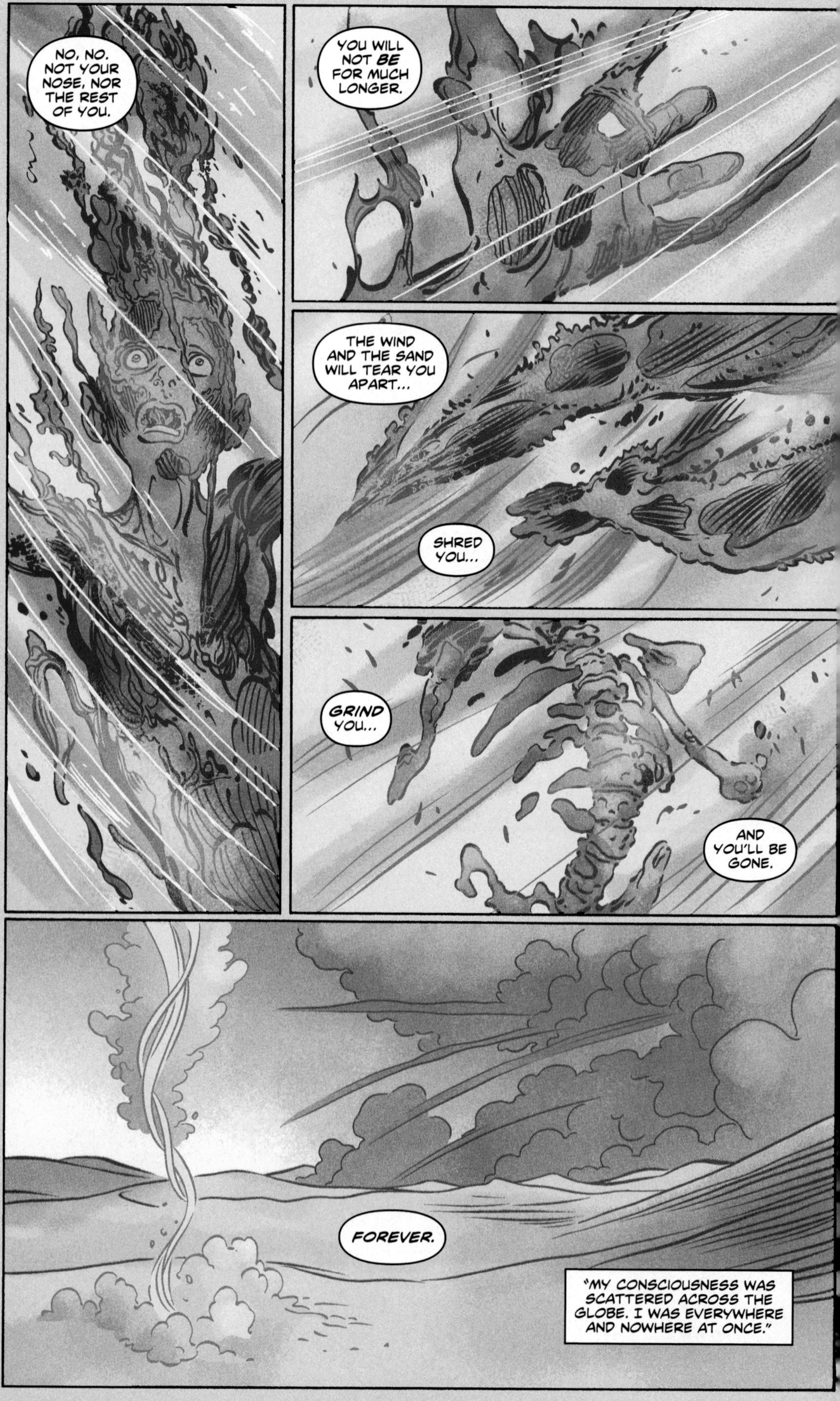
NO, NO. NOT YOUR NOSE, NOR THE REST OF YOU.
YOU WILL NOT *BE* FOR MUCH LONGER.
THE WIND AND THE SAND WILL TEAR YOU APART...
SHRED YOU...
GRIND YOU...
AND YOU'LL BE GONE.
FOREVER.
"MY CONSCIOUSNESS WAS SCATTERED ACROSS THE GLOBE. I WAS EVERYWHERE AND NOWHERE AT ONCE."

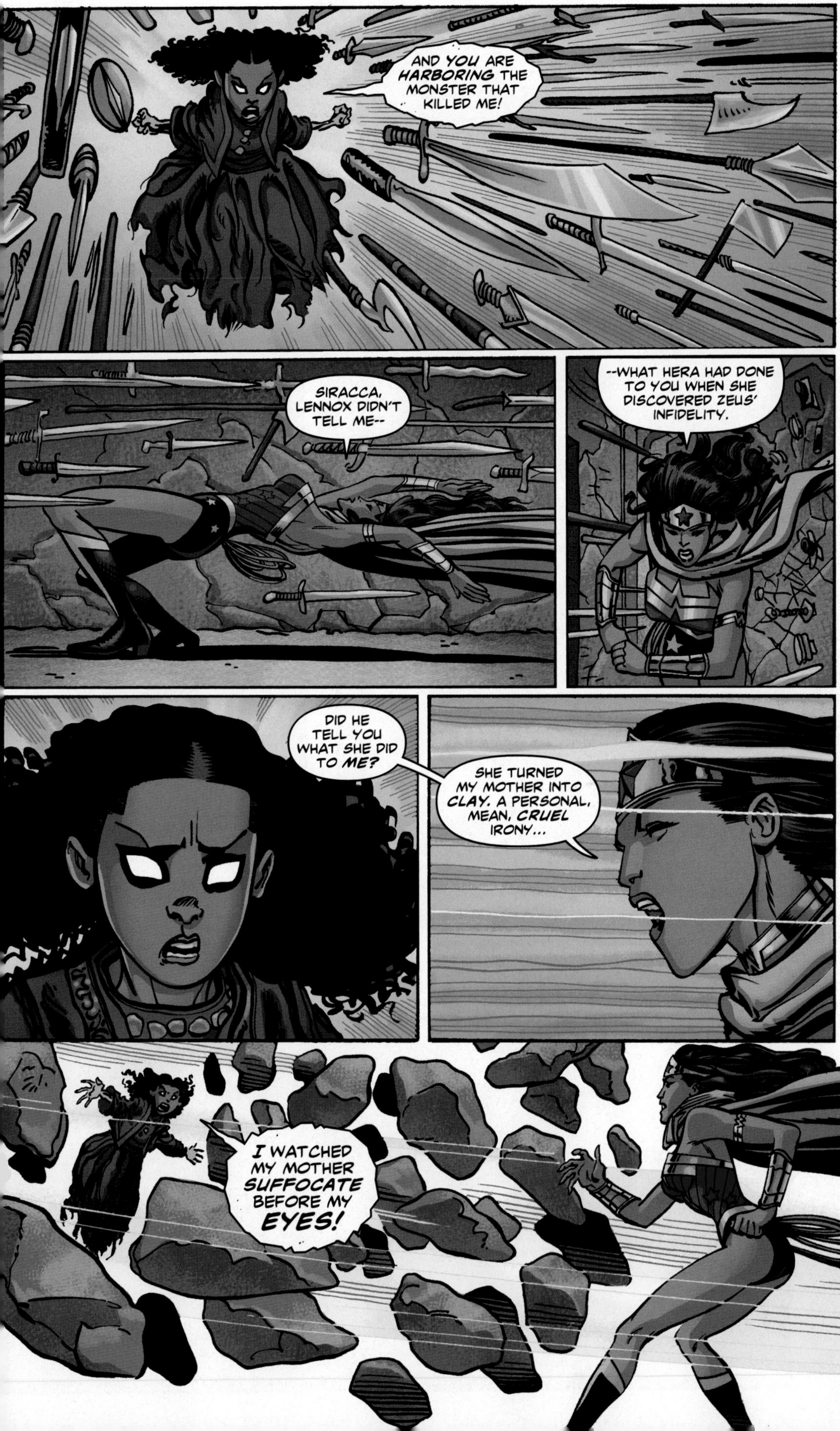
AND YOU ARE HARBORING THE MONSTER THAT KILLED ME!
SIRACCA, LENNOX DIDN'T TELL ME--
--WHAT HERA HAD DONE TO YOU WHEN SHE DISCOVERED ZEUS' INFIDELITY.
DID HE TELL YOU WHAT SHE DID TO ME?
SHE TURNED MY MOTHER INTO CLAY. A PERSONAL, MEAN, CRUEL IRONY...
I WATCHED MY MOTHER SUFFOCATE BEFORE MY EYES!

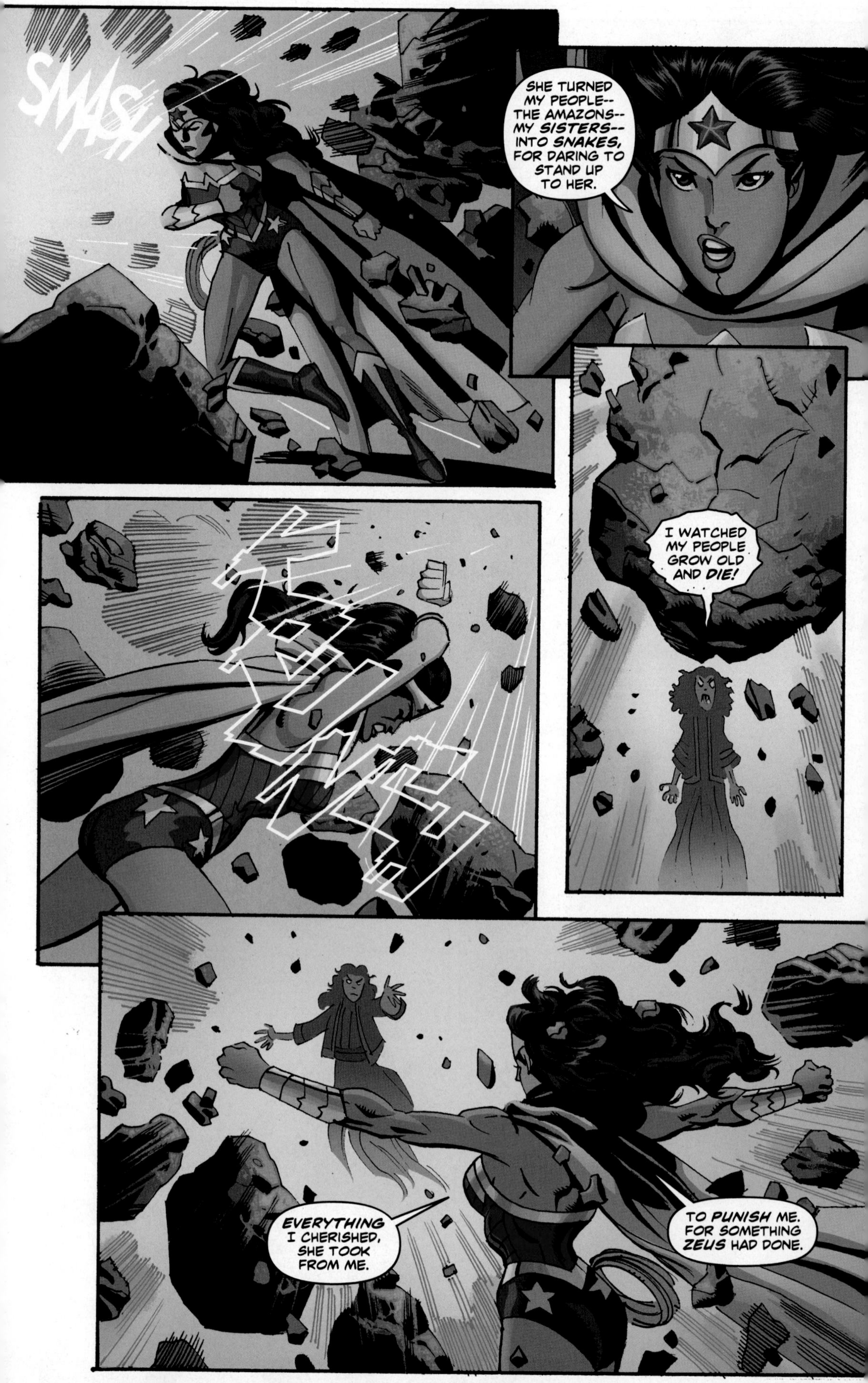
SMASH
SHE TURNED MY PEOPLE-- THE AMAZONS-- MY SISTERS-- INTO SNAKES, FOR DARING TO STAND UP TO HER.
I WATCHED MY PEOPLE GROW OLD AND DIE!
EVERYTHING I CHERISHED, SHE TOOK FROM ME.
TO PUNISH ME. FOR SOMETHING ZEUS HAD DONE.

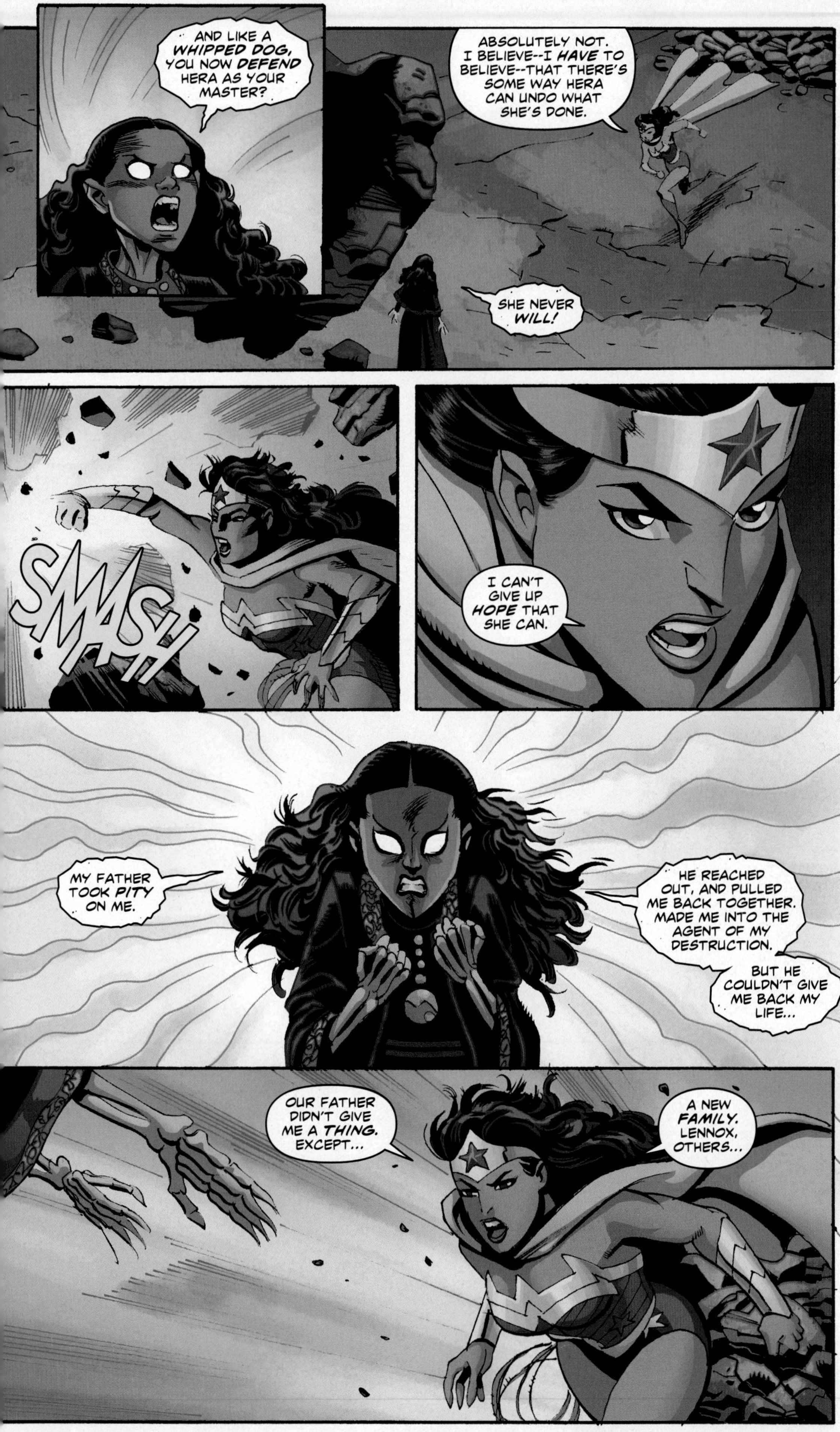
AND LIKE A WHIPPED DOG, YOU NOW DEFEND HERA AS YOUR MASTER?
ABSOLUTELY NOT. I BELIEVE--I HAVE TO BELIEVE--THAT THERE'S SOME WAY HERA CAN UNDO WHAT SHE'S DONE.
SHE NEVER WILL!
SMASH
I CAN'T GIVE UP HOPE THAT SHE CAN.
MY FATHER TOOK PITY ON ME.
HE REACHED OUT, AND PULLED ME BACK TOGETHER. MADE ME INTO THE AGENT OF MY DESTRUCTION.
BUT HE COULDN'T GIVE ME BACK MY LIFE...
OUR FATHER DIDN'T GIVE ME A THING. EXCEPT...
A NEW FAMILY. LENNOX, OTHERS...

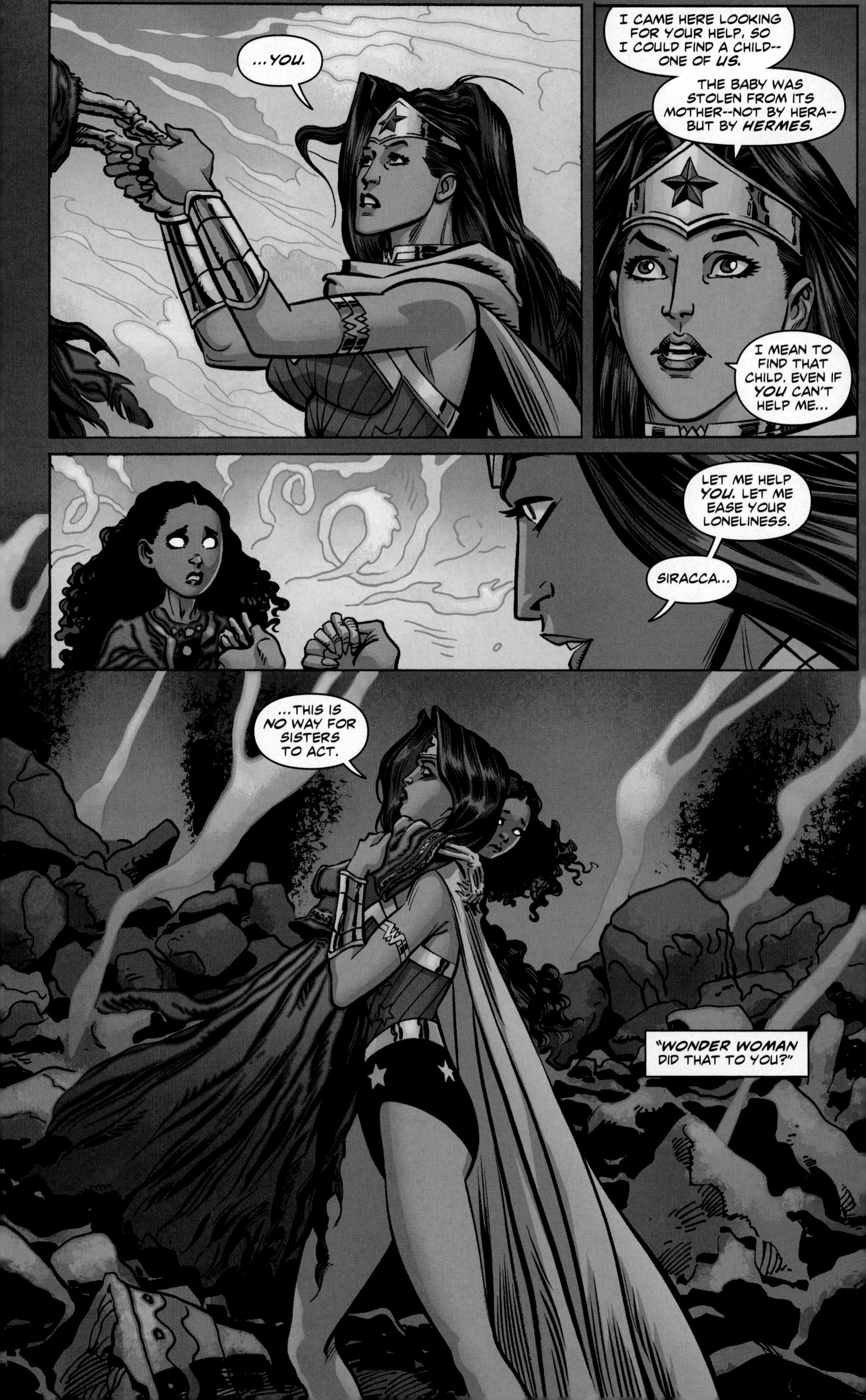
...YOU.
I CAME HERE LOOKING FOR YOUR HELP, SO I COULD FIND A CHILD-- ONE OF US.
THE BABY WAS STOLEN FROM ITS MOTHER--NOT BY HERA-- BUT BY HERMES.
I MEAN TO FIND THAT CHILD. EVEN IF YOU CAN'T HELP ME...
LET ME HELP YOU. LET ME EASE YOUR LONELINESS.
SIRACCA...
...THIS IS NO WAY FOR SISTERS TO ACT.
"WONDER WOMAN DID THAT TO YOU?"

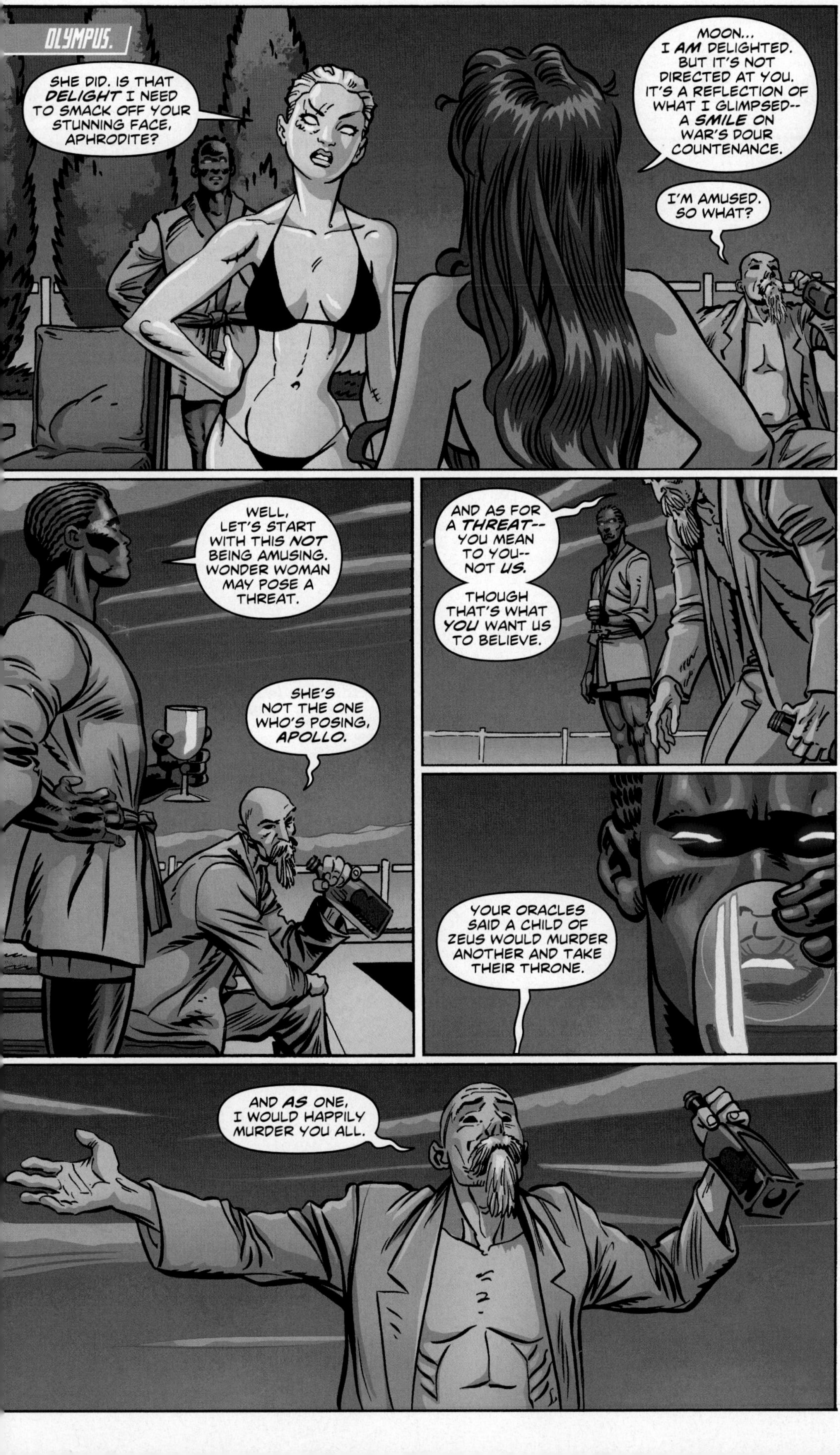
OLYMPUS.
SHE DID. IS THAT DELIGHT I NEED TO SMACK OFF YOUR STUNNING FACE, APHRODITE?
MOON... I AM DELIGHTED. BUT IT'S NOT DIRECTED AT YOU. IT'S A REFLECTION OF WHAT I GLIMPSED-- A SMILE ON WAR'S DOUR COUNTENANCE.
I'M AMUSED. SO WHAT?
WELL, LET'S START WITH THIS NOT BEING AMUSING. WONDER WOMAN MAY POSE A THREAT.
SHE'S NOT THE ONE WHO'S POSING, APOLLO.
AND AS FOR A THREAT-- YOU MEAN TO YOU-- NOT US.
THOUGH THAT'S WHAT YOU WANT US TO BELIEVE.
YOUR ORACLES SAID A CHILD OF ZEUS WOULD MURDER ANOTHER AND TAKE THEIR THRONE.
AND AS ONE, I WOULD HAPPILY MURDER YOU ALL.

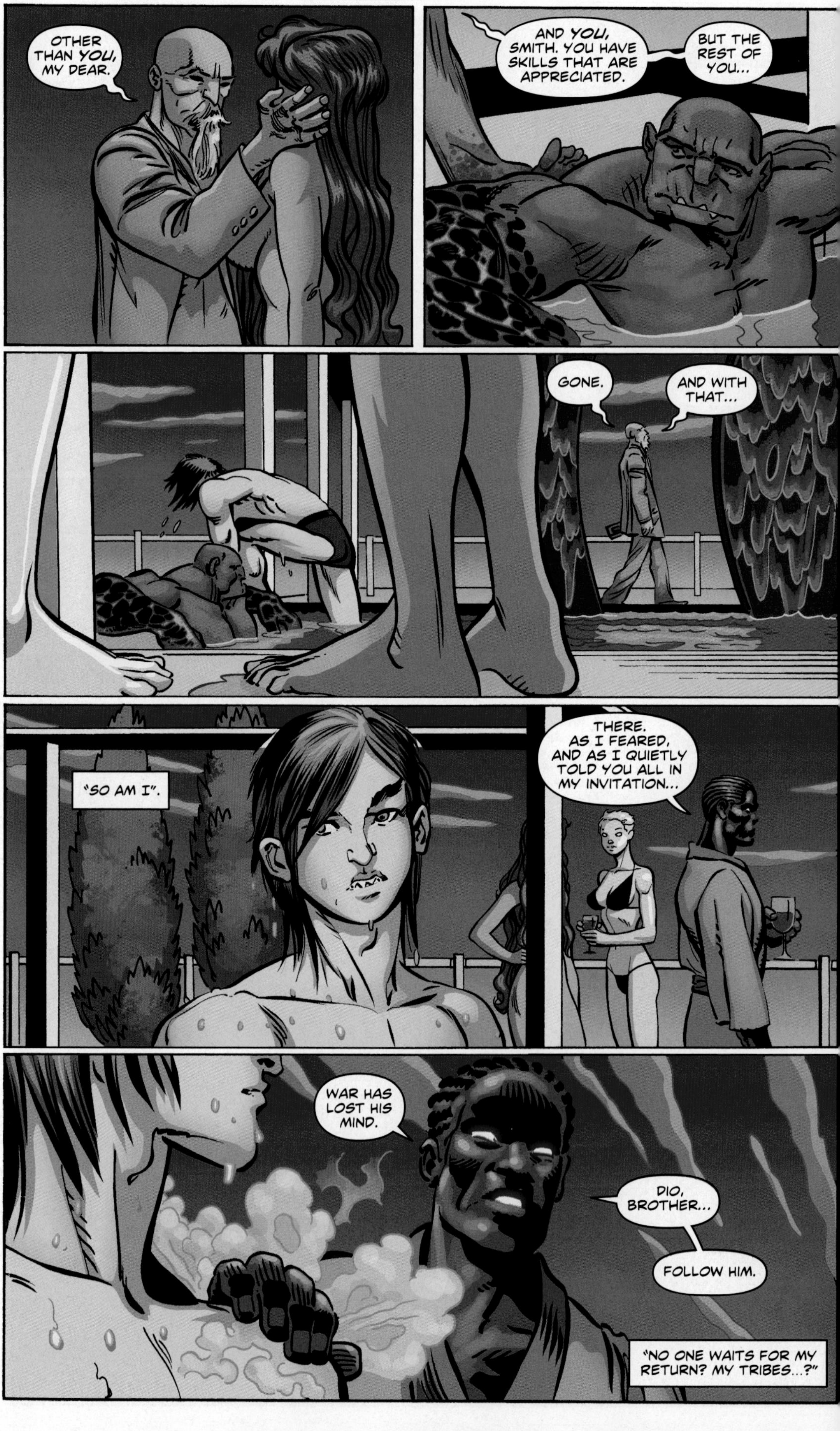
OTHER THAN YOU, MY DEAR.
AND YOU, SMITH. YOU HAVE SKILLS THAT ARE APPRECIATED.
BUT THE REST OF YOU...
GONE.
AND WITH THAT...
"SO AM I".
THERE. AS I FEARED, AND AS I QUIETLY TOLD YOU ALL IN MY INVITATION...
WAR HAS LOST HIS MIND.
DIO, BROTHER...
FOLLOW HIM.
"NO ONE WAITS FOR MY RETURN? MY TRIBES...?"

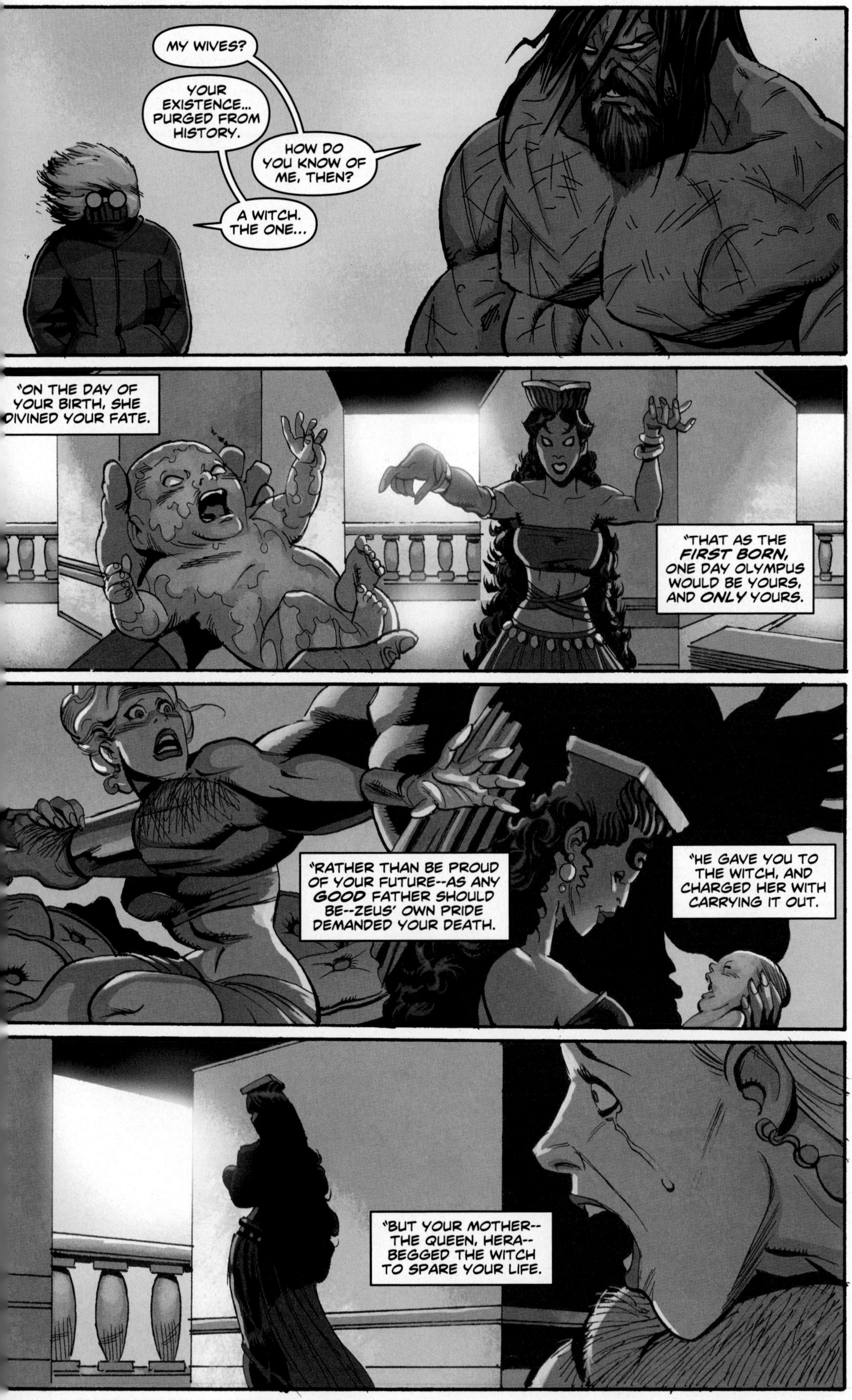
MY WIVES?
YOUR EXISTENCE... PURGED FROM HISTORY.
HOW DO YOU KNOW OF ME, THEN?
A WITCH. THE ONE...
"ON THE DAY OF YOUR BIRTH, SHE DIVINED YOUR FATE.
"THAT AS THE FIRST BORN, ONE DAY OLYMPUS WOULD BE YOURS, AND ONLY YOURS.
"RATHER THAN BE PROUD OF YOUR FUTURE--AS ANY GOOD FATHER SHOULD BE--ZEUS' OWN PRIDE DEMANDED YOUR DEATH.
"HE GAVE YOU TO THE WITCH, AND CHARGED HER WITH CARRYING IT OUT.
"BUT YOUR MOTHER--THE QUEEN, HERA--BEGGED THE WITCH TO SPARE YOUR LIFE.

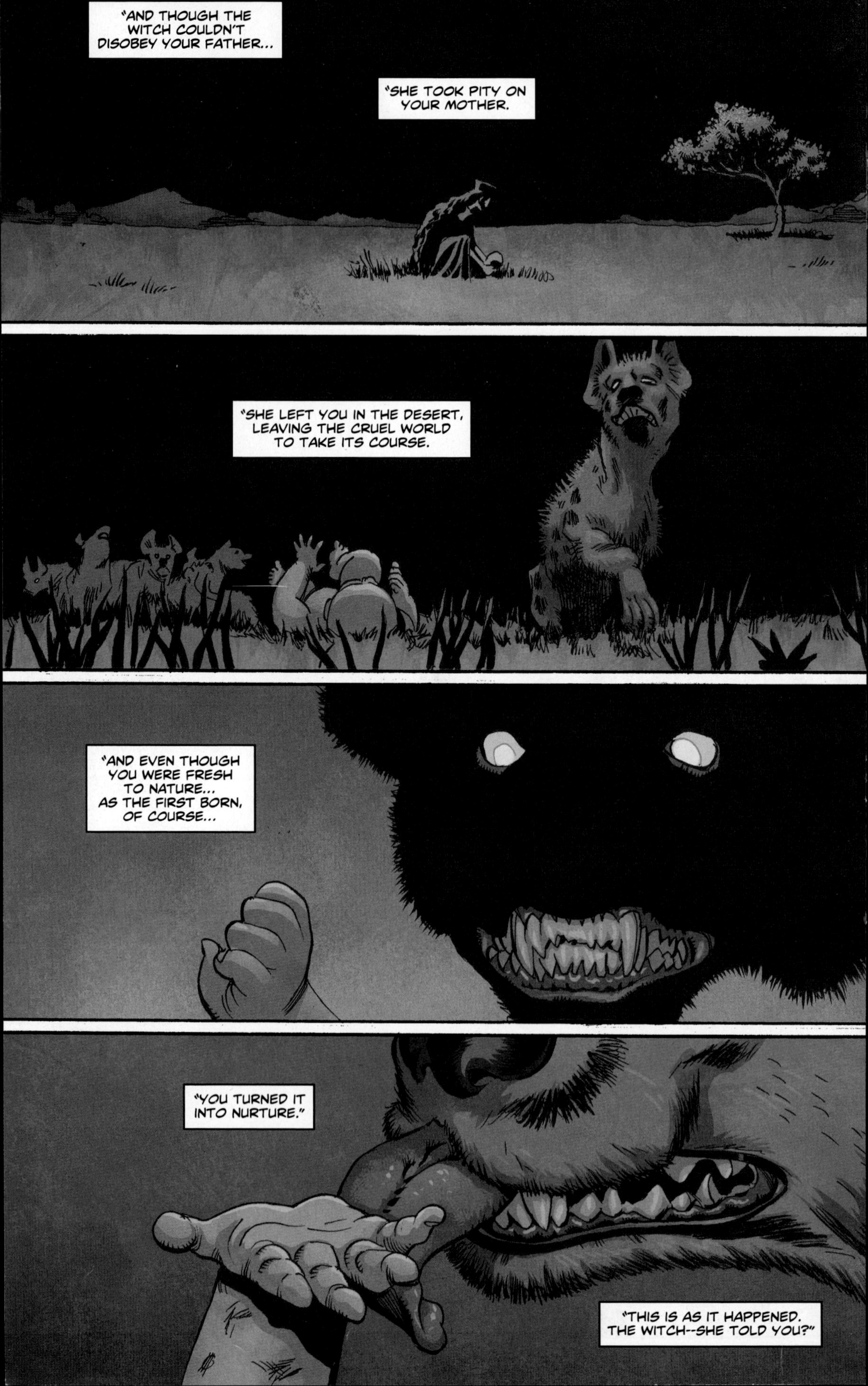
"AND THOUGH THE WITCH COULDN'T DISOBEY YOUR FATHER...
"SHE TOOK PITY ON YOUR MOTHER.
"SHE LEFT YOU IN THE DESERT, LEAVING THE CRUEL WORLD TO TAKE ITS COURSE.
"AND EVEN THOUGH YOU WERE FRESH TO NATURE... AS THE FIRST BORN, OF COURSE...
"YOU TURNED IT INTO NURTURE."
"THIS IS AS IT HAPPENED. THE WITCH--SHE TOLD YOU?"

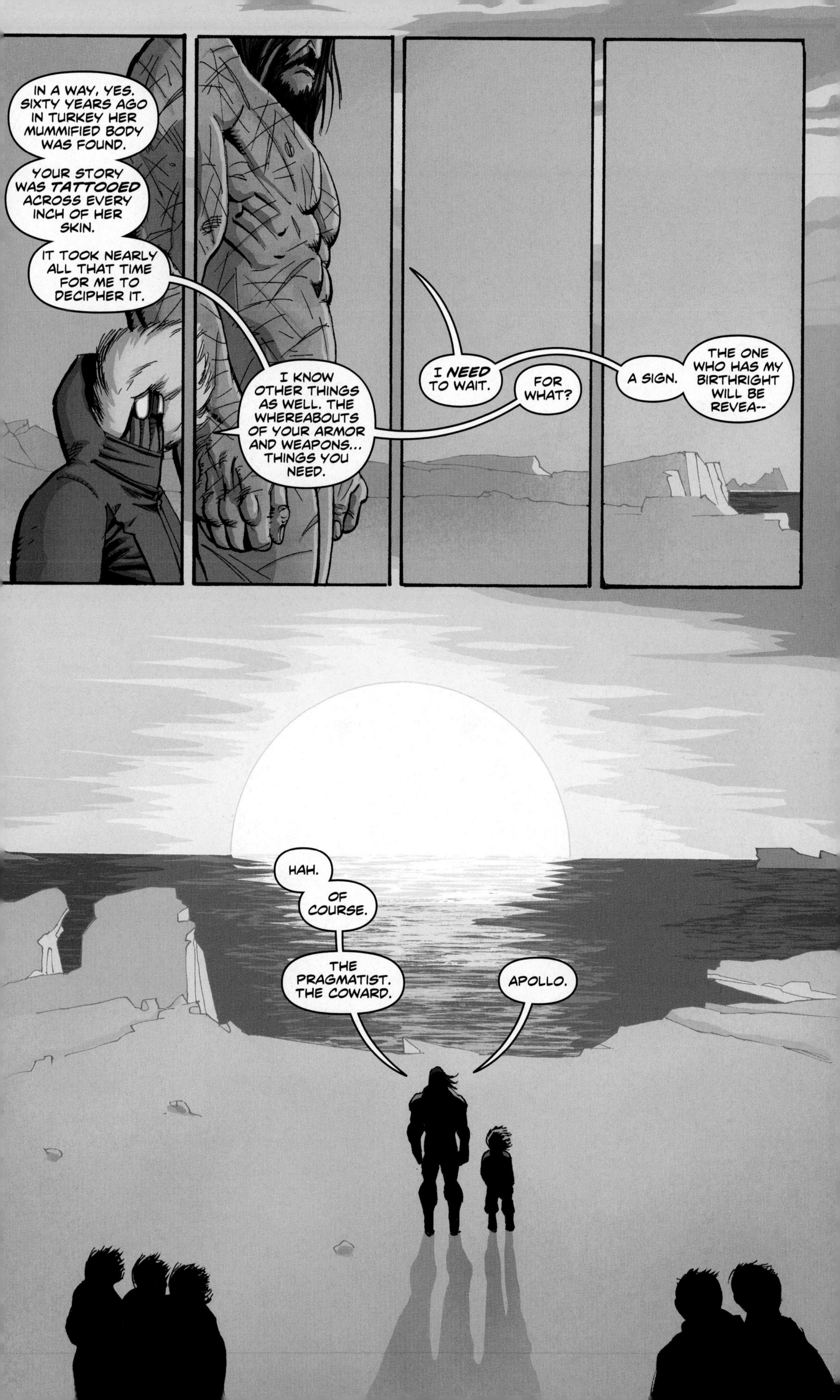

IN A WAY, YES. SIXTY YEARS AGO IN TURKEY HER MUMMIFIED BODY WAS FOUND.
YOUR STORY WAS *TATTOOED* ACROSS EVERY INCH OF HER SKIN.
IT TOOK NEARLY ALL THAT TIME FOR ME TO DECIPHER IT.
I KNOW OTHER THINGS AS WELL. THE WHEREABOUTS OF YOUR ARMOR AND WEAPONS... THINGS YOU NEED.
I *NEED* TO WAIT.
FOR WHAT?
A SIGN.
THE ONE WHO HAS MY BIRTHRIGHT WILL BE REVEA--
HAH.
OF COURSE.
THE PRAGMATIST. THE COWARD.
APOLLO.

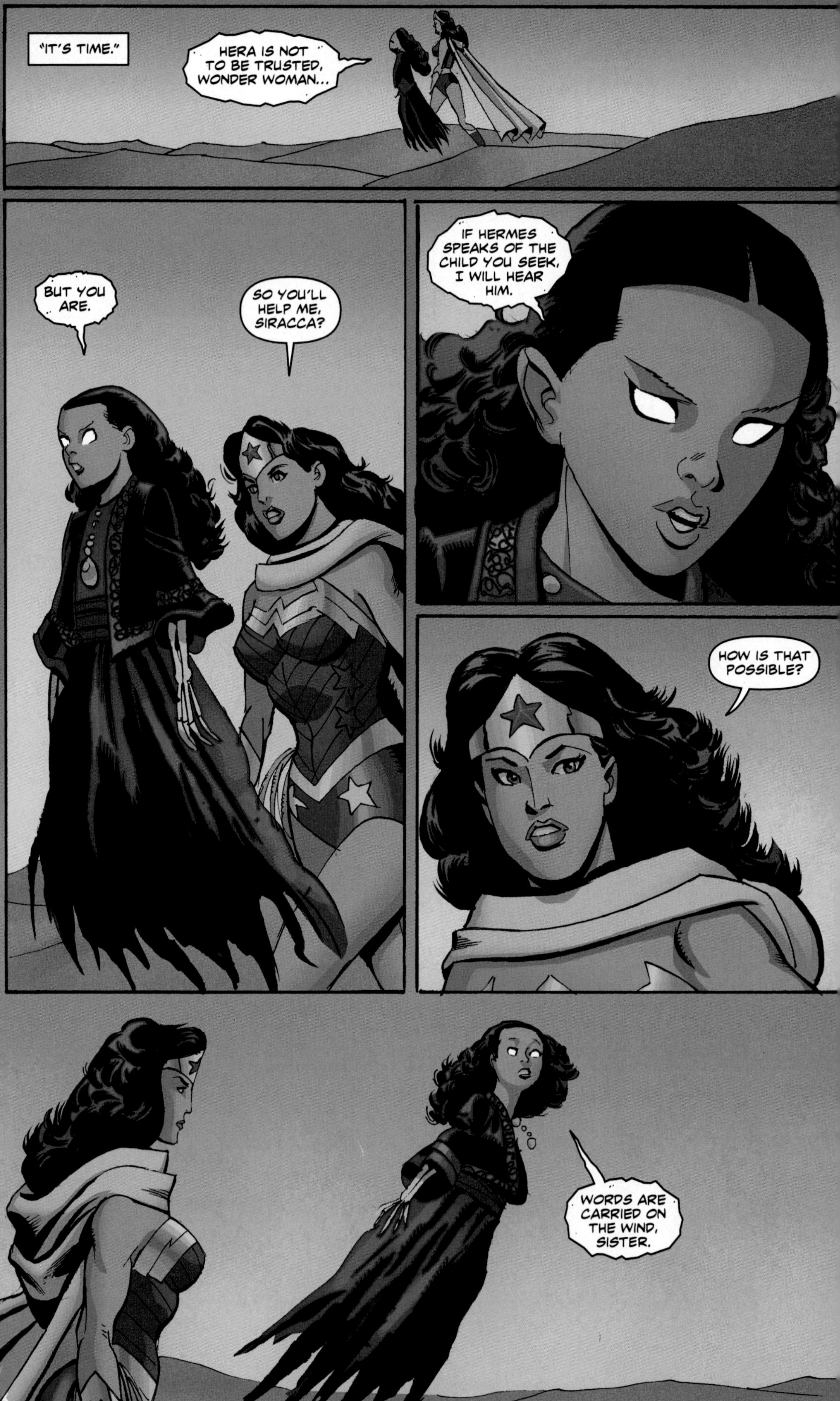
"IT'S TIME."
HERA IS NOT TO BE TRUSTED, WONDER WOMAN...
BUT YOU ARE.
SO YOU'LL HELP ME, SIRACCA?
IF HERMES SPEAKS OF THE CHILD YOU SEEK, I WILL HEAR HIM.
HOW IS THAT POSSIBLE?
WORDS ARE CARRIED ON THE WIND, SISTER.

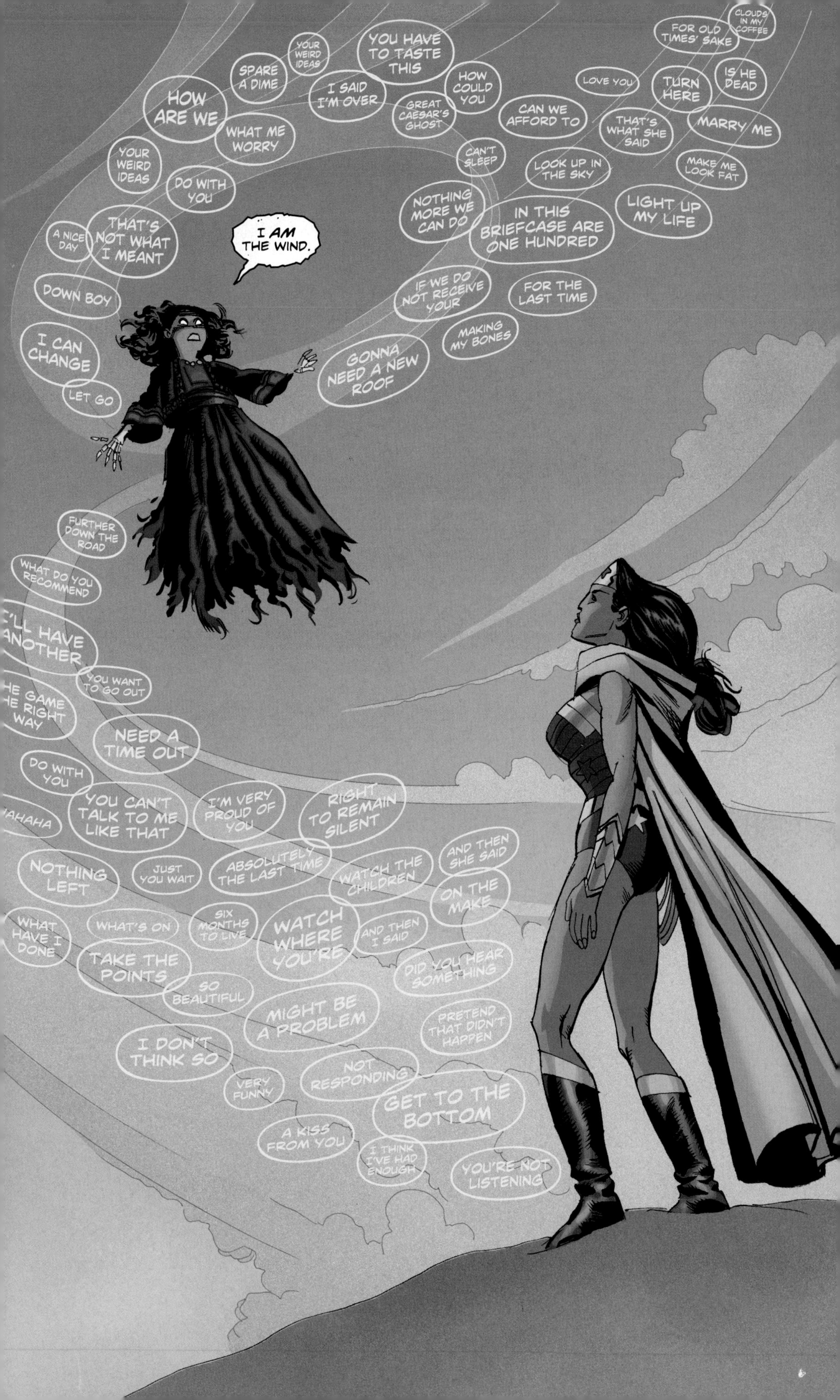

I AM THE WIND.
YOUR WEIRD IDEAS
SPARE A DIME
YOU HAVE TO TASTE THIS
HOW ARE WE
I SAID I'M OVER
HOW COULD YOU
GREAT CAESAR'S GHOST
WHAT ME WORRY
YOUR WEIRD IDEAS
DO WITH YOU
CAN'T SLEEP
FOR OLD TIMES' SAKE
CLOUDS IN MY COFFEE
LOVE YOU
TURN HERE
IS HE DEAD
CAN WE AFFORD TO
THAT'S WHAT SHE SAID
MARRY ME
LOOK UP IN THE SKY
MAKE ME LOOK FAT
NOTHING MORE WE CAN DO
IN THIS BRIEFCASE ARE ONE HUNDRED
LIGHT UP MY LIFE
A NICE DAY
THAT'S NOT WHAT I MEANT
DOWN BOY
IF WE DO NOT RECEIVE YOUR
FOR THE LAST TIME
I CAN CHANGE
LET GO
MAKING MY BONES
GONNA NEED A NEW ROOF
FURTHER DOWN THE ROAD
WHAT DO YOU RECOMMEND
YOU WANT TO GO OUT
NEED A TIME OUT
DO WITH YOU
YOU CAN'T TALK TO ME LIKE THAT
I'M VERY PROUD OF YOU
RIGHT TO REMAIN SILENT
NOTHING LEFT
JUST YOU WAIT
ABSOLUTELY THE LAST TIME
WATCH THE CHILDREN
AND THEN SHE SAID
ON THE MAKE
WHAT HAVE I DONE
WHAT'S ON
SIX MONTHS TO LIVE
WATCH WHERE YOU'RE
AND THEN I SAID
TAKE THE POINTS
SO BEAUTIFUL
DID YOU HEAR SOMETHING
MIGHT BE A PROBLEM
PRETEND THAT DIDN'T HAPPEN
I DON'T THINK SO
VERY FUNNY
NOT RESPONDING
GET TO THE BOTTOM
A KISS FROM YOU
I THINK I'VE HAD ENOUGH
YOU'RE NOT LISTENING

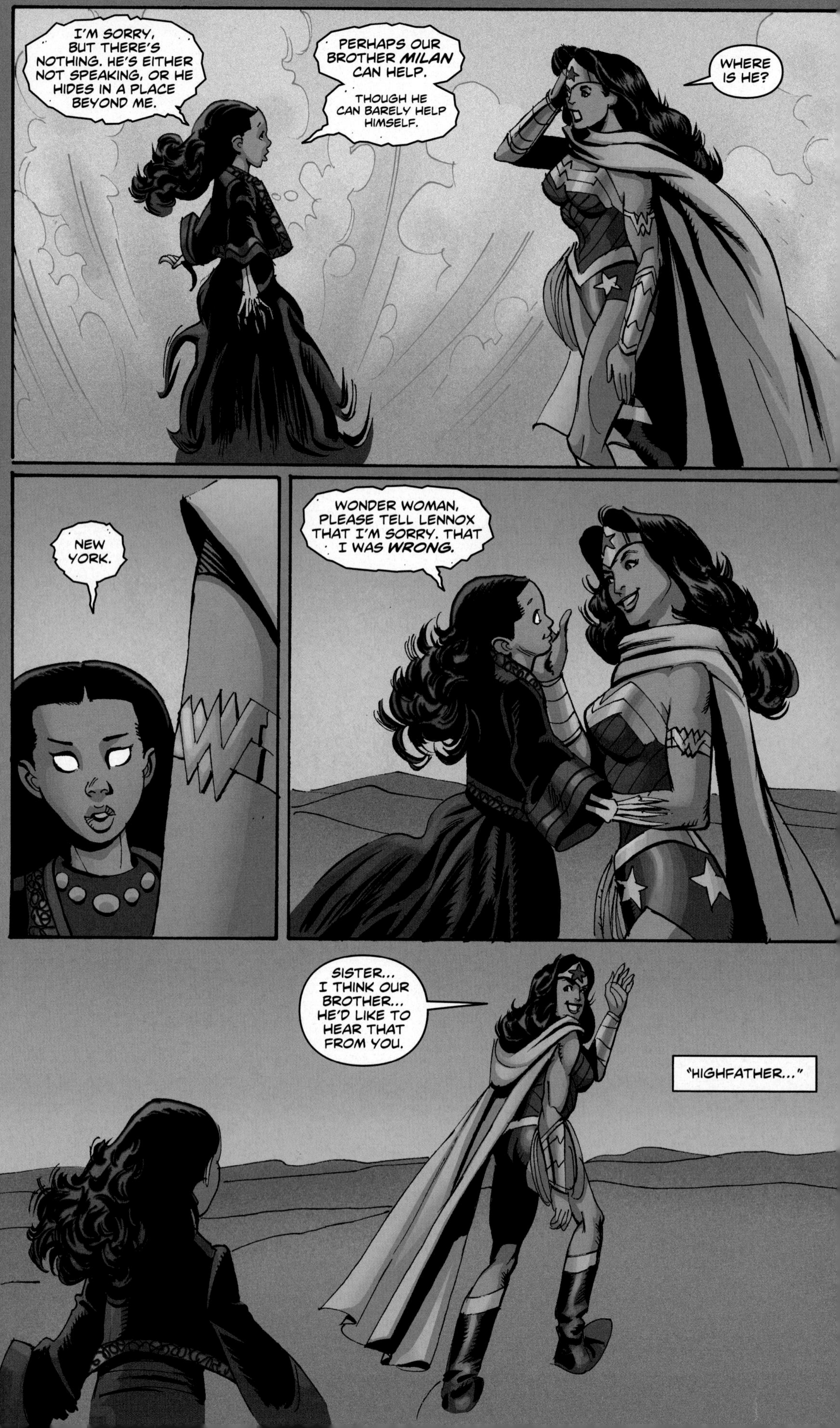
I'M SORRY, BUT THERE'S NOTHING. HE'S EITHER NOT SPEAKING, OR HE HIDES IN A PLACE BEYOND ME.
PERHAPS OUR BROTHER MILAN CAN HELP.
THOUGH HE CAN BARELY HELP HIMSELF.
WHERE IS HE?
NEW YORK.
WONDER WOMAN, PLEASE TELL LENNOX THAT I'M SORRY. THAT I WAS WRONG.
SISTER... I THINK OUR BROTHER... HE'D LIKE TO HEAR THAT FROM YOU.
"HIGHFATHER..."

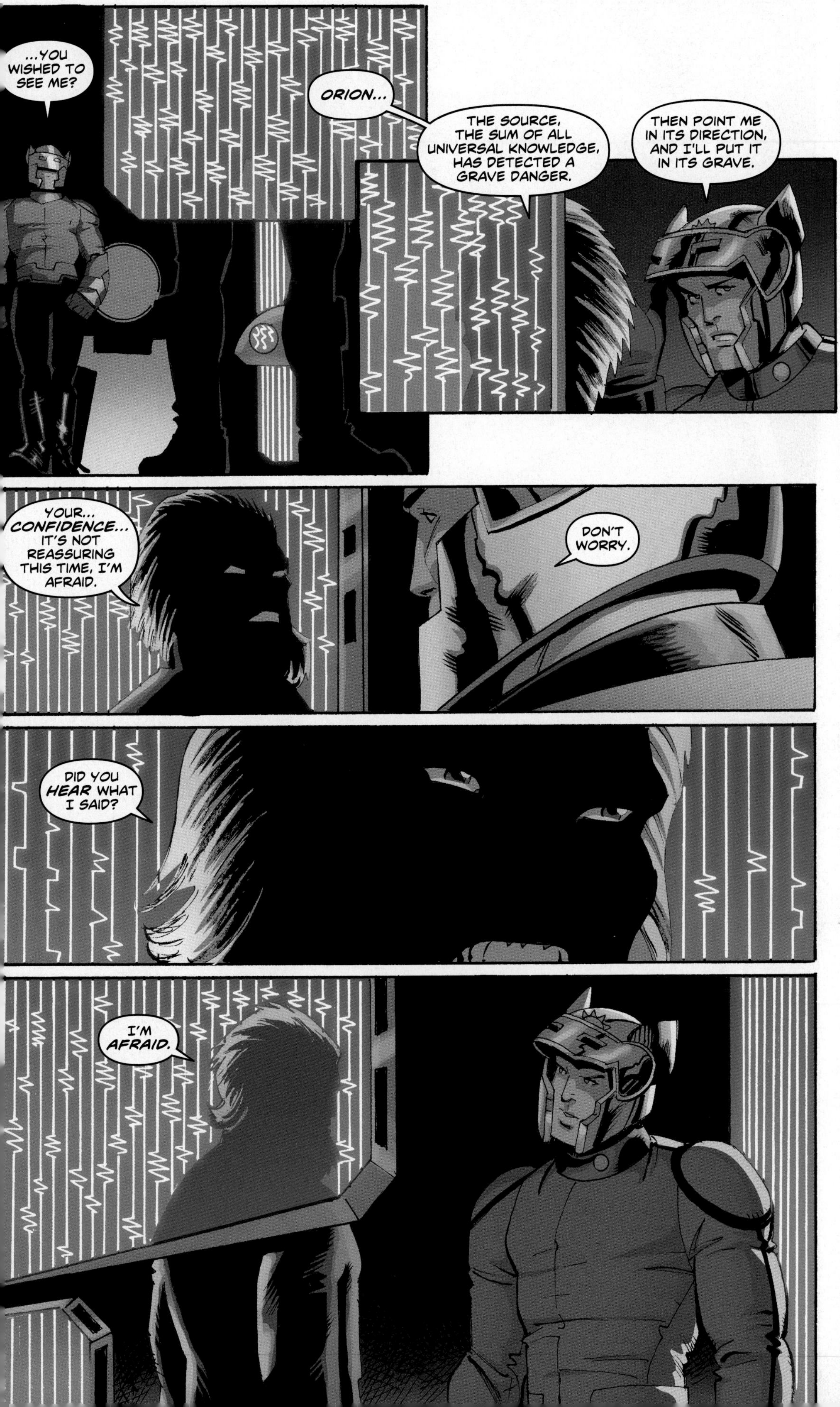
...YOU WISHED TO SEE ME?
ORION...
THE SOURCE, THE SUM OF ALL UNIVERSAL KNOWLEDGE, HAS DETECTED A GRAVE DANGER.
THEN POINT ME IN ITS DIRECTION, AND I'LL PUT IT IN ITS GRAVE.
YOUR... CONFIDENCE... IT'S NOT REASSURING THIS TIME, I'M AFRAID.
DON'T WORRY.
DID YOU HEAR WHAT I SAID?
I'M AFRAID.

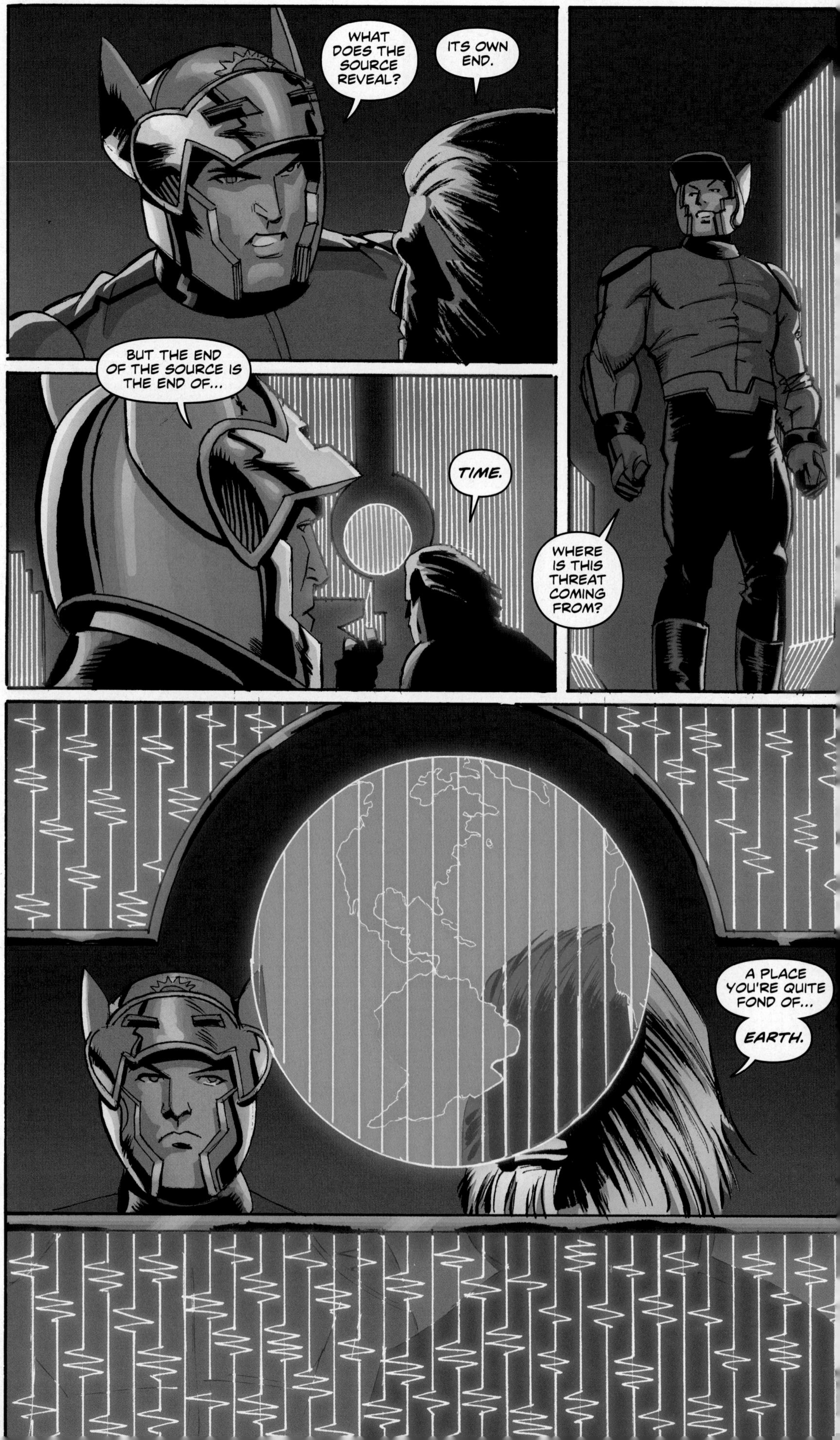
WHAT DOES THE SOURCE REVEAL?
ITS OWN END.
BUT THE END OF THE SOURCE IS THE END OF...
TIME.
WHERE IS THIS THREAT COMING FROM?
A PLACE YOU'RE QUITE FOND OF...
EARTH.

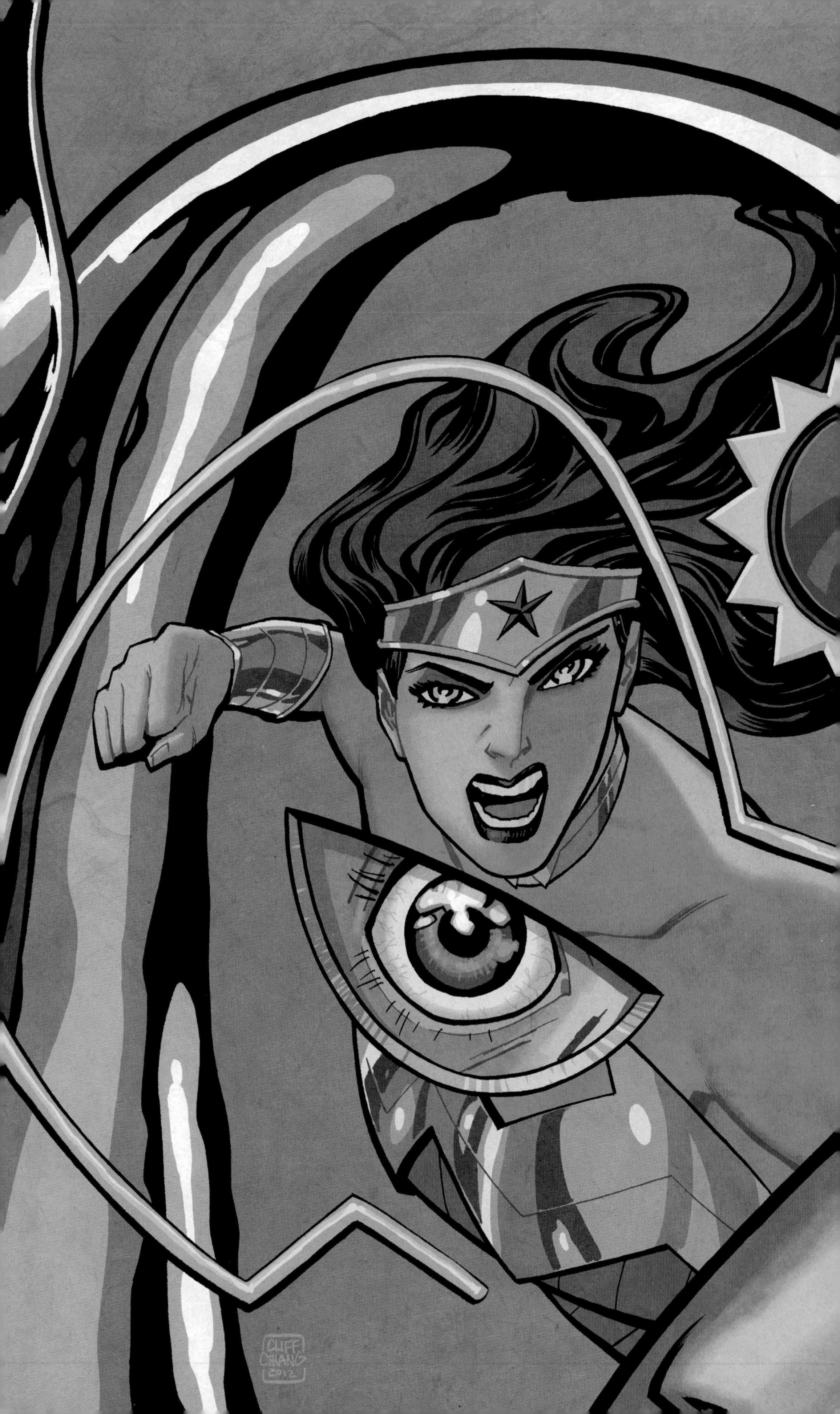
CLIFF CHIANG 2012

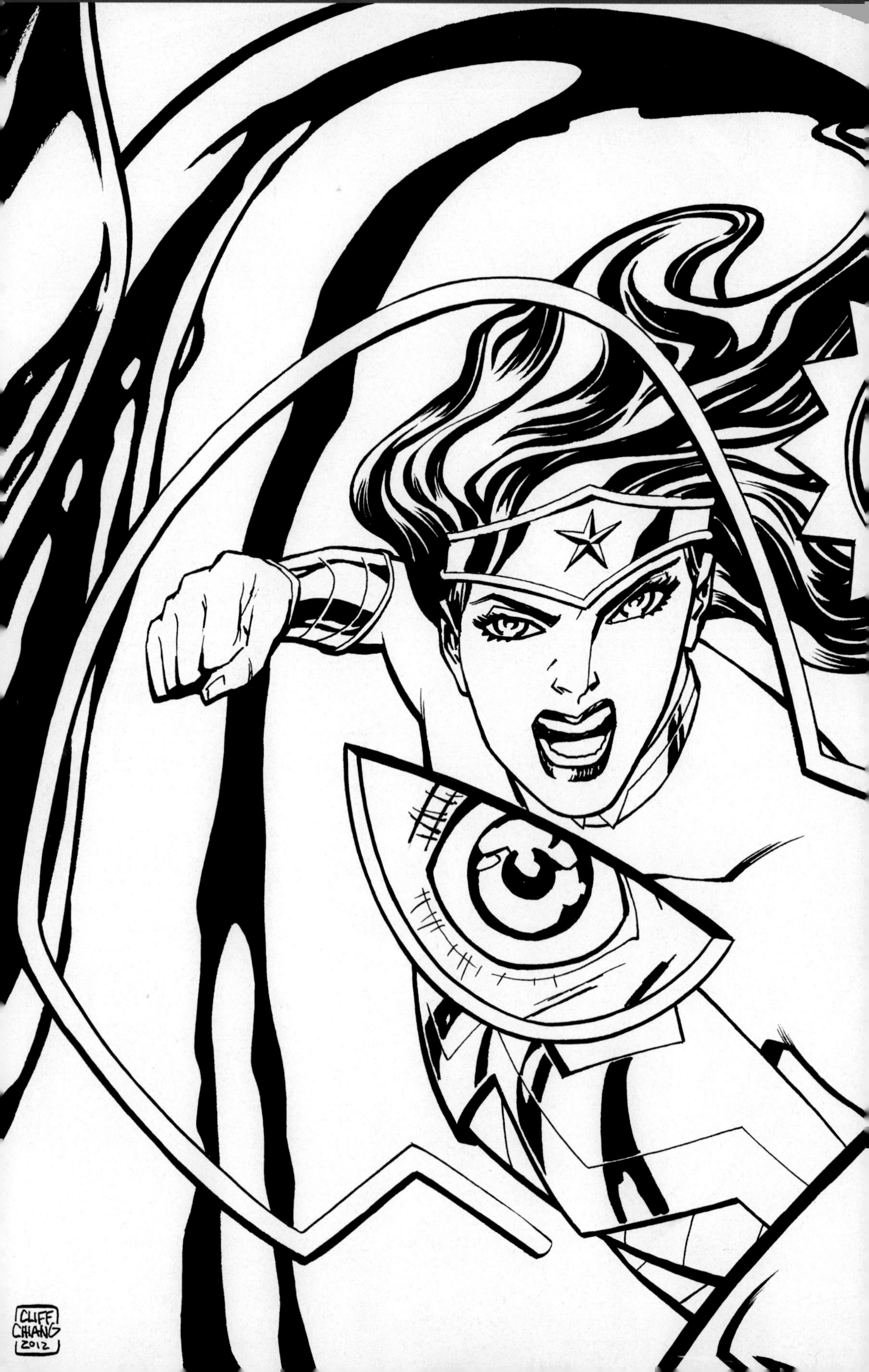
CLIFF
CHIANG
2012

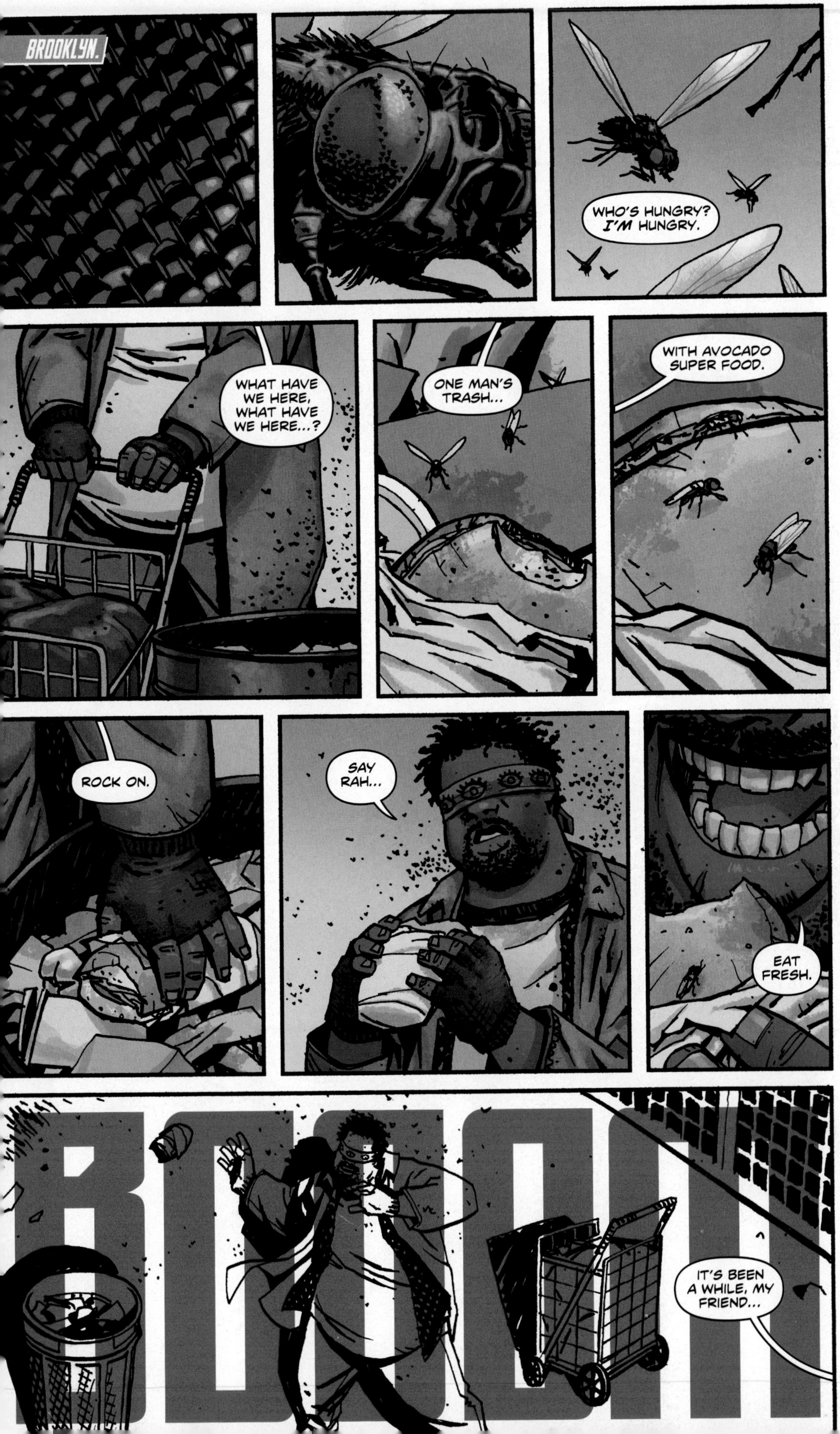
BROOKLYN.
WHO'S HUNGRY? I'M HUNGRY.
WHAT HAVE WE HERE, WHAT HAVE WE HERE...?
ONE MAN'S TRASH...
WITH AVOCADO SUPER FOOD.
ROCK ON.
SAY RAH...
EAT FRESH.
BOOOM
IT'S BEEN A WHILE, MY FRIEND...

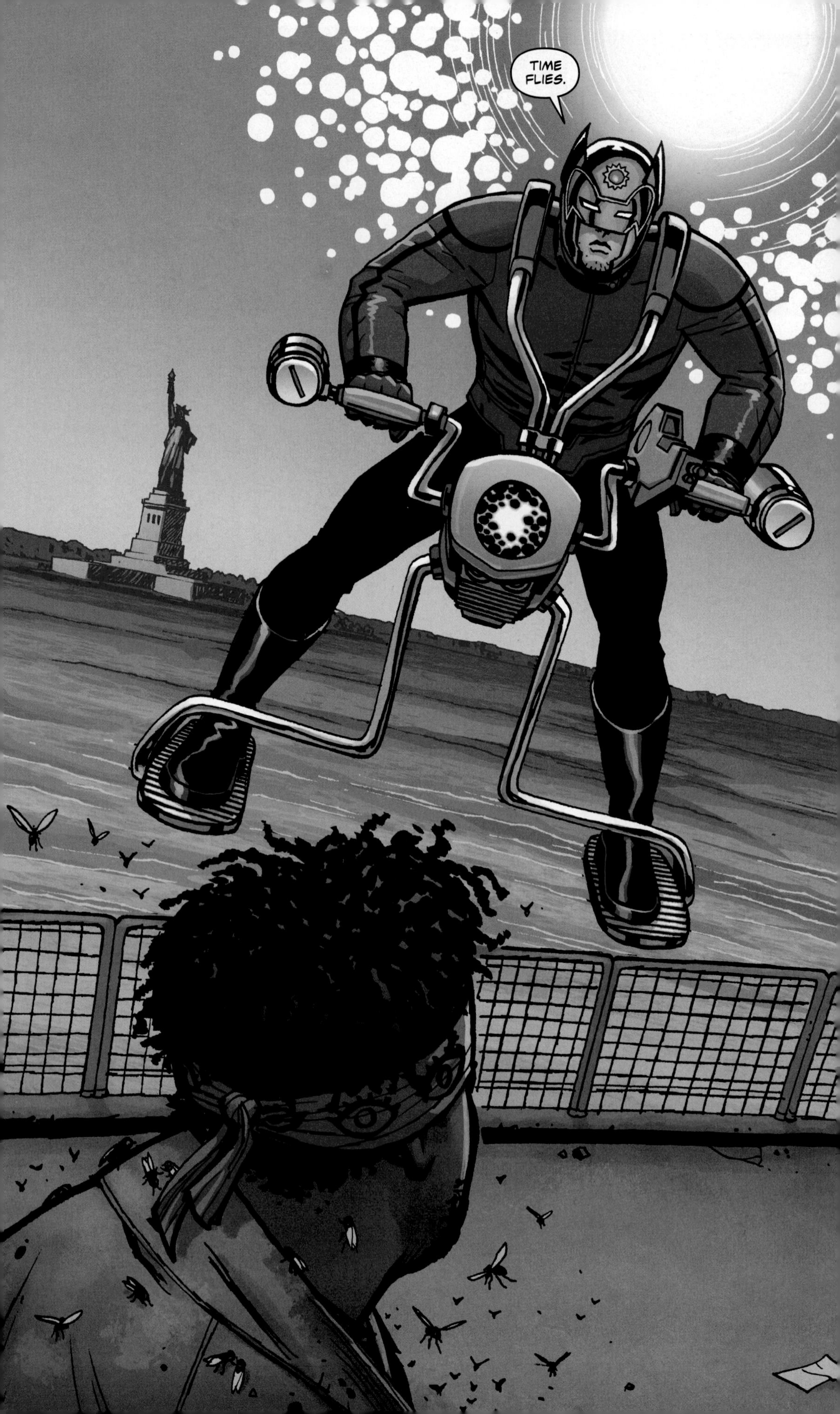
TIME FLIES.

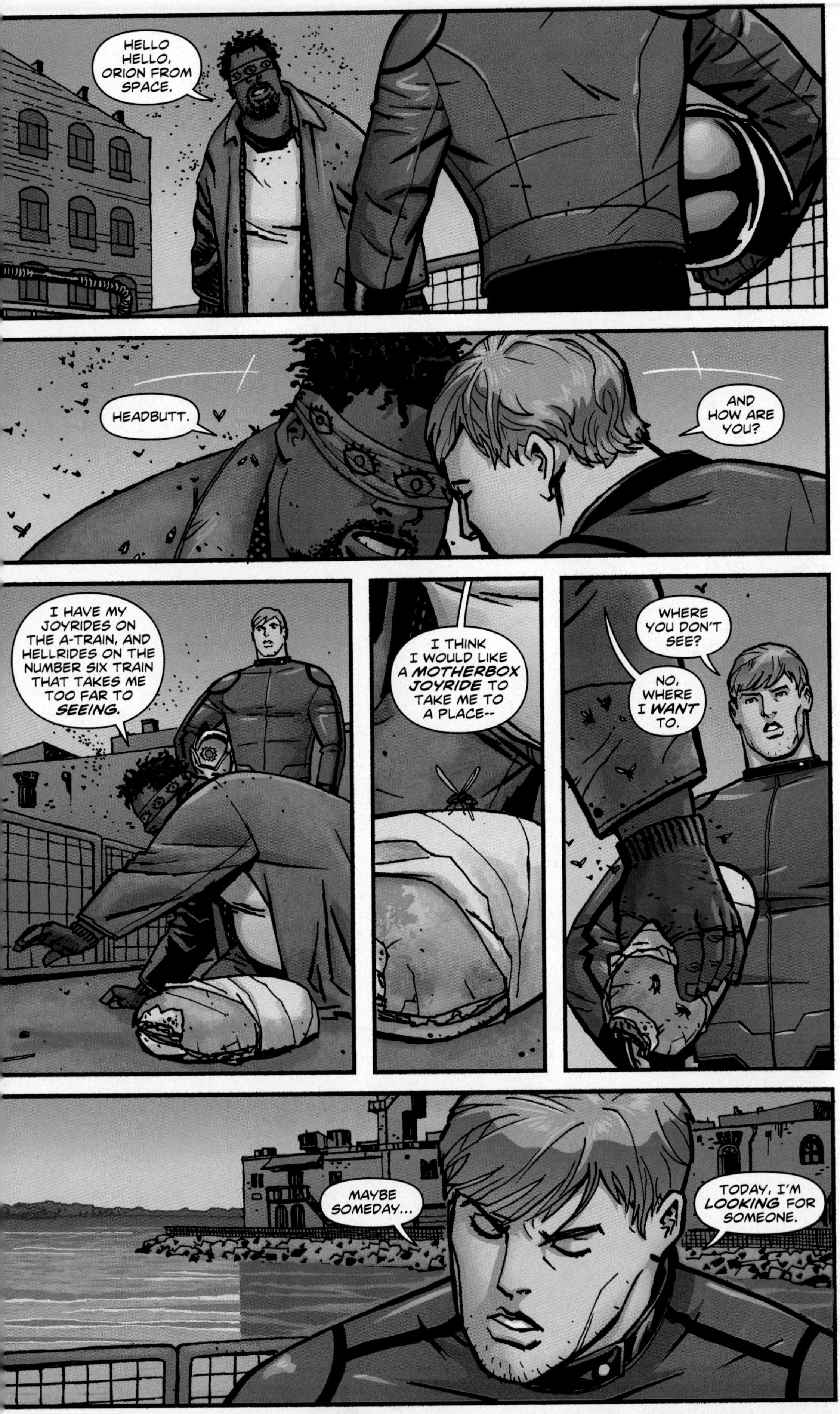
HELLO HELLO, ORION FROM SPACE.
HEADBUTT.
AND HOW ARE YOU?
I HAVE MY JOYRIDES ON THE A-TRAIN, AND HELLRIDES ON THE NUMBER SIX TRAIN THAT TAKES ME TOO FAR TO SEEING.
I THINK I WOULD LIKE A MOTHERBOX JOYRIDE TO TAKE ME TO A PLACE--
WHERE YOU DON'T SEE?
NO, WHERE I WANT TO.
MAYBE SOMEDAY...
TODAY, I'M LOOKING FOR SOMEONE.

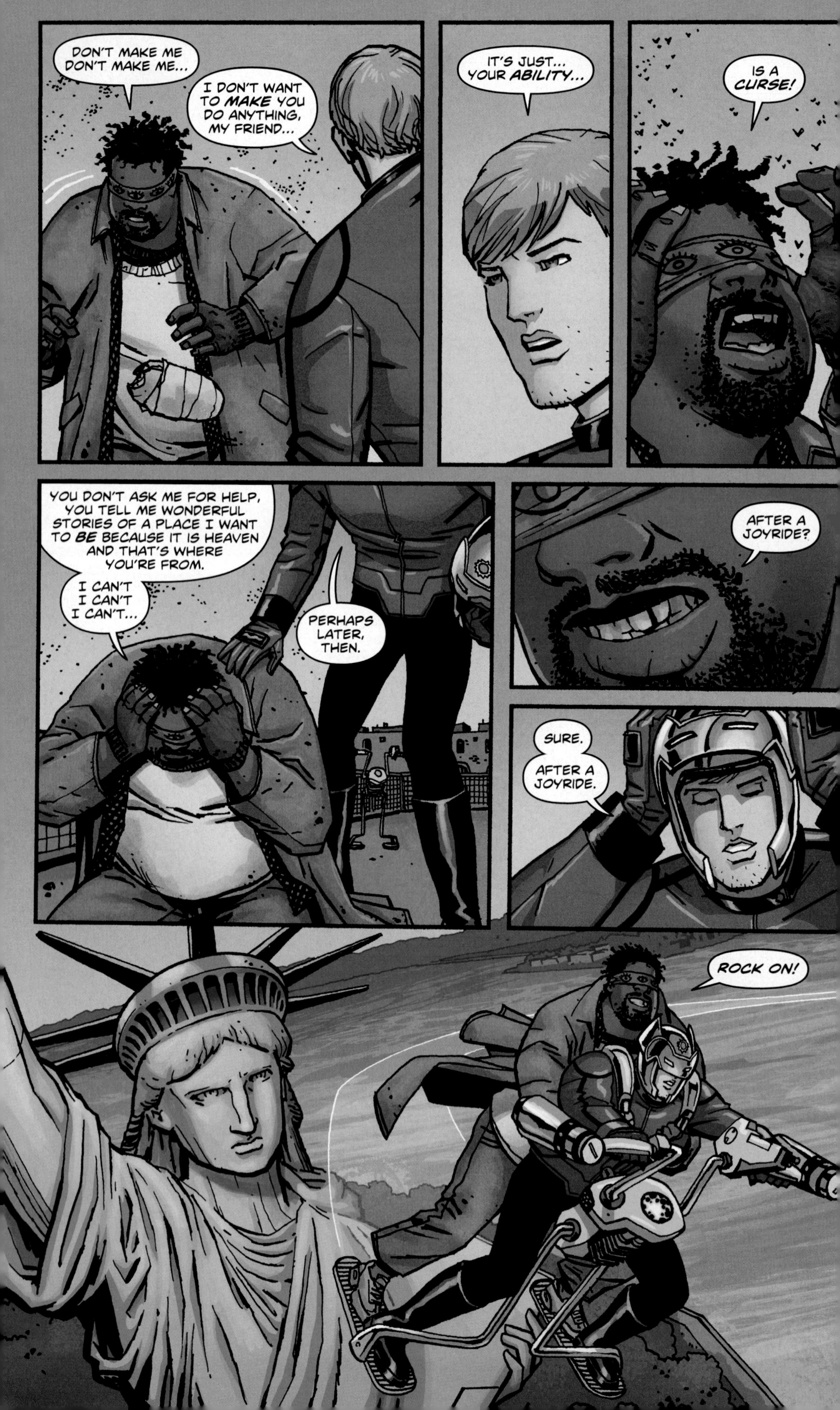
DON'T MAKE ME
DON'T MAKE ME...
I DON'T WANT TO MAKE YOU DO ANYTHING, MY FRIEND...
IT'S JUST... YOUR ABILITY...
IS A CURSE!
YOU DON'T ASK ME FOR HELP, YOU TELL ME WONDERFUL STORIES OF A PLACE I WANT TO BE BECAUSE IT IS HEAVEN AND THAT'S WHERE YOU'RE FROM.
I CAN'T I CAN'T I CAN'T...
PERHAPS LATER, THEN.
AFTER A JOYRIDE?
SURE.
AFTER A JOYRIDE.
ROCK ON!

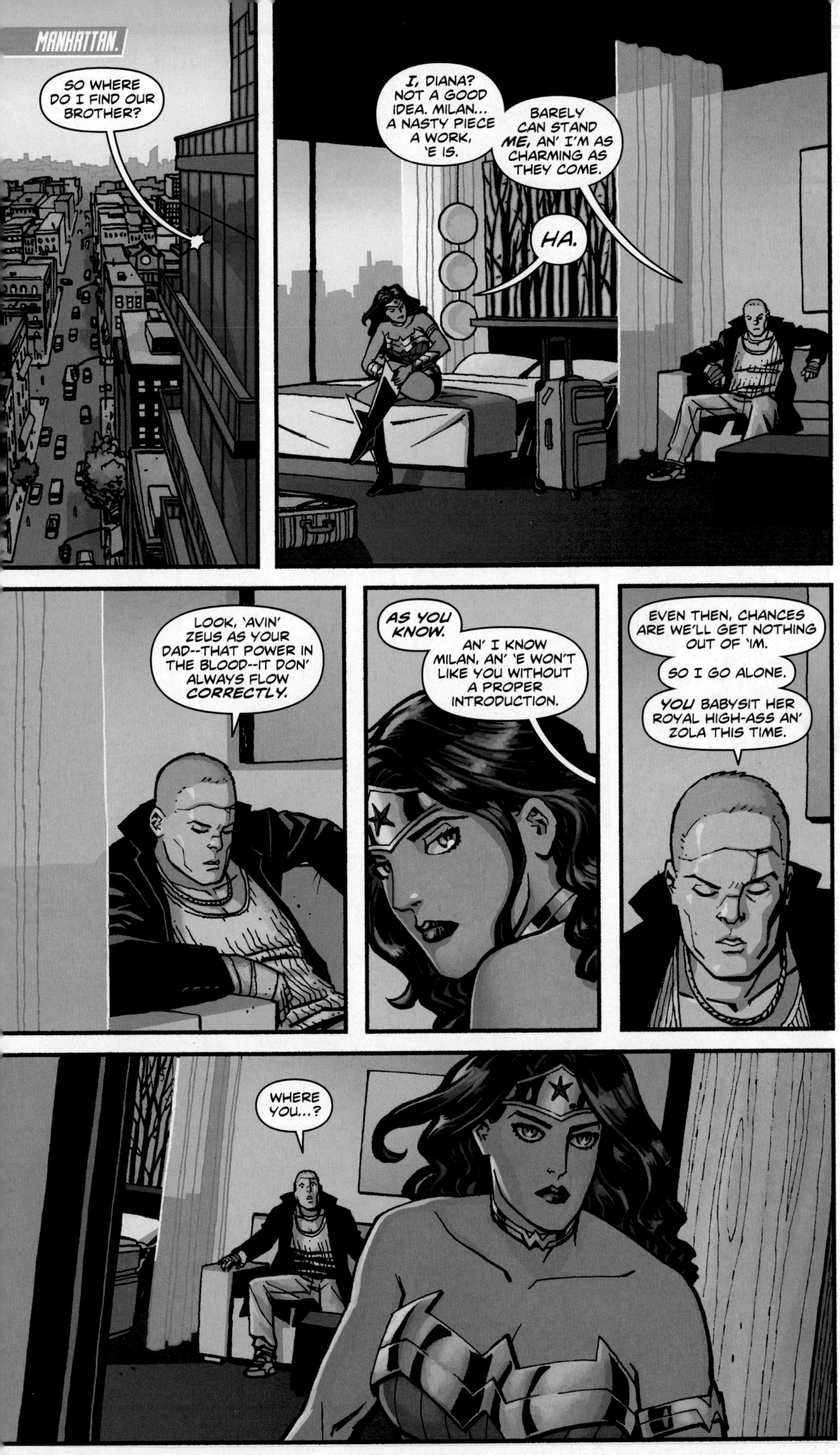
MANHATTAN.
SO WHERE DO I FIND OUR BROTHER?
I, DIANA? NOT A GOOD IDEA. MILAN... A NASTY PIECE A WORK, 'E IS.
BARELY CAN STAND ME, AN' I'M AS CHARMING AS THEY COME.
HA.
LOOK, 'AVIN' ZEUS AS YOUR DAD--THAT POWER IN THE BLOOD--IT DON' ALWAYS FLOW CORRECTLY.
AS YOU KNOW.
AN' I KNOW MILAN, AN' 'E WON'T LIKE YOU WITHOUT A PROPER INTRODUCTION.
EVEN THEN, CHANCES ARE WE'LL GET NOTHING OUT OF 'IM.
SO I GO ALONE.
YOU BABYSIT HER ROYAL HIGH-ASS AN' ZOLA THIS TIME.
WHERE YOU...?

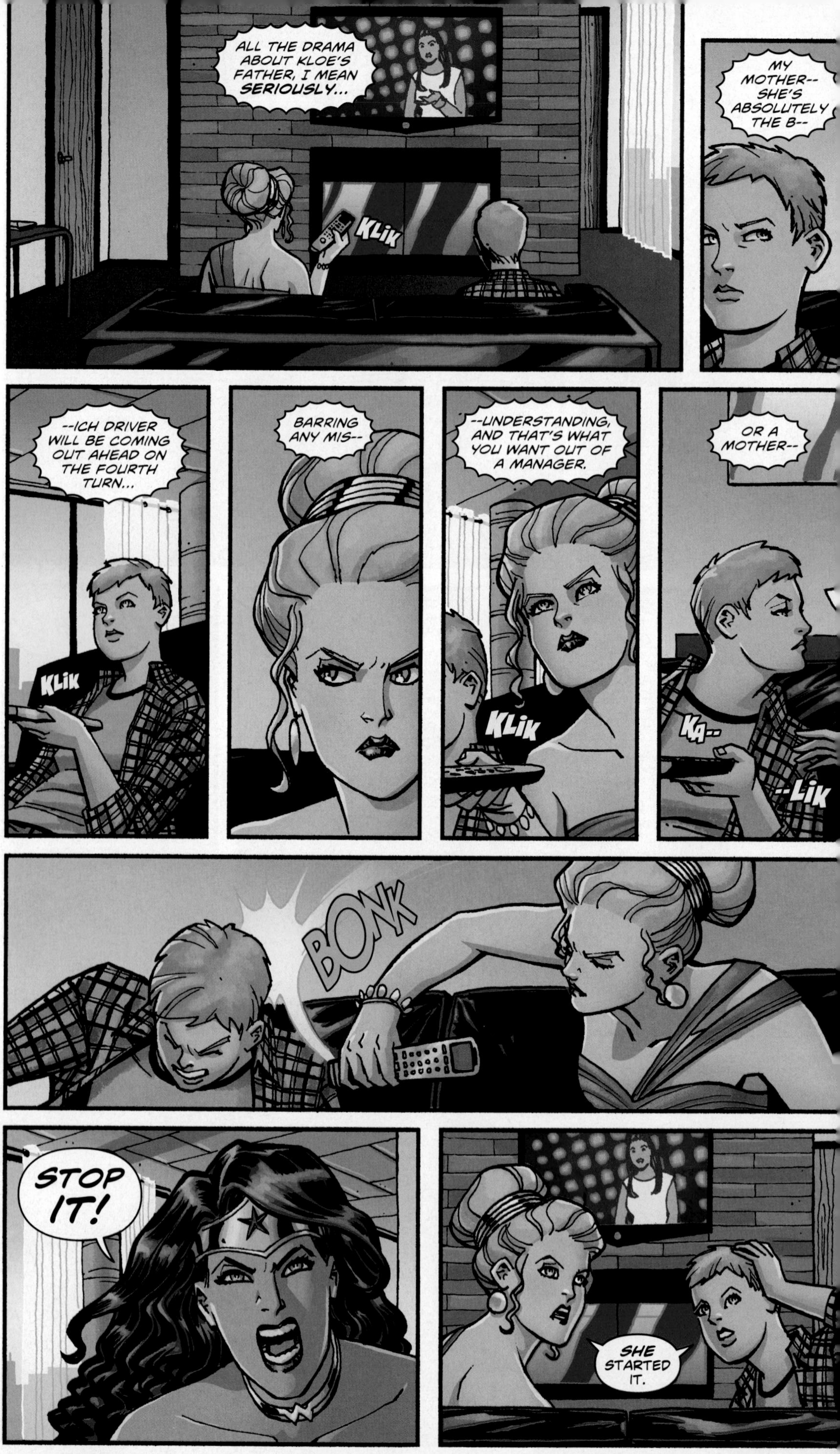
ALL THE DRAMA ABOUT KLOE'S FATHER, I MEAN SERIOUSLY...
KLIK
MY MOTHER-- SHE'S ABSOLUTELY THE B--
--ICH DRIVER WILL BE COMING OUT AHEAD ON THE FOURTH TURN...
KLIK
BARRING ANY MIS--
--UNDERSTANDING, AND THAT'S WHAT YOU WANT OUT OF A MANAGER.
KLIK
OR A MOTHER--
KA--
--LIK
BONK
STOP IT!
SHE STARTED IT.

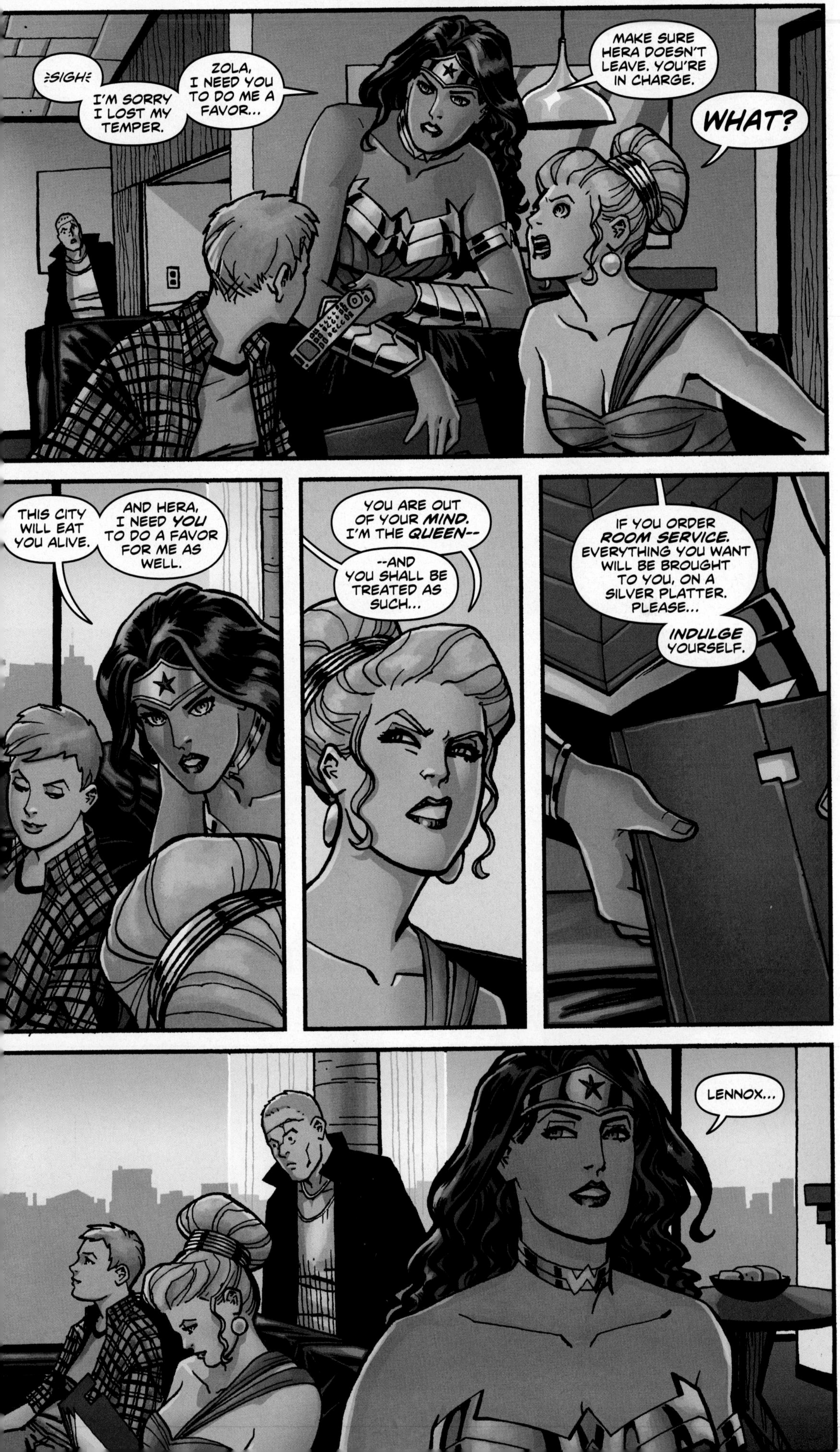

SIGH
I'M SORRY I LOST MY TEMPER.
ZOLA, I NEED YOU TO DO ME A FAVOR...
MAKE SURE HERA DOESN'T LEAVE. YOU'RE IN CHARGE.
WHAT?
THIS CITY WILL EAT YOU ALIVE.
AND HERA, I NEED YOU TO DO A FAVOR FOR ME AS WELL.
YOU ARE OUT OF YOUR MIND. I'M THE QUEEN--
--AND YOU SHALL BE TREATED AS SUCH...
IF YOU ORDER ROOM SERVICE, EVERYTHING YOU WANT WILL BE BROUGHT TO YOU, ON A SILVER PLATTER. PLEASE...
INDULGE YOURSELF.
LENNOX...

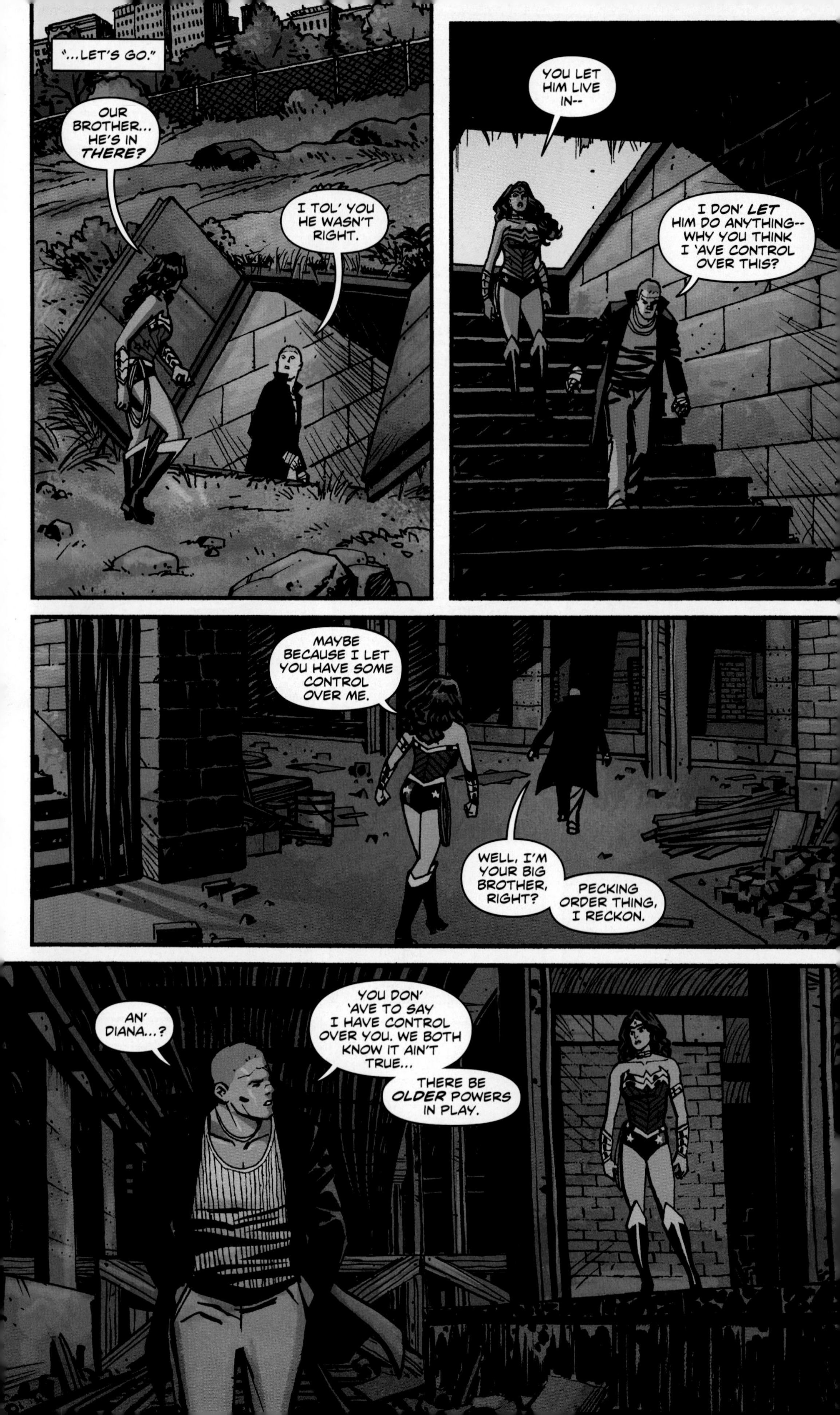
"...LET'S GO."
OUR BROTHER... HE'S IN THERE?
I TOL' YOU HE WASN'T RIGHT.
YOU LET HIM LIVE IN--
I DON' LET HIM DO ANYTHING-- WHY YOU THINK I 'AVE CONTROL OVER THIS?
MAYBE BECAUSE I LET YOU HAVE SOME CONTROL OVER ME.
WELL, I'M YOUR BIG BROTHER, RIGHT?
PECKING ORDER THING, I RECKON.
AN' DIANA...?
YOU DON' 'AVE TO SAY I HAVE CONTROL OVER YOU. WE BOTH KNOW IT AIN'T TRUE...
THERE BE OLDER POWERS IN PLAY.

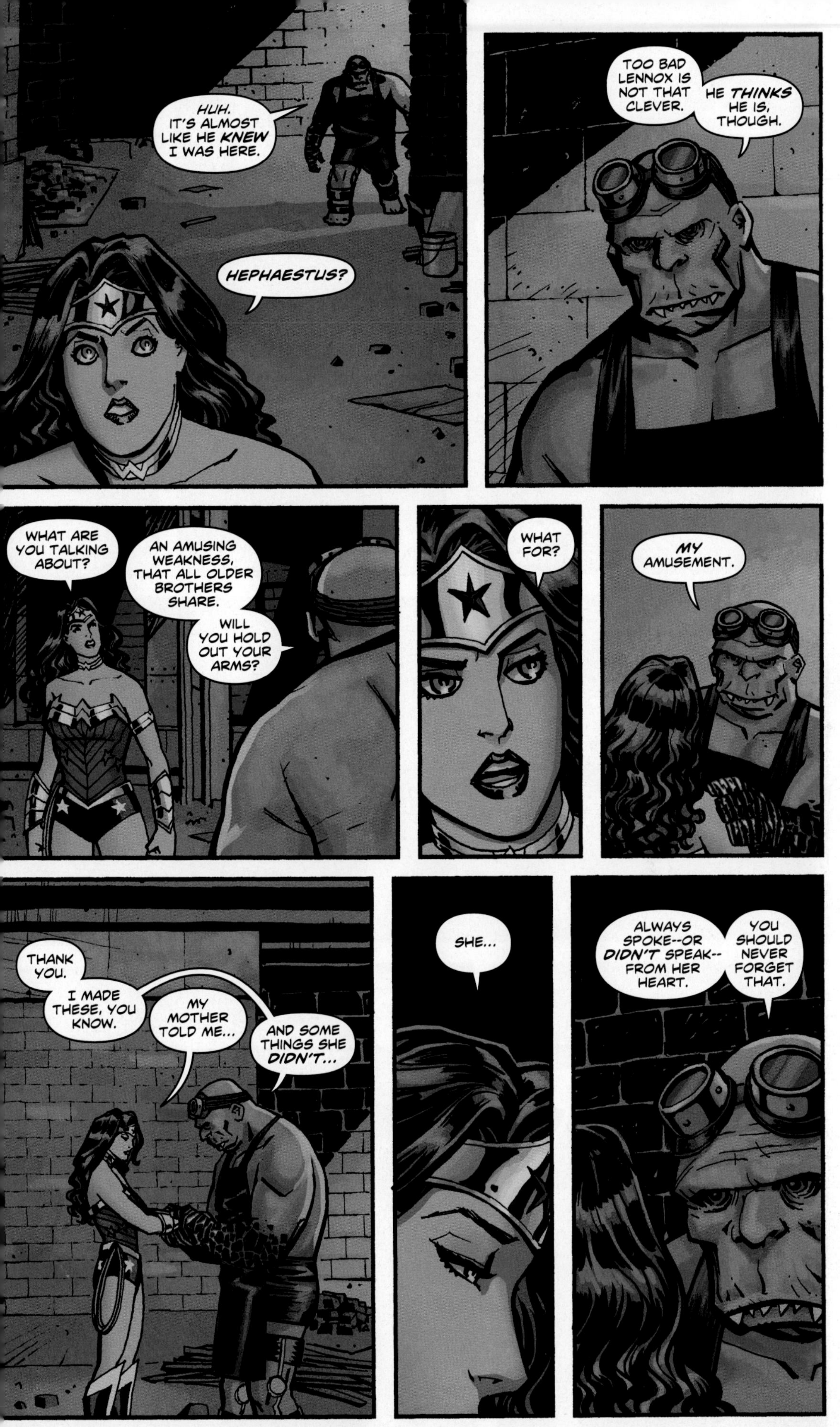
HUH. IT'S ALMOST LIKE HE KNEW I WAS HERE.
HEPHAESTUS?
TOO BAD LENNOX IS NOT THAT CLEVER.
HE THINKS HE IS, THOUGH.
WHAT ARE YOU TALKING ABOUT?
AN AMUSING WEAKNESS, THAT ALL OLDER BROTHERS SHARE.
WILL YOU HOLD OUT YOUR ARMS?
WHAT FOR?
MY AMUSEMENT.
THANK YOU.
I MADE THESE, YOU KNOW.
MY MOTHER TOLD ME...
AND SOME THINGS SHE DIDN'T...
SHE...
ALWAYS SPOKE--OR DIDN'T SPEAK--FROM HER HEART.
YOU SHOULD NEVER FORGET THAT.

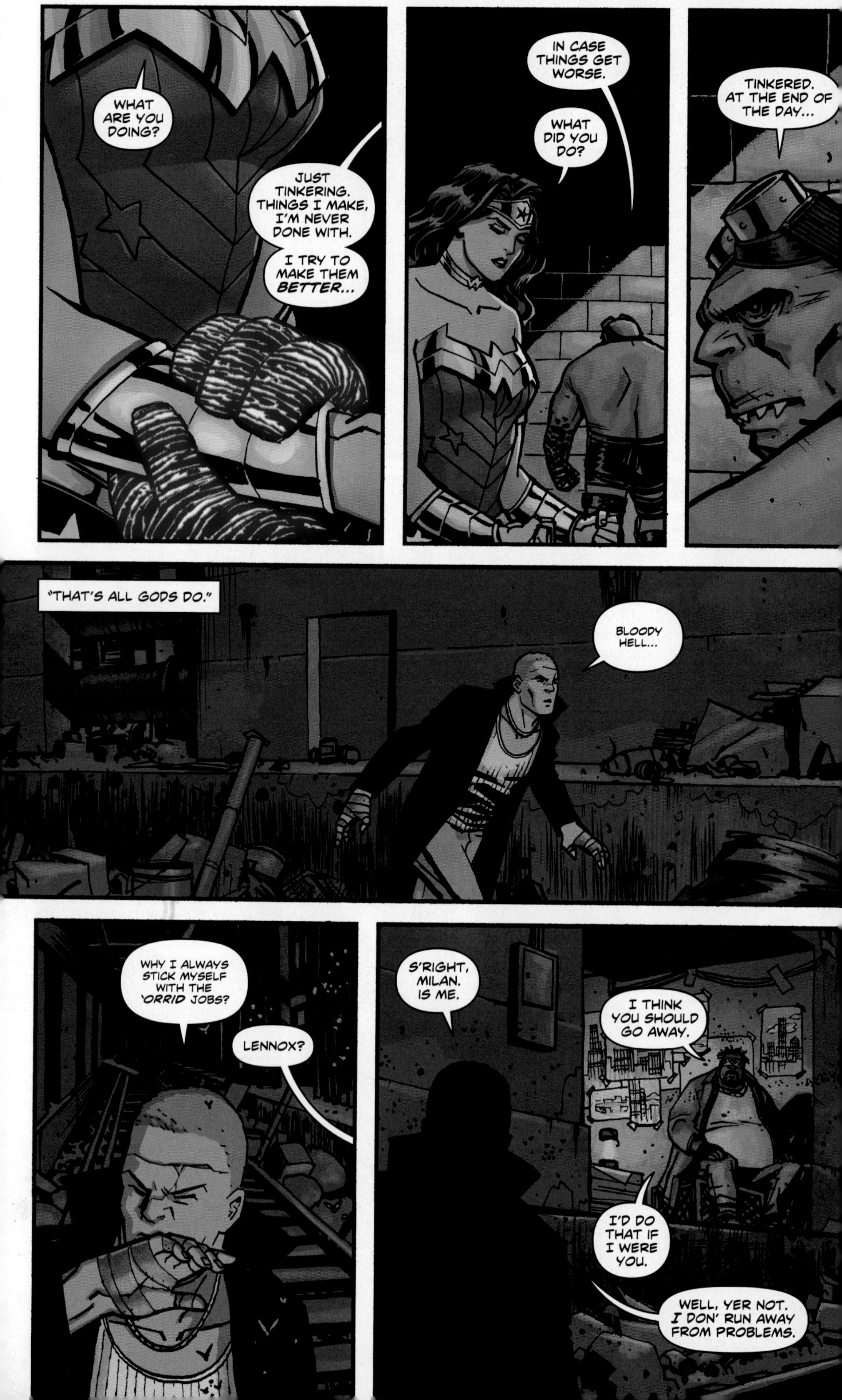
WHAT ARE YOU DOING?
JUST TINKERING. THINGS I MAKE, I'M NEVER DONE WITH.
I TRY TO MAKE THEM *BETTER*...
IN CASE THINGS GET WORSE.
WHAT DID YOU DO?
TINKERED. AT THE END OF THE DAY...
"THAT'S ALL GODS DO."
BLOODY HELL...
WHY I ALWAYS STICK MYSELF WITH THE *'ORRID* JOBS?
LENNOX?
S'RIGHT, MILAN. IS ME.
I THINK YOU SHOULD GO AWAY.
I'D DO THAT IF I WERE YOU.
WELL, YER NOT. *I* DON' RUN AWAY FROM PROBLEMS.

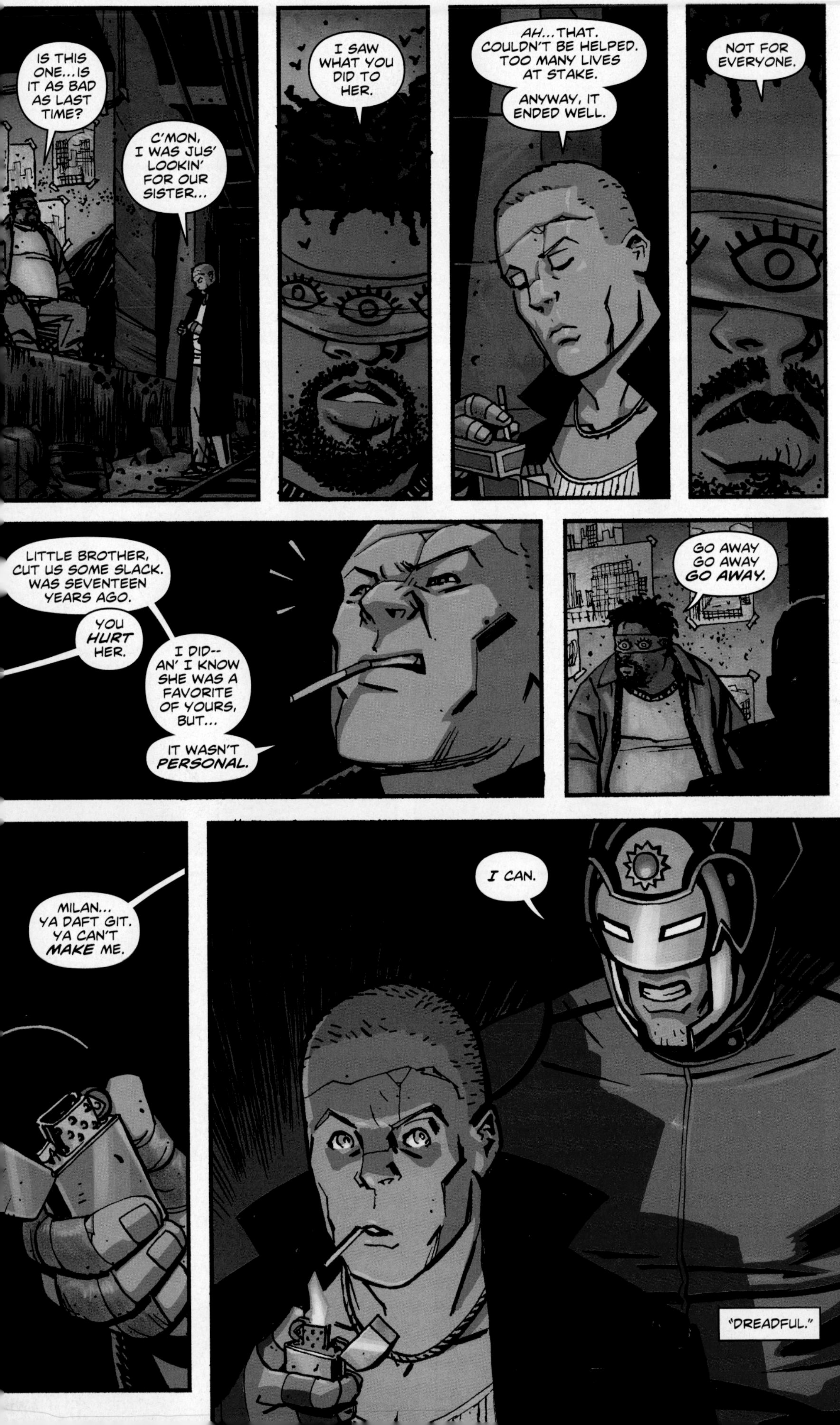
IS THIS ONE...IS IT AS BAD AS LAST TIME?
C'MON, I WAS JUS' LOOKIN' FOR OUR SISTER...
I SAW WHAT YOU DID TO HER.
AH...THAT. COULDN'T BE HELPED. TOO MANY LIVES AT STAKE.
ANYWAY, IT ENDED WELL.
NOT FOR EVERYONE.
LITTLE BROTHER, CUT US SOME SLACK. WAS SEVENTEEN YEARS AGO.
YOU HURT HER.
I DID-- AN' I KNOW SHE WAS A FAVORITE OF YOURS, BUT...
IT WASN'T PERSONAL.
GO AWAY GO AWAY GO AWAY.
MILAN... YA DAFT GIT. YA CAN'T MAKE ME.
I CAN.
"DREADFUL."

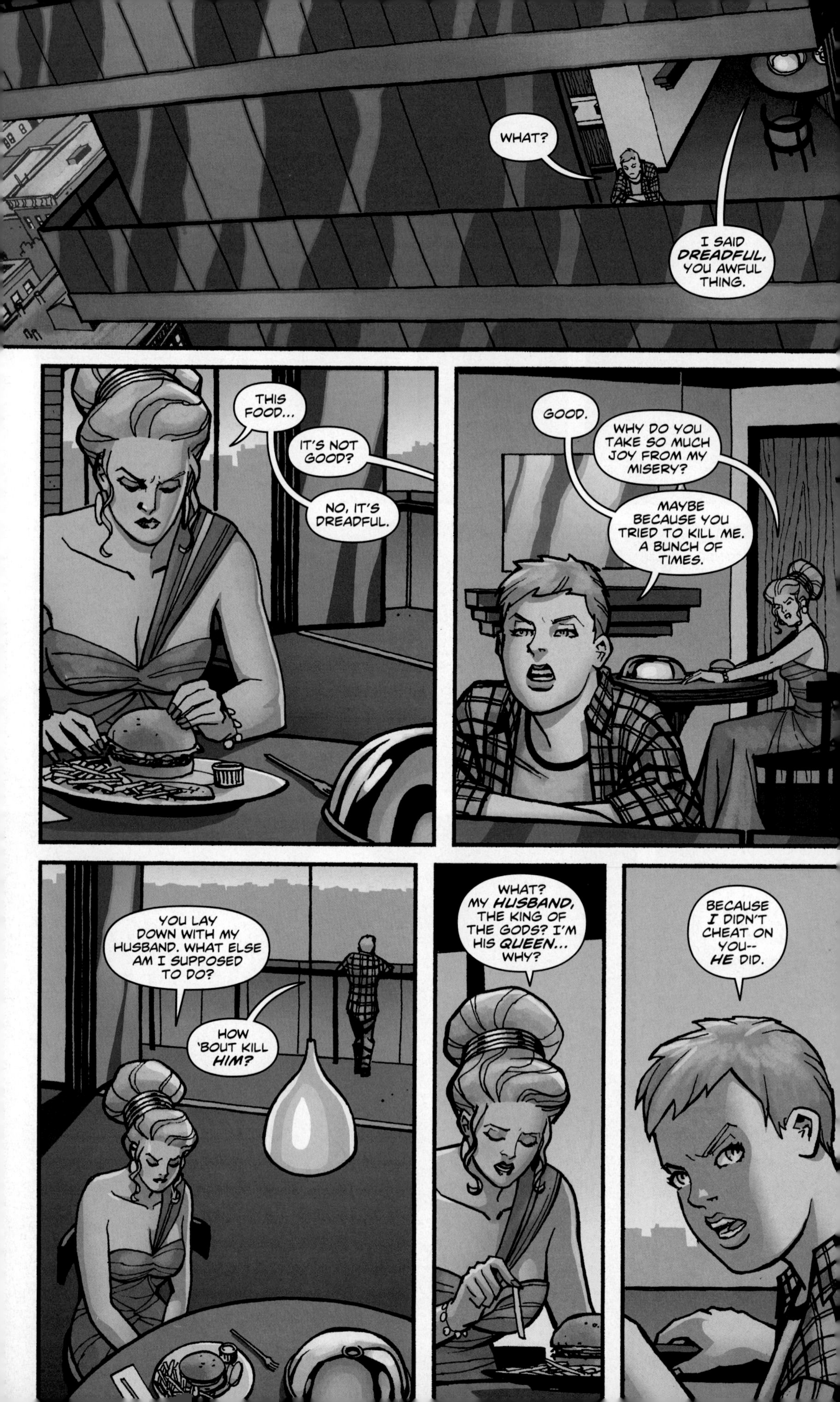

WHAT?
I SAID DREADFUL, YOU AWFUL THING.
THIS FOOD...
IT'S NOT GOOD?
NO, IT'S DREADFUL.
GOOD.
WHY DO YOU TAKE SO MUCH JOY FROM MY MISERY?
MAYBE BECAUSE YOU TRIED TO KILL ME. A BUNCH OF TIMES.
YOU LAY DOWN WITH MY HUSBAND. WHAT ELSE AM I SUPPOSED TO DO?
HOW 'BOUT KILL HIM?
WHAT? MY HUSBAND, THE KING OF THE GODS? I'M HIS QUEEN... WHY?
BECAUSE I DIDN'T CHEAT ON YOU-- HE DID.

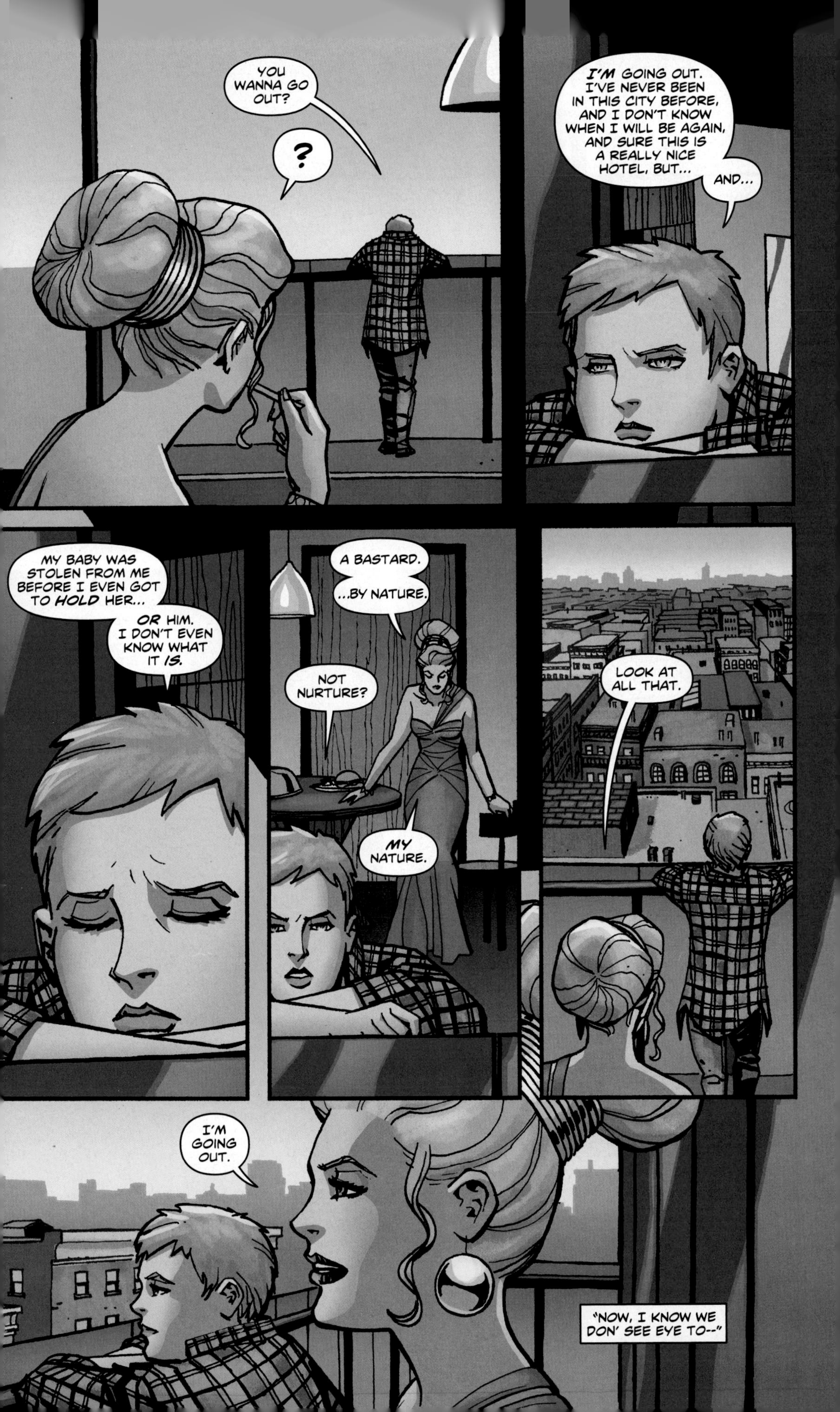
YOU WANNA GO OUT?
?
I'M GOING OUT. I'VE NEVER BEEN IN THIS CITY BEFORE, AND I DON'T KNOW WHEN I WILL BE AGAIN, AND SURE THIS IS A REALLY NICE HOTEL, BUT...
AND...
MY BABY WAS STOLEN FROM ME BEFORE I EVEN GOT TO HOLD HER...
OR HIM. I DON'T EVEN KNOW WHAT IT IS.
A BASTARD.
...BY NATURE.
NOT NURTURE?
MY NATURE.
LOOK AT ALL THAT.
I'M GOING OUT.
"NOW, I KNOW WE DON' SEE EYE TO--"

--AYE!

YA WANT ME BLIND AS YOU?

HE WANTS YOU TO *LEAVE*...

I DON'T WANT YOU TO *TRIP* ON YOUR WAY OUT.

WELL AIN'T YOU KIND...

LOVELY PLACE YA GOT HERE, DEAR BROTHER.

A REGULA SANCTUM STANKTORI

WE DON'T GET ALONG.

GO FIGURE.

YEA...AN' THOUGH YOU CUT QUITE A *DASHING* ONE, THIS BIT BETWEEN ME AN' MILAN IS *FAMILY*, SPACEMAN...

"SO BE POLITE TO OUR *SISTER* ON YOUR WAY OUT."

"OUR *SISTER*, LENNOX? SIRACCA--? OR--"

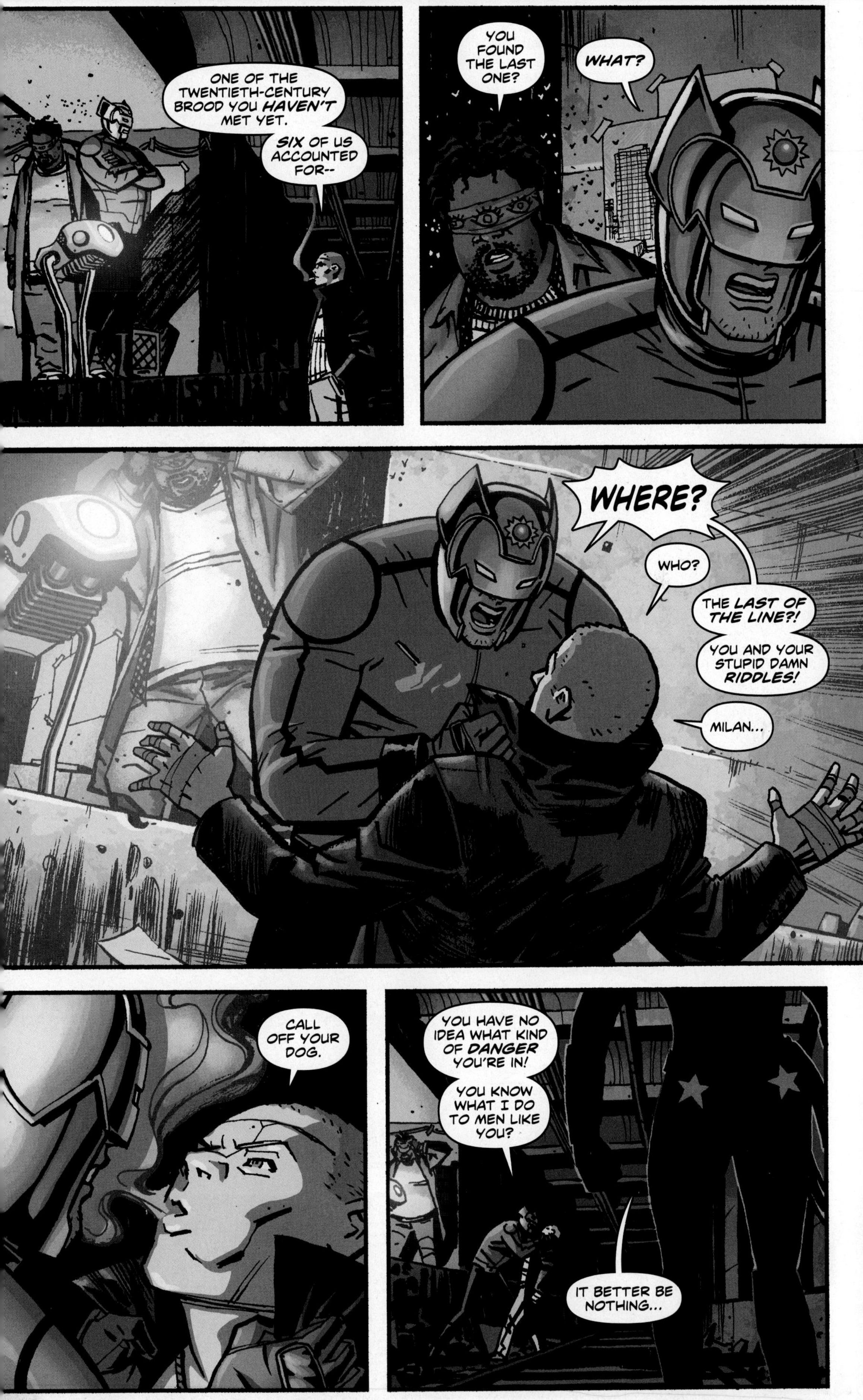
ONE OF THE TWENTIETH-CENTURY BROOD YOU *HAVEN'T* MET YET.
SIX OF US ACCOUNTED FOR--
YOU FOUND THE LAST ONE?
WHAT?
WHERE?
WHO?
THE *LAST OF THE LINE?!*
YOU AND YOUR STUPID DAMN *RIDDLES!*
MILAN...
CALL OFF YOUR DOG.
YOU HAVE NO IDEA WHAT KIND OF *DANGER* YOU'RE IN!
YOU KNOW WHAT I DO TO MEN LIKE YOU?
IT BETTER BE NOTHING...

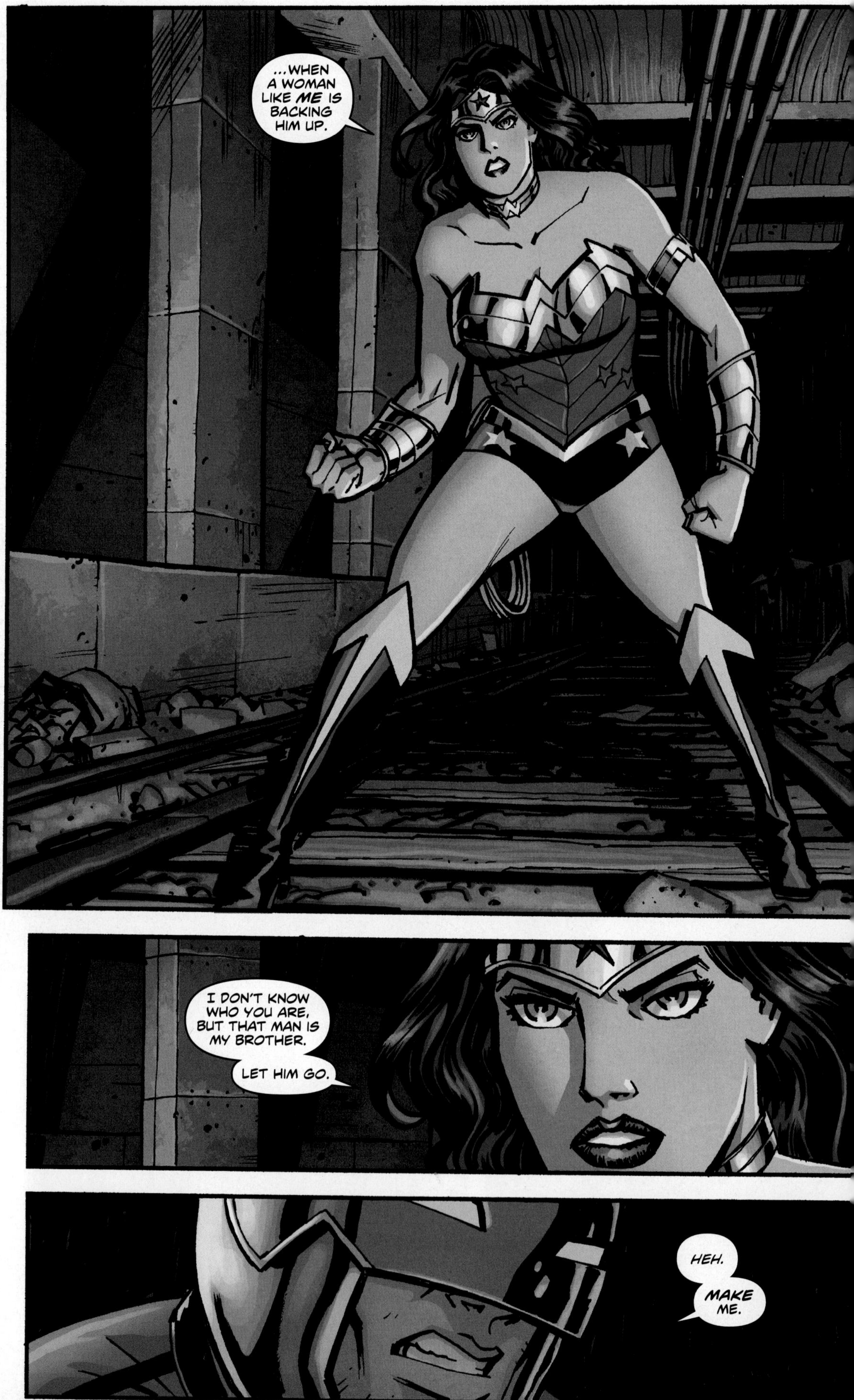
...WHEN A WOMAN LIKE ME IS BACKING HIM UP.
I DON'T KNOW WHO YOU ARE, BUT THAT MAN IS MY BROTHER.
LET HIM GO.
HEH.
MAKE ME.

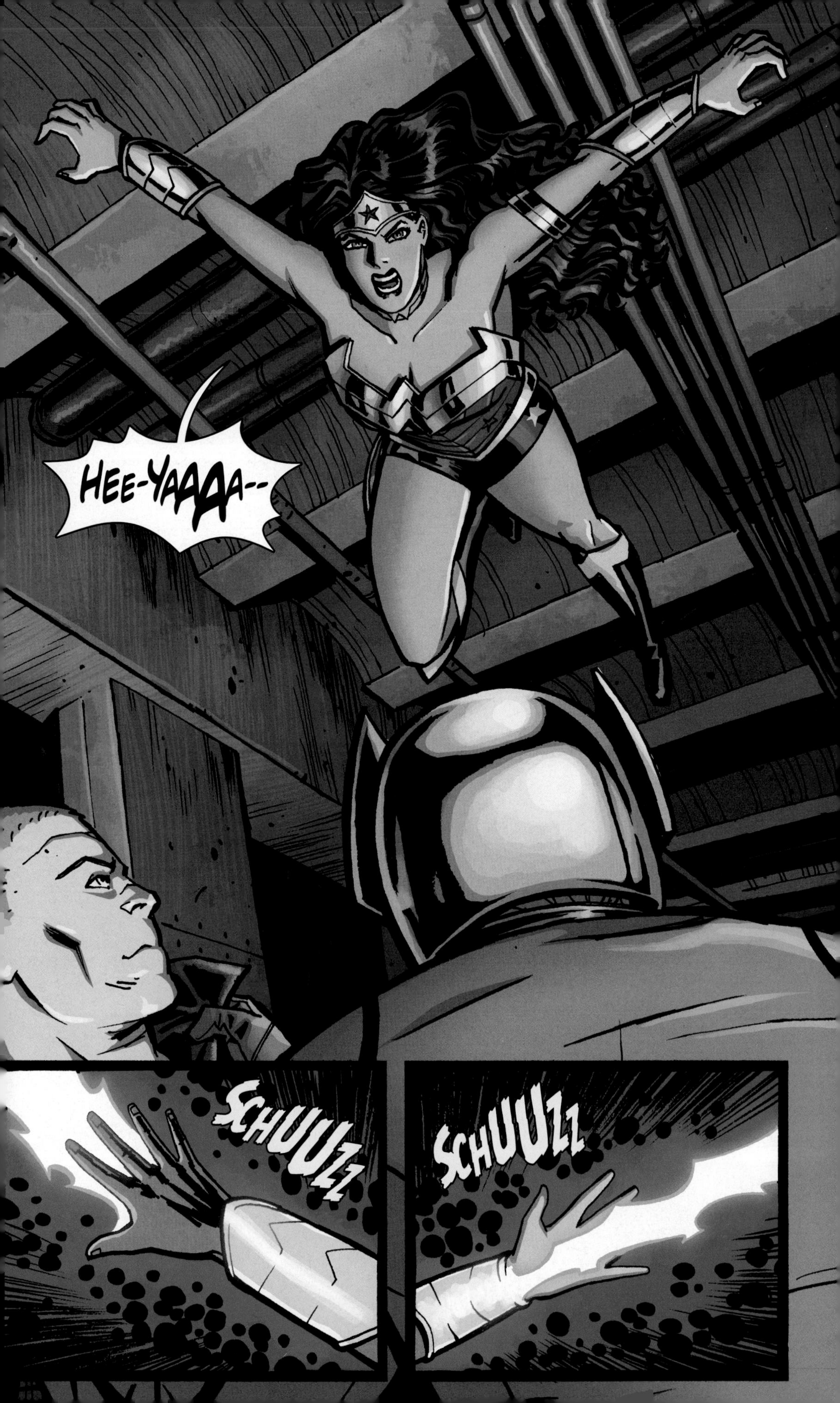
HEE-YAAAA--
SCHUUZz
SCHUUZz

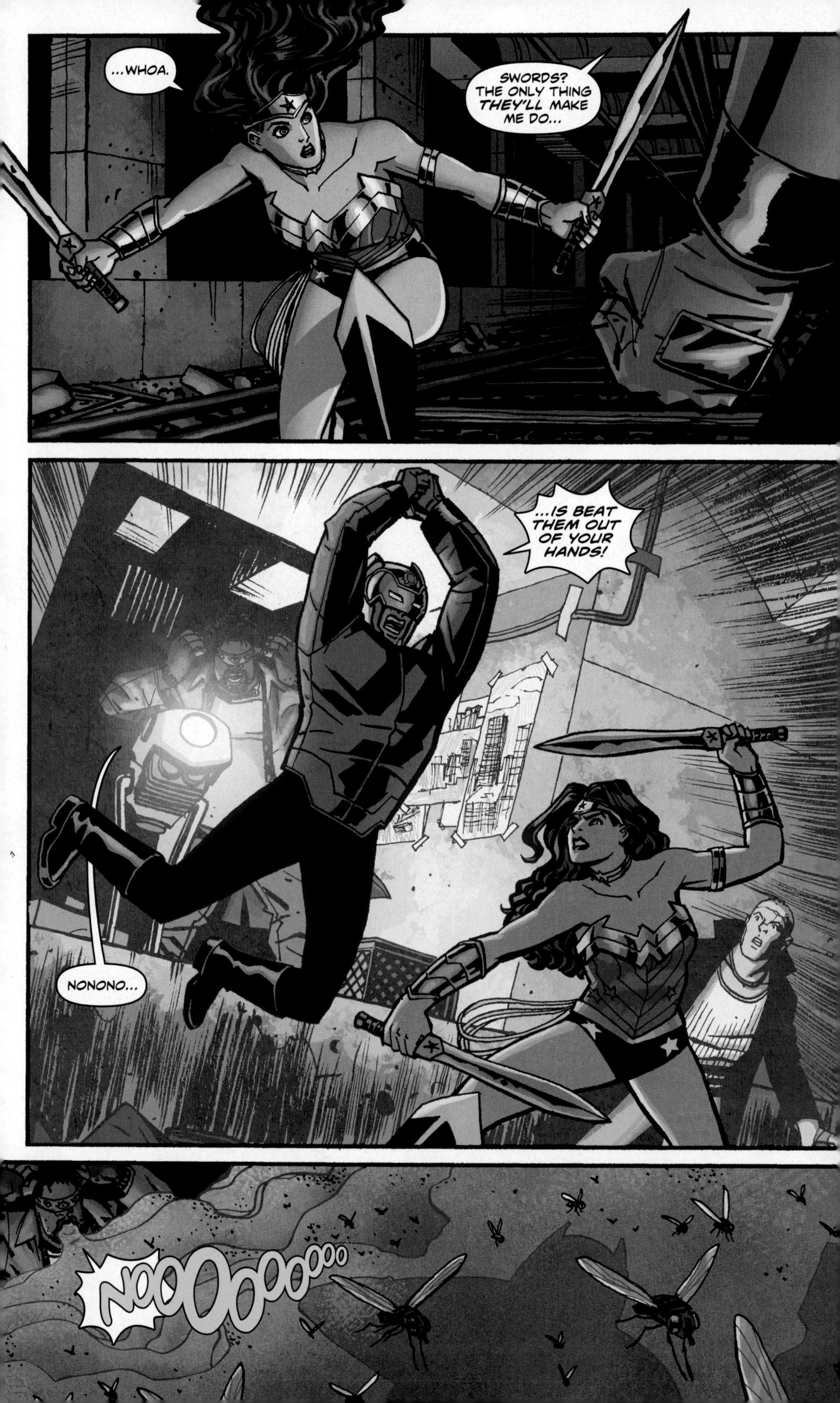
...WHOA.
SWORDS? THE ONLY THING THEY'LL MAKE ME DO...
...IS BEAT THEM OUT OF YOUR HANDS!
NONONO...
NOOOOOOOOO

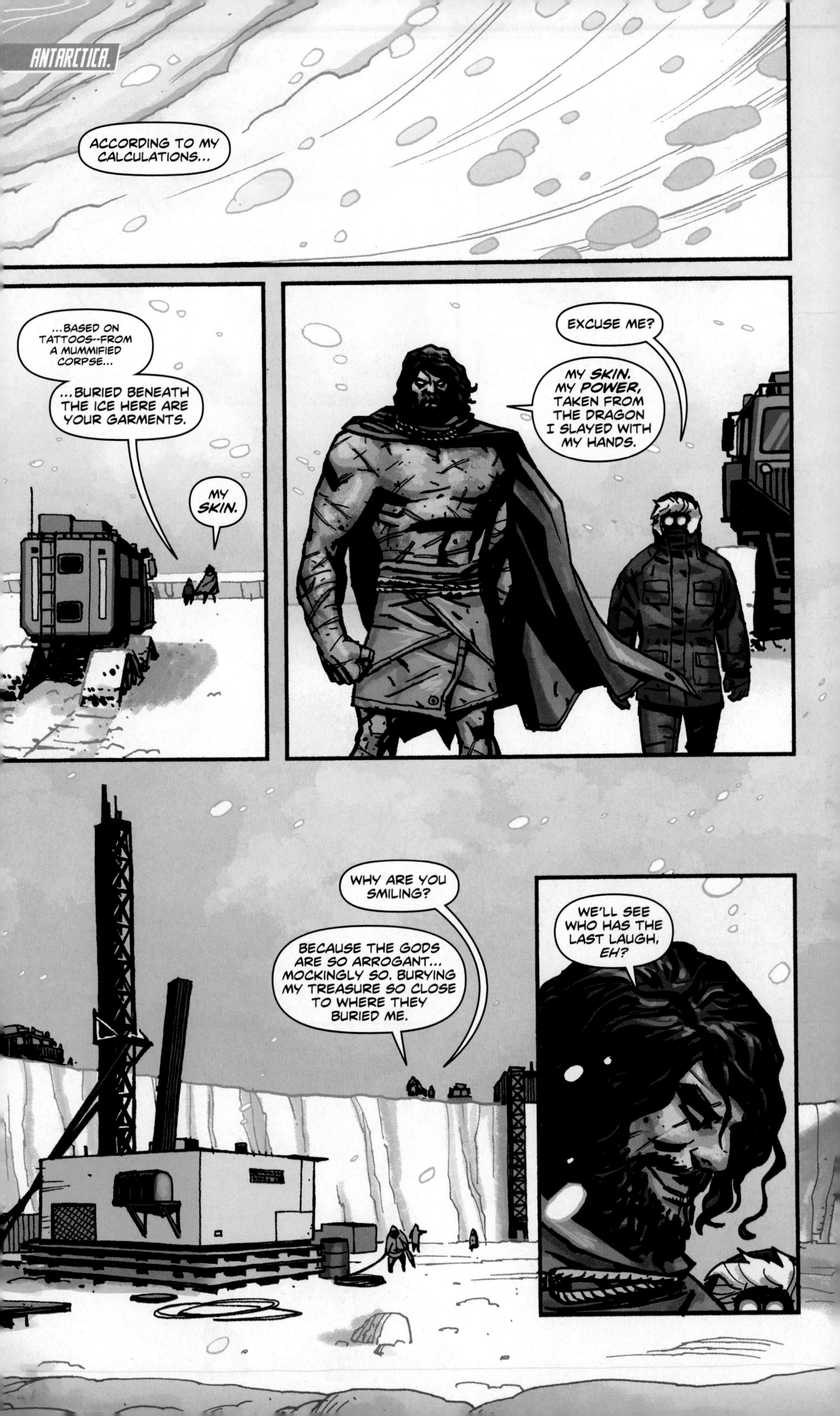
ANTARCTICA.
ACCORDING TO MY CALCULATIONS...
...BASED ON TATTOOS--FROM A MUMMIFIED CORPSE...
...BURIED BENEATH THE ICE HERE ARE YOUR GARMENTS.
MY SKIN.
EXCUSE ME?
MY SKIN. MY POWER, TAKEN FROM THE DRAGON I SLAYED WITH MY HANDS.
WHY ARE YOU SMILING?
BECAUSE THE GODS ARE SO ARROGANT... MOCKINGLY SO. BURYING MY TREASURE SO CLOSE TO WHERE THEY BURIED ME.
WE'LL SEE WHO HAS THE LAST LAUGH, EH?

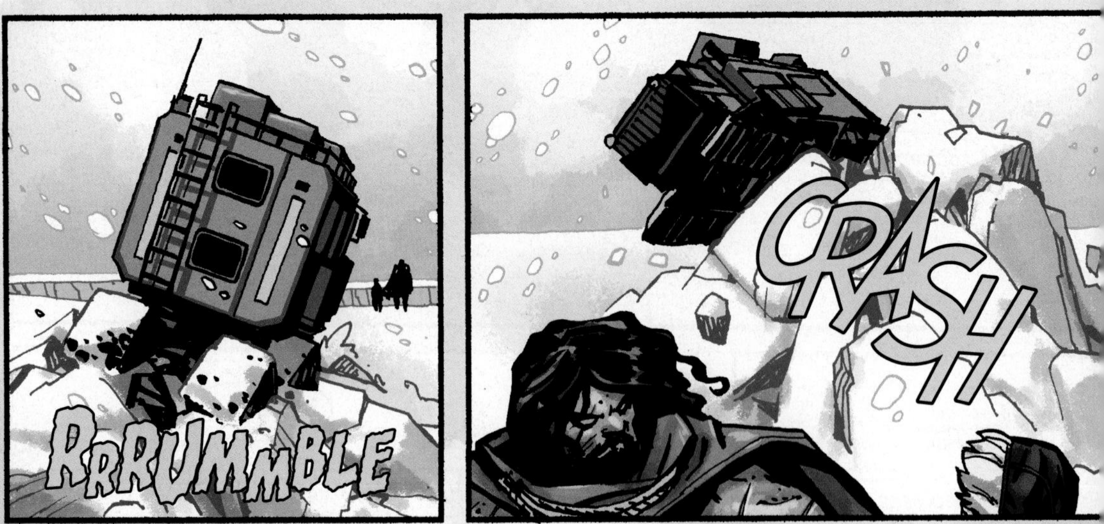
RRRUMMBLE
CRASH

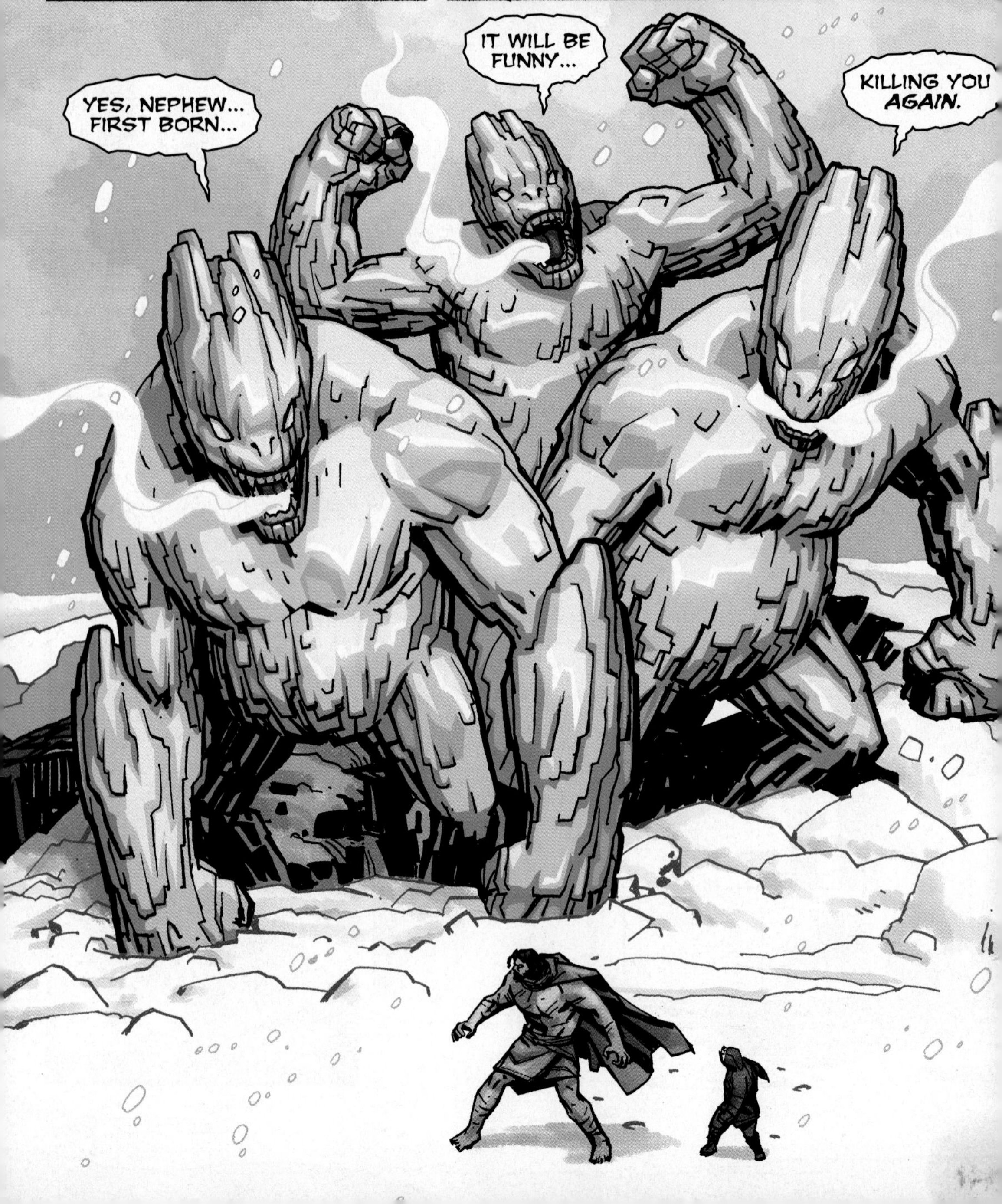
YES, NEPHEW... FIRST BORN...
IT WILL BE FUNNY...
KILLING YOU *AGAIN.*

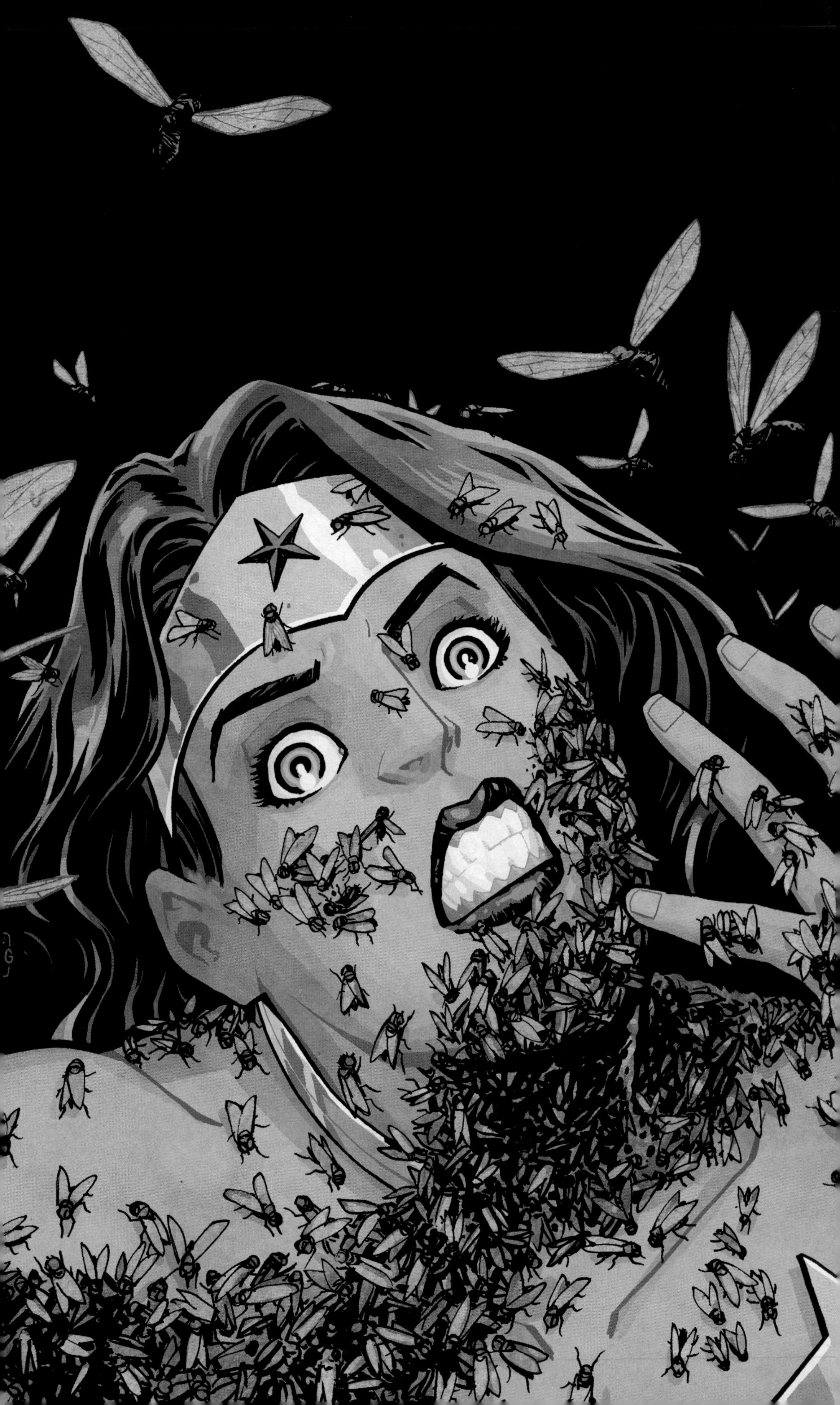

FAMILY REACHES

CLIFF CHIANG artist

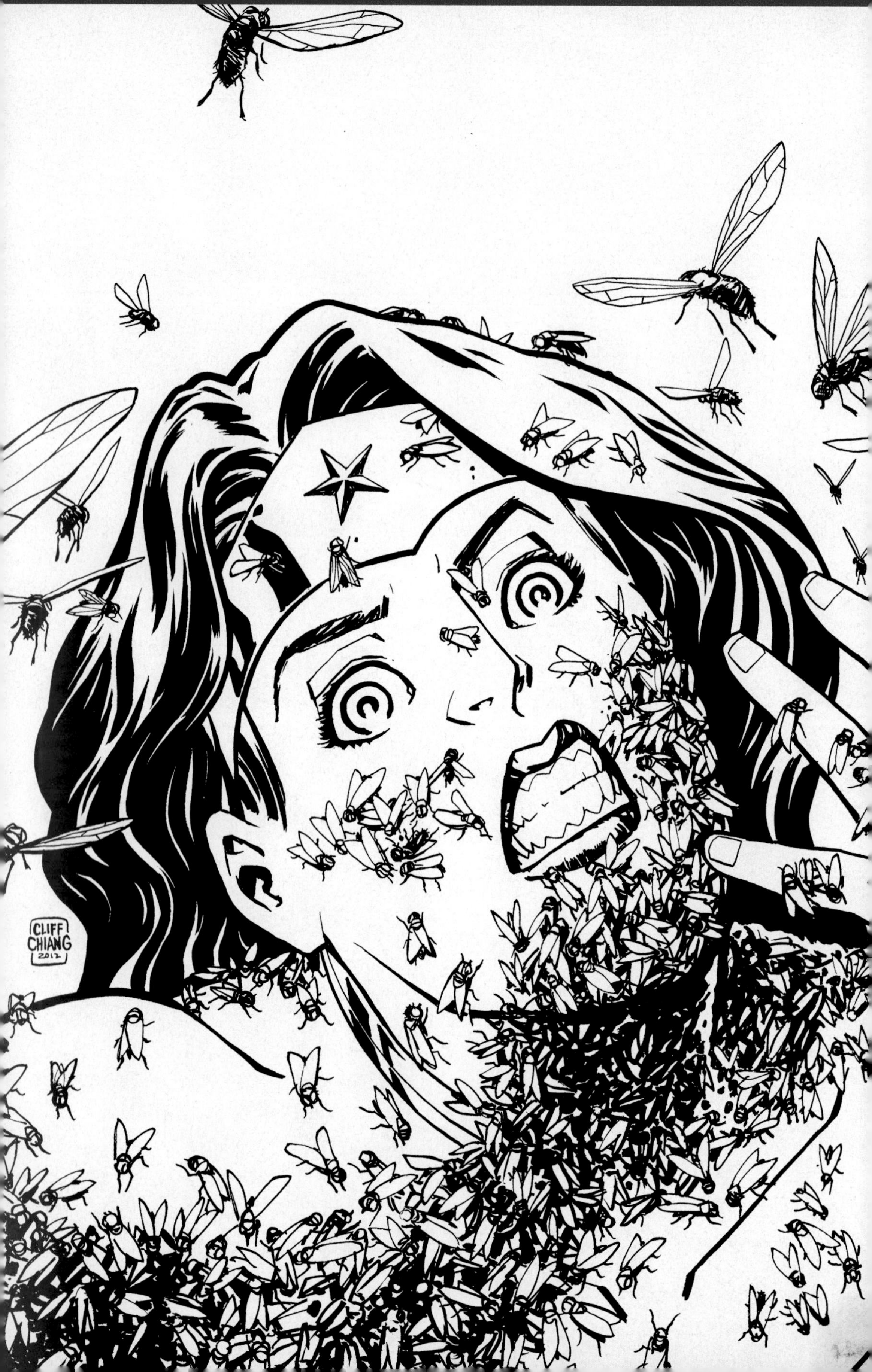

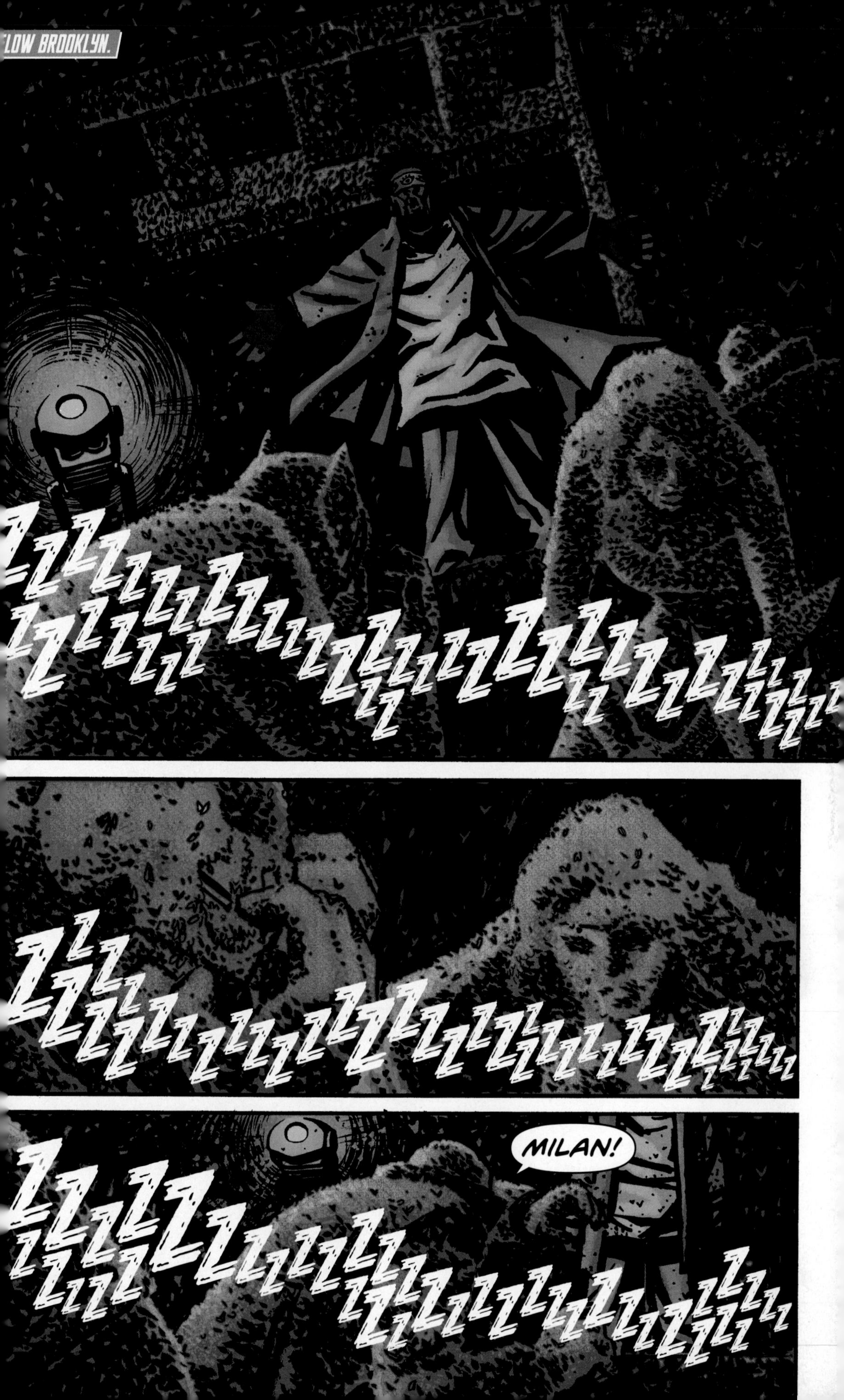
LOW BROOKLYN.
MILAN!

YOU BLOODY IDIOT!

≡GAG≡

YOU DIDN'T *LISTEN* TO ME!

CAN'T BRE--

THEN STOP...

STOP FIGHTING!

NO MORE FIGHTING!

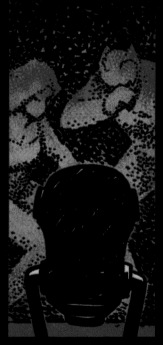

TZAAOOOoo

"I'M SORRY..."

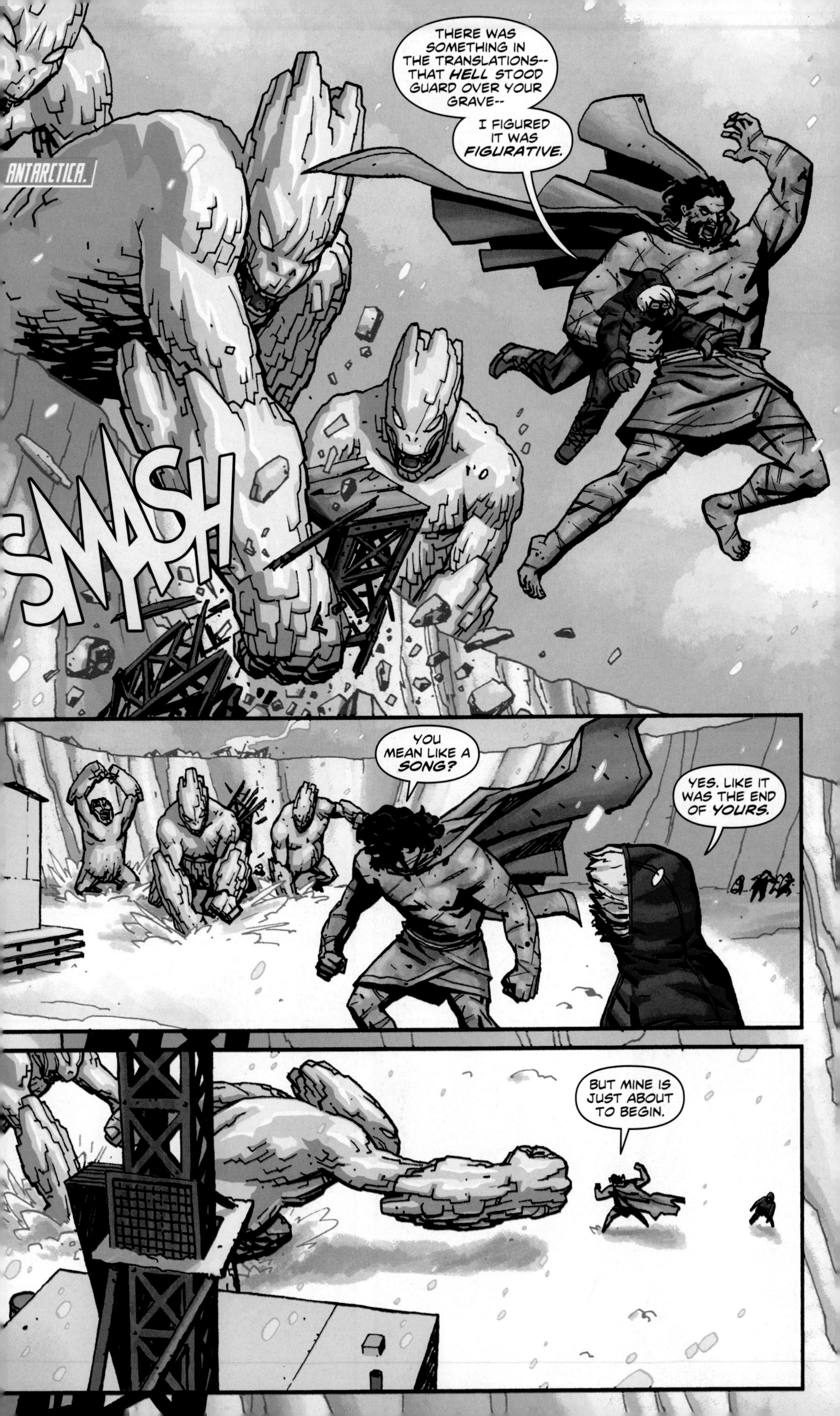
ANTARCTICA.
THERE WAS SOMETHING IN THE TRANSLATIONS-- THAT HELL STOOD GUARD OVER YOUR GRAVE--
I FIGURED IT WAS FIGURATIVE.
SMASH
YOU MEAN LIKE A SONG?
YES. LIKE IT WAS THE END OF YOURS.
BUT MINE IS JUST ABOUT TO BEGIN.

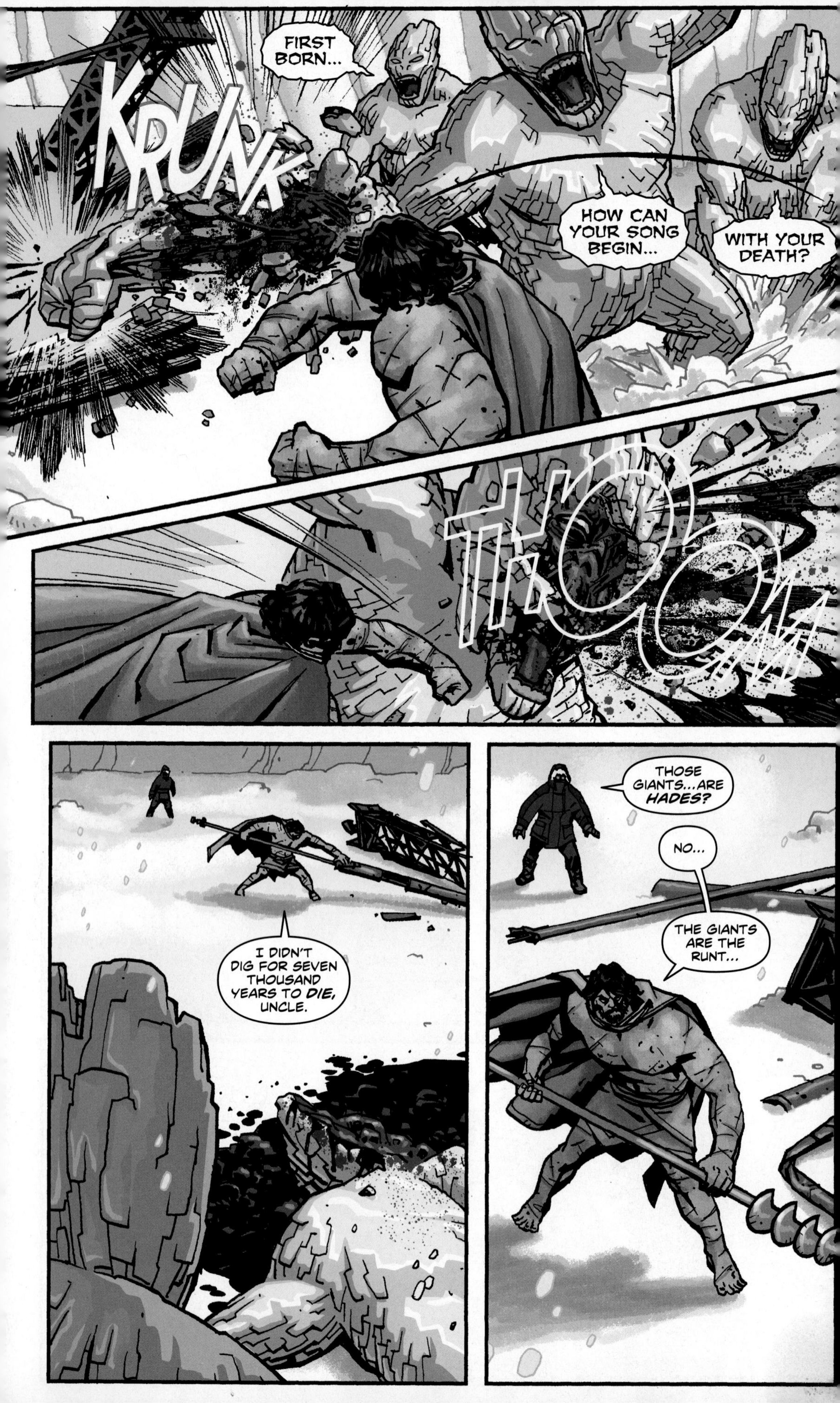
KRUNK
FIRST BORN...
HOW CAN YOUR SONG BEGIN...
WITH YOUR DEATH?
THOOM
I DIDN'T DIG FOR SEVEN THOUSAND YEARS TO *DIE*, UNCLE.
THOSE GIANTS...ARE *HADES?*
NO...
THE GIANTS ARE THE RUNT...

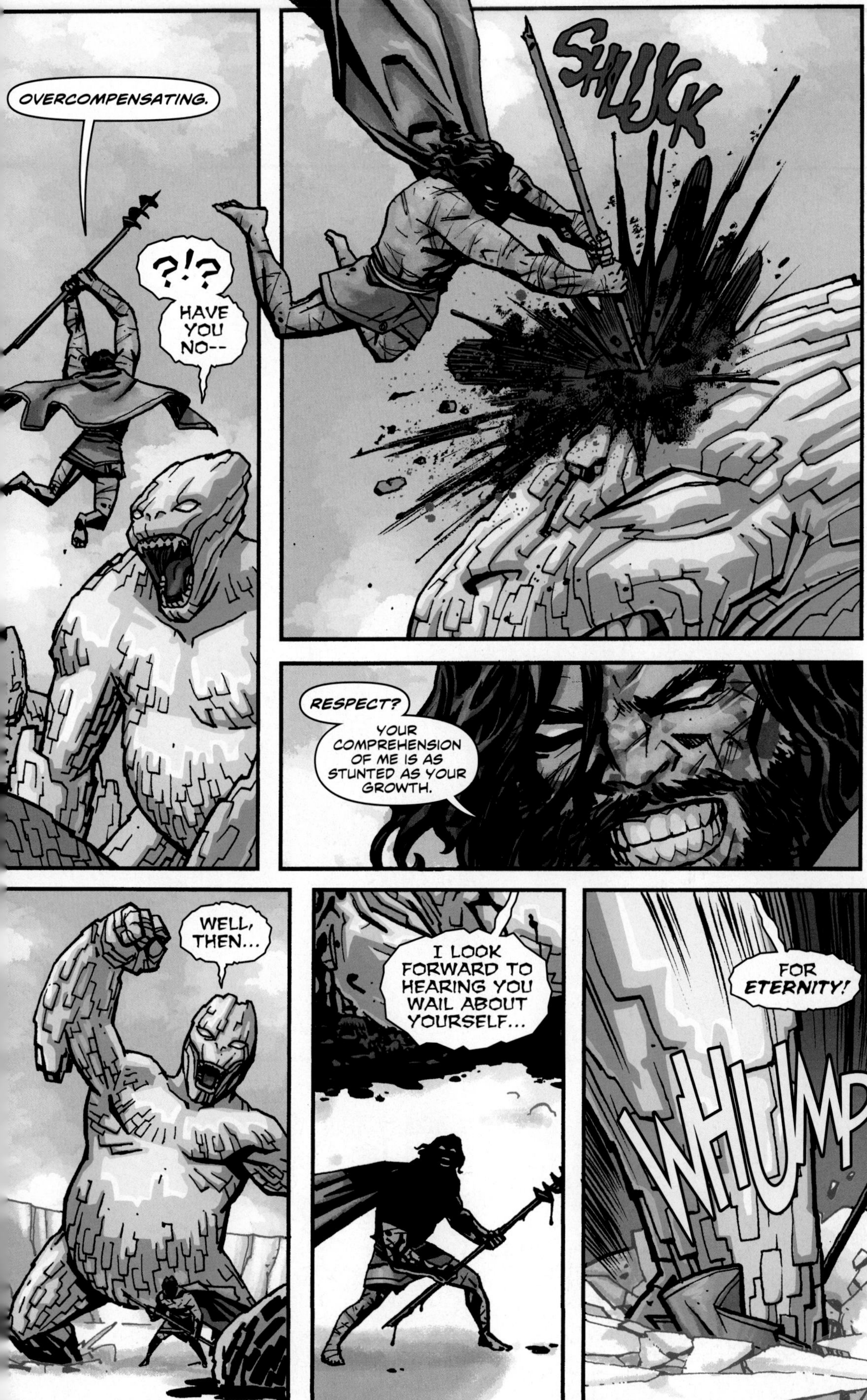
OVERCOMPENSATING.
?!?
HAVE YOU NO--
SHLUCK
RESPECT?
YOUR COMPREHENSION OF ME IS AS STUNTED AS YOUR GROWTH.
WELL, THEN...
I LOOK FORWARD TO HEARING YOU WAIL ABOUT YOURSELF...
FOR ETERNITY!
WHUMP

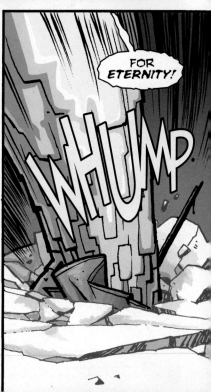

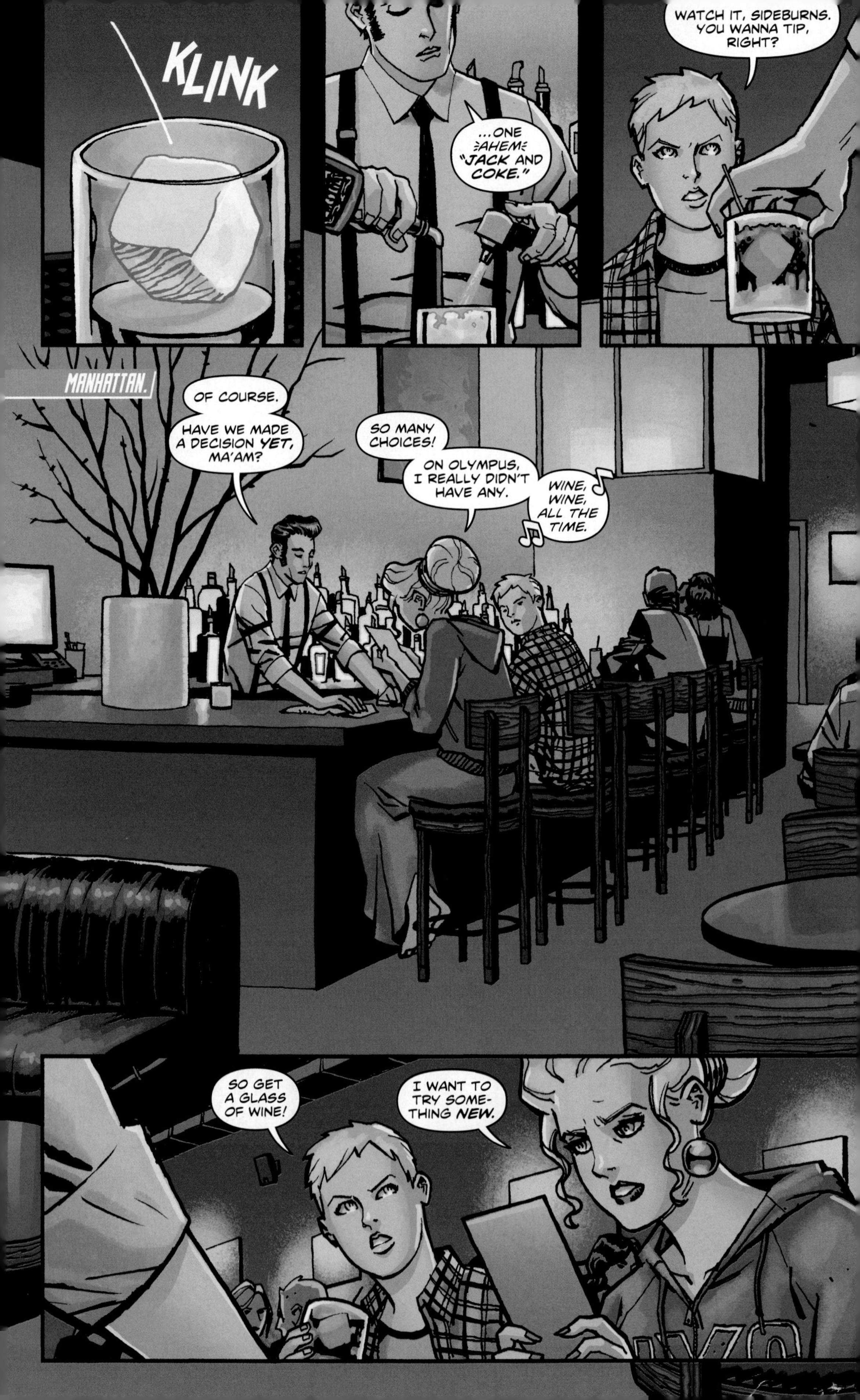
KLINK
...ONE AHEM "JACK AND COKE."
WATCH IT, SIDEBURNS. YOU WANNA TIP, RIGHT?
MANHATTAN.
OF COURSE.
HAVE WE MADE A DECISION YET, MA'AM?
SO MANY CHOICES!
ON OLYMPUS, I REALLY DIDN'T HAVE ANY.
WINE, WINE, ALL THE TIME.
SO GET A GLASS OF WINE!
I WANT TO TRY SOME-THING NEW.

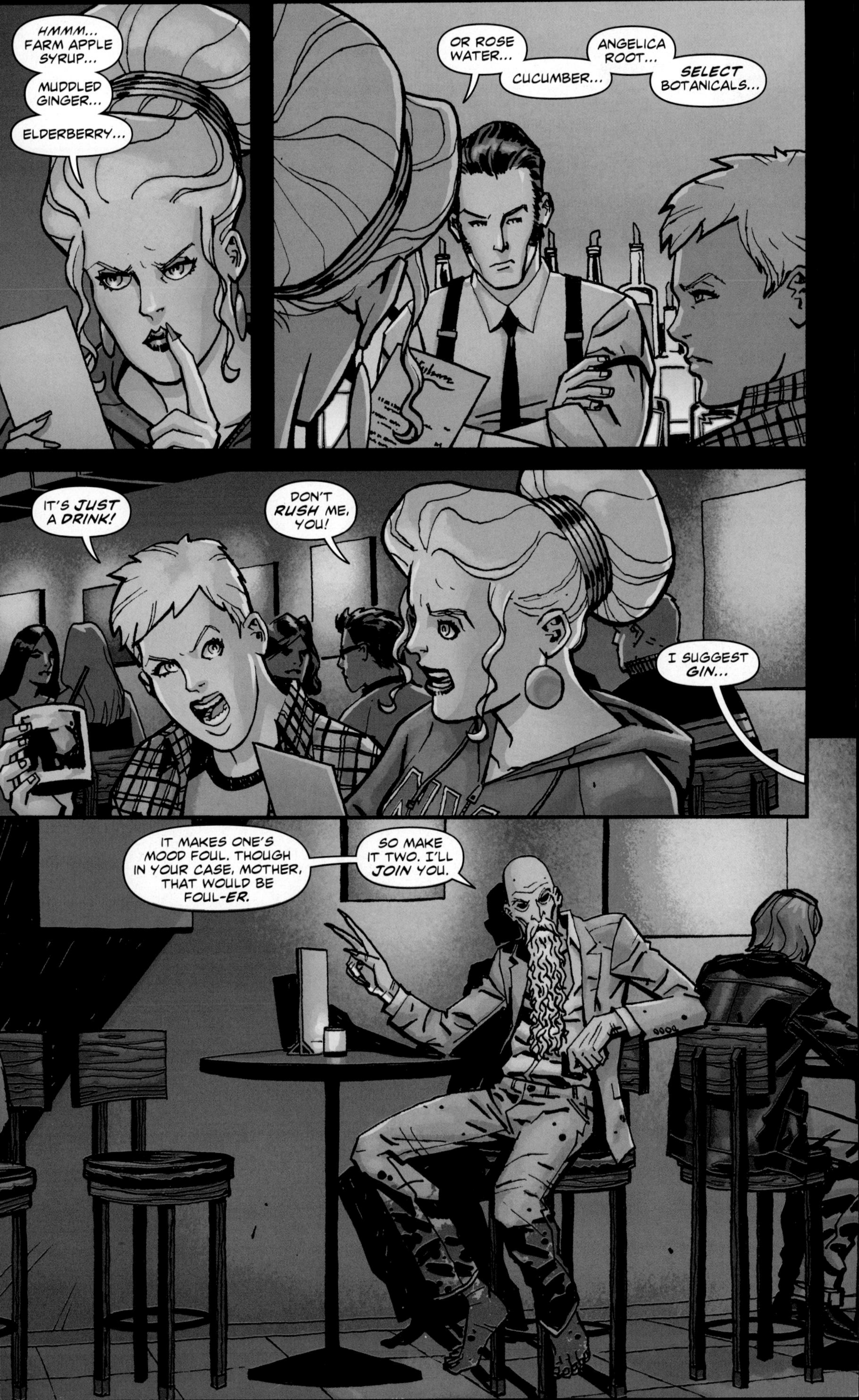
HMMM... FARM APPLE SYRUP...
MUDDLED GINGER...
ELDERBERRY...
OR ROSE WATER...
CUCUMBER...
ANGELICA ROOT...
SELECT BOTANICALS...
IT'S JUST A DRINK!
DON'T RUSH ME, YOU!
I SUGGEST GIN...
IT MAKES ONE'S MOOD FOUL. THOUGH IN YOUR CASE, MOTHER, THAT WOULD BE FOUL-ER.
SO MAKE IT TWO. I'LL JOIN YOU.

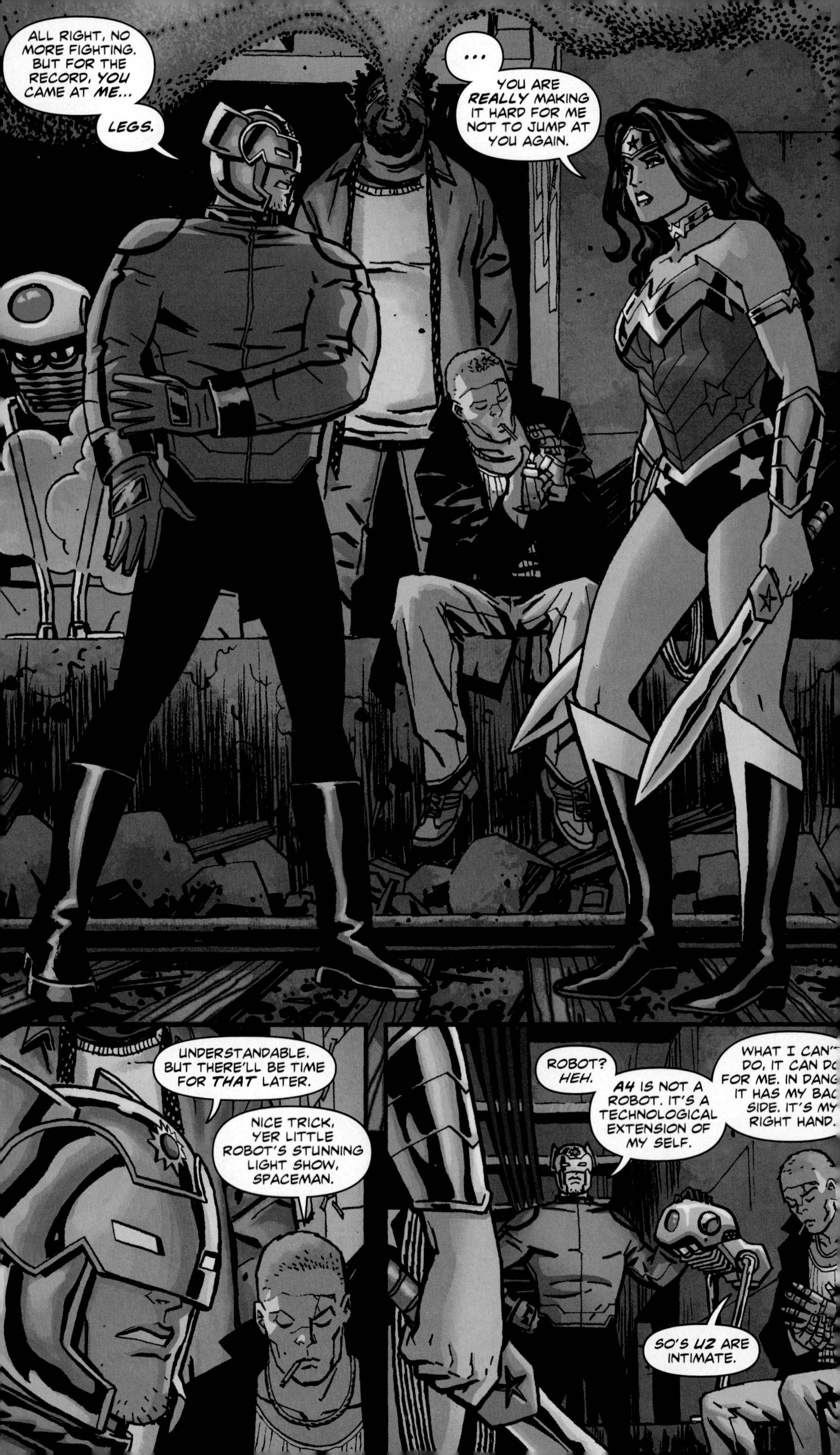
ALL RIGHT, NO MORE FIGHTING. BUT FOR THE RECORD, *YOU* CAME AT *ME*...
LEGS.
...
YOU ARE *REALLY* MAKING IT HARD FOR ME NOT TO JUMP AT YOU AGAIN.
UNDERSTANDABLE. BUT THERE'LL BE TIME FOR *THAT* LATER.
NICE TRICK, YER LITTLE ROBOT'S STUNNING LIGHT SHOW, SPACEMAN.
ROBOT? *HEH.*
A4 IS NOT A ROBOT. IT'S A TECHNOLOGICAL EXTENSION OF MY SELF.
WHAT I CAN' DO, IT CAN DO FOR ME. IN DANG IT HAS MY BAC SIDE. IT'S MY RIGHT HAND.
SO'S *U2* ARE INTIMATE.

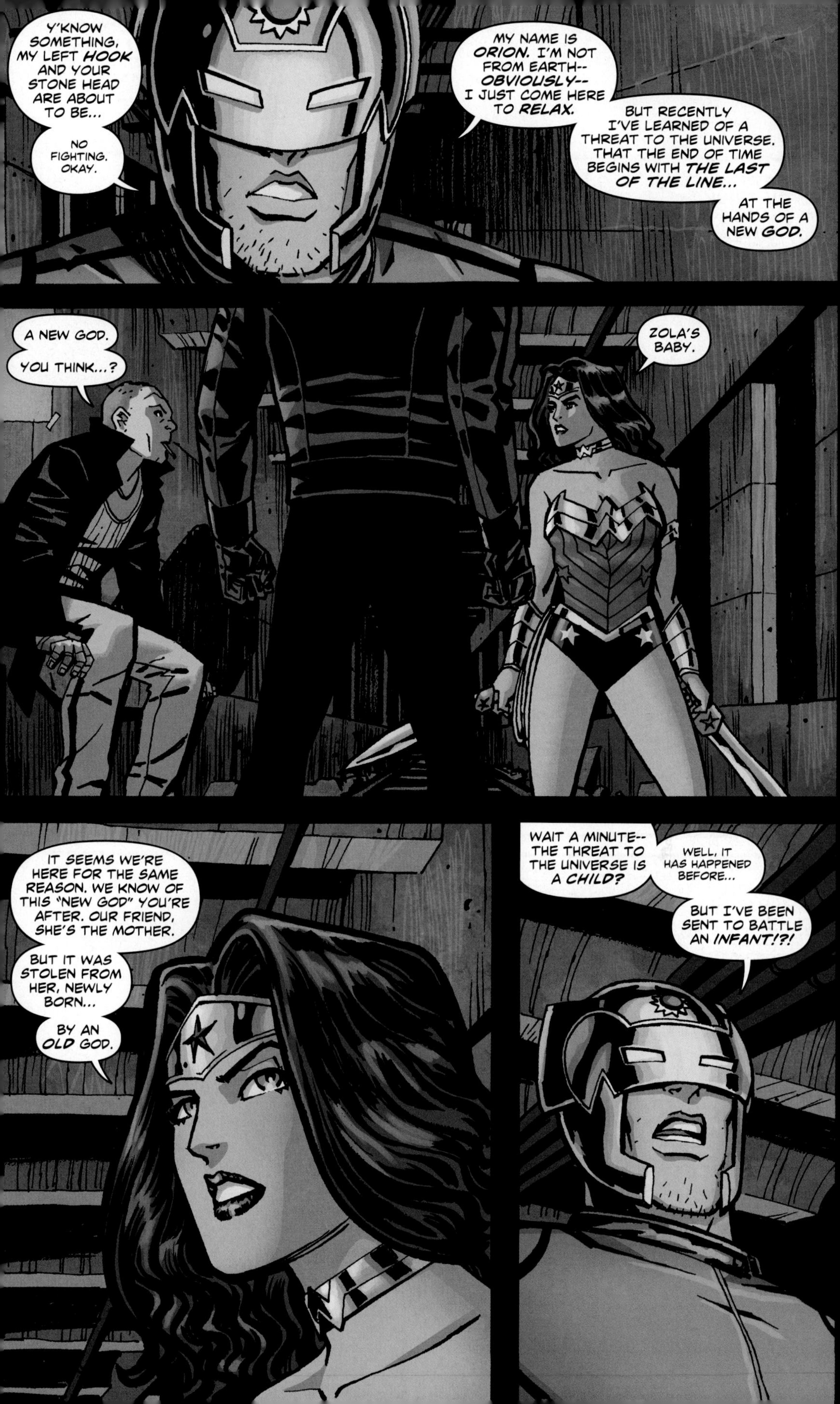
Y'KNOW SOMETHING, MY LEFT HOOK AND YOUR STONE HEAD ARE ABOUT TO BE...
NO FIGHTING. OKAY.
MY NAME IS ORION. I'M NOT FROM EARTH-- OBVIOUSLY-- I JUST COME HERE TO RELAX.
BUT RECENTLY I'VE LEARNED OF A THREAT TO THE UNIVERSE. THAT THE END OF TIME BEGINS WITH THE LAST OF THE LINE...
AT THE HANDS OF A NEW GOD.
A NEW GOD.
YOU THINK...?
ZOLA'S BABY.
IT SEEMS WE'RE HERE FOR THE SAME REASON. WE KNOW OF THIS "NEW GOD" YOU'RE AFTER. OUR FRIEND, SHE'S THE MOTHER.
BUT IT WAS STOLEN FROM HER, NEWLY BORN...
BY AN OLD GOD.
WAIT A MINUTE-- THE THREAT TO THE UNIVERSE IS A CHILD?
WELL, IT HAS HAPPENED BEFORE...
BUT I'VE BEEN SENT TO BATTLE AN INFANT!?!

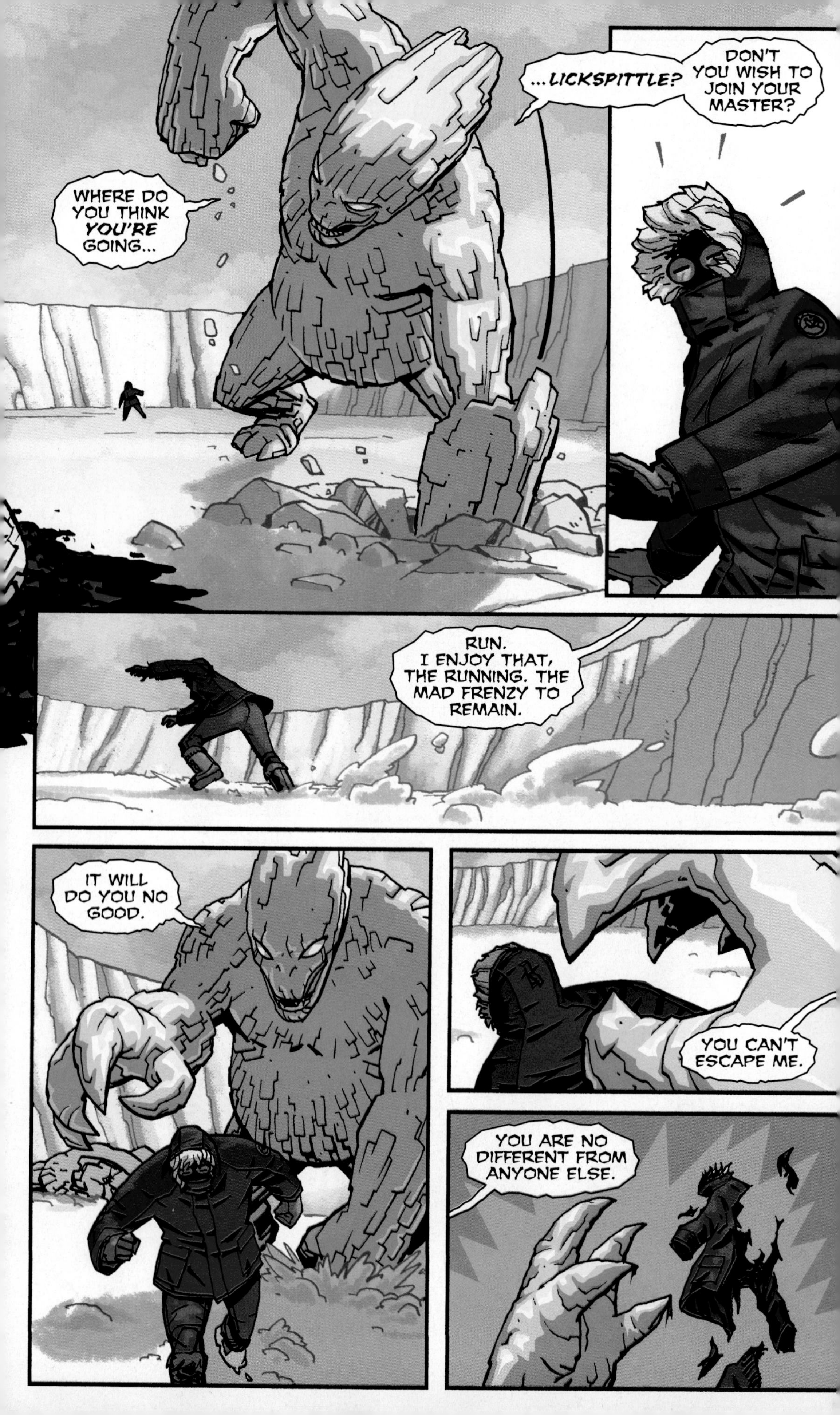
WHERE DO YOU THINK *YOU'RE* GOING...
...*LICKSPITTLE?*
DON'T YOU WISH TO JOIN YOUR MASTER?
RUN. I ENJOY THAT, THE RUNNING. THE MAD FRENZY TO REMAIN.
IT WILL DO YOU NO GOOD.
YOU CAN'T ESCAPE ME.
YOU ARE NO DIFFERENT FROM ANYONE ELSE.

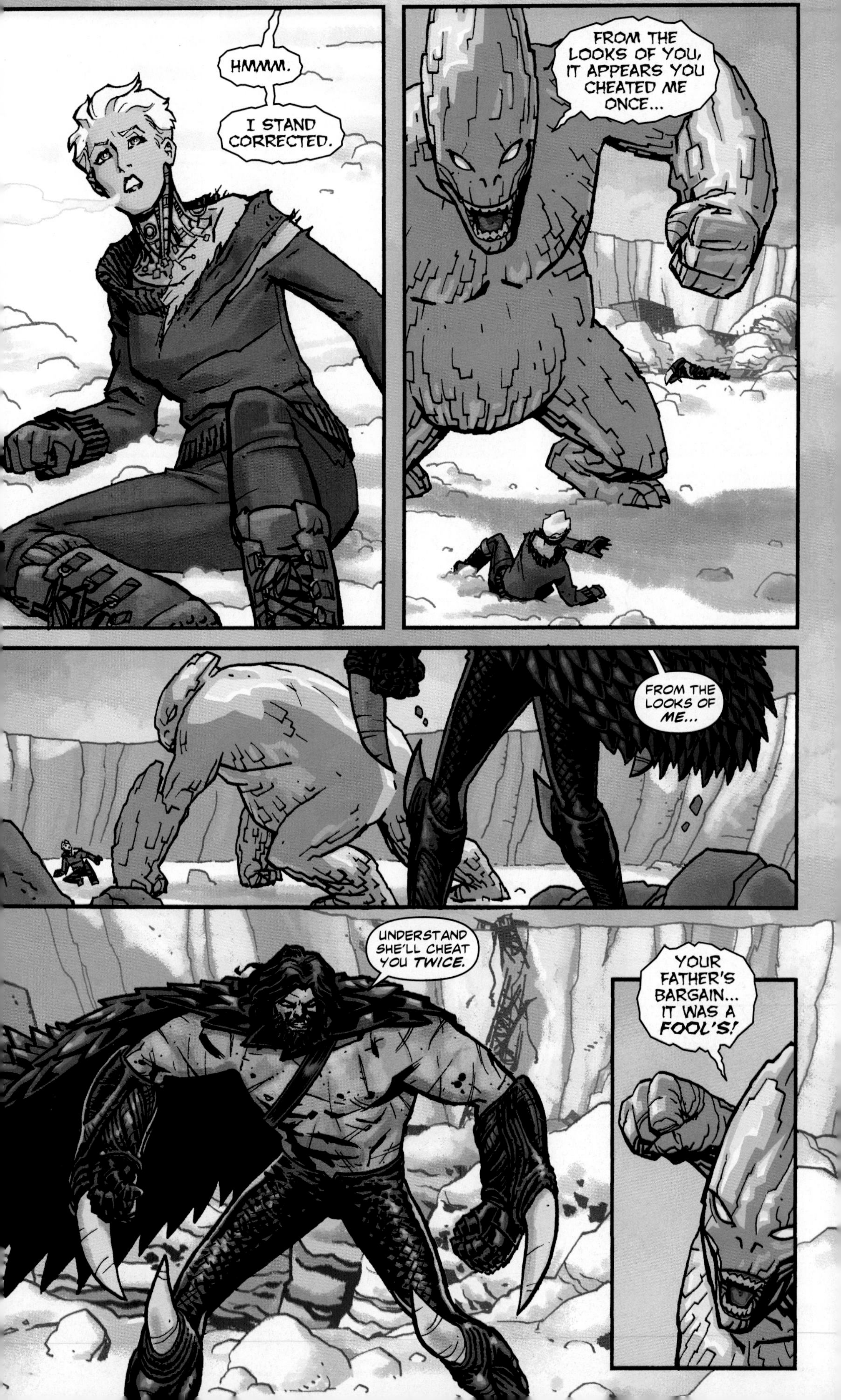
HMMM.
I STAND CORRECTED.
FROM THE LOOKS OF YOU, IT APPEARS YOU CHEATED ME ONCE...
FROM THE LOOKS OF ME...
UNDERSTAND SHE'LL CHEAT YOU TWICE.
YOUR FATHER'S BARGAIN... IT WAS A FOOL'S!

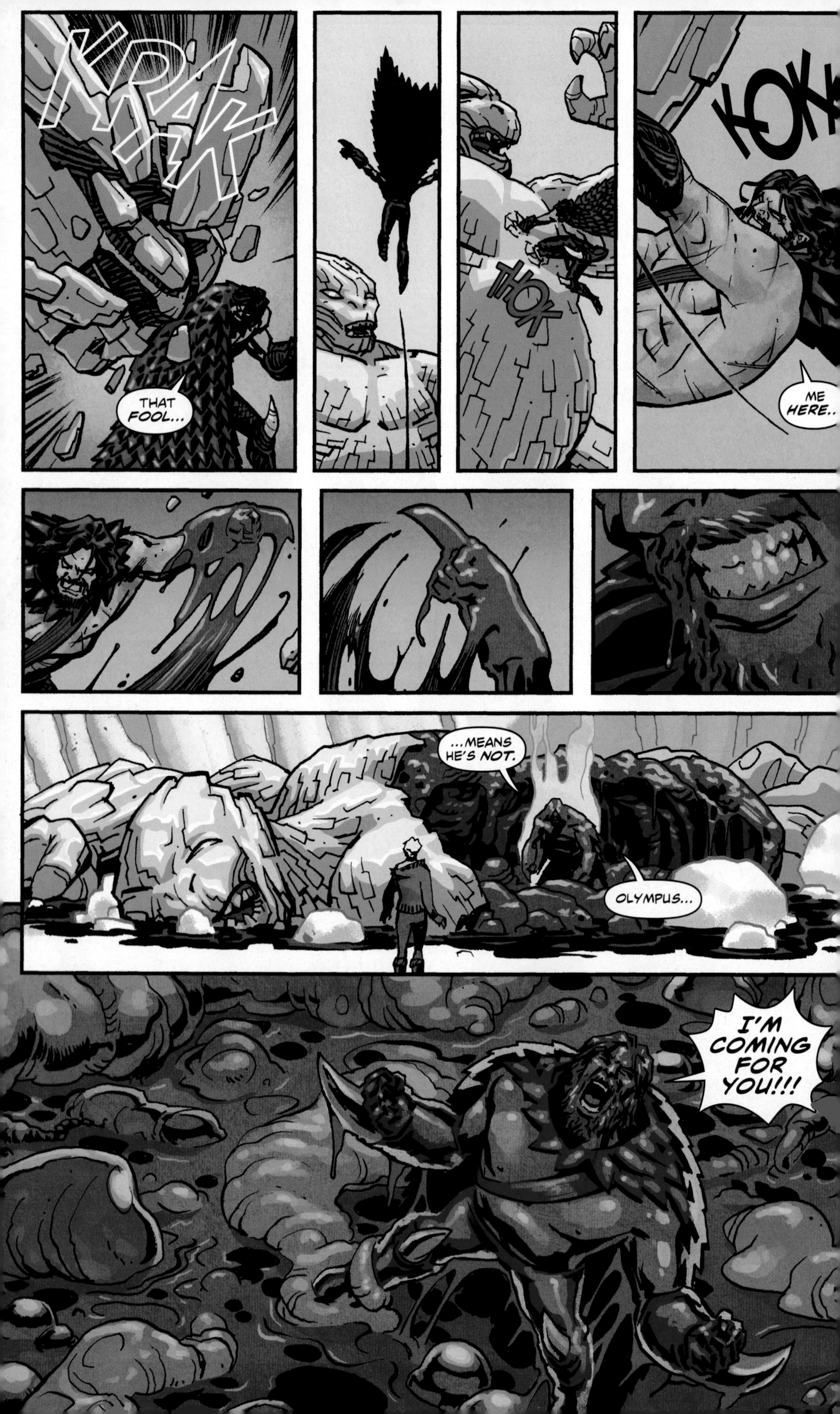
KRAKAKAK
THAT FOOL...
THOK
KOKK
ME HERE..
...MEANS HE'S NOT.
OLYMPUS...
I'M COMING FOR YOU!!!

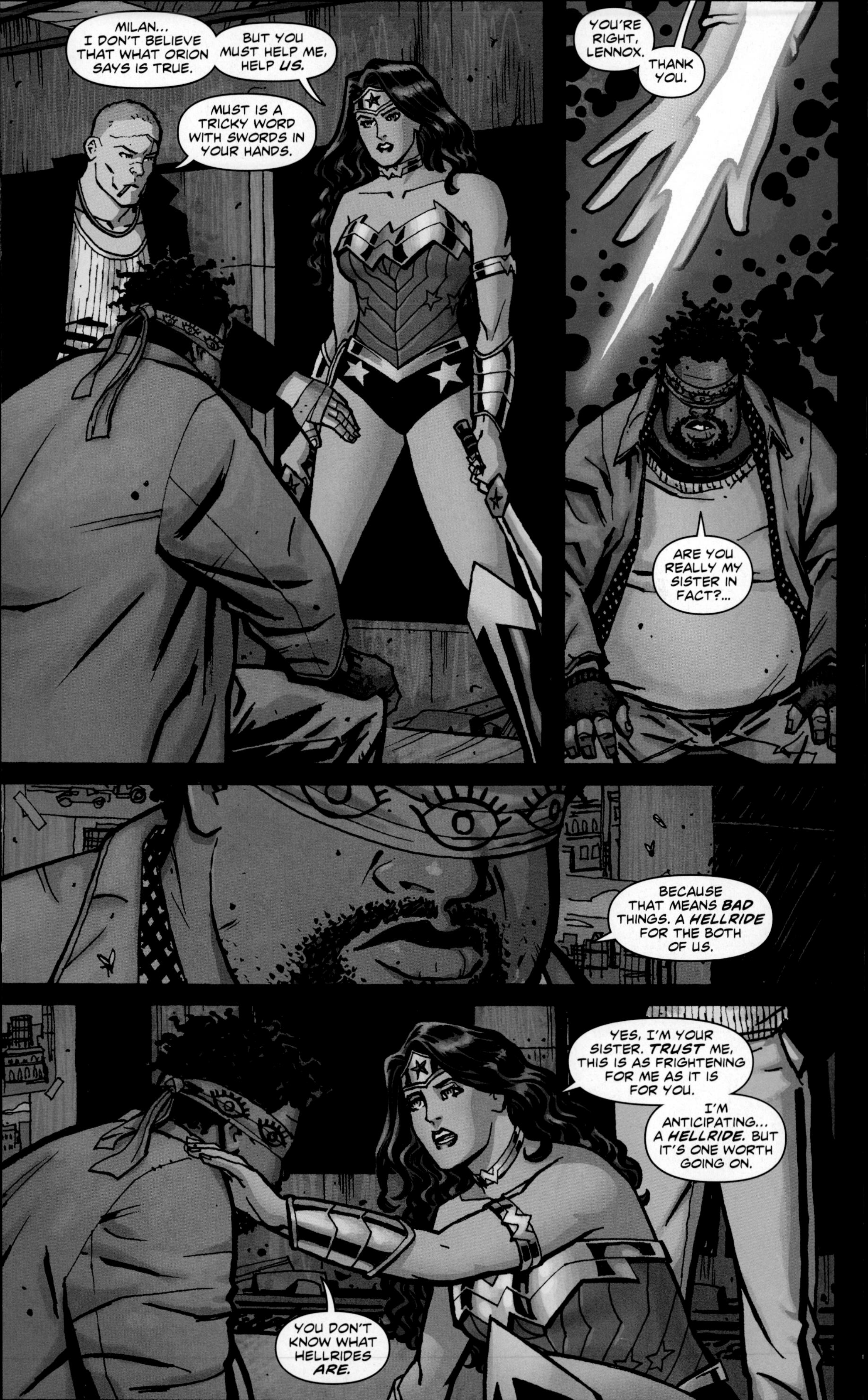

MILAN... I DON'T BELIEVE THAT WHAT ORION SAYS IS TRUE.
BUT YOU MUST HELP ME, HELP *US*.
MUST IS A TRICKY WORD WITH SWORDS IN YOUR HANDS.
YOU'RE RIGHT, LENNOX.
THANK YOU.
ARE YOU REALLY MY SISTER IN FACT?...
BECAUSE THAT MEANS ***BAD*** THINGS. A ***HELLRIDE*** FOR THE BOTH OF US.
YES, I'M YOUR SISTER. ***TRUST*** ME, THIS IS AS FRIGHTENING FOR ME AS IT IS FOR YOU.
I'M ANTICIPATING... A ***HELLRIDE.*** BUT IT'S ONE WORTH GOING ON.
YOU DON'T KNOW WHAT HELLRIDES ***ARE.***

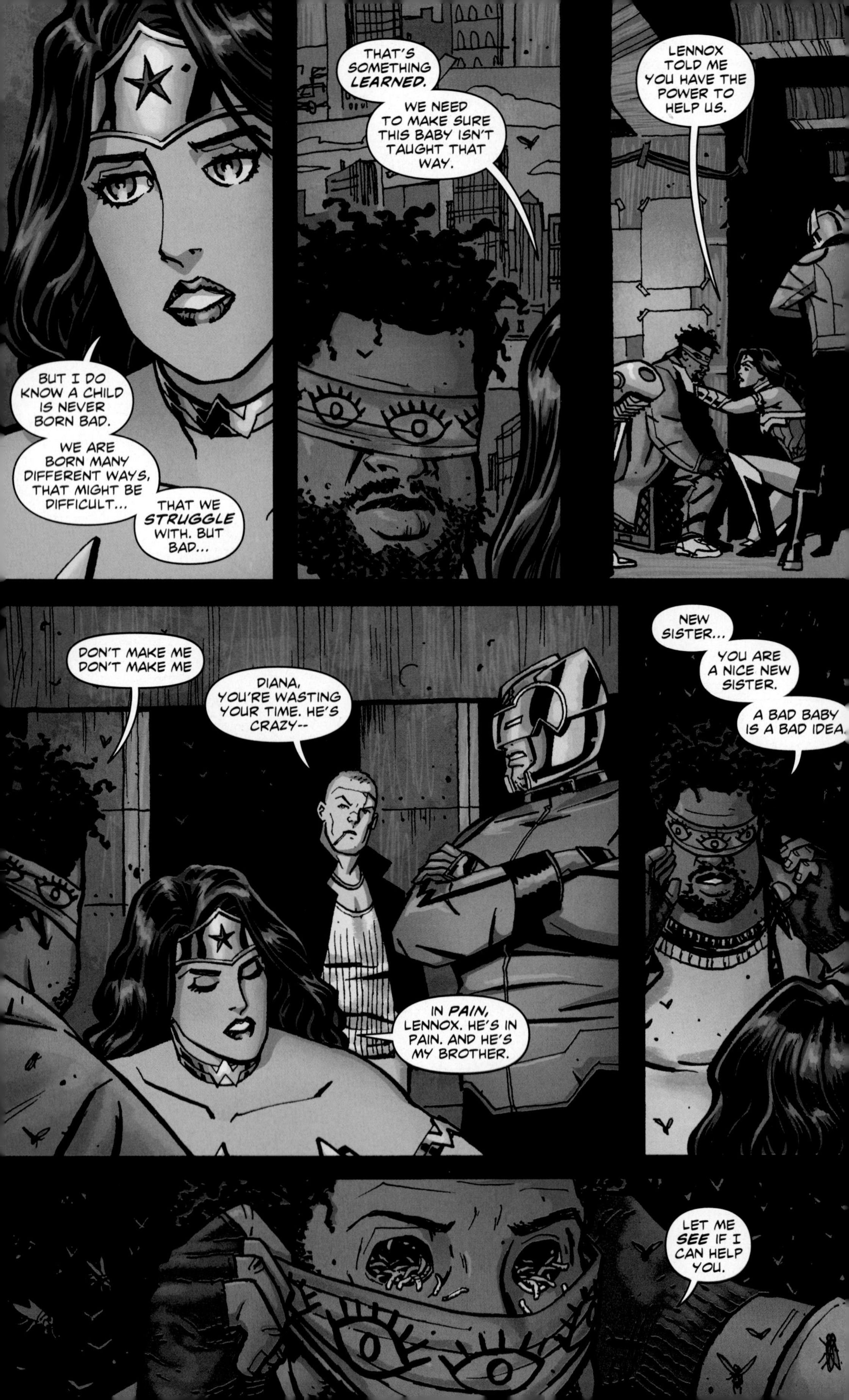
BUT I DO KNOW A CHILD IS NEVER BORN BAD.
WE ARE BORN MANY DIFFERENT WAYS, THAT MIGHT BE DIFFICULT...
THAT WE STRUGGLE WITH. BUT BAD...
THAT'S SOMETHING LEARNED.
WE NEED TO MAKE SURE THIS BABY ISN'T TAUGHT THAT WAY.
LENNOX TOLD ME YOU HAVE THE POWER TO HELP US.
DON'T MAKE ME DON'T MAKE ME
DIANA, YOU'RE WASTING YOUR TIME. HE'S CRAZY--
IN PAIN, LENNOX. HE'S IN PAIN. AND HE'S MY BROTHER.
NEW SISTER...
YOU ARE A NICE NEW SISTER.
A BAD BABY IS A BAD IDEA.
LET ME SEE IF I CAN HELP YOU.

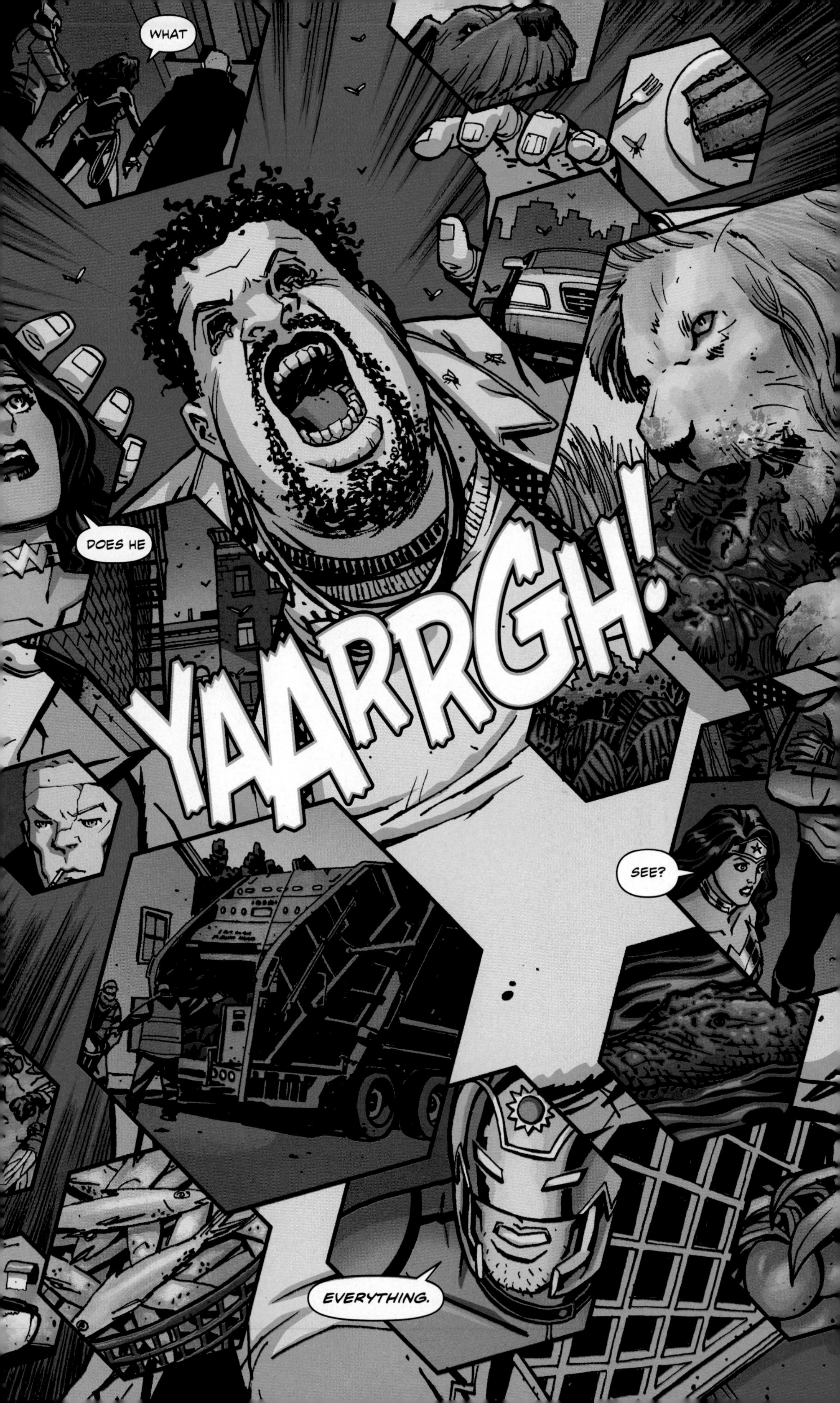
WHAT
DOES HE
YAARRGH!
SEE?
EVERYTHING.

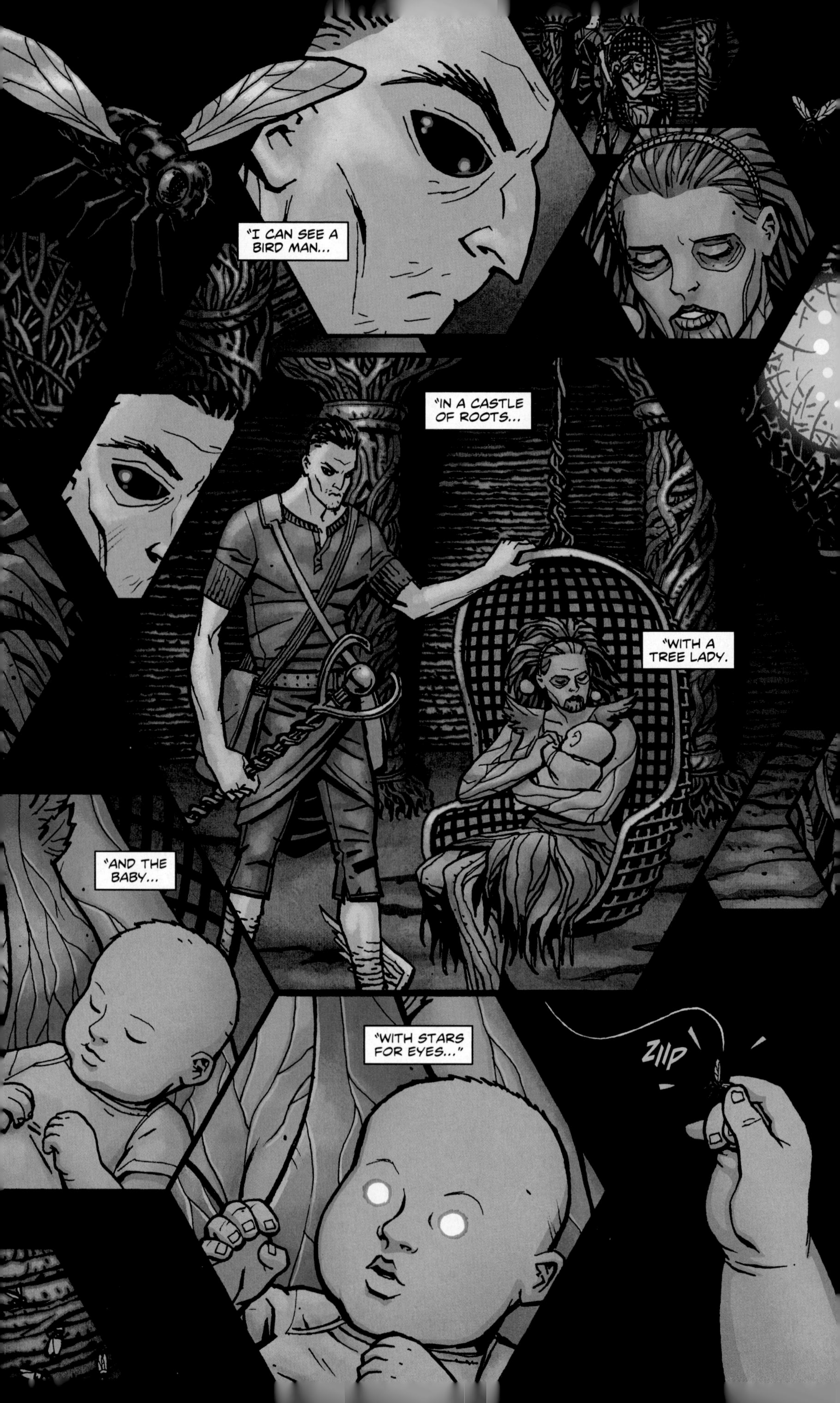
"I CAN SEE A BIRD MAN...
"IN A CASTLE OF ROOTS...
"WITH A TREE LADY.
"AND THE BABY...
"WITH STARS FOR EYES..."
ZIIP

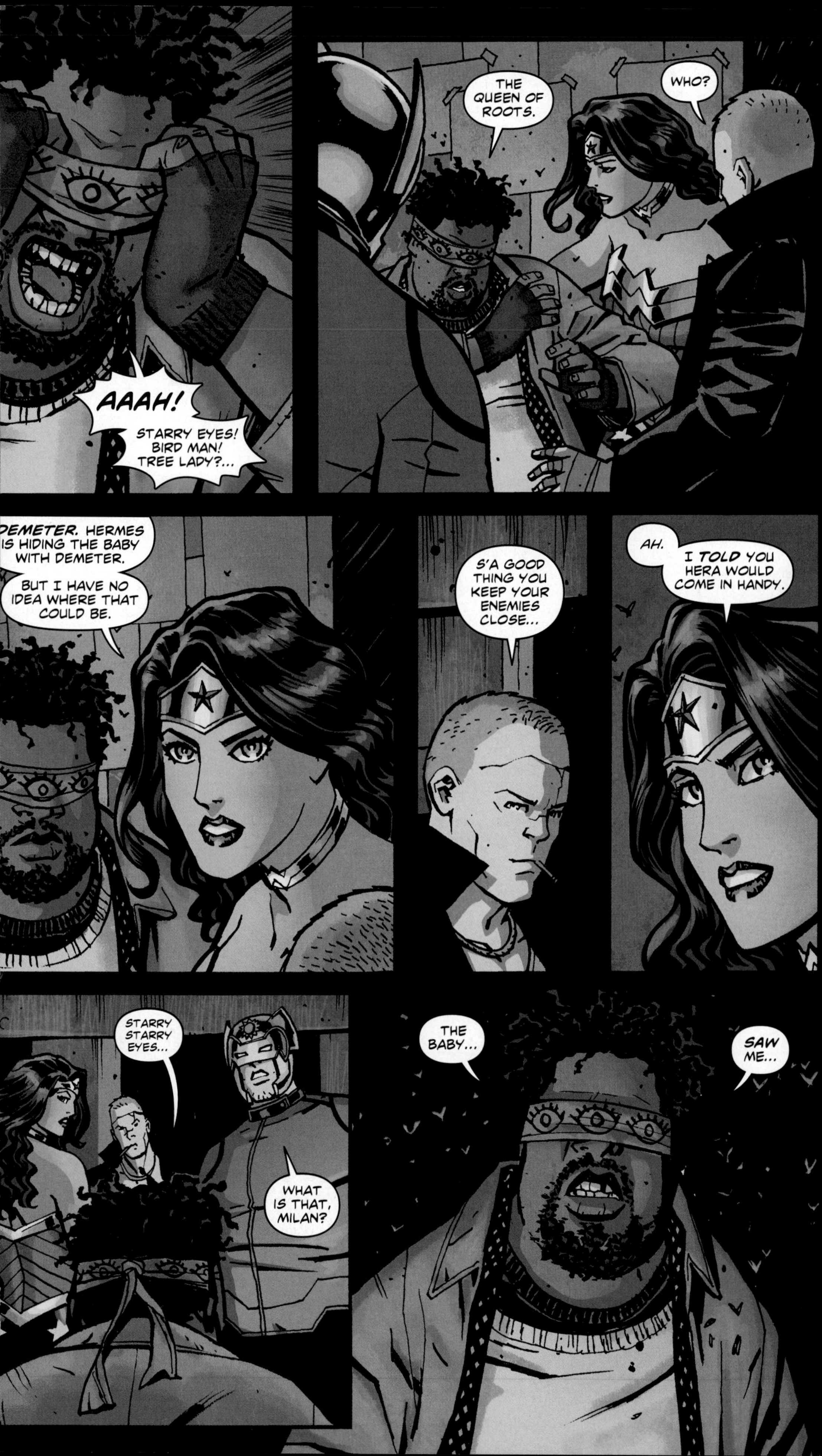
AAAH!
STARRY EYES! BIRD MAN! TREE LADY?...
THE QUEEN OF ROOTS.
WHO?
DEMETER. HERMES IS HIDING THE BABY WITH DEMETER.
BUT I HAVE NO IDEA WHERE THAT COULD BE.
S'A GOOD THING YOU KEEP YOUR ENEMIES CLOSE...
AH.
I TOLD YOU HERA WOULD COME IN HANDY.
STARRY STARRY EYES...
WHAT IS THAT, MILAN?
THE BABY...
SAW ME...

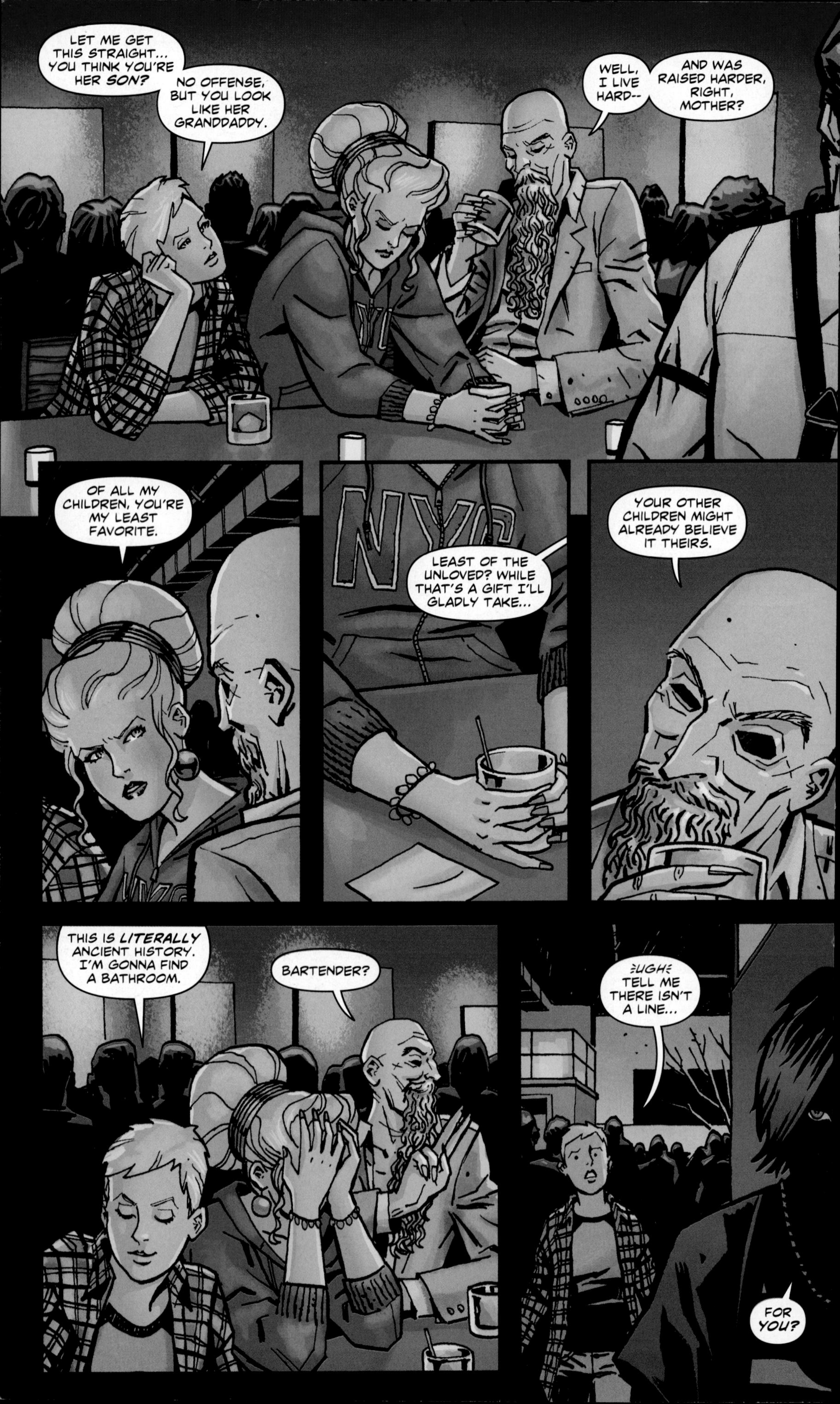
LET ME GET THIS STRAIGHT... YOU THINK YOU'RE HER *SON*?
NO OFFENSE, BUT YOU LOOK LIKE HER GRANDDADDY.
WELL, I LIVE HARD--
AND WAS RAISED HARDER, RIGHT, MOTHER?
OF ALL MY CHILDREN, YOU'RE MY LEAST FAVORITE.
LEAST OF THE UNLOVED? WHILE THAT'S A GIFT I'LL GLADLY TAKE...
YOUR OTHER CHILDREN MIGHT ALREADY BELIEVE IT THEIRS.
THIS IS *LITERALLY* ANCIENT HISTORY. I'M GONNA FIND A BATHROOM.
BARTENDER?
UGH
TELL ME THERE ISN'T A LINE...
FOR *YOU*?

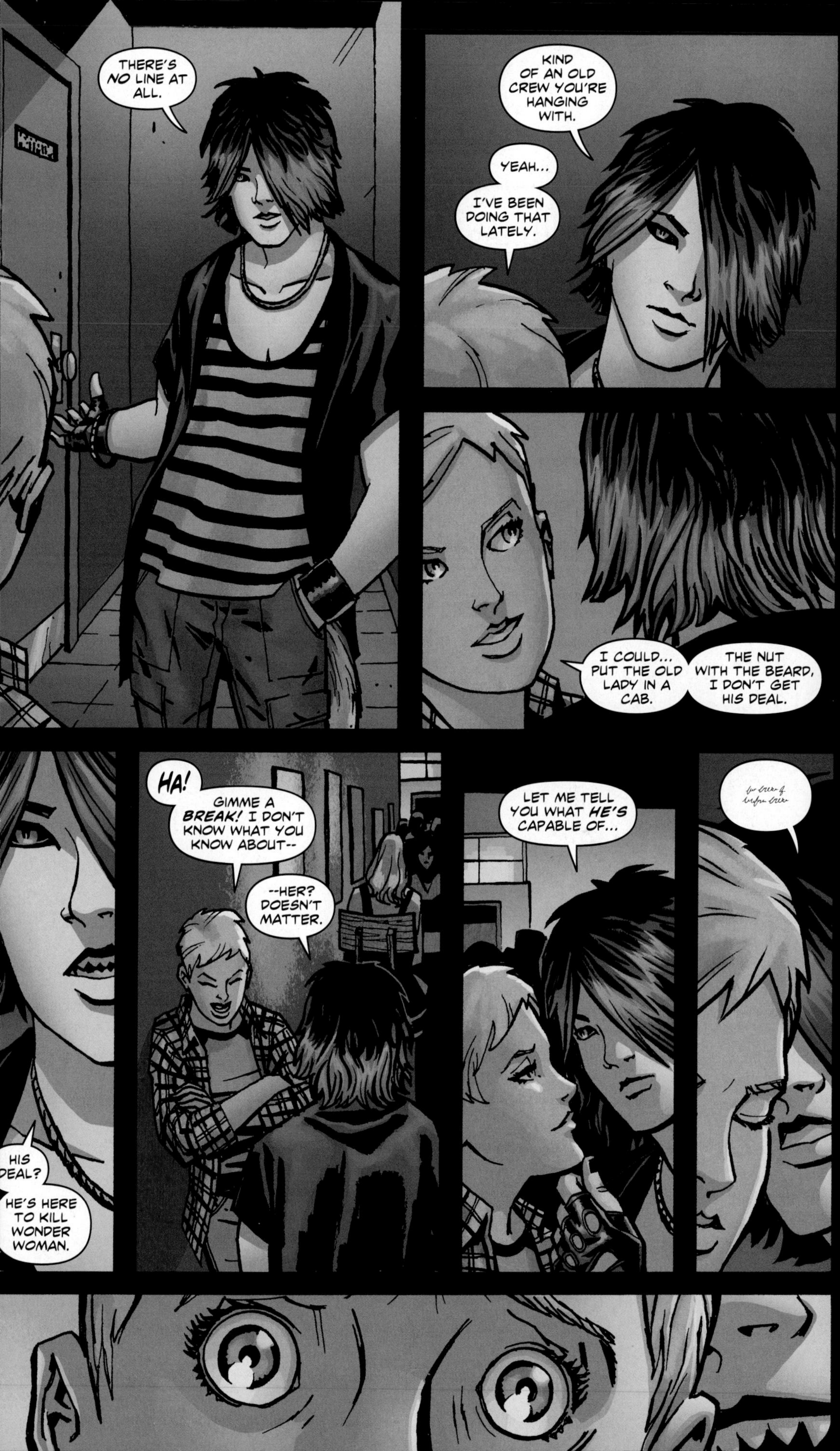

THERE'S NO LINE AT ALL.
KIND OF AN OLD CREW YOU'RE HANGING WITH.
YEAH...
I'VE BEEN DOING THAT LATELY.
I COULD... PUT THE OLD LADY IN A CAB.
THE NUT WITH THE BEARD, I DON'T GET HIS DEAL.
HIS DEAL?
HE'S HERE TO KILL WONDER WOMAN.
HA!
GIMME A BREAK! I DON'T KNOW WHAT YOU KNOW ABOUT--
--HER? DOESN'T MATTER.
LET ME TELL YOU WHAT HE'S CAPABLE OF...

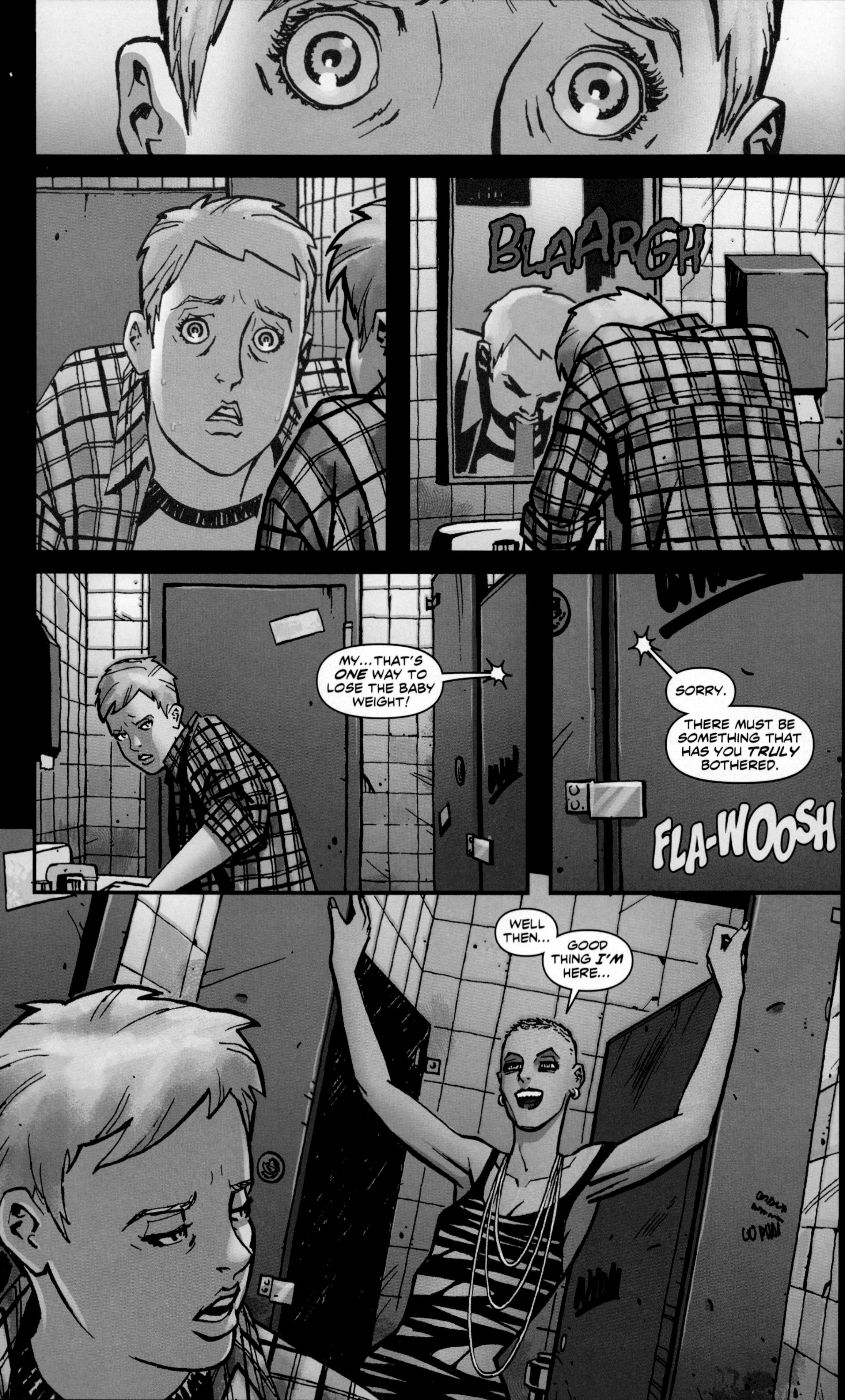
BLAARGH
MY...THAT'S *ONE* WAY TO LOSE THE BABY WEIGHT!
SORRY.
THERE MUST BE SOMETHING THAT HAS YOU *TRULY* BOTHERED.
FLA-WOOSH
WELL THEN...
GOOD THING *I'M* HERE...

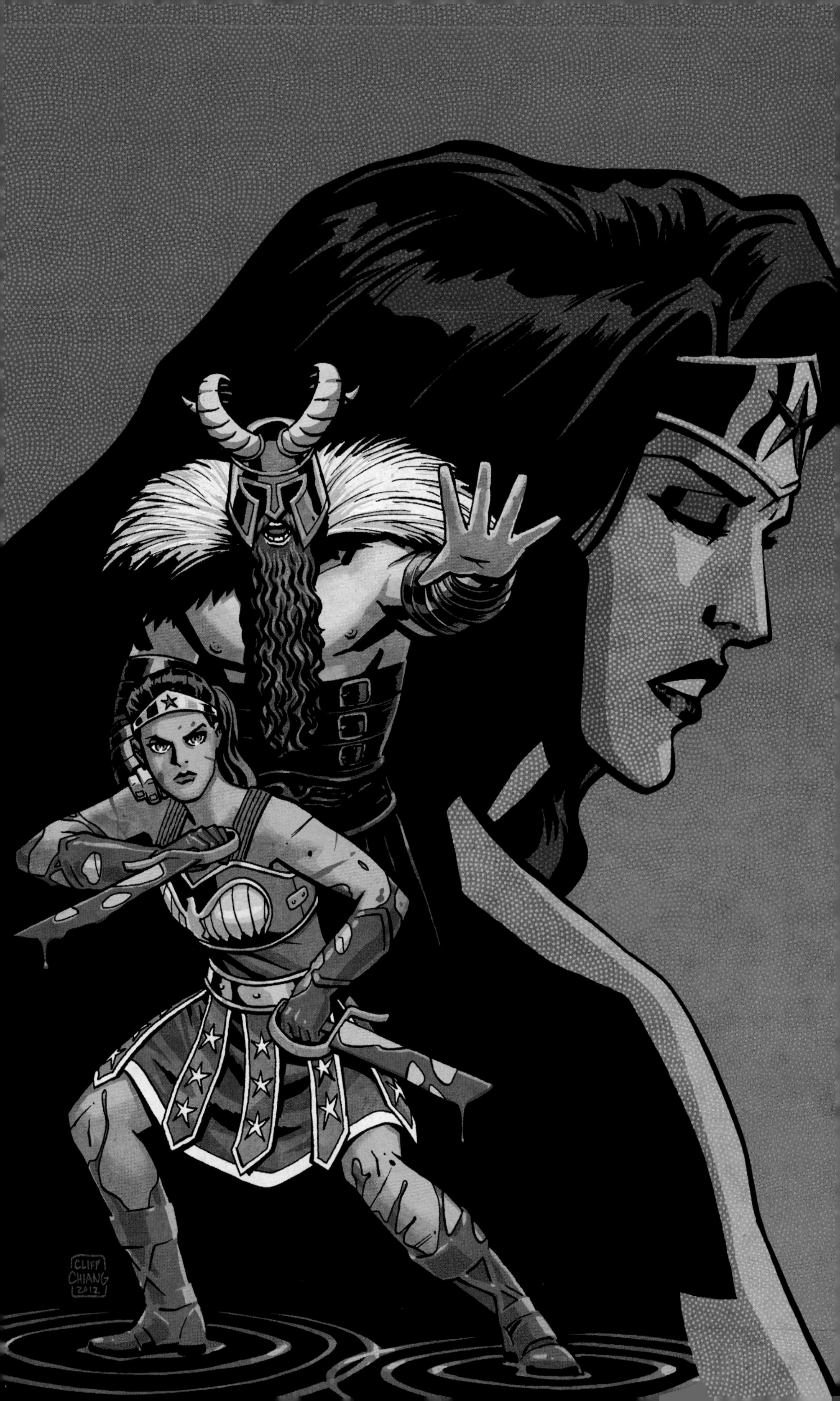
CLIFF
CHIANG
2012

DETERMINATION

TONY AKINS with AMILCAR PINNA (pages 9-11) pencillers DAN GREEN with AMILCAR PINNA (pages 9-11) inkers

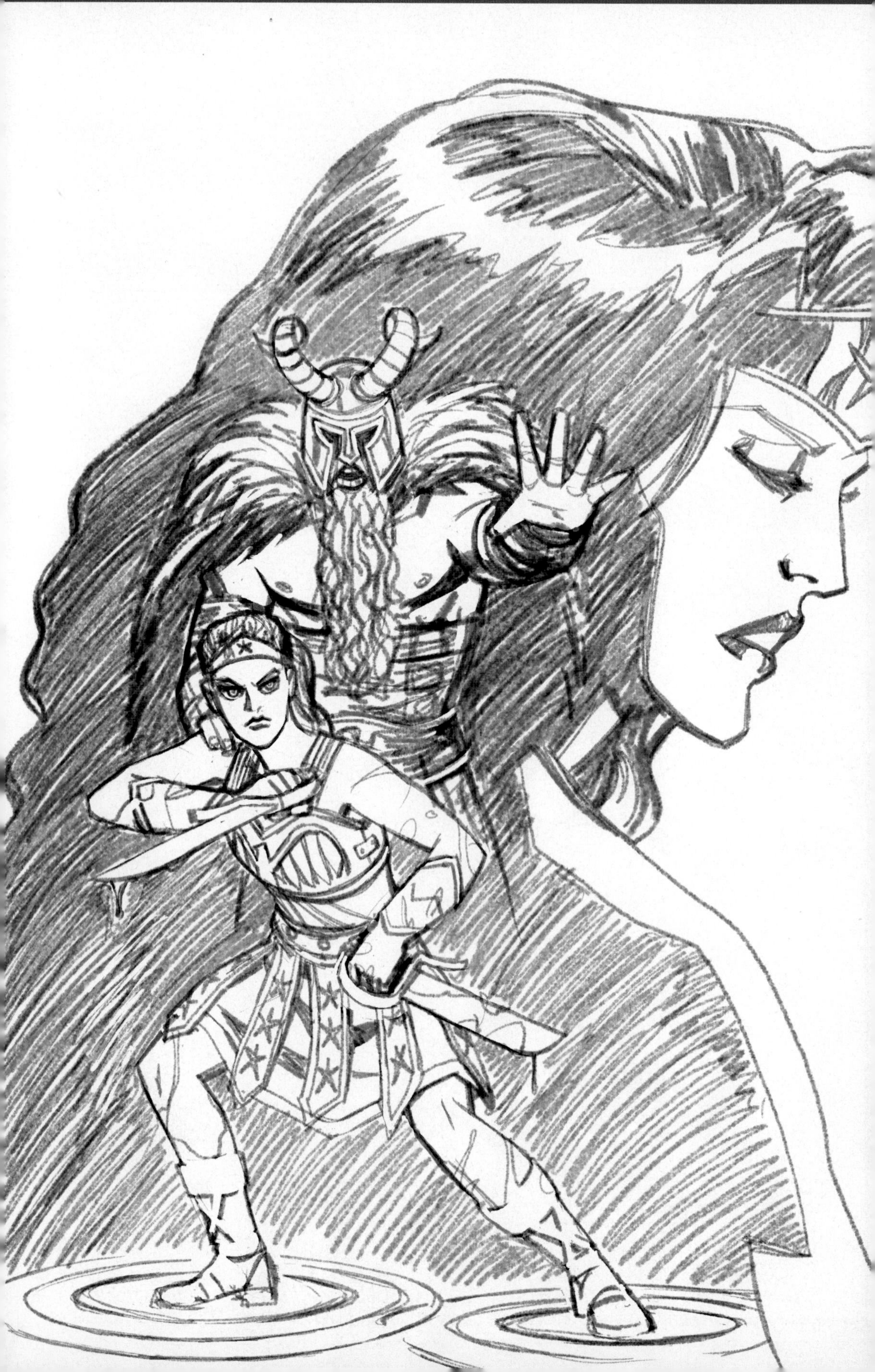

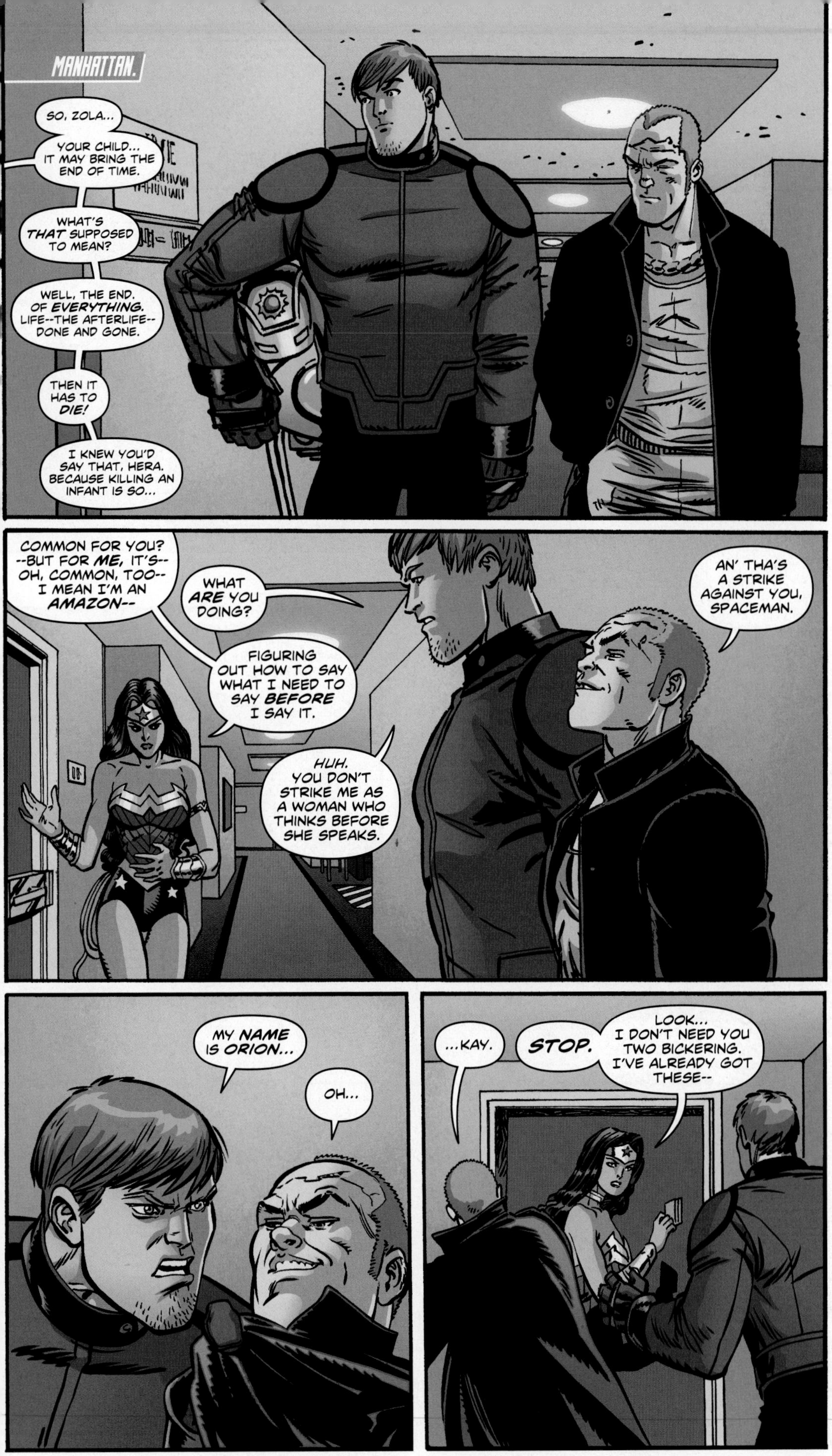
MANHATTAN.
SO, ZOLA...
YOUR CHILD... IT MAY BRING THE END OF TIME.
WHAT'S THAT SUPPOSED TO MEAN?
WELL, THE END. OF EVERYTHING. LIFE--THE AFTERLIFE--DONE AND GONE.
THEN IT HAS TO DIE!
I KNEW YOU'D SAY THAT, HERA. BECAUSE KILLING AN INFANT IS SO...
COMMON FOR YOU? --BUT FOR ME, IT'S--OH, COMMON, TOO--I MEAN I'M AN AMAZON--
WHAT ARE YOU DOING?
FIGURING OUT HOW TO SAY WHAT I NEED TO SAY BEFORE I SAY IT.
HUH. YOU DON'T STRIKE ME AS A WOMAN WHO THINKS BEFORE SHE SPEAKS.
AN' THA'S A STRIKE AGAINST YOU, SPACEMAN.
MY NAME IS ORION...
OH...
...KAY.
STOP.
LOOK... I DON'T NEED YOU TWO BICKERING. I'VE ALREADY GOT THESE--

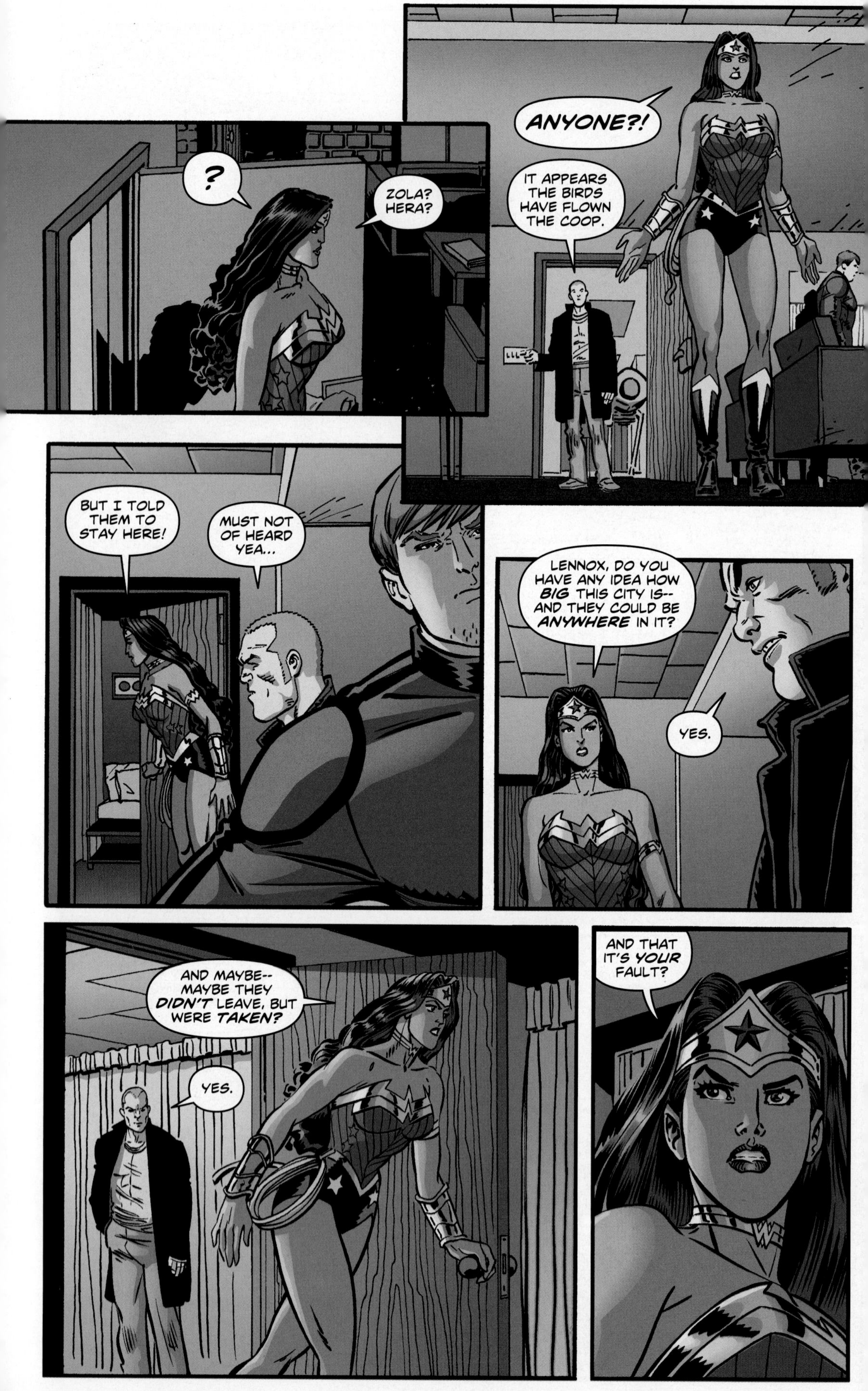
?
ZOLA? HERA?
ANYONE?!
IT APPEARS THE BIRDS HAVE FLOWN THE COOP.
BUT I TOLD THEM TO STAY HERE!
MUST NOT OF HEARD YEA...
LENNOX, DO YOU HAVE ANY IDEA HOW BIG THIS CITY IS-- AND THEY COULD BE ANYWHERE IN IT?
YES.
AND MAYBE-- MAYBE THEY DIDN'T LEAVE, BUT WERE TAKEN?
YES.
AND THAT IT'S YOUR FAULT?

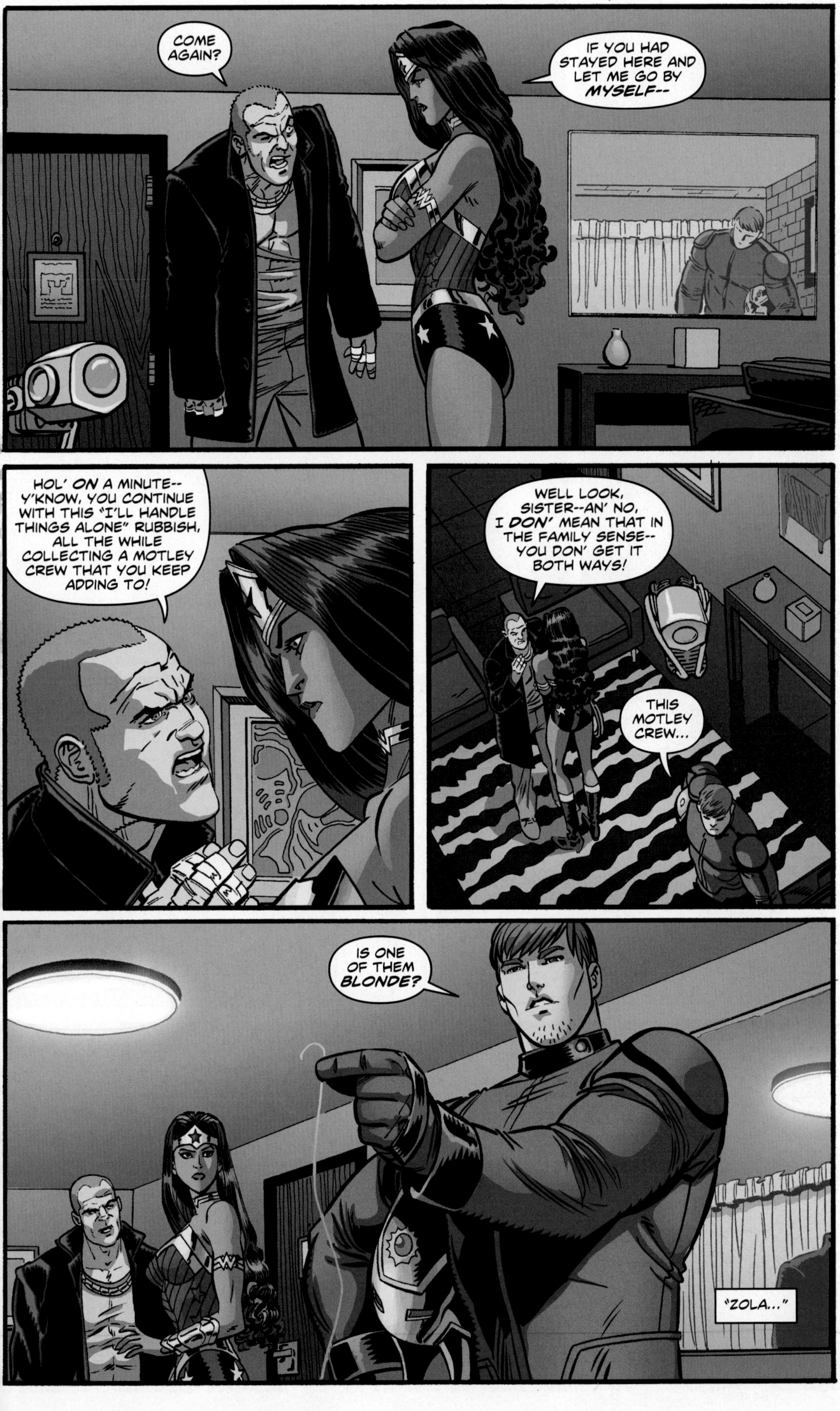
COME AGAIN?
IF YOU HAD STAYED HERE AND LET ME GO BY MYSELF--
HOL' ON A MINUTE-- Y'KNOW, YOU CONTINUE WITH THIS "I'LL HANDLE THINGS ALONE" RUBBISH, ALL THE WHILE COLLECTING A MOTLEY CREW THAT YOU KEEP ADDING TO!
WELL LOOK, SISTER--AN' NO, I DON' MEAN THAT IN THE FAMILY SENSE-- YOU DON' GET IT BOTH WAYS!
THIS MOTLEY CREW...
IS ONE OF THEM BLONDE?
"ZOLA..."

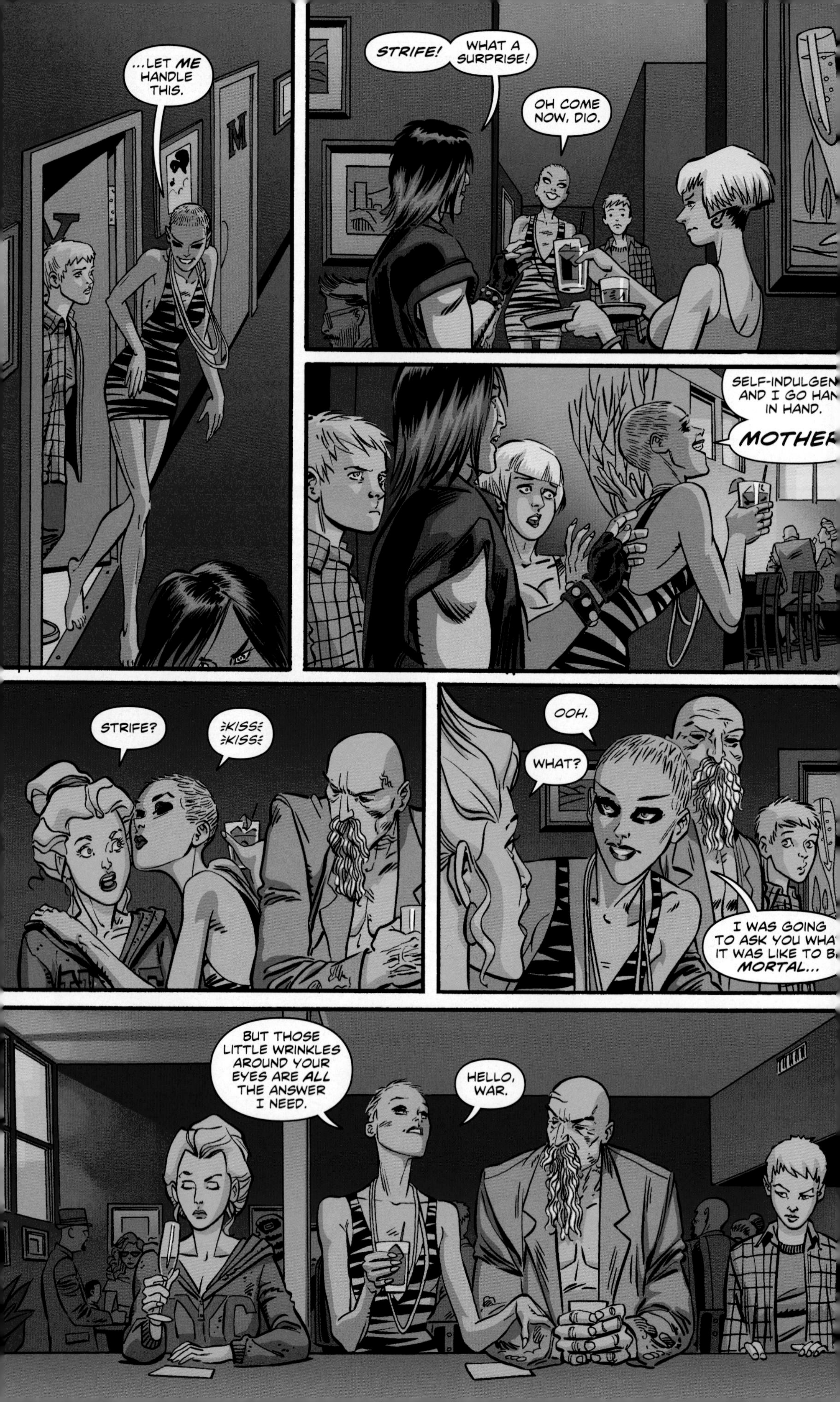
...LET ME HANDLE THIS.
STRIFE!
WHAT A SURPRISE!
OH COME NOW, DIO.
SELF-INDULGEN AND I GO HAN IN HAND.
MOTHER
STRIFE?
KISS KISS
OOH.
WHAT?
I WAS GOING TO ASK YOU WHA IT WAS LIKE TO B MORTAL...
BUT THOSE LITTLE WRINKLES AROUND YOUR EYES ARE ALL THE ANSWER I NEED.
HELLO, WAR.

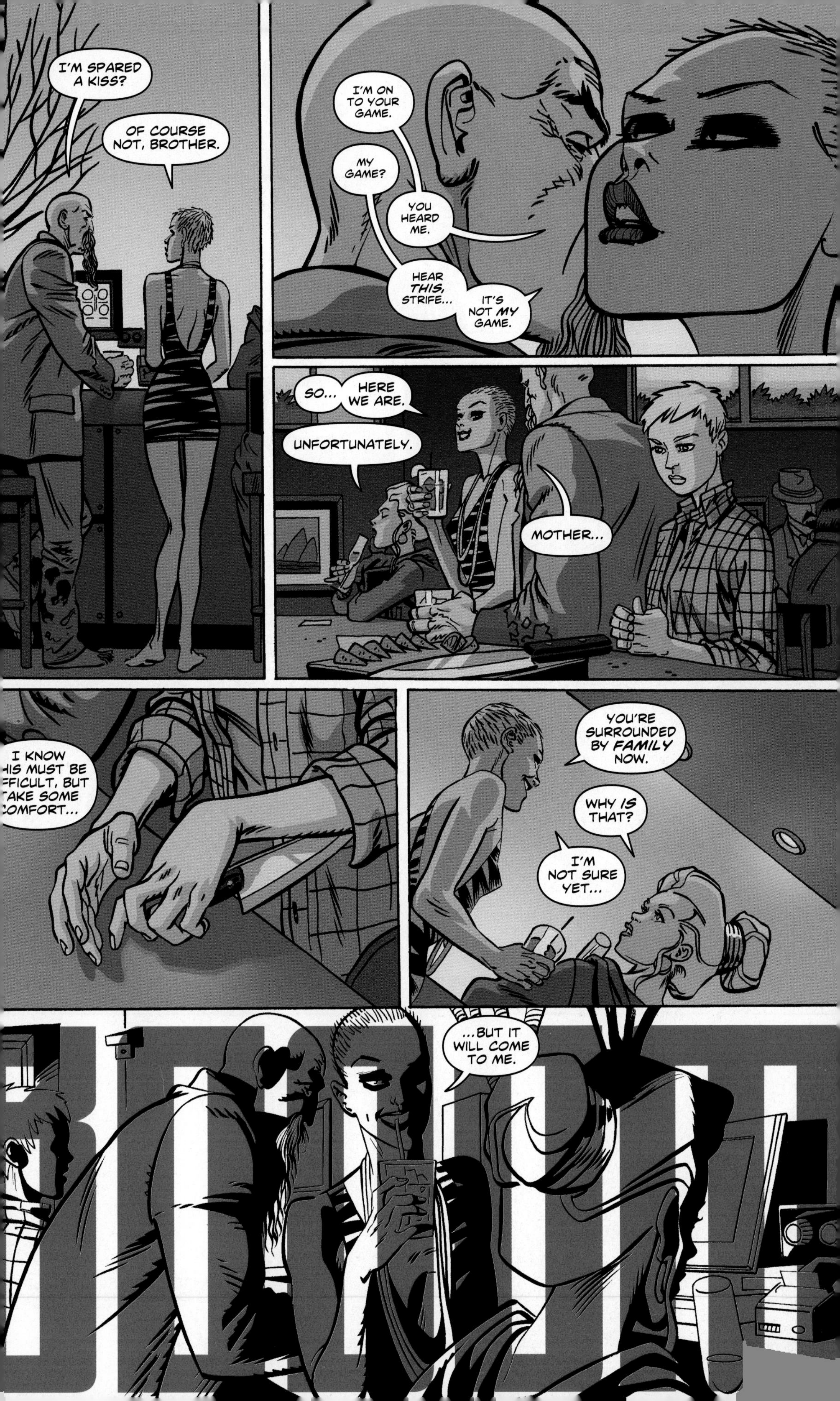
I'M SPARED A KISS?
OF COURSE NOT, BROTHER.
I'M ON TO YOUR GAME.
MY GAME?
YOU HEARD ME.
HEAR *THIS*, STRIFE...
IT'S NOT *MY* GAME.
SO...
HERE WE ARE.
UNFORTUNATELY.
MOTHER...
I KNOW
HIS MUST BE
FFICULT, BUT
TAKE SOME
COMFORT...
YOU'RE SURROUNDED BY *FAMILY* NOW.
WHY *IS* THAT?
I'M NOT SURE YET...
...BUT IT WILL COME TO ME.

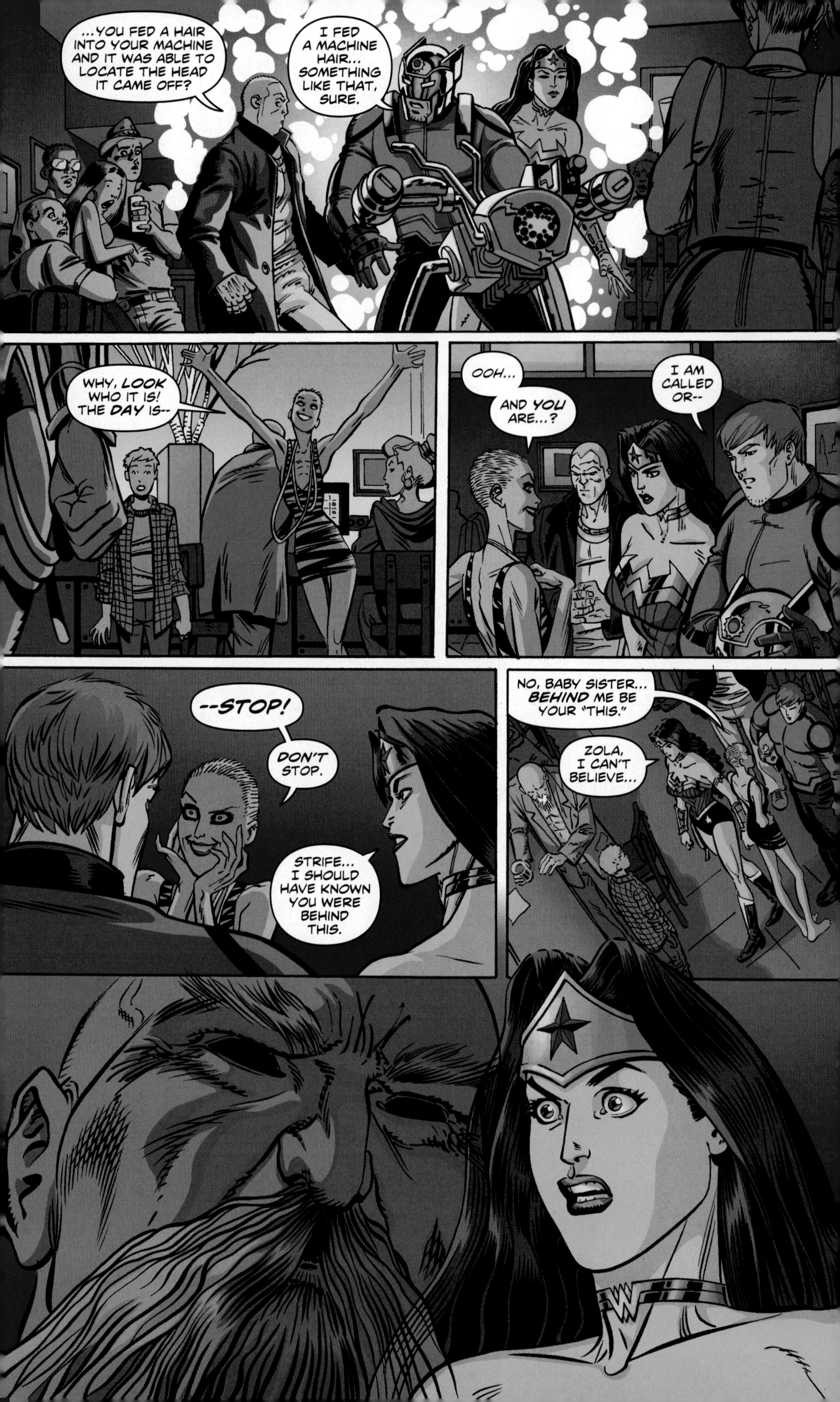
...YOU FED A HAIR INTO YOUR MACHINE AND IT WAS ABLE TO LOCATE THE HEAD IT CAME OFF?
I FED A MACHINE HAIR... SOMETHING LIKE THAT, SURE.
WHY, LOOK WHO IT IS! THE DAY IS--
OOH...
AND YOU ARE...?
I AM CALLED OR--
--STOP!
DON'T STOP.
STRIFE... I SHOULD HAVE KNOWN YOU WERE BEHIND THIS.
NO, BABY SISTER... BEHIND ME BE YOUR "THIS."
ZOLA, I CAN'T BELIEVE...

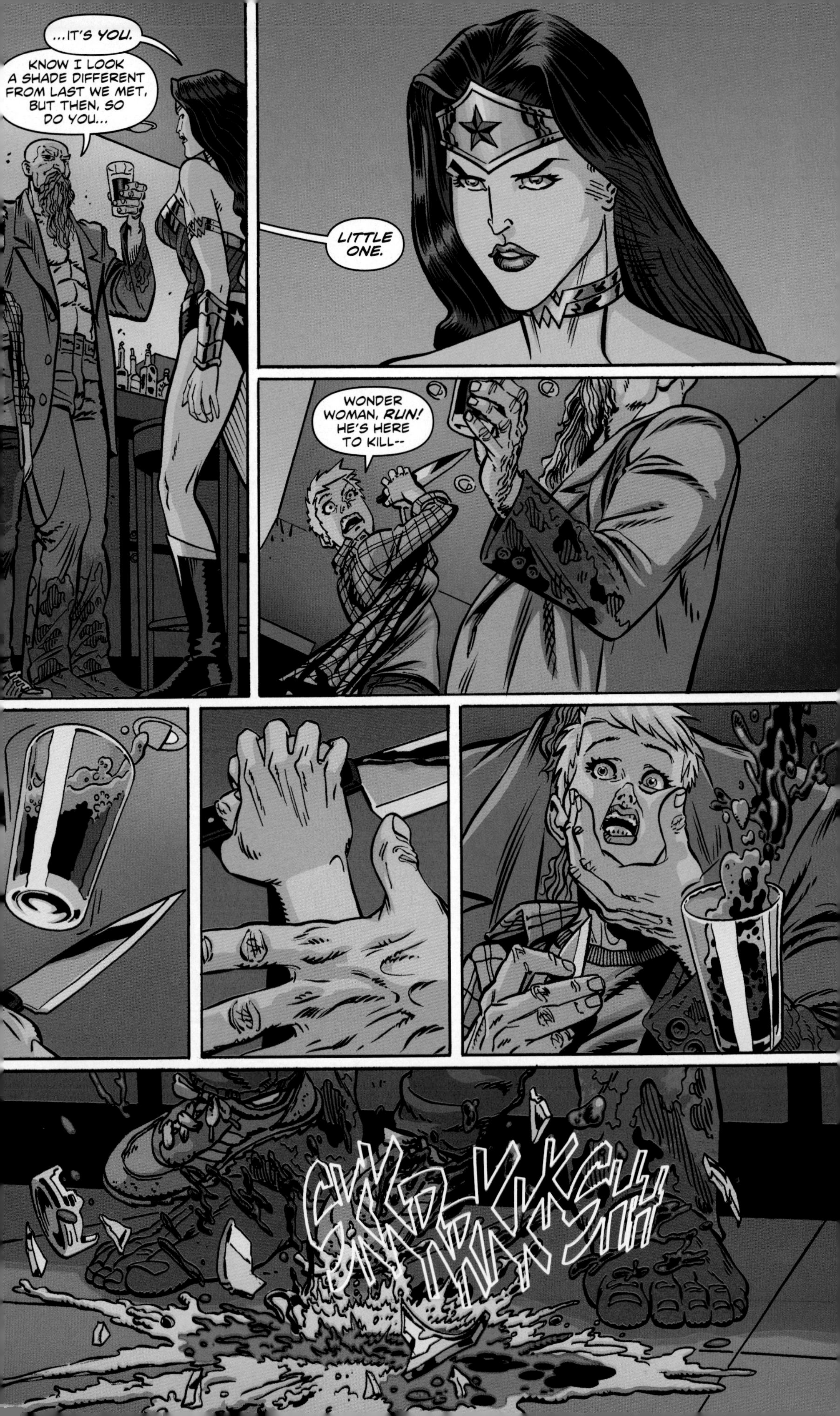
...IT'S YOU.
KNOW I LOOK A SHADE DIFFERENT FROM LAST WE MET, BUT THEN, SO DO YOU...
LITTLE ONE.
WONDER WOMAN, RUN! HE'S HERE TO KILL--
SKKRUNNKSH

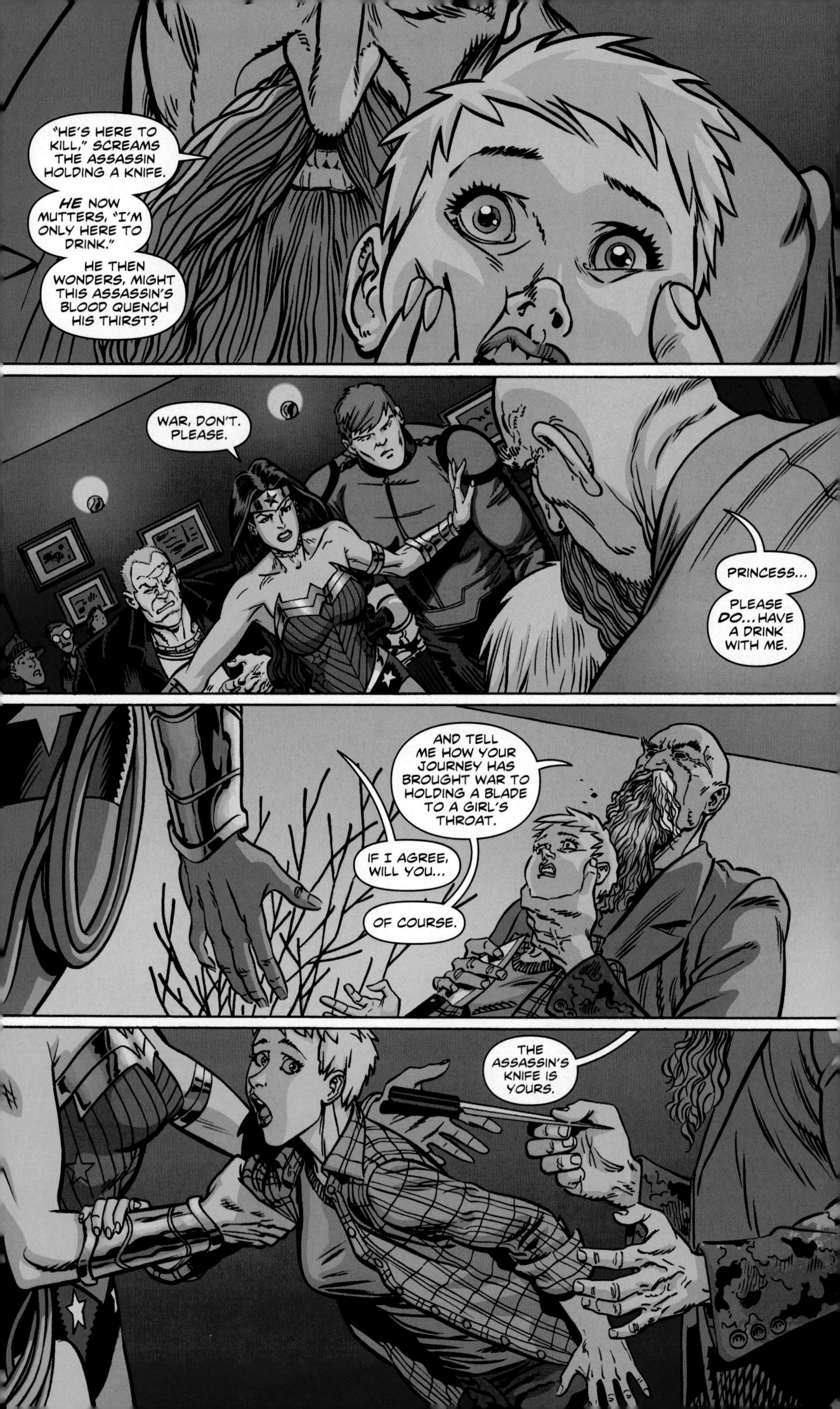

"HE'S HERE TO KILL," SCREAMS THE ASSASSIN HOLDING A KNIFE.
HE NOW MUTTERS, "I'M ONLY HERE TO DRINK."
HE THEN WONDERS, MIGHT THIS ASSASSIN'S BLOOD QUENCH HIS THIRST?
WAR, DON'T. PLEASE.
PRINCESS...
PLEASE DO... HAVE A DRINK WITH ME.
AND TELL ME HOW YOUR JOURNEY HAS BROUGHT WAR TO HOLDING A BLADE TO A GIRL'S THROAT.
IF I AGREE, WILL YOU...
OF COURSE.
THE ASSASSIN'S KNIFE IS YOURS.

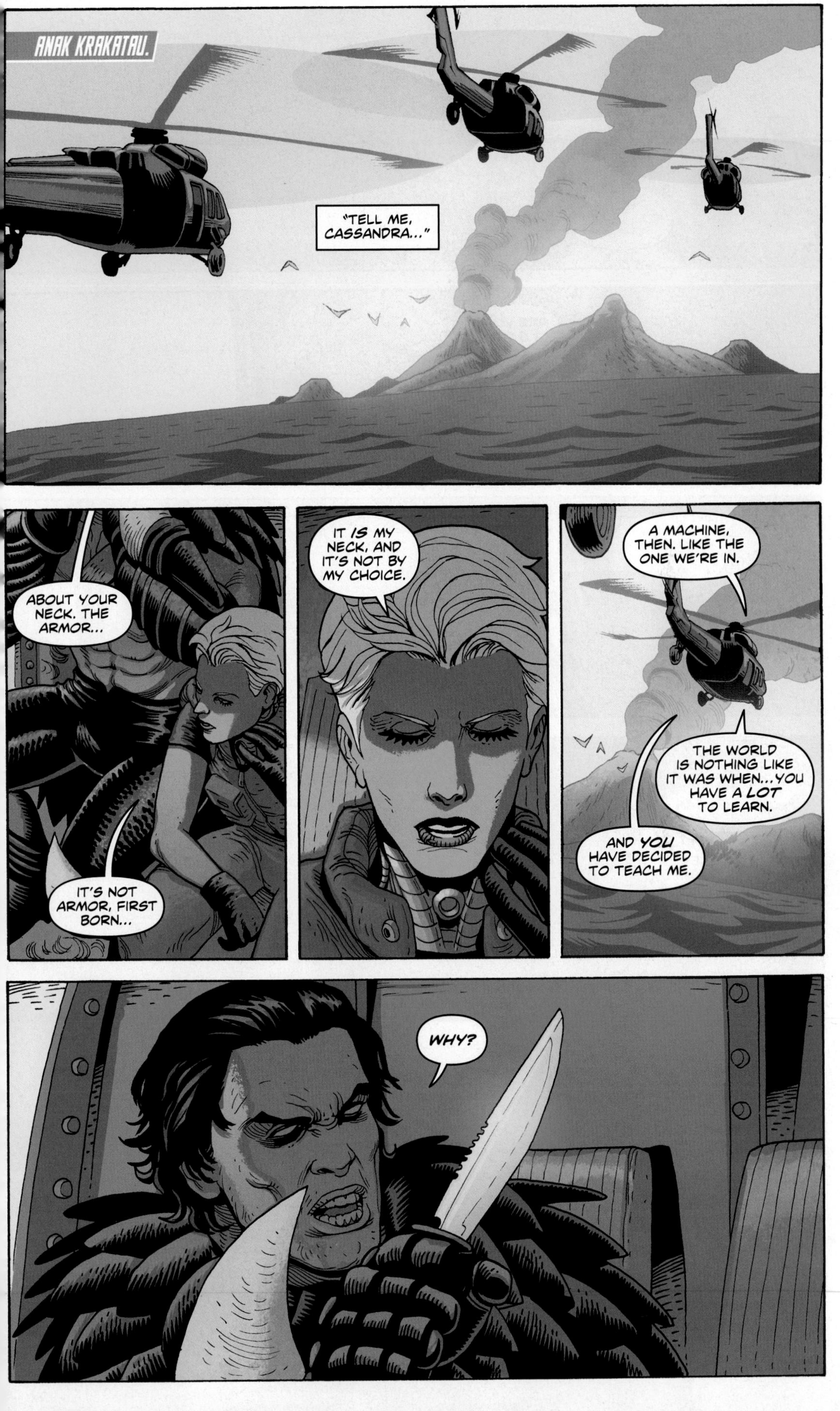
ANAK KRAKATAU.
"TELL ME, CASSANDRA..."
ABOUT YOUR NECK. THE ARMOR...
IT'S NOT ARMOR, FIRST BORN...
IT IS MY NECK, AND IT'S NOT BY MY CHOICE.
A MACHINE, THEN. LIKE THE ONE WE'RE IN.
THE WORLD IS NOTHING LIKE IT WAS WHEN...YOU HAVE A LOT TO LEARN.
AND YOU HAVE DECIDED TO TEACH ME.
WHY?

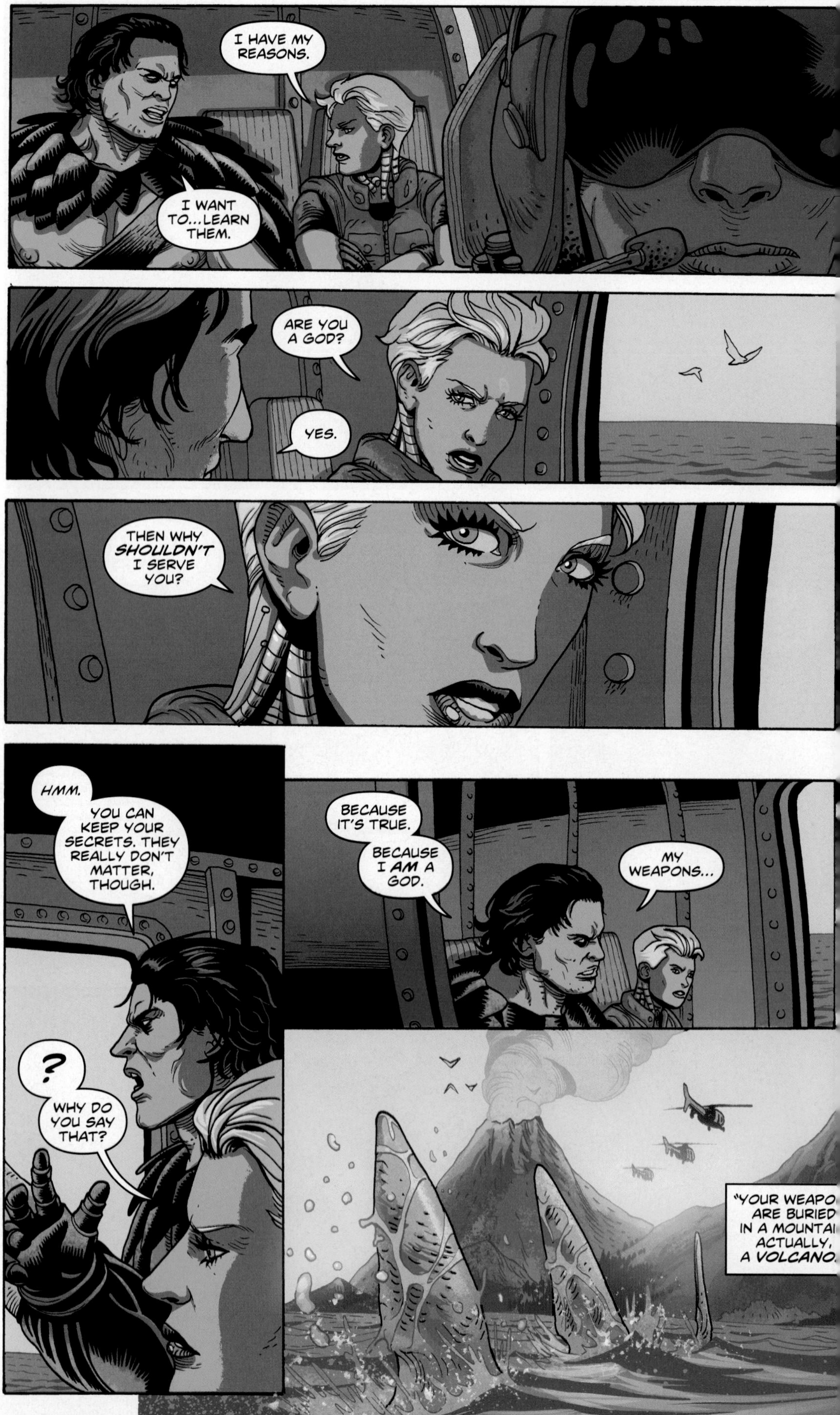
I HAVE MY REASONS.
I WANT TO...LEARN THEM.
ARE YOU A GOD?
YES.
THEN WHY SHOULDN'T I SERVE YOU?
HMM.
YOU CAN KEEP YOUR SECRETS. THEY REALLY DON'T MATTER, THOUGH.
BECAUSE IT'S TRUE.
BECAUSE I AM A GOD.
MY WEAPONS...
?
WHY DO YOU SAY THAT?
"YOUR WEAPO ARE BURIED IN A MOUNTAI ACTUALLY, A VOLCANO.

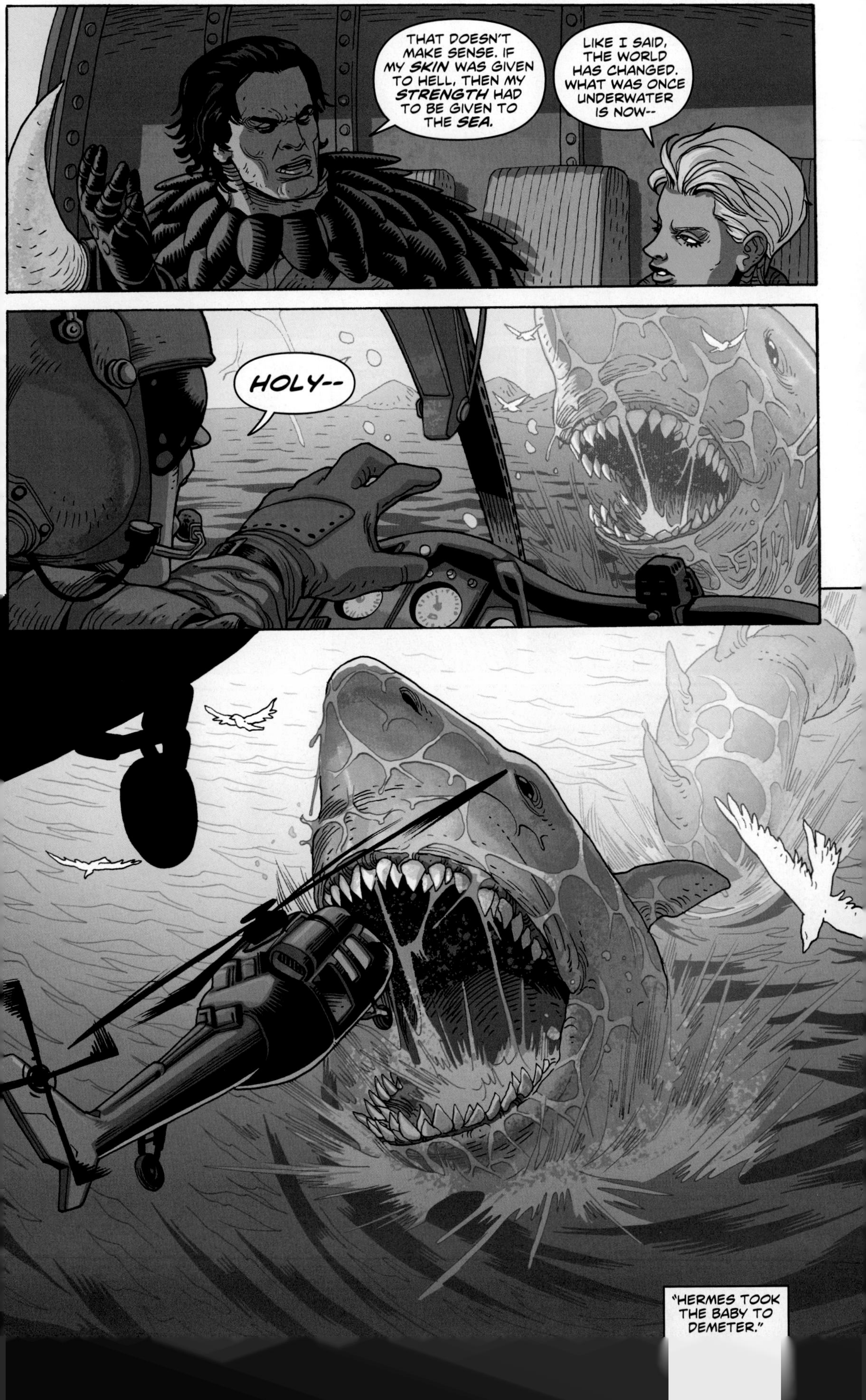
THAT DOESN'T MAKE SENSE. IF MY SKIN WAS GIVEN TO HELL, THEN MY STRENGTH HAD TO BE GIVEN TO THE SEA.
LIKE I SAID, THE WORLD HAS CHANGED. WHAT WAS ONCE UNDERWATER IS NOW--
HOLY--
"HERMES TOOK THE BABY TO DEMETER."

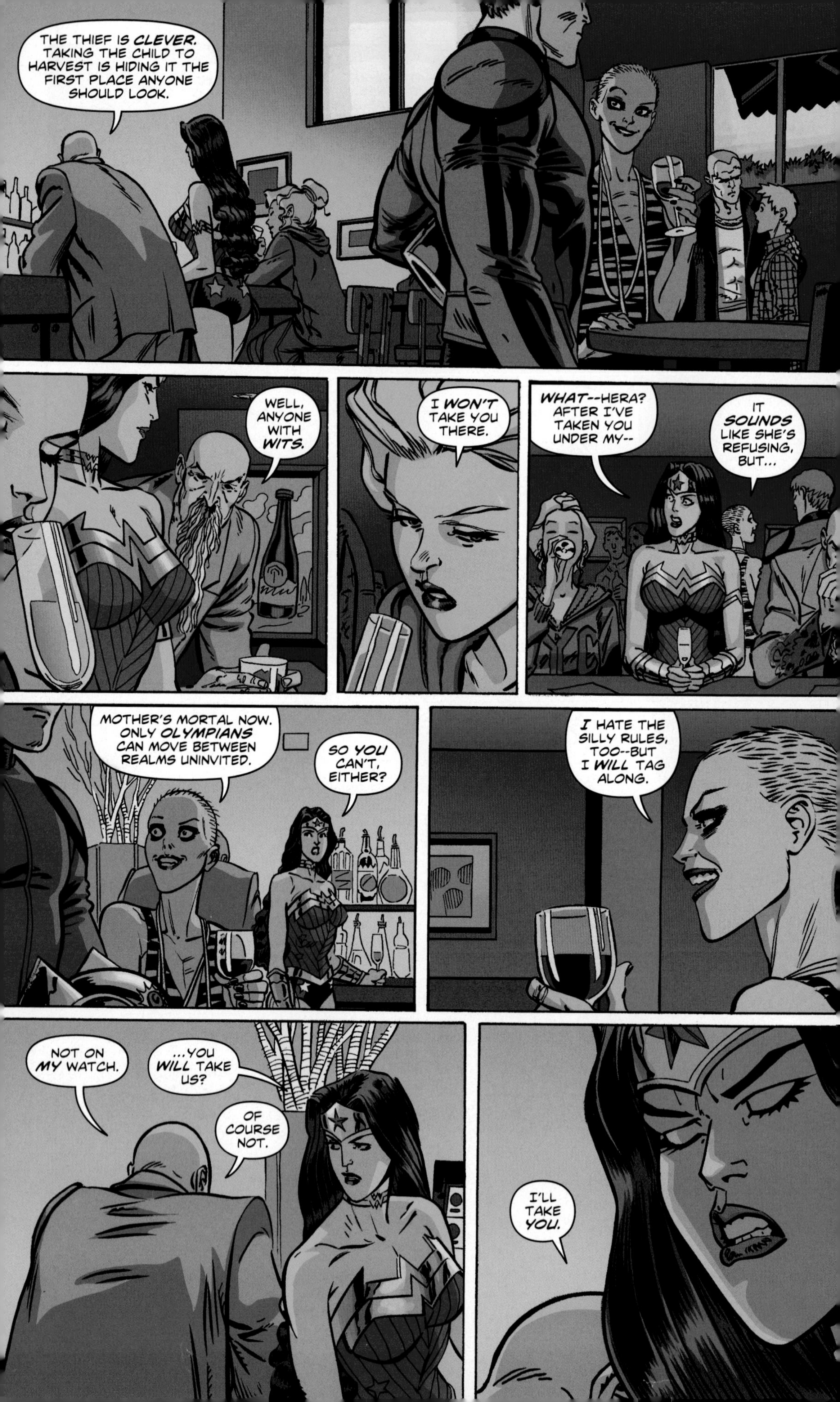
THE THIEF IS CLEVER. TAKING THE CHILD TO HARVEST IS HIDING IT THE FIRST PLACE ANYONE SHOULD LOOK.
WELL, ANYONE WITH WITS.
I WON'T TAKE YOU THERE.
WHAT--HERA? AFTER I'VE TAKEN YOU UNDER MY--
IT SOUNDS LIKE SHE'S REFUSING, BUT...
MOTHER'S MORTAL NOW. ONLY OLYMPIANS CAN MOVE BETWEEN REALMS UNINVITED.
SO YOU CAN'T, EITHER?
I HATE THE SILLY RULES, TOO--BUT I WILL TAG ALONG.
NOT ON MY WATCH.
...YOU WILL TAKE US?
OF COURSE NOT.
I'LL TAKE YOU.

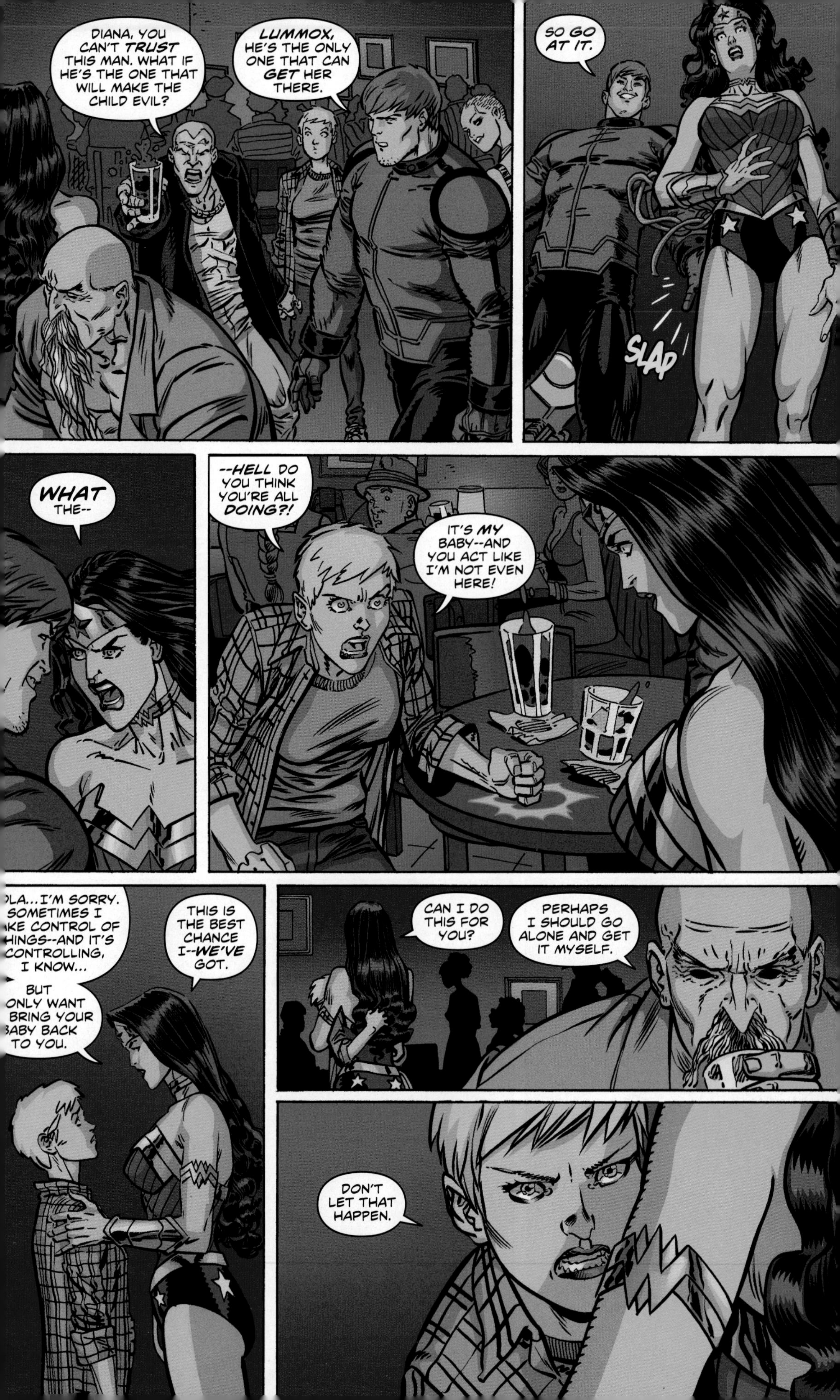
DIANA, YOU CAN'T TRUST THIS MAN. WHAT IF HE'S THE ONE THAT WILL MAKE THE CHILD EVIL?
LUMMOX, HE'S THE ONLY ONE THAT CAN GET HER THERE.
SO GO AT IT.
SLAP
WHAT THE--
--HELL DO YOU THINK YOU'RE ALL DOING?!
IT'S MY BABY--AND YOU ACT LIKE I'M NOT EVEN HERE!
OLA...I'M SORRY. SOMETIMES I AKE CONTROL OF HINGS--AND IT'S CONTROLLING, I KNOW...
BUT ONLY WANT BRING YOUR BABY BACK TO YOU.
THIS IS THE BEST CHANCE I--WE'VE GOT.
CAN I DO THIS FOR YOU?
PERHAPS I SHOULD GO ALONE AND GET IT MYSELF.
DON'T LET THAT HAPPEN.

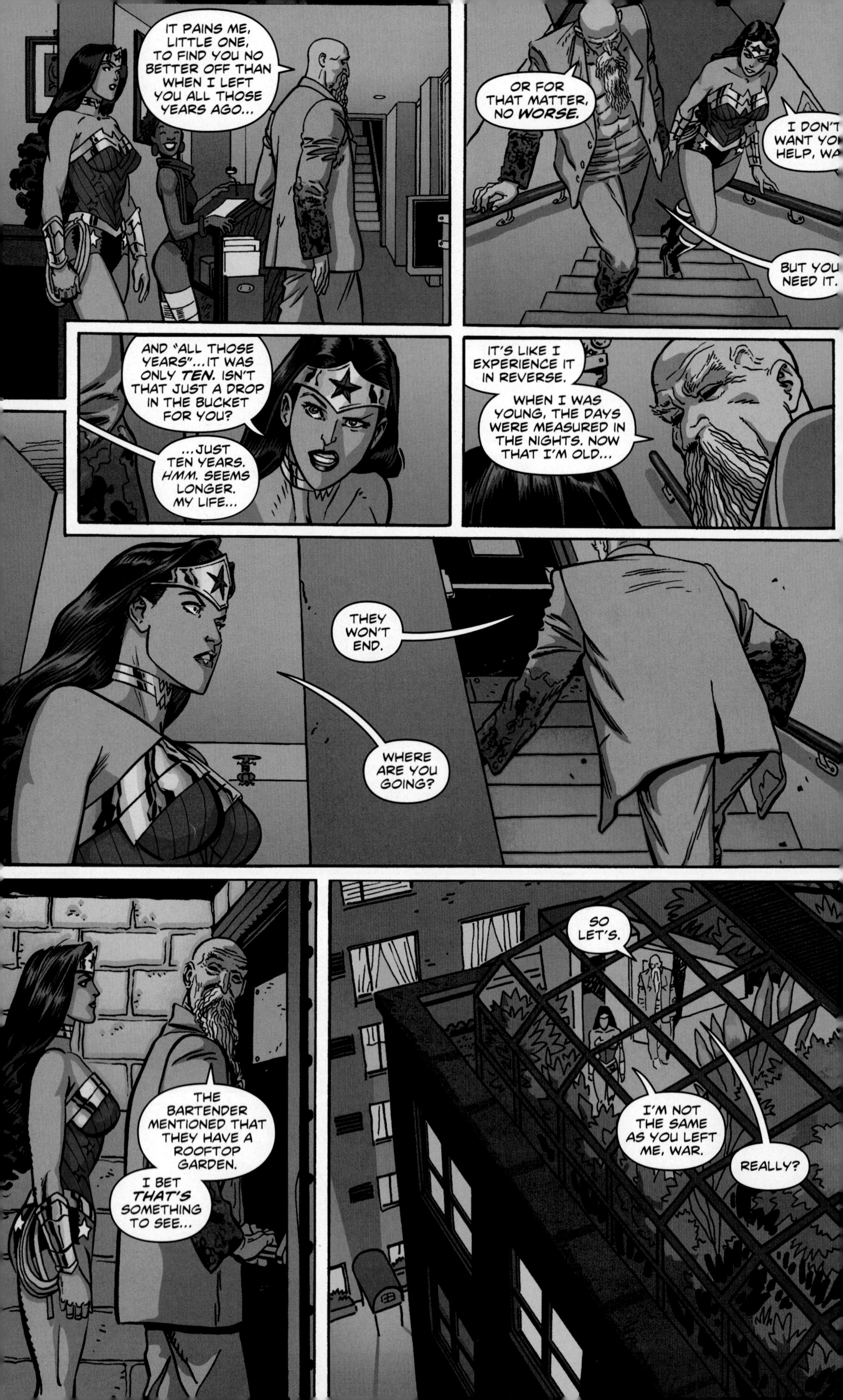

IT PAINS ME, LITTLE ONE, TO FIND YOU NO BETTER OFF THAN WHEN I LEFT YOU ALL THOSE YEARS AGO...
OR FOR THAT MATTER, NO *WORSE.*
I DON'T WANT YO HELP, WA
BUT YOU NEED IT.
AND "ALL THOSE YEARS"...IT WAS ONLY *TEN.* ISN'T THAT JUST A DROP IN THE BUCKET FOR YOU?
...JUST TEN YEARS. *HMM.* SEEMS LONGER. MY LIFE...
IT'S LIKE I EXPERIENCE IT IN REVERSE.
WHEN I WAS YOUNG, THE DAYS WERE MEASURED IN THE NIGHTS. NOW THAT I'M OLD...
THEY WON'T END.
WHERE ARE YOU GOING?
THE BARTENDER MENTIONED THAT THEY HAVE A ROOFTOP GARDEN.
I BET *THAT'S* SOMETHING TO SEE...
SO LET'S.
I'M NOT THE SAME AS YOU LEFT ME, WAR.
REALLY?

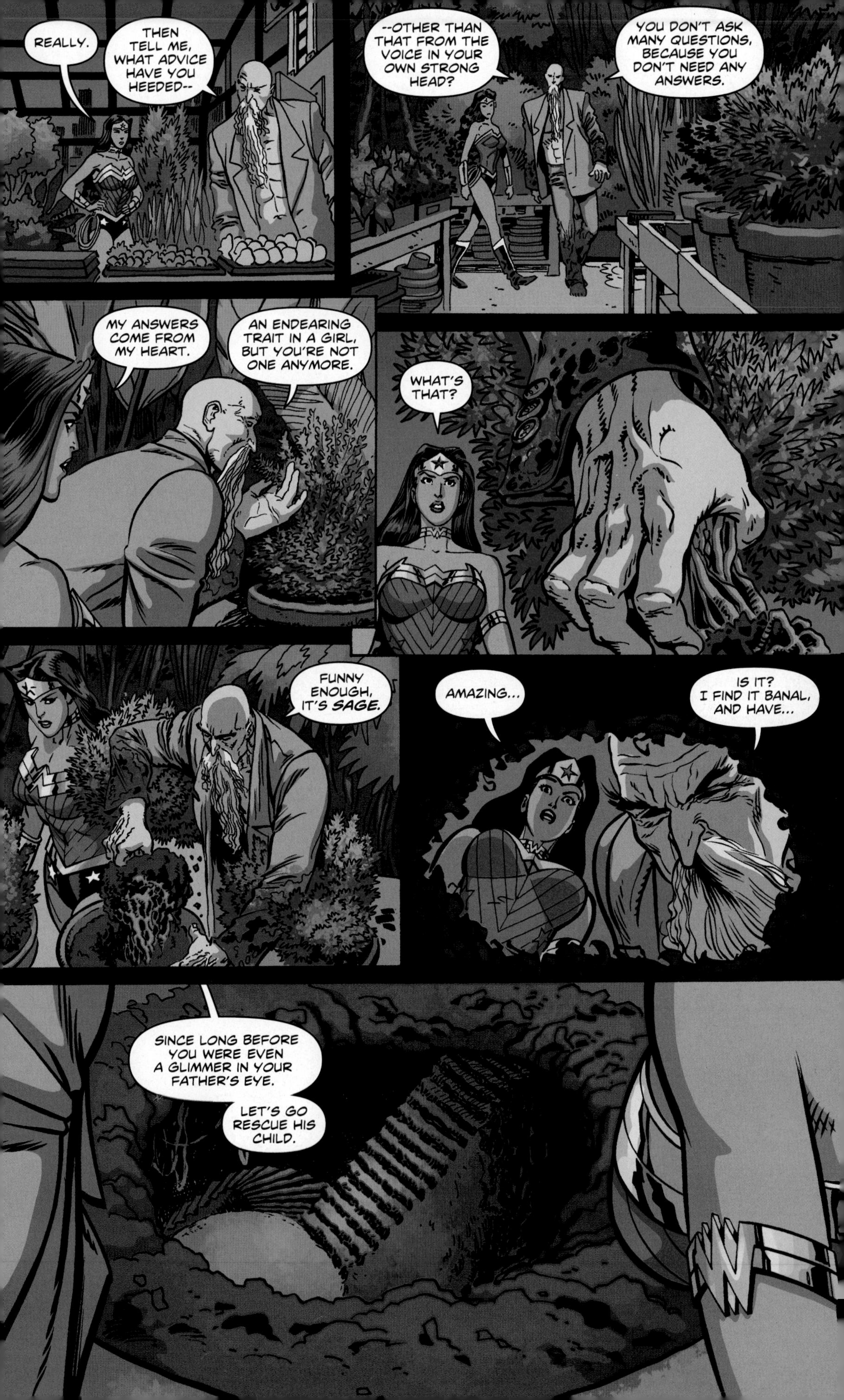

REALLY.
THEN TELL ME, WHAT ADVICE HAVE YOU HEEDED--
--OTHER THAN THAT FROM THE VOICE IN YOUR OWN STRONG HEAD?
YOU DON'T ASK MANY QUESTIONS, BECAUSE YOU DON'T NEED ANY ANSWERS.
MY ANSWERS COME FROM MY HEART.
AN ENDEARING TRAIT IN A GIRL, BUT YOU'RE NOT ONE ANYMORE.
WHAT'S THAT?
FUNNY ENOUGH, IT'S *SAGE*.
AMAZING...
IS IT? I FIND IT BANAL, AND HAVE...
SINCE LONG BEFORE YOU WERE EVEN A GLIMMER IN YOUR FATHER'S EYE.
LET'S GO RESCUE HIS CHILD.

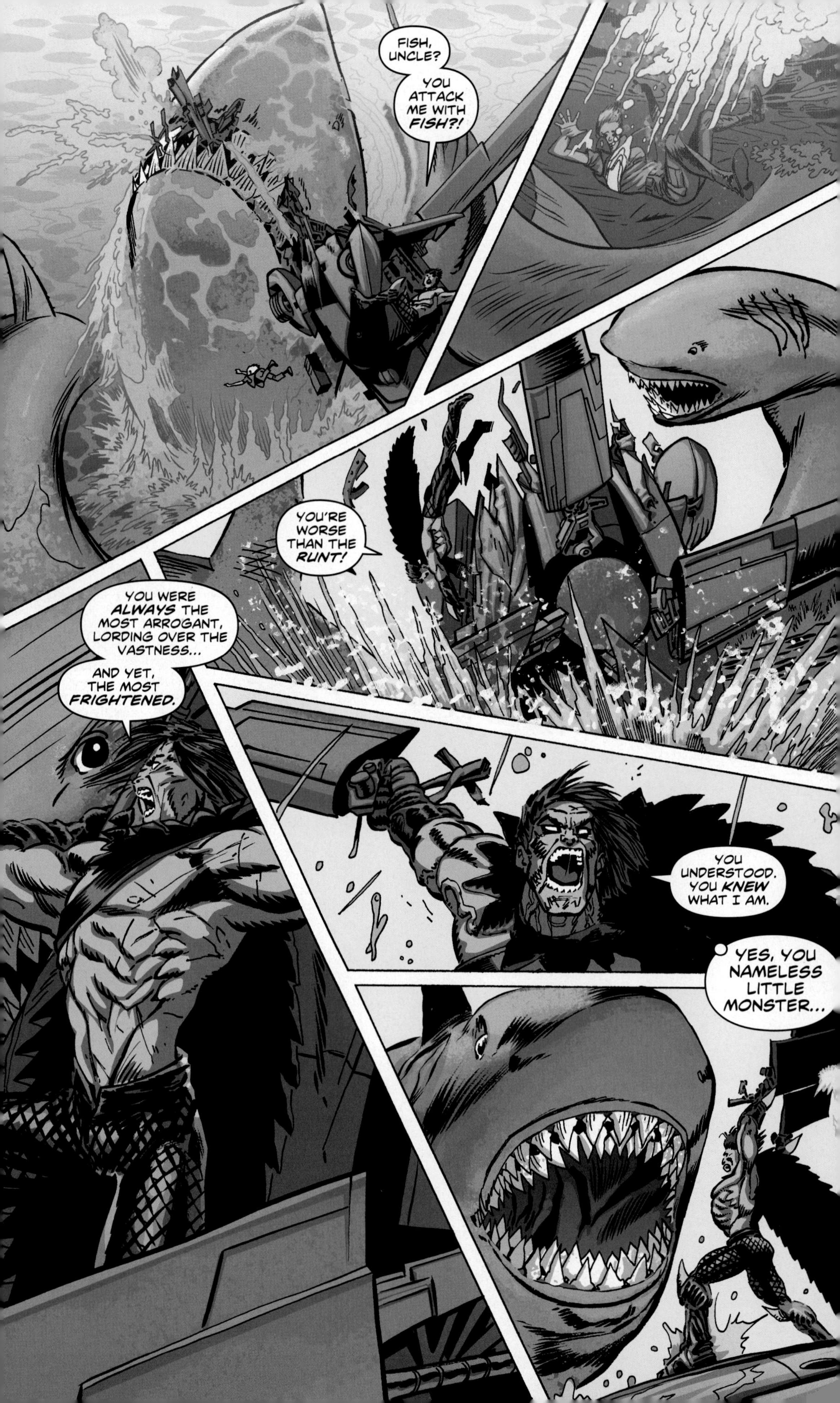
FISH, UNCLE?
YOU ATTACK ME WITH FISH?!
YOU'RE WORSE THAN THE RUNT!
YOU WERE ALWAYS THE MOST ARROGANT, LORDING OVER THE VASTNESS...
AND YET, THE MOST FRIGHTENED.
YOU UNDERSTOOD. YOU KNEW WHAT I AM.
YES, YOU NAMELESS LITTLE MONSTER...

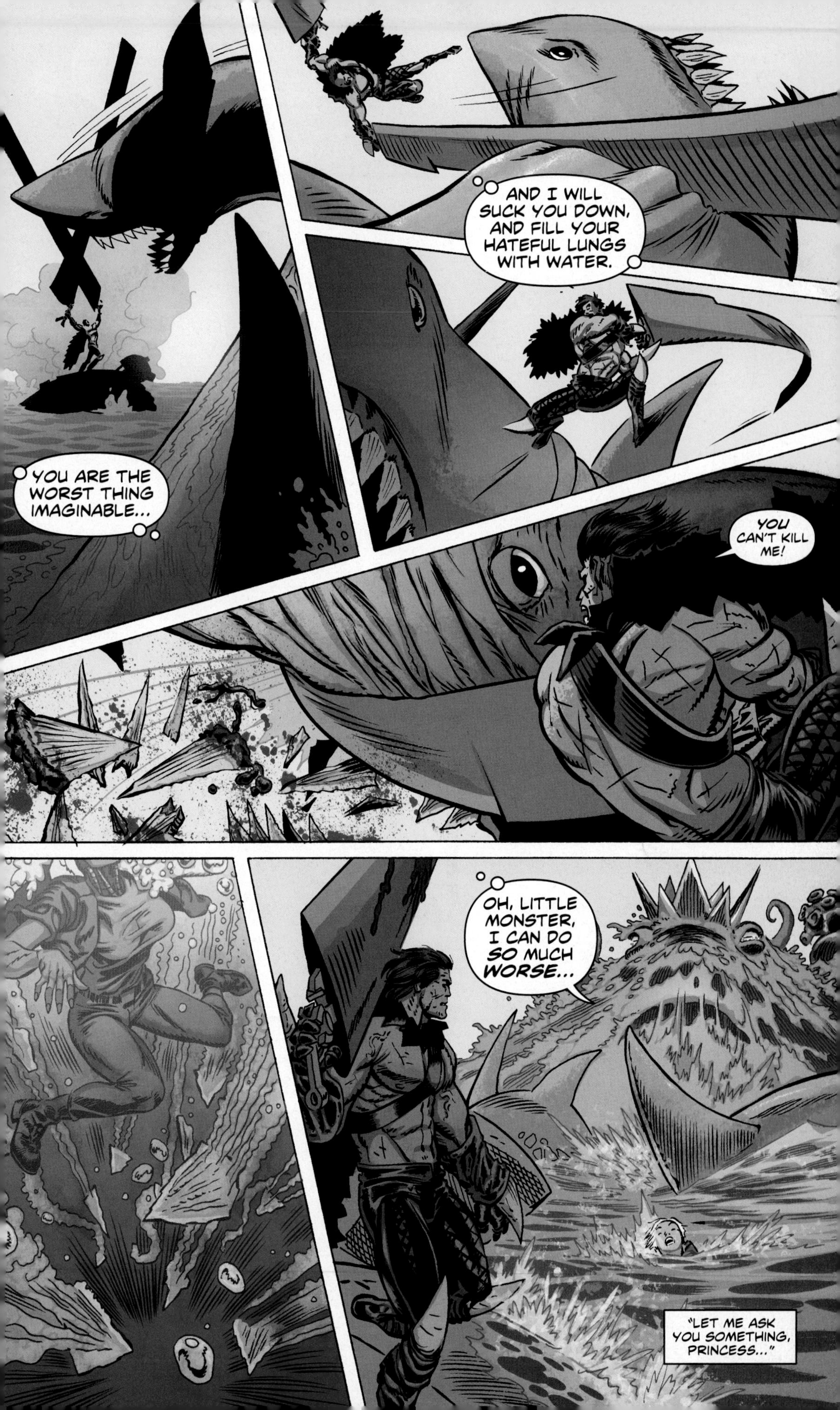
AND I WILL SUCK YOU DOWN, AND FILL YOUR HATEFUL LUNGS WITH WATER.
YOU ARE THE WORST THING IMAGINABLE...
YOU CAN'T KILL ME!
OH, LITTLE MONSTER, I CAN DO SO MUCH WORSE...
"LET ME ASK YOU SOMETHING, PRINCESS..."

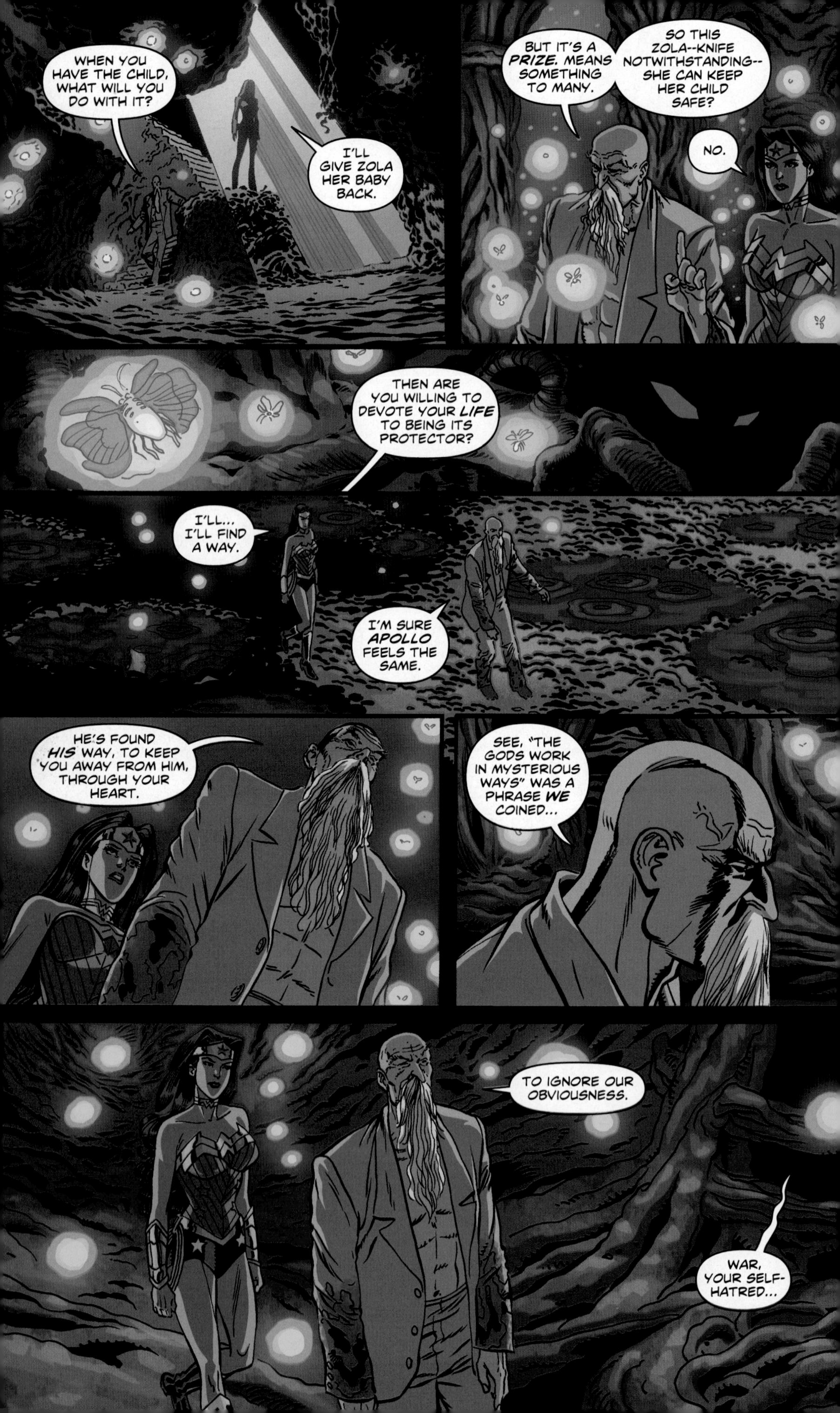
WHEN YOU HAVE THE CHILD, WHAT WILL YOU DO WITH IT?
I'LL GIVE ZOLA HER BABY BACK.
BUT IT'S A PRIZE. MEANS SOMETHING TO MANY.
SO THIS ZOLA--KNIFE NOTWITHSTANDING--SHE CAN KEEP HER CHILD SAFE?
NO.
THEN ARE YOU WILLING TO DEVOTE YOUR LIFE TO BEING ITS PROTECTOR?
I'LL... I'LL FIND A WAY.
I'M SURE APOLLO FEELS THE SAME.
HE'S FOUND HIS WAY, TO KEEP YOU AWAY FROM HIM, THROUGH YOUR HEART.
SEE, "THE GODS WORK IN MYSTERIOUS WAYS" WAS A PHRASE WE COINED...
TO IGNORE OUR OBVIOUSNESS.
WAR, YOUR SELF-HATRED...

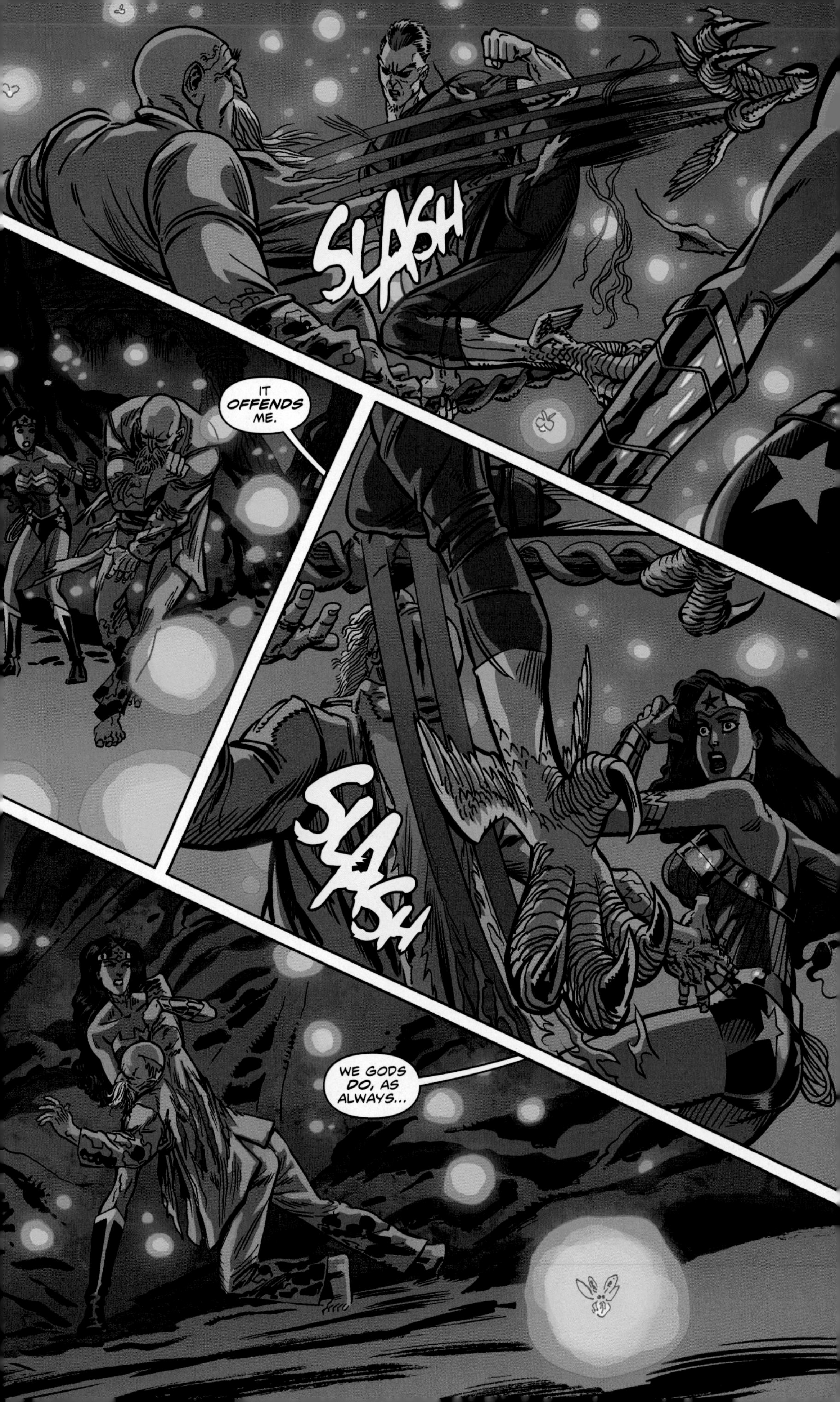
SLASH
IT OFFENDS ME.
SLASH
WE GODS DO, AS ALWAYS...

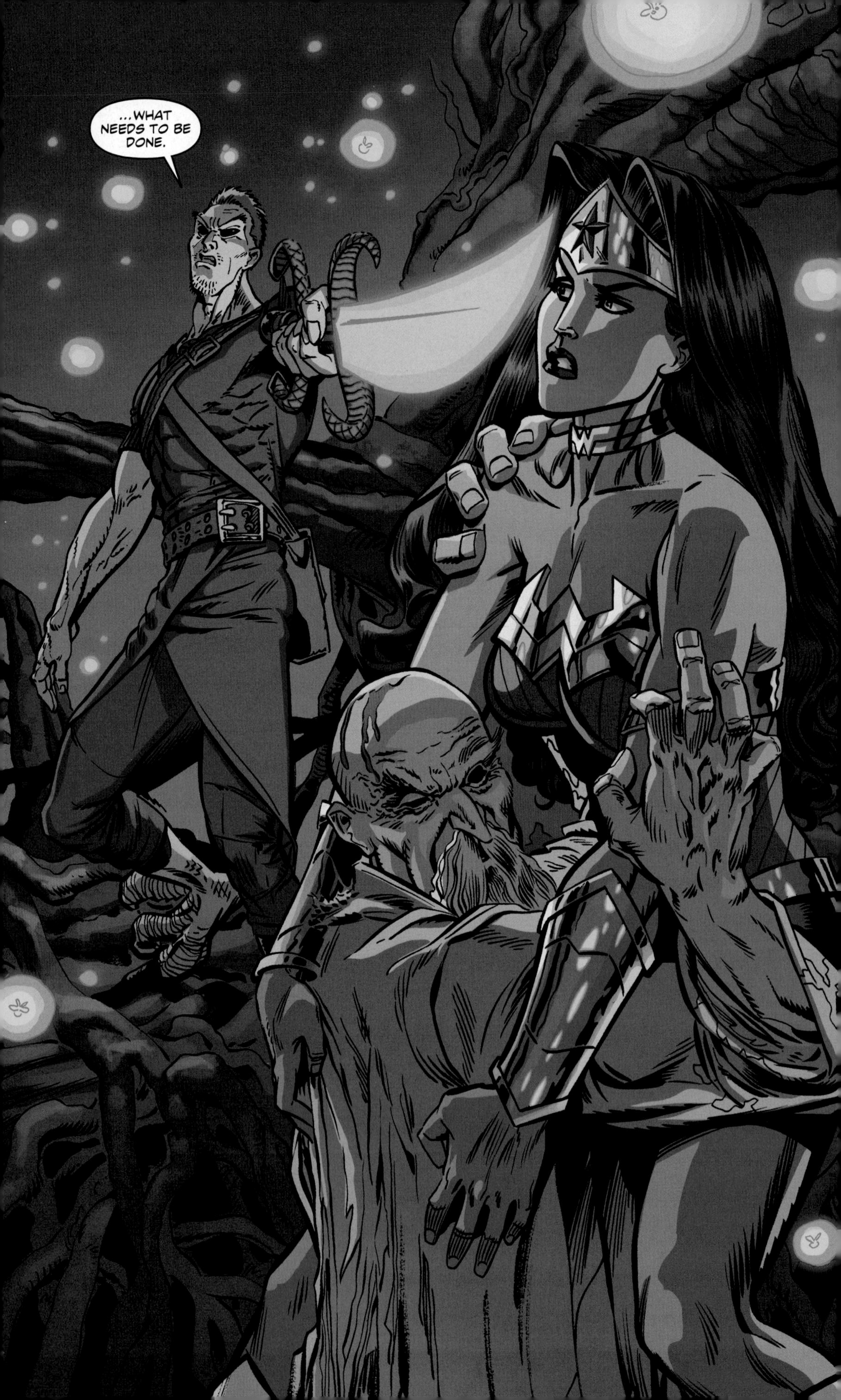
...WHAT NEEDS TO BE DONE.

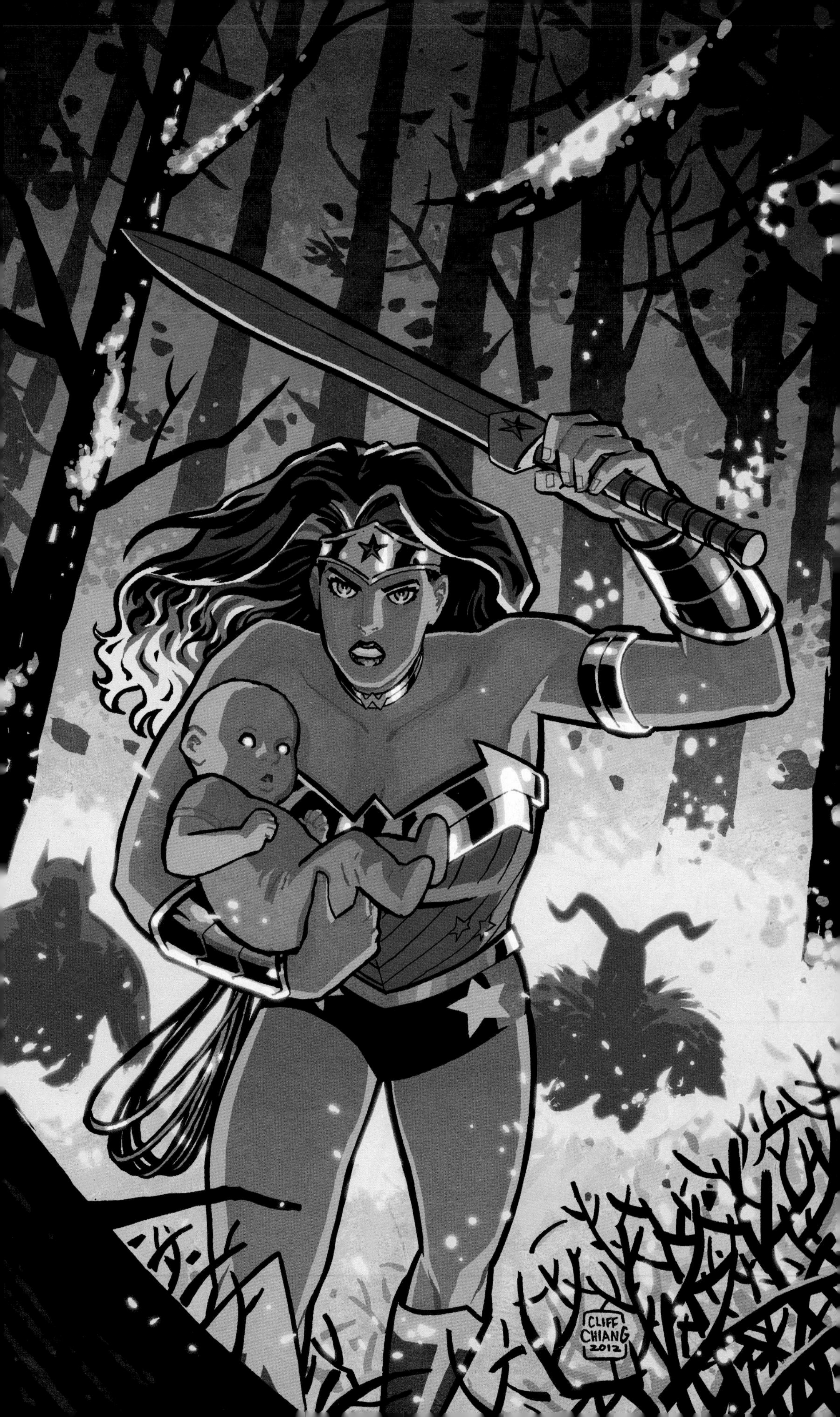
CLIFF CHIANG 2012

THE QUEEN OF ROOTS

GORAN SUDŽUKA artist (pages 4-5, 8-10, 13-17) CLIFF CHIANG artist (pages 18-20)
TONY AKINS with DAN GREEN layouts and finishes (pages 1-3, 6-7, 11-12)

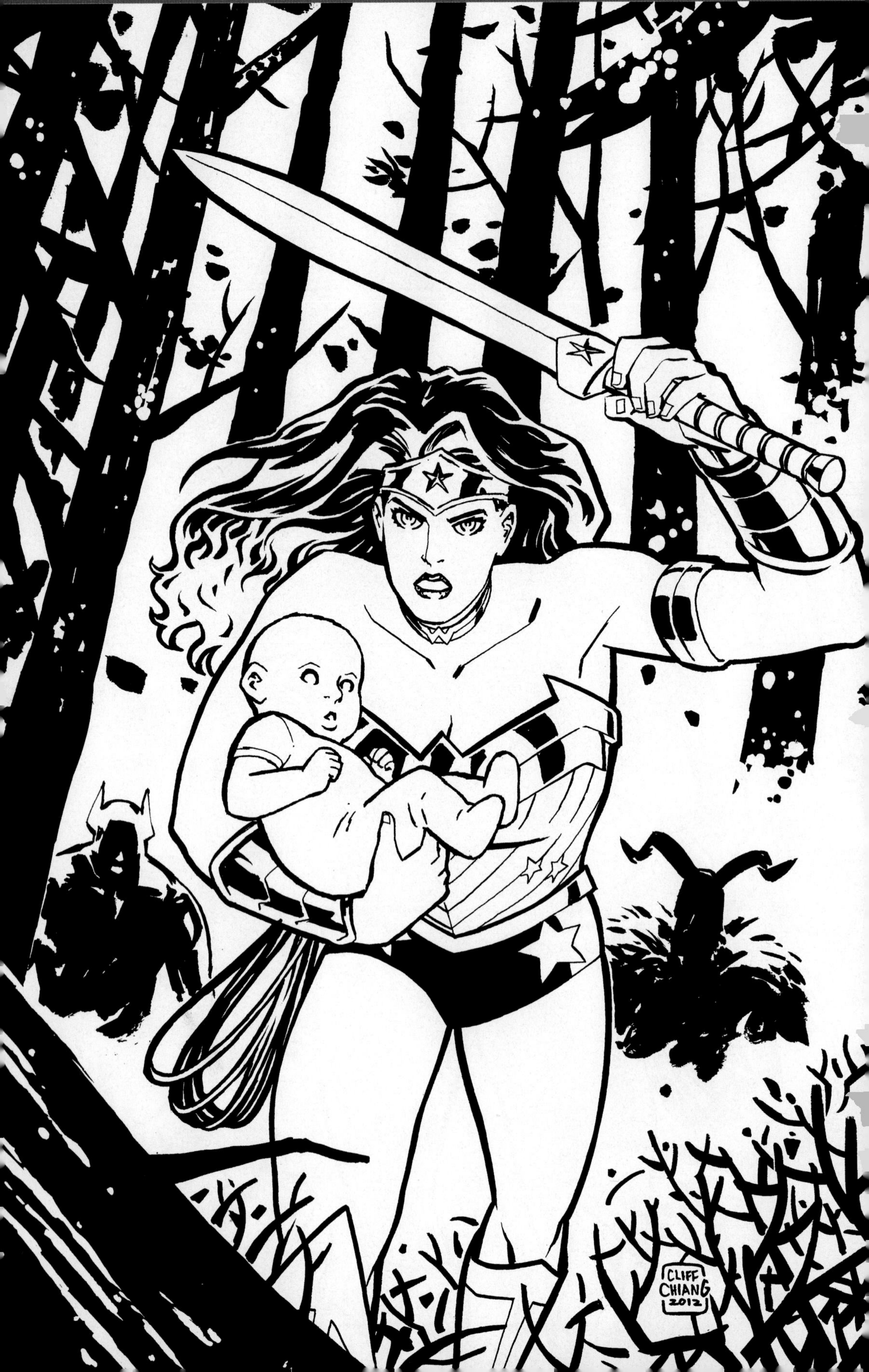
CLIFF CHIANG 2012

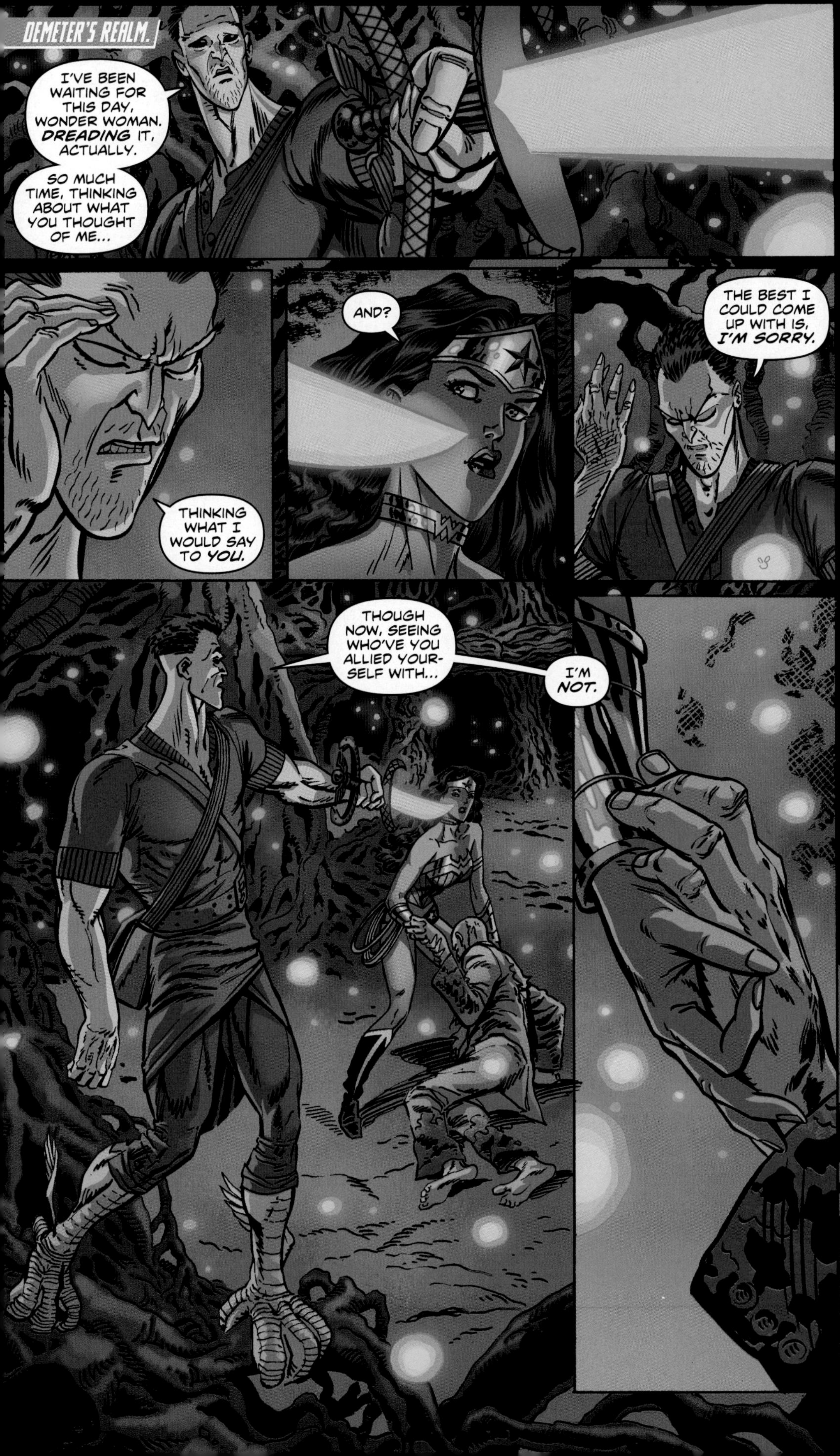
DEMETER'S REALM.
I'VE BEEN WAITING FOR THIS DAY, WONDER WOMAN. DREADING IT, ACTUALLY.
SO MUCH TIME, THINKING ABOUT WHAT YOU THOUGHT OF ME...
THINKING WHAT I WOULD SAY TO YOU.
AND?
THE BEST I COULD COME UP WITH IS, I'M SORRY.
THOUGH NOW, SEEING WHO'VE YOU ALLIED YOUR-SELF WITH...
I'M NOT.

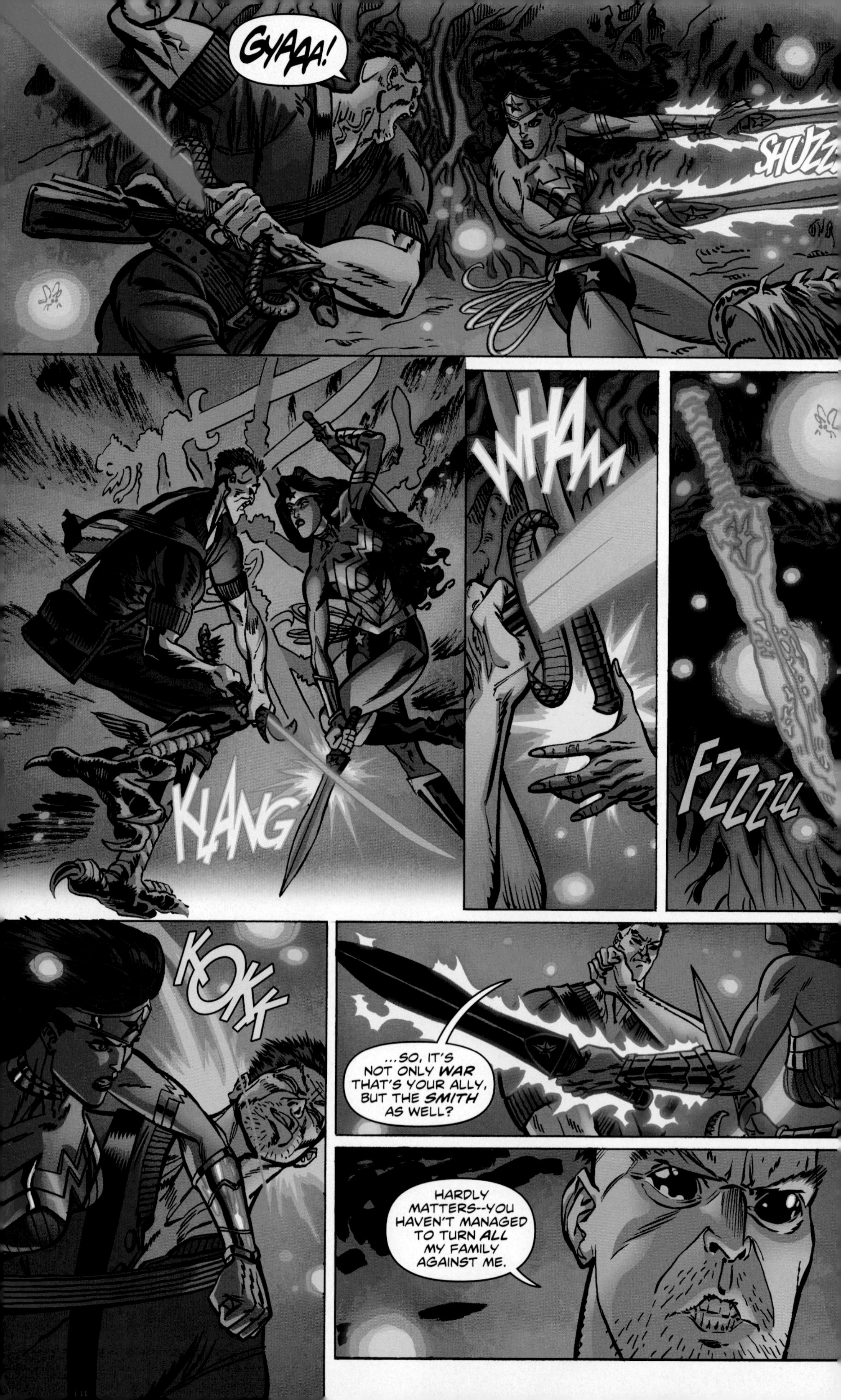
GYAAA!
SHUZZ
KLANG
WHAM
FZZZZZ
KOKK
...SO, IT'S NOT ONLY WAR THAT'S YOUR ALLY, BUT THE SMITH AS WELL?
HARDLY MATTERS--YOU HAVEN'T MANAGED TO TURN ALL MY FAMILY AGAINST ME.

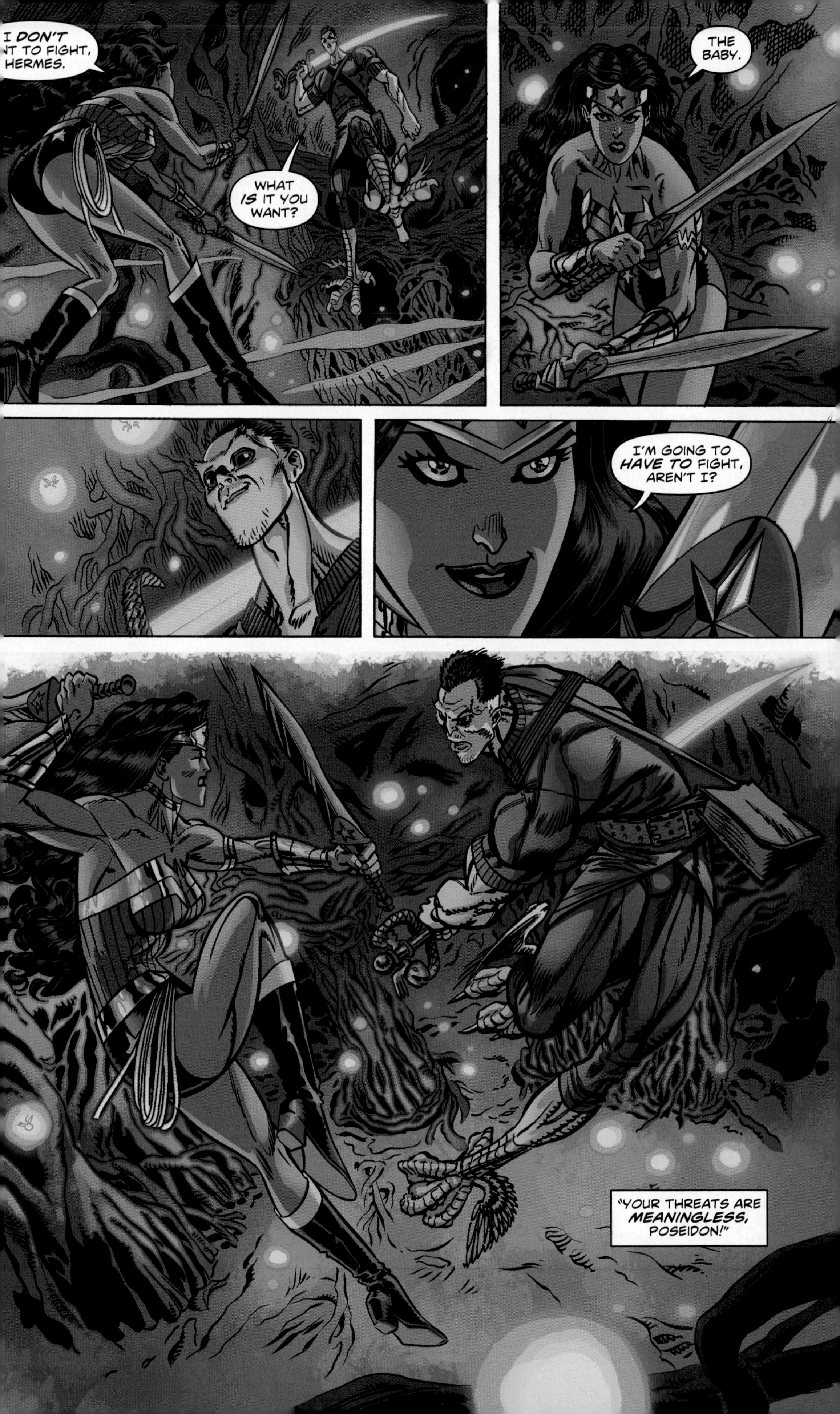
I DON'T
NT TO FIGHT,
HERMES.
WHAT IS IT YOU WANT?
THE BABY.
I'M GOING TO HAVE TO FIGHT, AREN'T I?
"YOUR THREATS ARE MEANINGLESS, POSEIDON!"

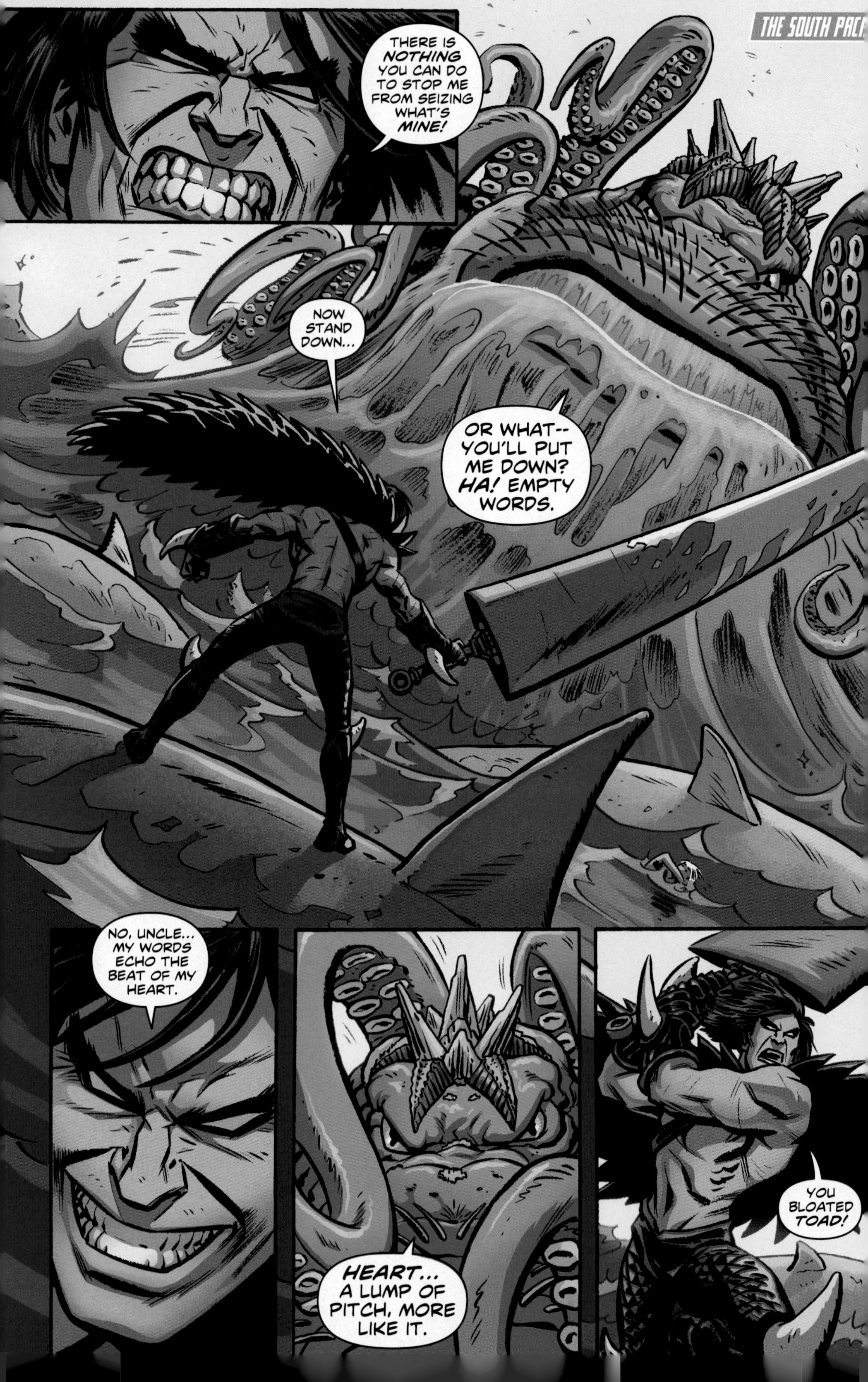
THE SOUTH PACI
THERE IS NOTHING YOU CAN DO TO STOP ME FROM SEIZING WHAT'S MINE!
NOW STAND DOWN...
OR WHAT-- YOU'LL PUT ME DOWN? HA! EMPTY WORDS.
NO, UNCLE... MY WORDS ECHO THE BEAT OF MY HEART.
HEART... A LUMP OF PITCH, MORE LIKE IT.
YOU BLOATED TOAD!

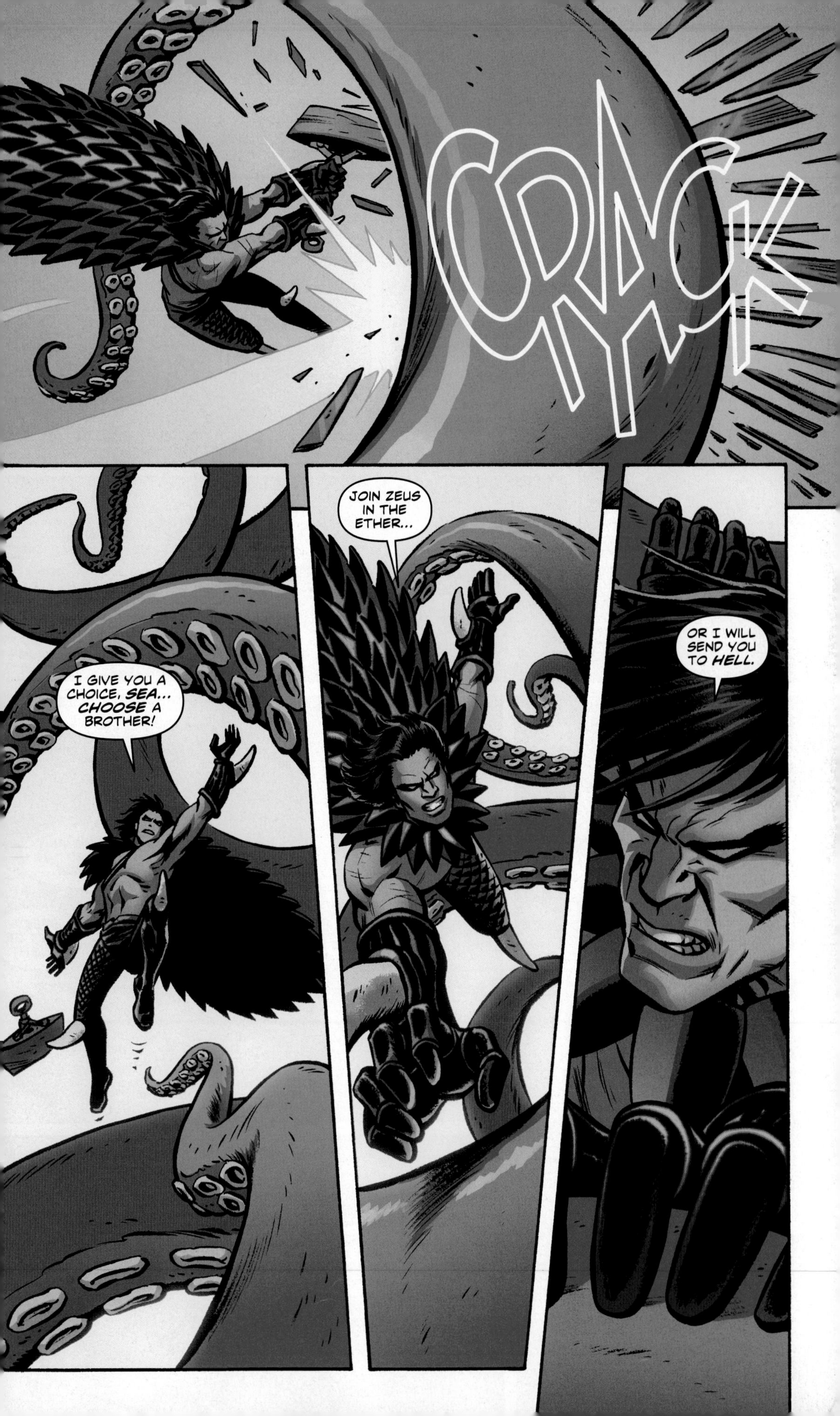
CRACK
I GIVE YOU A CHOICE, SEA... CHOOSE A BROTHER!
JOIN ZEUS IN THE ETHER...
OR I WILL SEND YOU TO HELL.

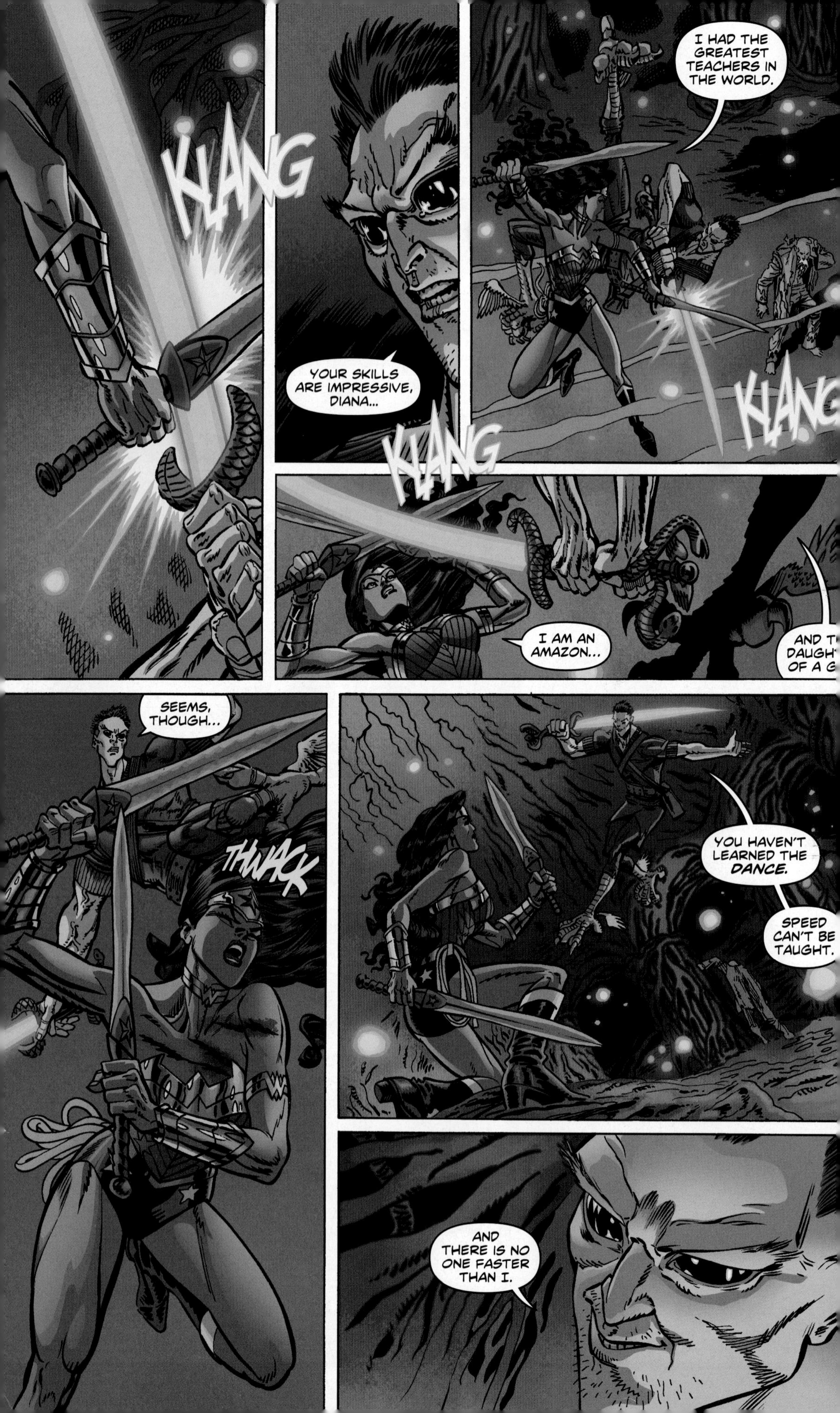
KLANG
YOUR SKILLS ARE IMPRESSIVE, DIANA...
I HAD THE GREATEST TEACHERS IN THE WORLD.
KLANG
KLANG
I AM AN AMAZON...
AND T
DAUGH
OF A G
SEEMS, THOUGH...
THWACK
YOU HAVEN'T LEARNED THE *DANCE.*
SPEED CAN'T BE TAUGHT.
AND THERE IS NO ONE FASTER THAN I.

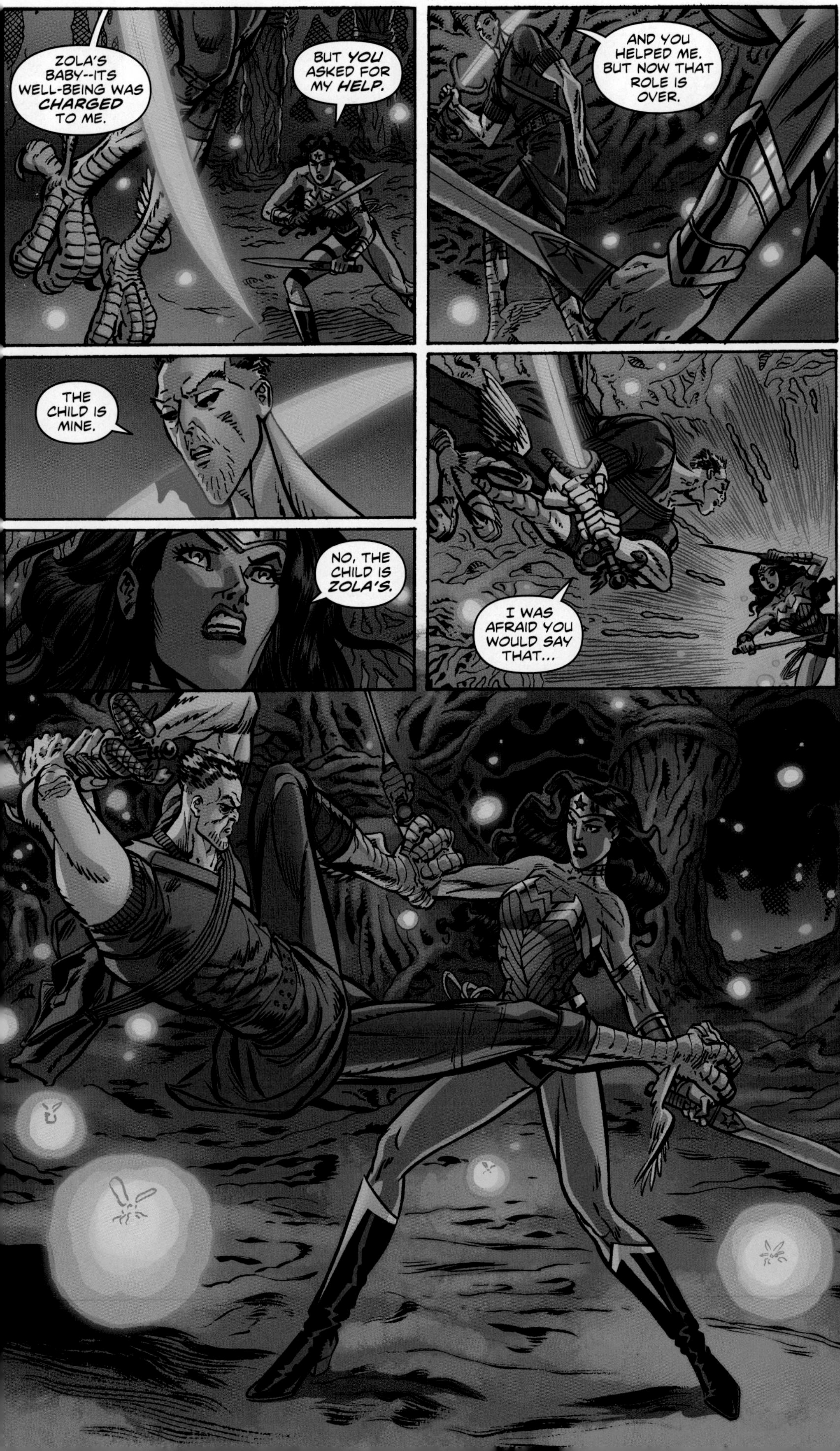
ZOLA'S BABY--ITS WELL-BEING WAS CHARGED TO ME.
BUT YOU ASKED FOR MY HELP.
AND YOU HELPED ME. BUT NOW THAT ROLE IS OVER.
THE CHILD IS MINE.
NO, THE CHILD IS ZOLA'S.
I WAS AFRAID YOU WOULD SAY THAT...

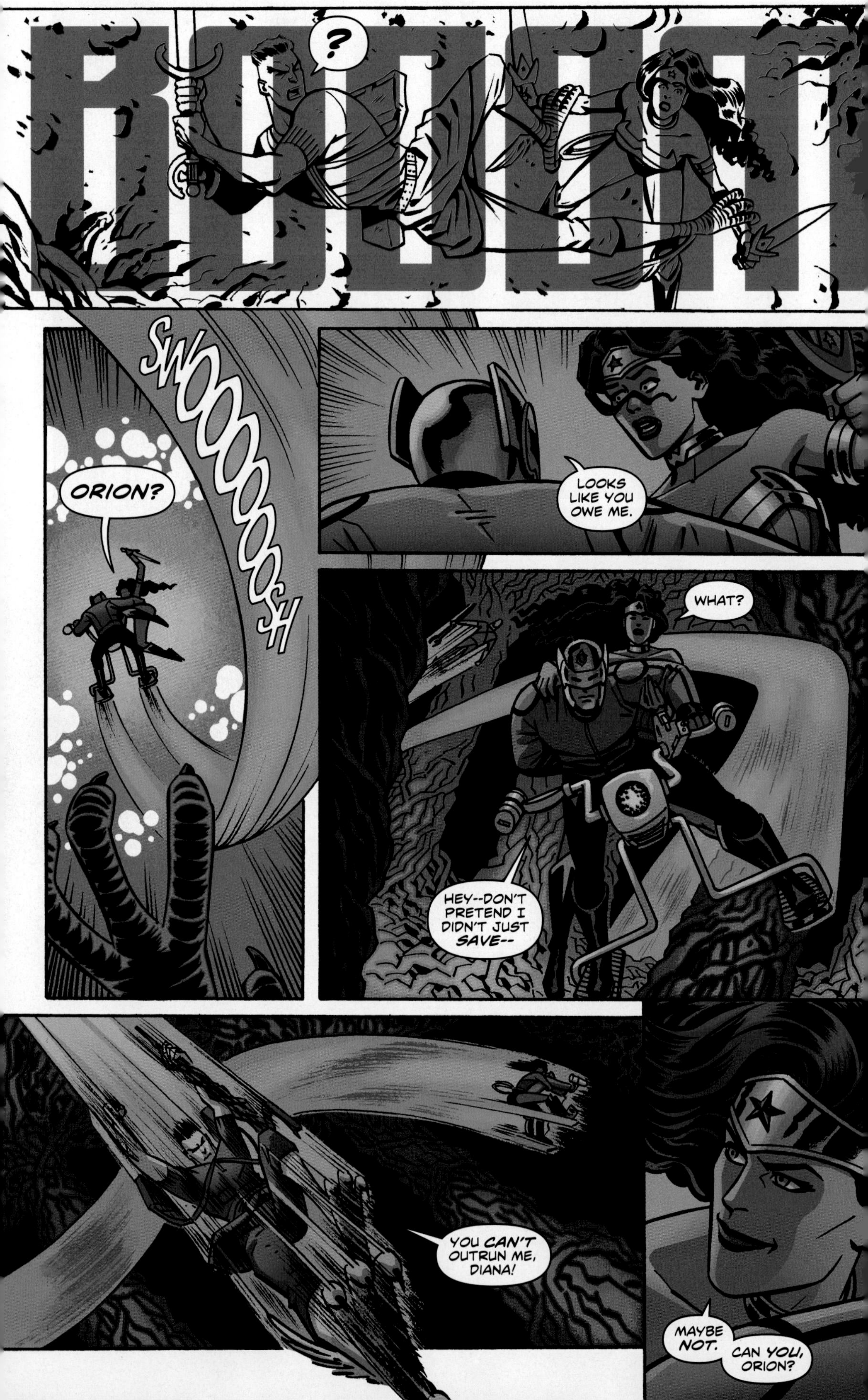

?
ORION?
SWOOOOOOOSH
LOOKS LIKE YOU OWE ME.
WHAT?
HEY--DON'T PRETEND I DIDN'T JUST SAVE--
YOU CAN'T OUTRUN ME, DIANA!
MAYBE NOT.
CAN YOU, ORION?

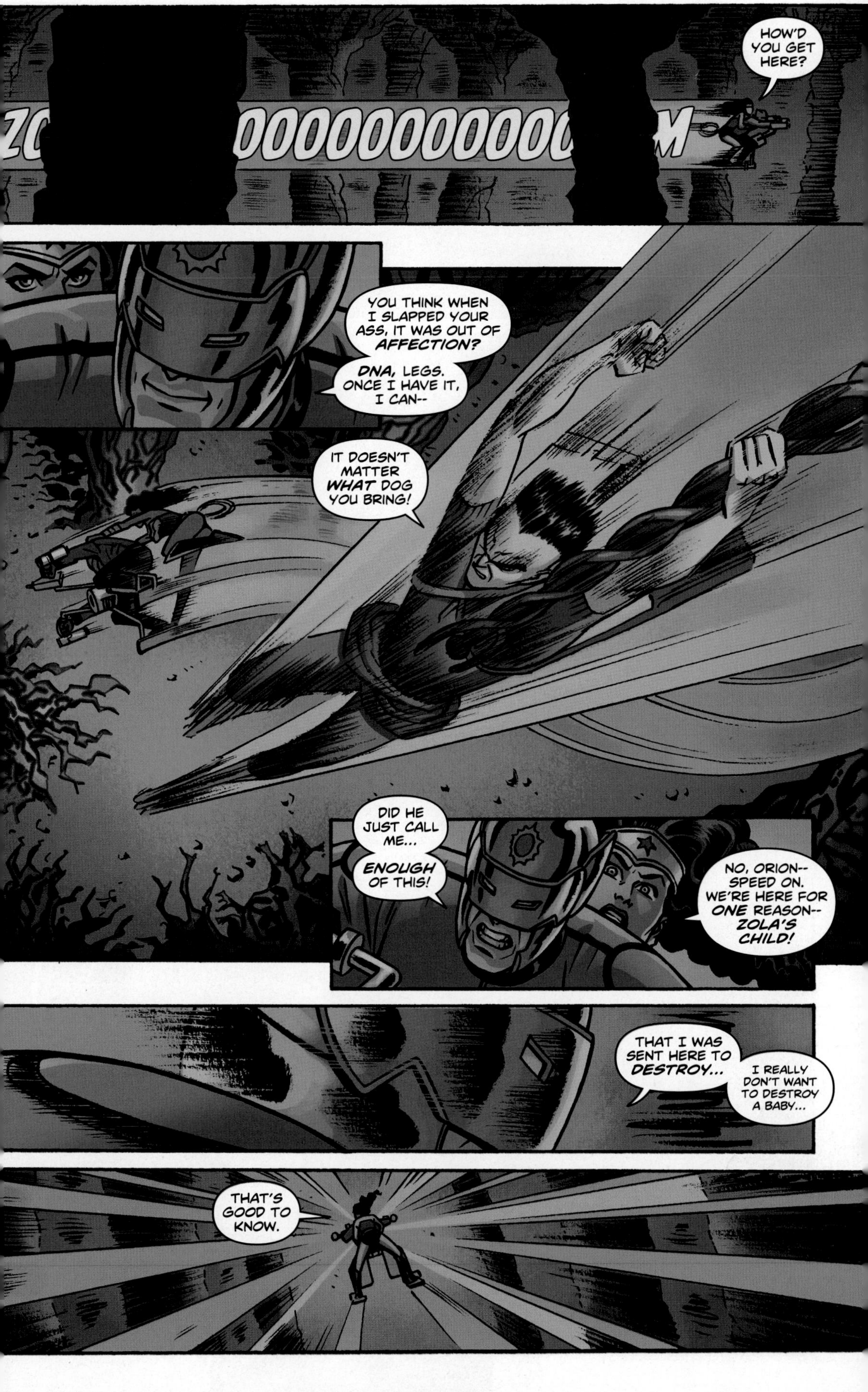
HOW'D YOU GET HERE?
YOU THINK WHEN I SLAPPED YOUR ASS, IT WAS OUT OF *AFFECTION?*
DNA, LEGS. ONCE I HAVE IT, I CAN--
IT DOESN'T MATTER *WHAT* DOG YOU BRING!
DID HE JUST CALL ME...
ENOUGH OF THIS!
NO, ORION-- SPEED ON. WE'RE HERE FOR *ONE* REASON-- *ZOLA'S CHILD!*
THAT I WAS SENT HERE TO *DESTROY...*
I REALLY DON'T WANT TO DESTROY A BABY...
THAT'S GOOD TO KNOW.

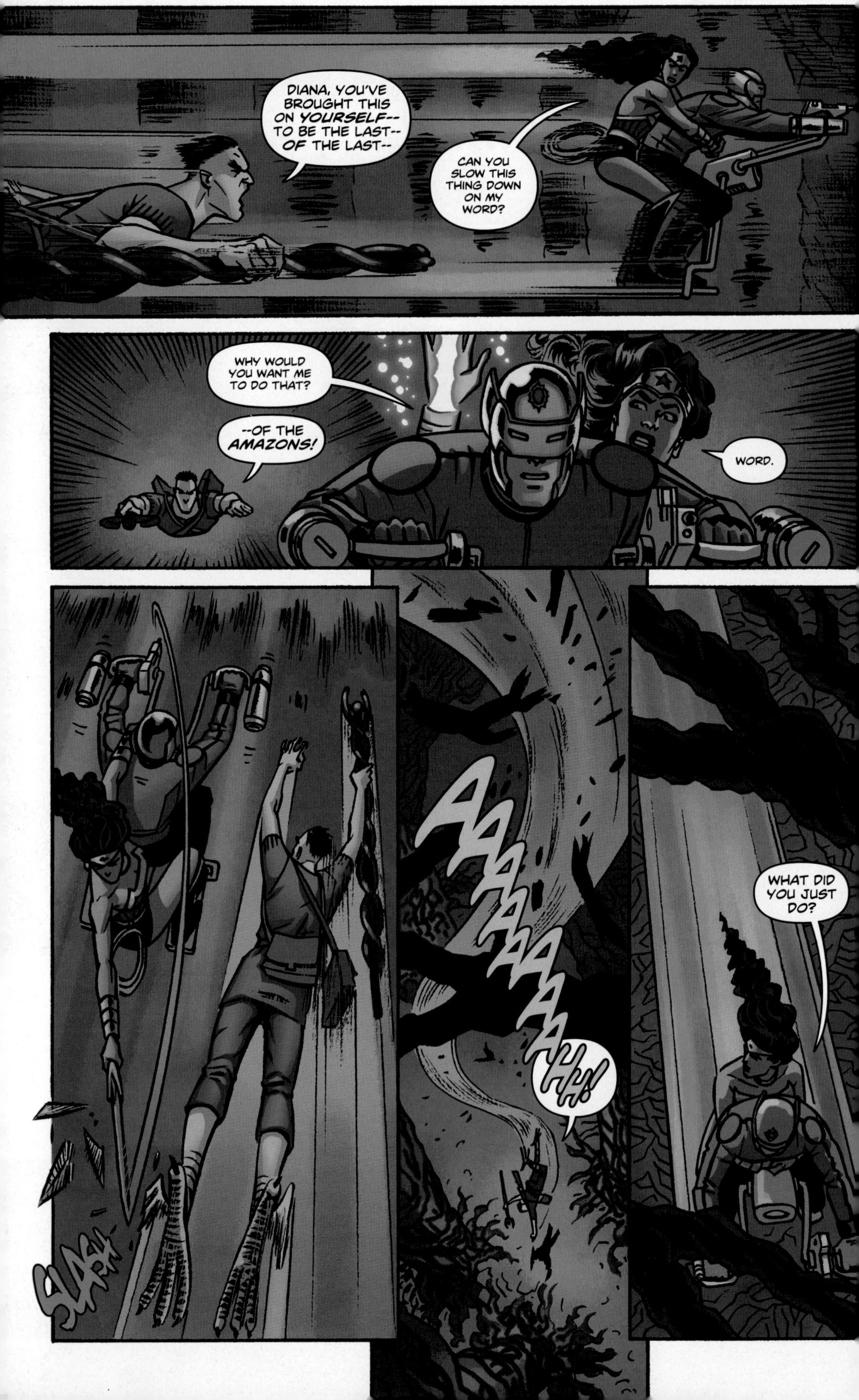
DIANA, YOU'VE BROUGHT THIS ON YOURSELF-- TO BE THE LAST-- OF THE LAST--
CAN YOU SLOW THIS THING DOWN ON MY WORD?
WHY WOULD YOU WANT ME TO DO THAT?
--OF THE AMAZONS!
WORD.
SLASH
AAAAAAAAAHH!
WHAT DID YOU JUST DO?

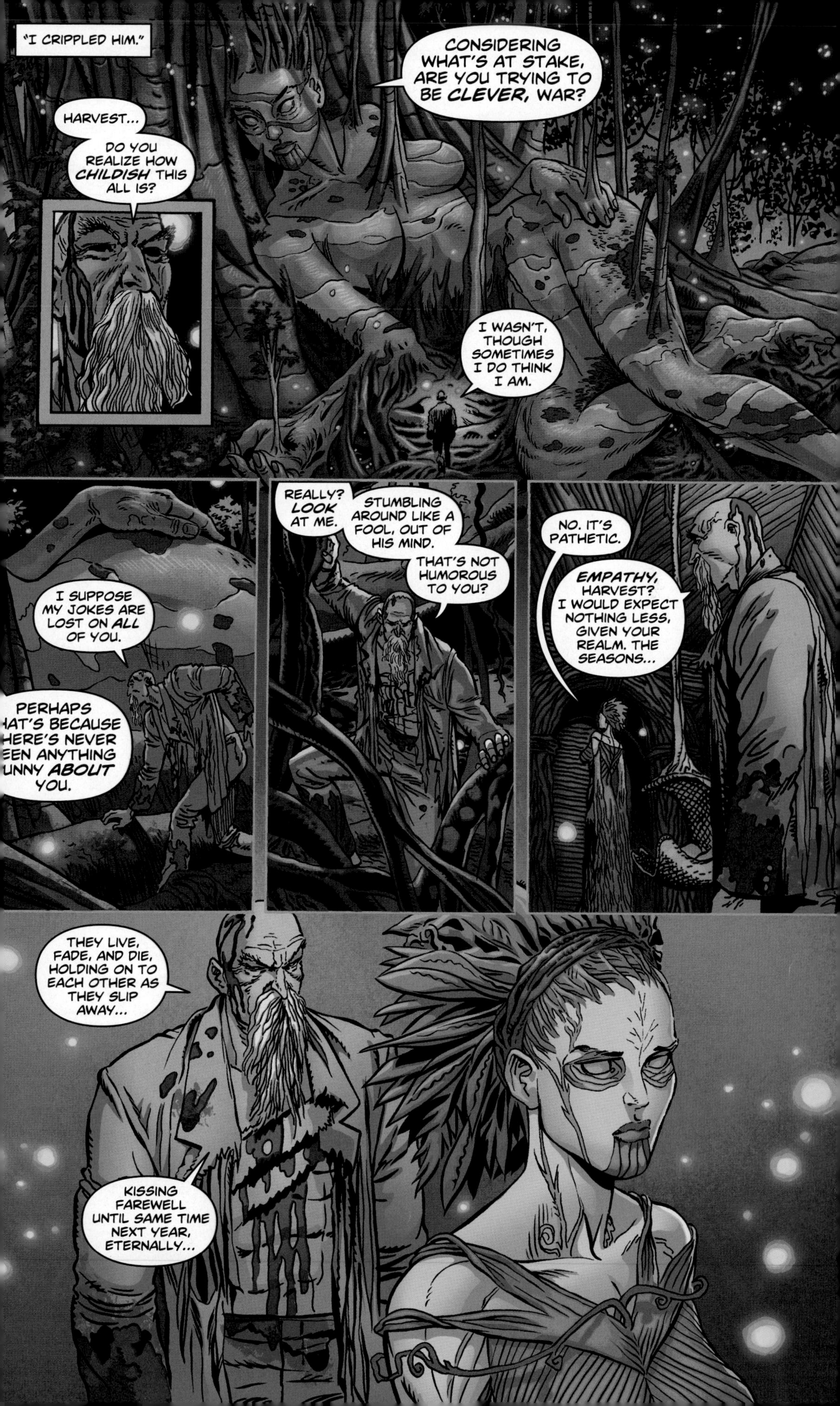
"I CRIPPLED HIM."
CONSIDERING WHAT'S AT STAKE, ARE YOU TRYING TO BE *CLEVER,* WAR?
HARVEST...
DO YOU REALIZE HOW *CHILDISH* THIS ALL IS?
I WASN'T, THOUGH SOMETIMES I DO THINK I AM.
I SUPPOSE MY JOKES ARE LOST ON *ALL* OF YOU.
PERHAPS HAT'S BECAUSE HERE'S NEVER EEN ANYTHING UNNY *ABOUT* YOU.
REALLY? *LOOK* AT ME.
STUMBLING AROUND LIKE A FOOL, OUT OF HIS MIND.
THAT'S NOT HUMOROUS TO YOU?
NO. IT'S PATHETIC.
EMPATHY, HARVEST? I WOULD EXPECT NOTHING LESS, GIVEN YOUR REALM. THE SEASONS...
THEY LIVE, FADE, AND DIE, HOLDING ON TO EACH OTHER AS THEY SLIP AWAY...
KISSING FAREWELL UNTIL SAME TIME NEXT YEAR, ETERNALLY...

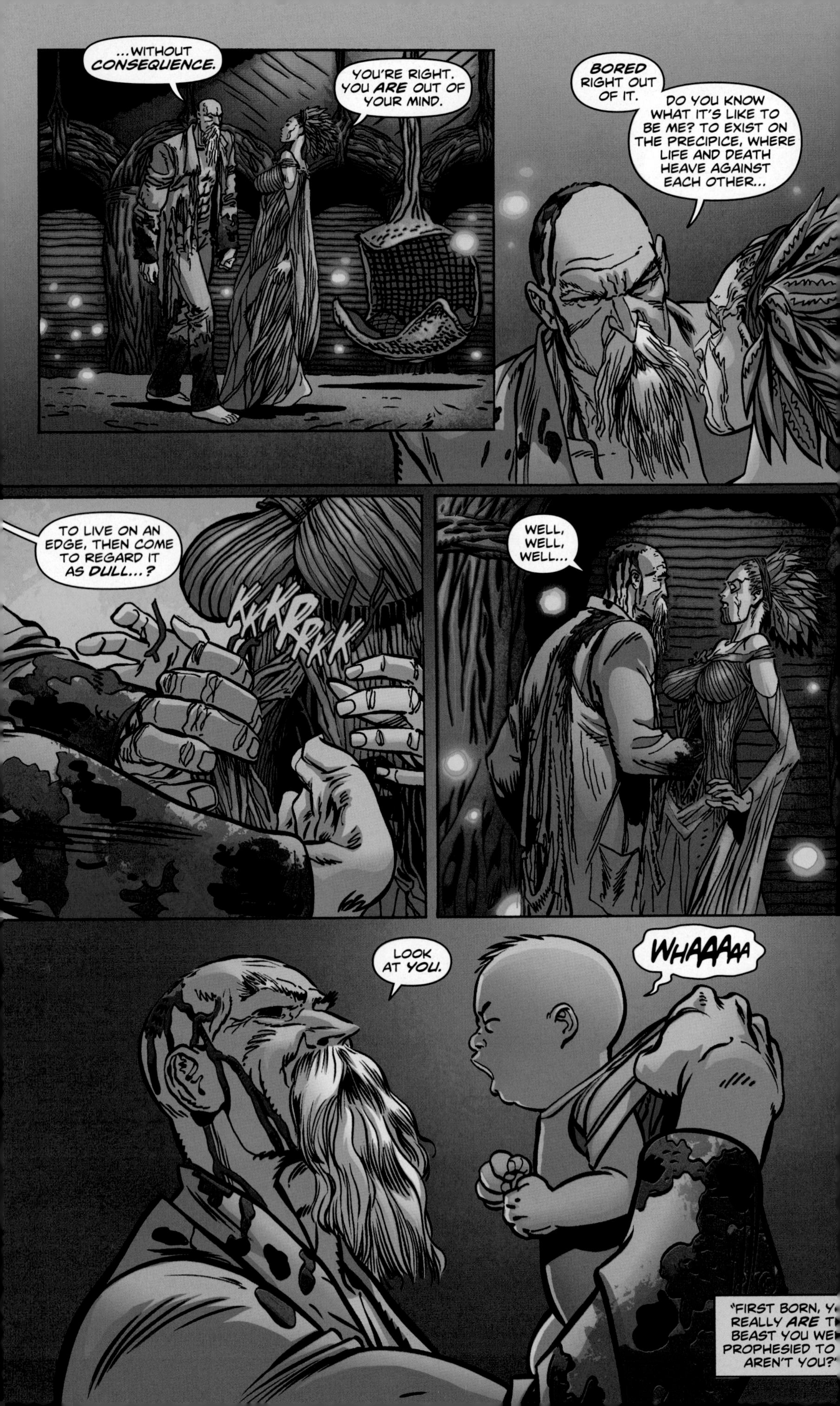
...WITHOUT CONSEQUENCE.
YOU'RE RIGHT. YOU ARE OUT OF YOUR MIND.
BORED RIGHT OUT OF IT.
DO YOU KNOW WHAT IT'S LIKE TO BE ME? TO EXIST ON THE PRECIPICE, WHERE LIFE AND DEATH HEAVE AGAINST EACH OTHER...
TO LIVE ON AN EDGE, THEN COME TO REGARD IT AS DULL...?
KKKRRKK
WELL, WELL, WELL...
LOOK AT YOU.
WHAAAAA
"FIRST BORN, Y REALLY ARE T BEAST YOU WE PROPHESIED TO AREN'T YOU?"

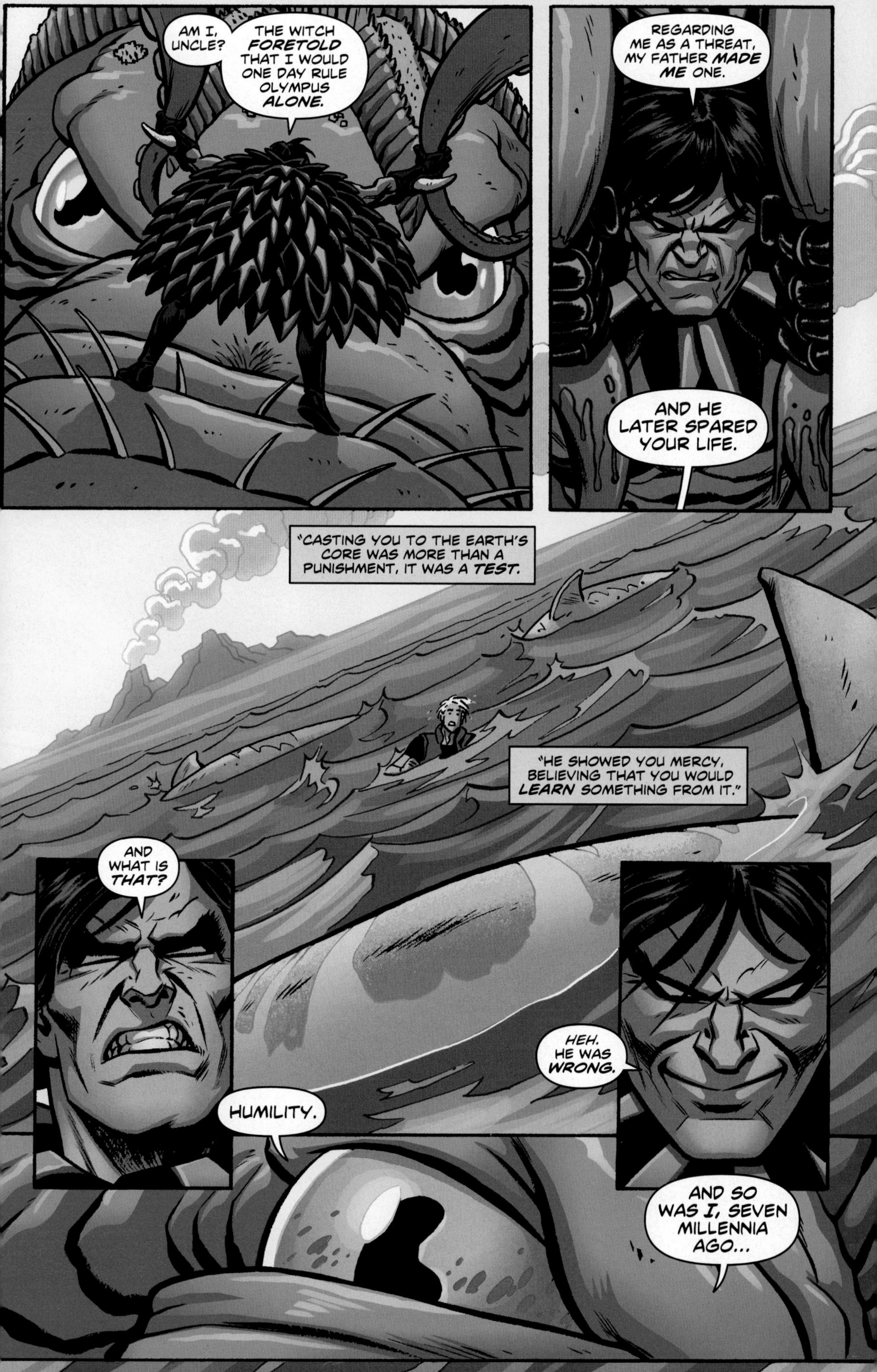
AM I, UNCLE?
THE WITCH FORETOLD THAT I WOULD ONE DAY RULE OLYMPUS ALONE.
REGARDING ME AS A THREAT, MY FATHER MADE ME ONE.
AND HE LATER SPARED YOUR LIFE.
"CASTING YOU TO THE EARTH'S CORE WAS MORE THAN A PUNISHMENT, IT WAS A TEST.
"HE SHOWED YOU MERCY, BELIEVING THAT YOU WOULD LEARN SOMETHING FROM IT."
AND WHAT IS THAT?
HUMILITY.
HEH. HE WAS WRONG.
AND SO WAS I, SEVEN MILLENNIA AGO...

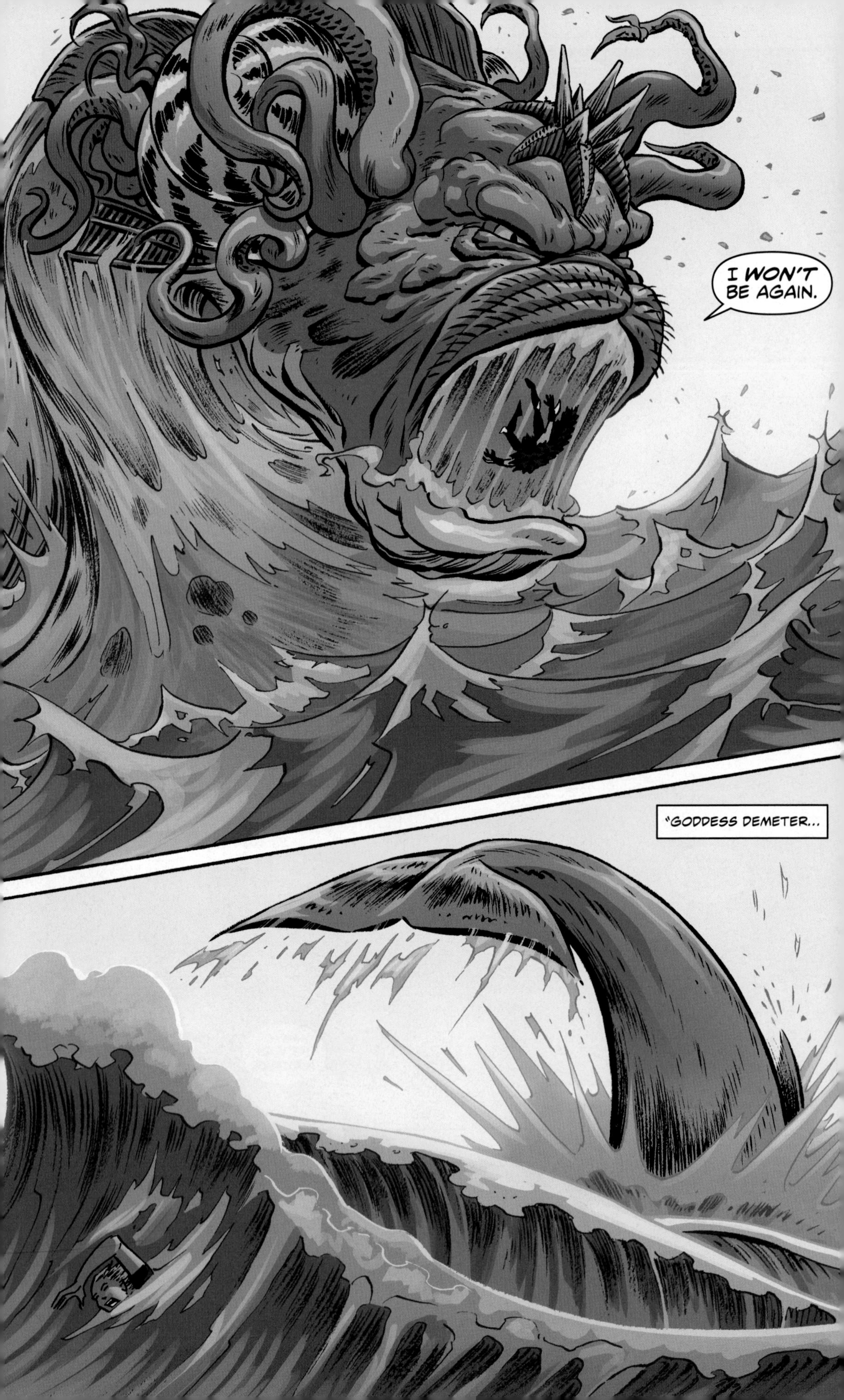
I WON'T BE AGAIN.
"GODDESS DEMETER...

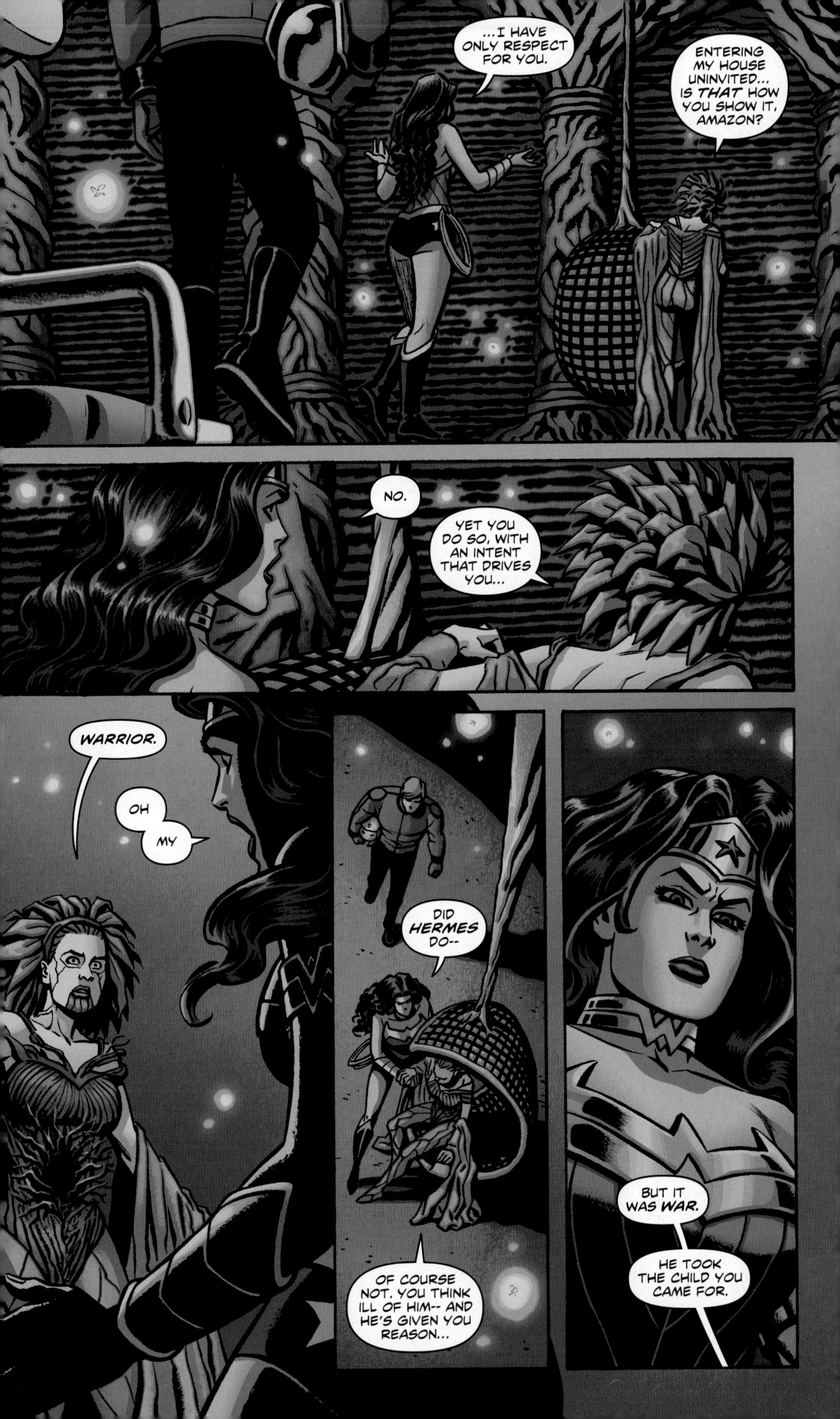
...I HAVE ONLY RESPECT FOR YOU.
ENTERING MY HOUSE UNINVITED... IS THAT HOW YOU SHOW IT, AMAZON?
NO.
YET YOU DO SO, WITH AN INTENT THAT DRIVES YOU...
WARRIOR.
OH
MY
DID HERMES DO--
OF COURSE NOT. YOU THINK ILL OF HIM-- AND HE'S GIVEN YOU REASON...
BUT IT WAS WAR.
HE TOOK THE CHILD YOU CAME FOR.

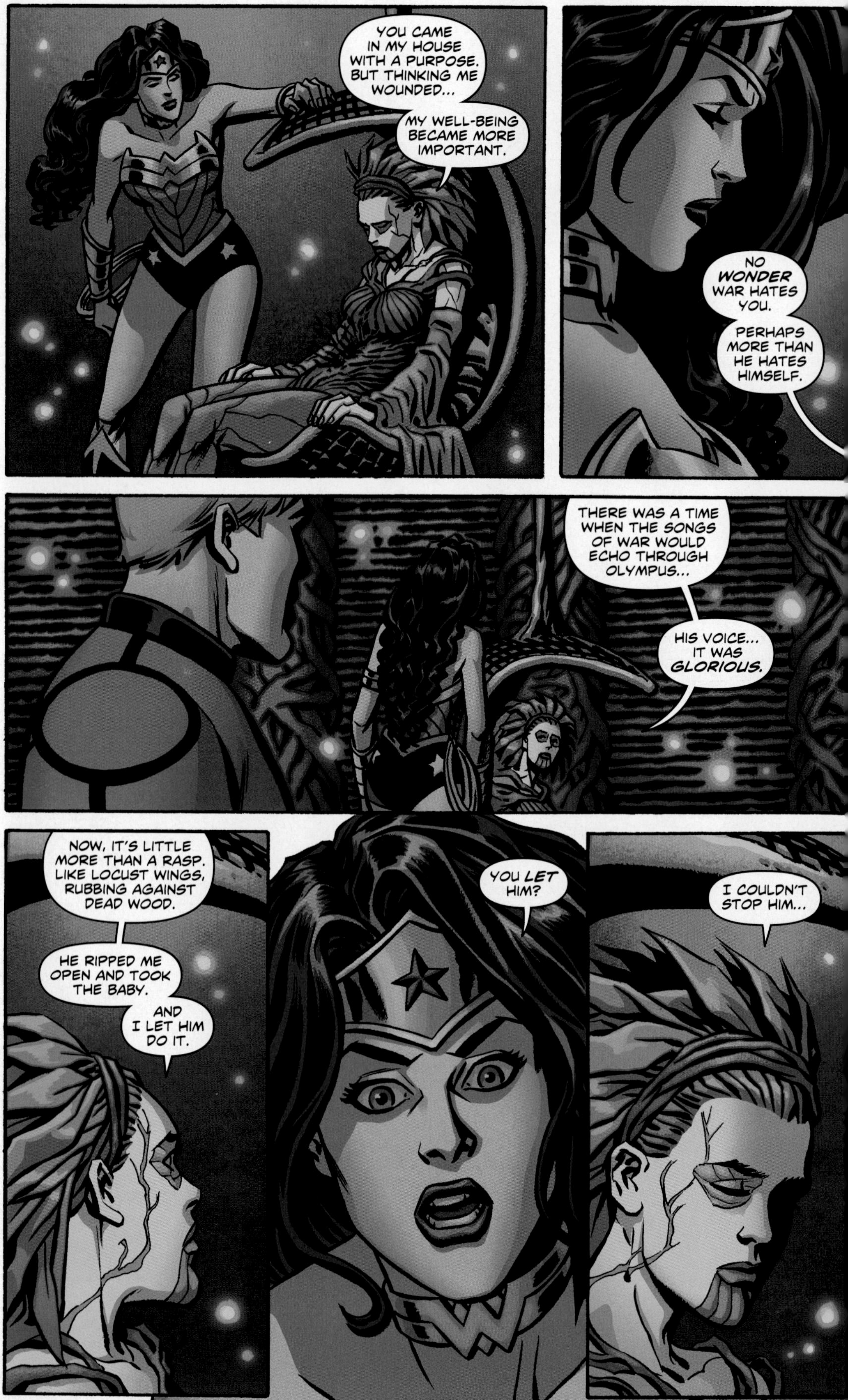
YOU CAME IN MY HOUSE WITH A PURPOSE. BUT THINKING ME WOUNDED...
MY WELL-BEING BECAME MORE IMPORTANT.
NO *WONDER* WAR HATES YOU.
PERHAPS MORE THAN HE HATES HIMSELF.
THERE WAS A TIME WHEN THE SONGS OF WAR WOULD ECHO THROUGH OLYMPUS...
HIS VOICE... IT WAS *GLORIOUS.*
NOW, IT'S LITTLE MORE THAN A RASP. LIKE LOCUST WINGS, RUBBING AGAINST DEAD WOOD.
HE RIPPED ME OPEN AND TOOK THE BABY.
AND I LET HIM DO IT.
YOU *LET* HIM?
I COULDN'T STOP HIM...

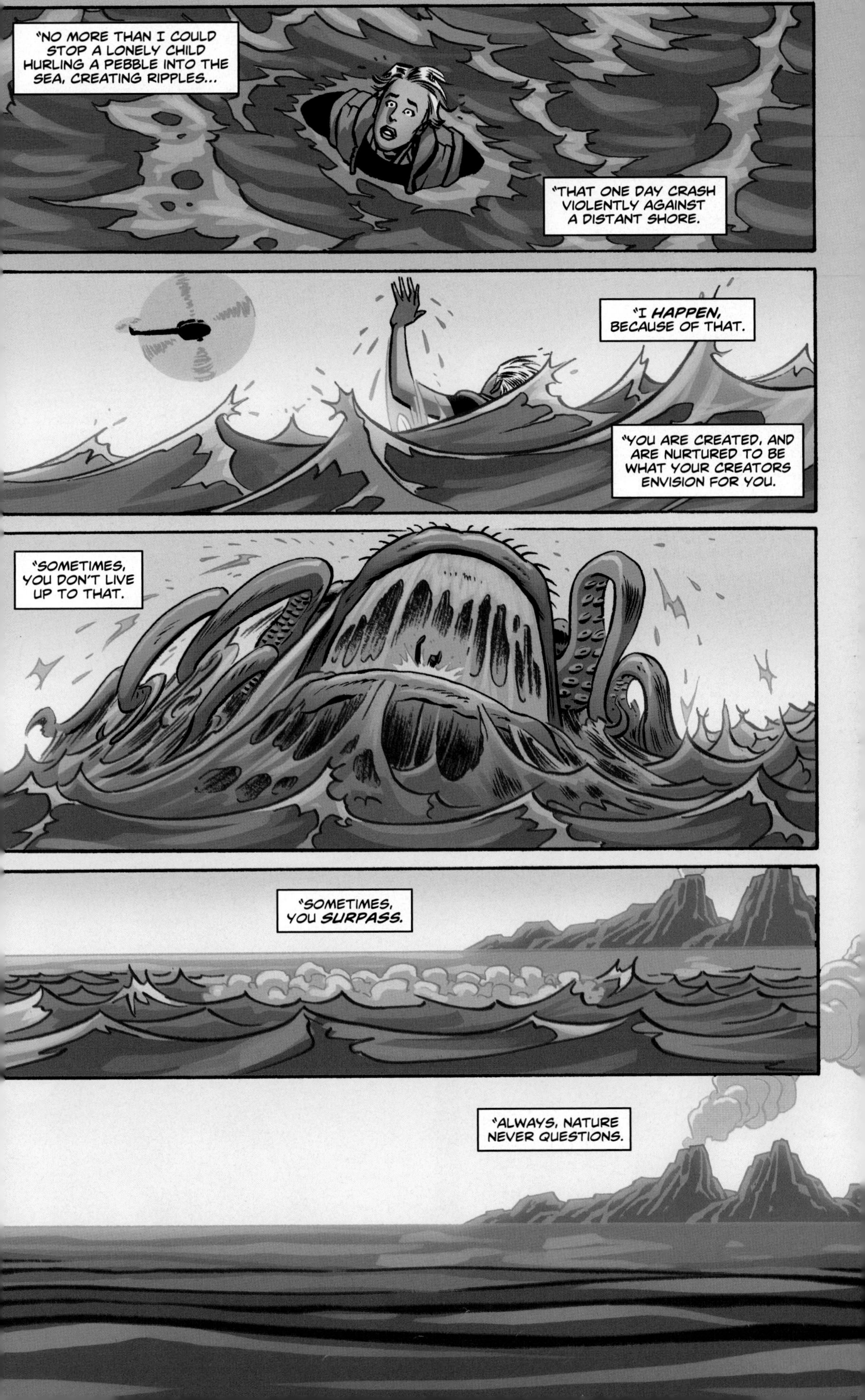

"NO MORE THAN I COULD STOP A LONELY CHILD HURLING A PEBBLE INTO THE SEA, CREATING RIPPLES...
"THAT ONE DAY CRASH VIOLENTLY AGAINST A DISTANT SHORE.
"I HAPPEN, BECAUSE OF THAT.
"YOU ARE CREATED, AND ARE NURTURED TO BE WHAT YOUR CREATORS ENVISION FOR YOU.
"SOMETIMES, YOU DON'T LIVE UP TO THAT.
"SOMETIMES, YOU SURPASS.
"ALWAYS, NATURE NEVER QUESTIONS.

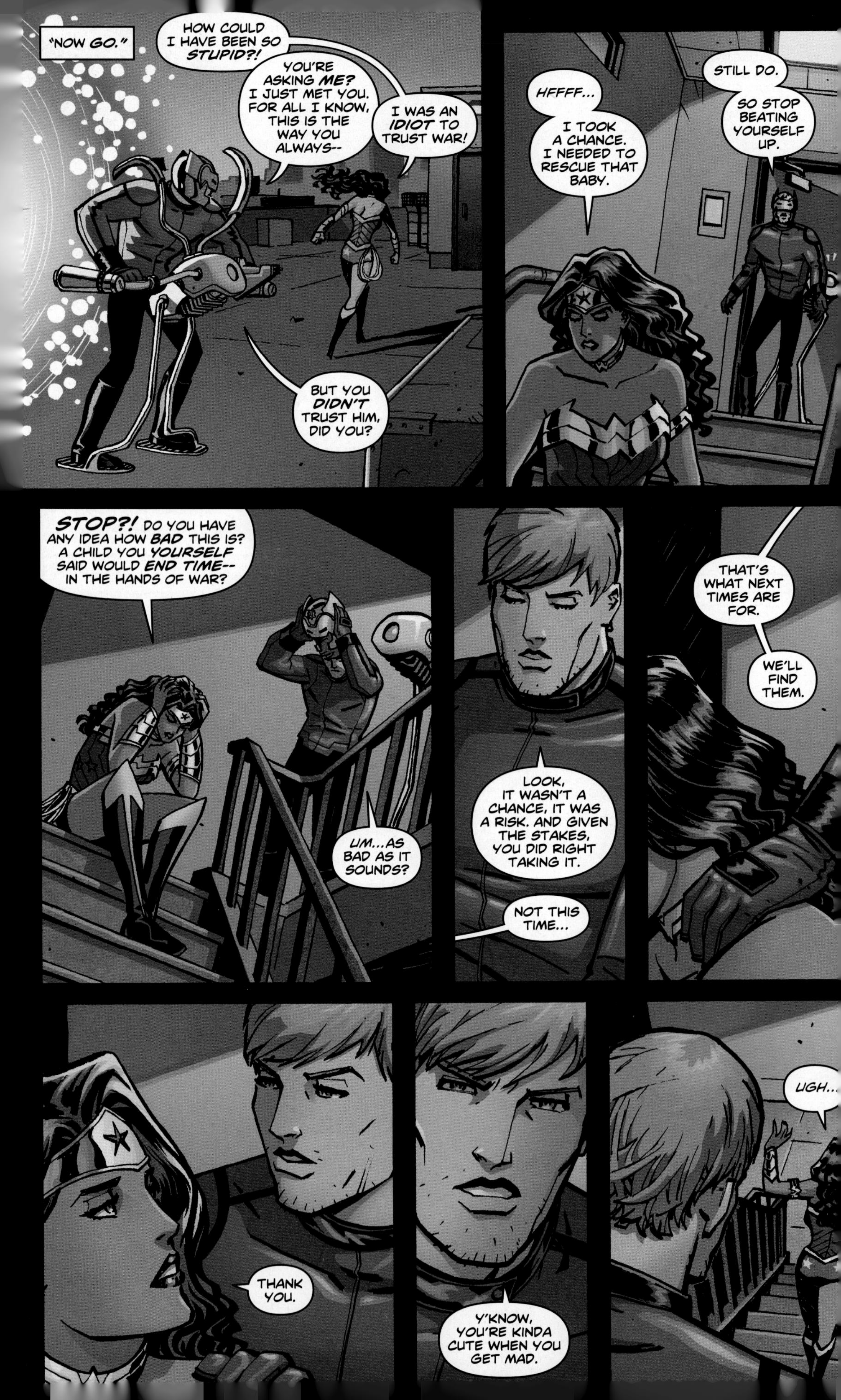
"NOW GO."
HOW COULD I HAVE BEEN SO STUPID?!
YOU'RE ASKING ME? I JUST MET YOU. FOR ALL I KNOW, THIS IS THE WAY YOU ALWAYS--
I WAS AN IDIOT TO TRUST WAR!
BUT YOU DIDN'T TRUST HIM, DID YOU?
HFFFF...
I TOOK A CHANCE. I NEEDED TO RESCUE THAT BABY.
STILL DO.
SO STOP BEATING YOURSELF UP.
STOP?! DO YOU HAVE ANY IDEA HOW BAD THIS IS? A CHILD YOU YOURSELF SAID WOULD END TIME-- IN THE HANDS OF WAR?
UM...AS BAD AS IT SOUNDS?
LOOK, IT WASN'T A CHANCE, IT WAS A RISK. AND GIVEN THE STAKES, YOU DID RIGHT TAKING IT.
NOT THIS TIME...
THAT'S WHAT NEXT TIMES ARE FOR.
WE'LL FIND THEM.
THANK YOU.
Y'KNOW, YOU'RE KINDA CUTE WHEN YOU GET MAD.
UGH...

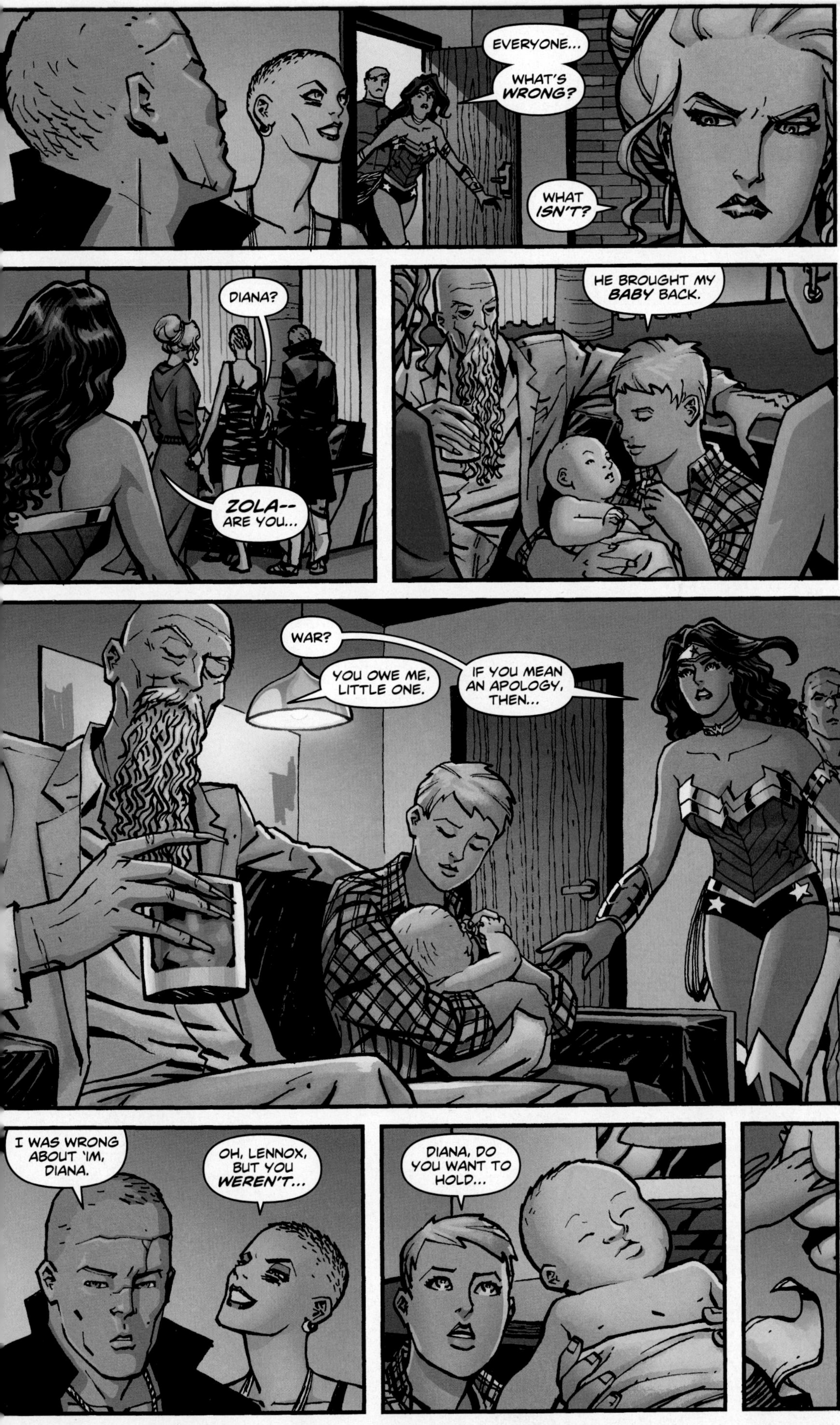
EVERYONE...
WHAT'S WRONG?
WHAT ISN'T?
DIANA?
ZOLA-- ARE YOU...
HE BROUGHT MY BABY BACK.
WAR?
YOU OWE ME, LITTLE ONE.
IF YOU MEAN AN APOLOGY, THEN...
I WAS WRONG ABOUT 'IM, DIANA.
OH, LENNOX, BUT YOU WEREN'T...
DIANA, DO YOU WANT TO HOLD...

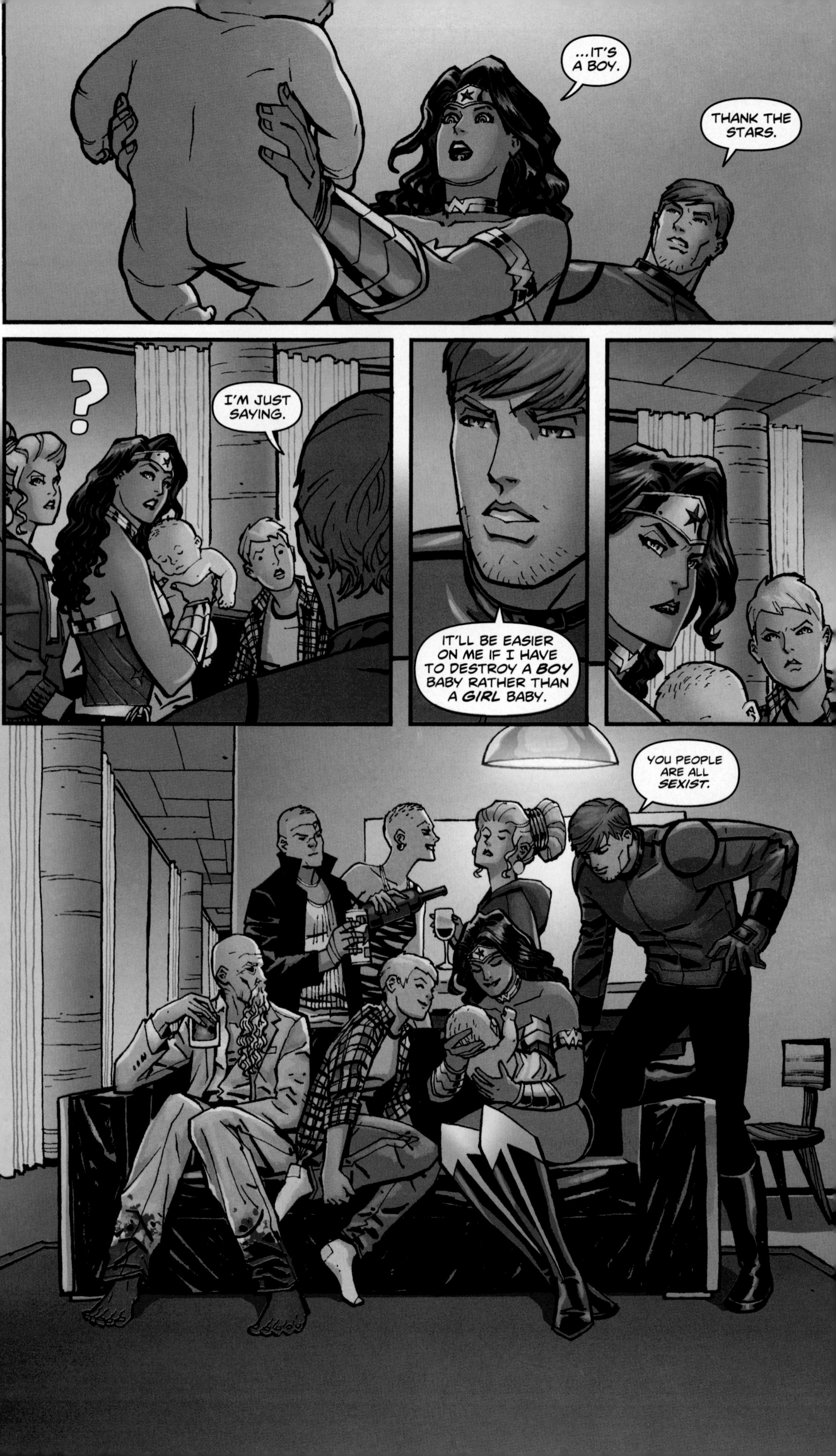
...IT'S A BOY.
THANK THE STARS.
?
I'M JUST SAYING.
IT'LL BE EASIER ON ME IF I HAVE TO DESTROY A BOY BABY RATHER THAN A GIRL BABY.
YOU PEOPLE ARE ALL SEXIST.

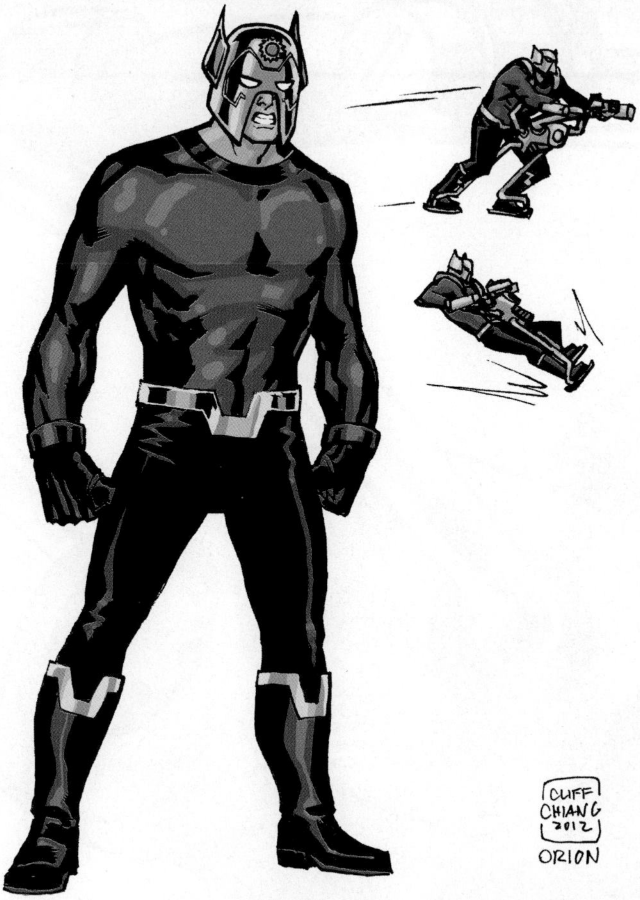
CLIFF CHIANG 2012
ORION

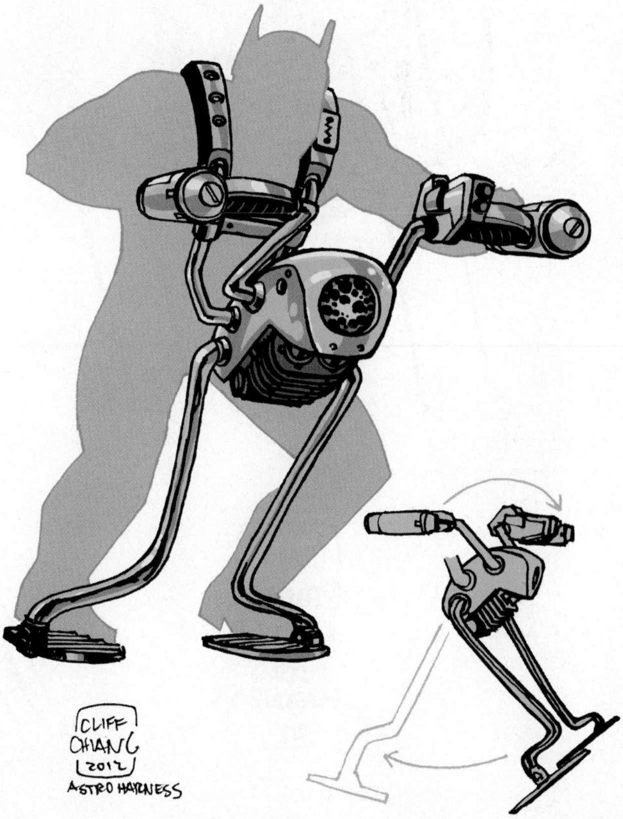
CLIFF CHIANG 2012
ASTRO HARNESS

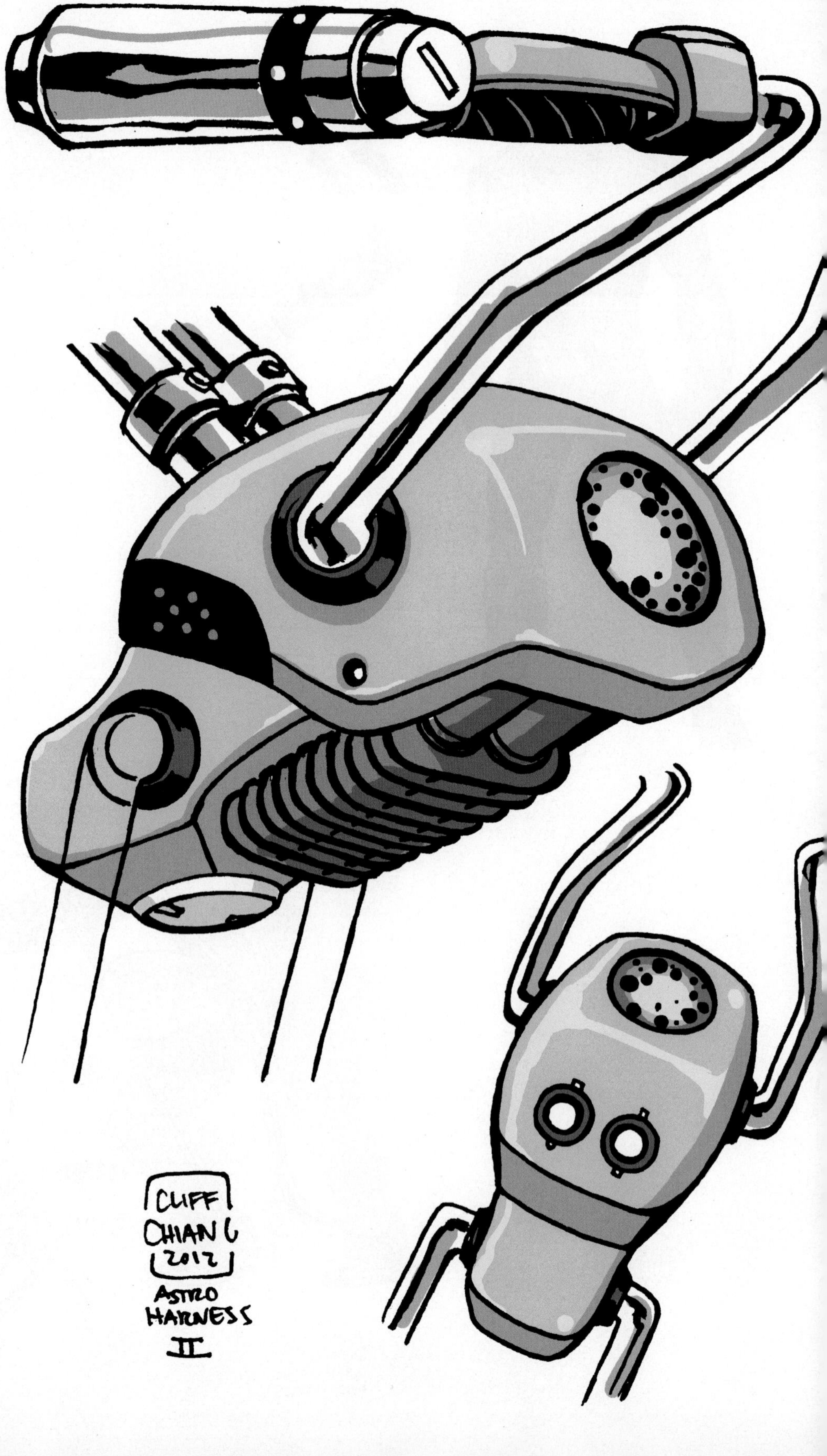
CLIFF CHIANG 2012
ASTRO HARNESS II

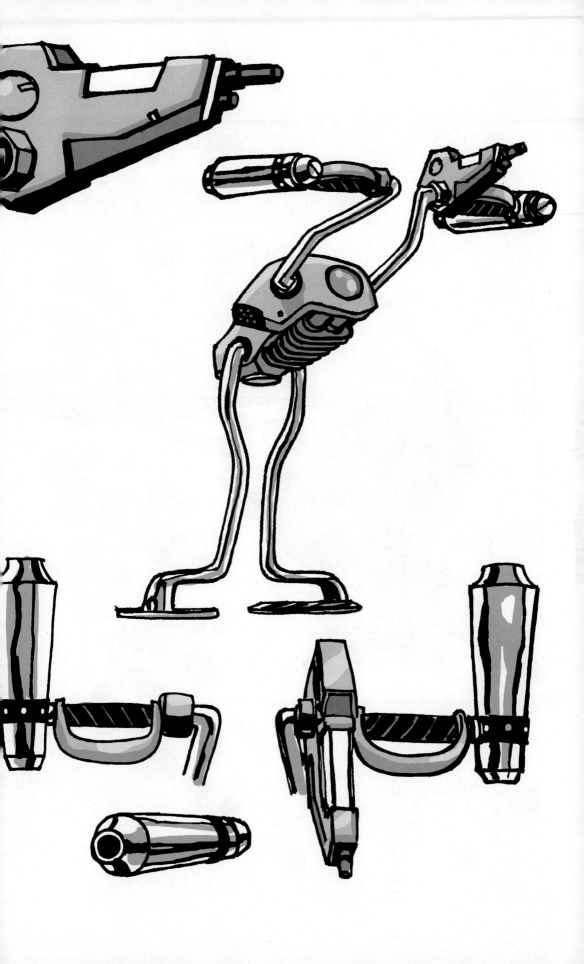

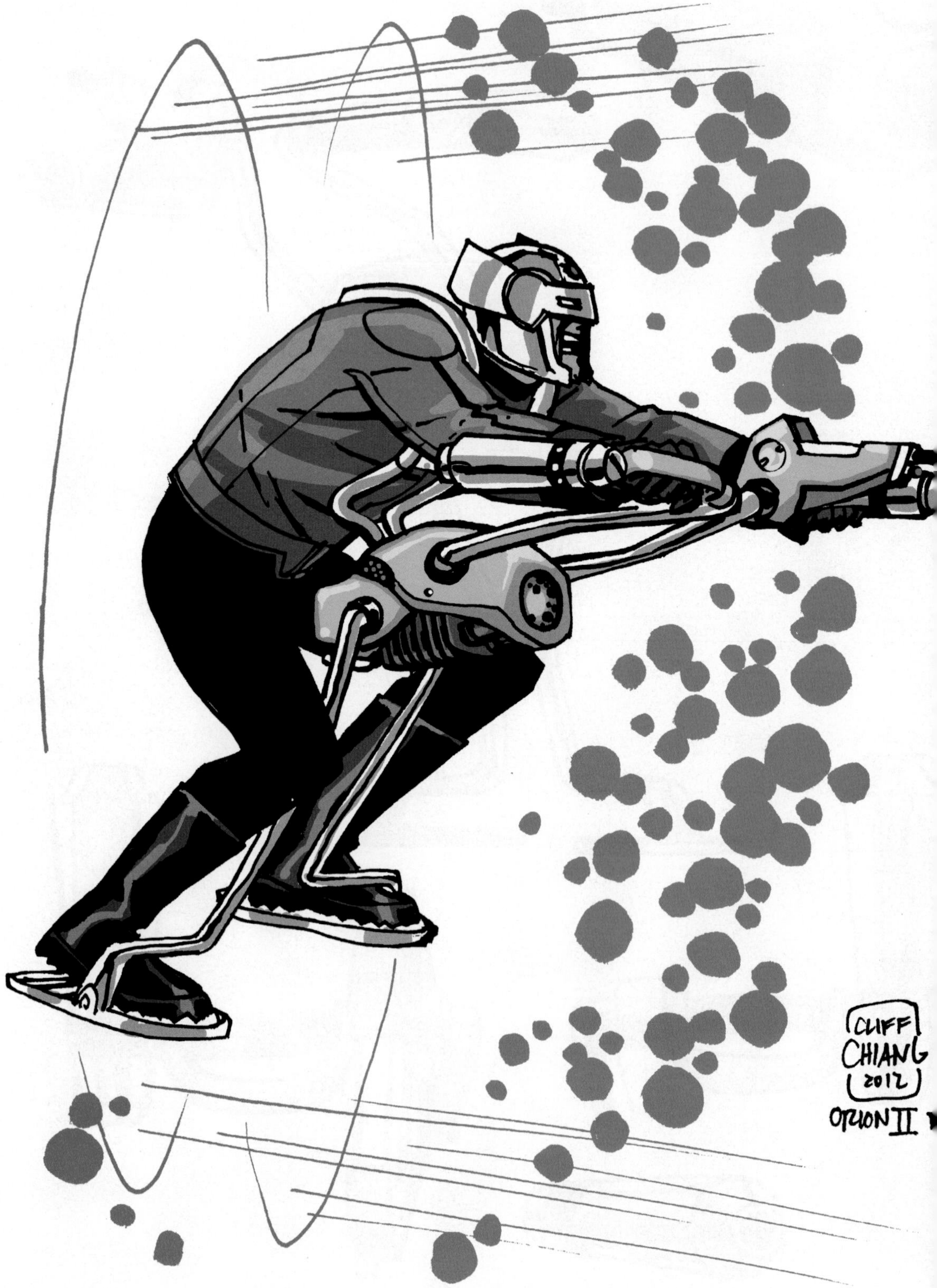
CLIFF
CHIANG
2012
ORION II

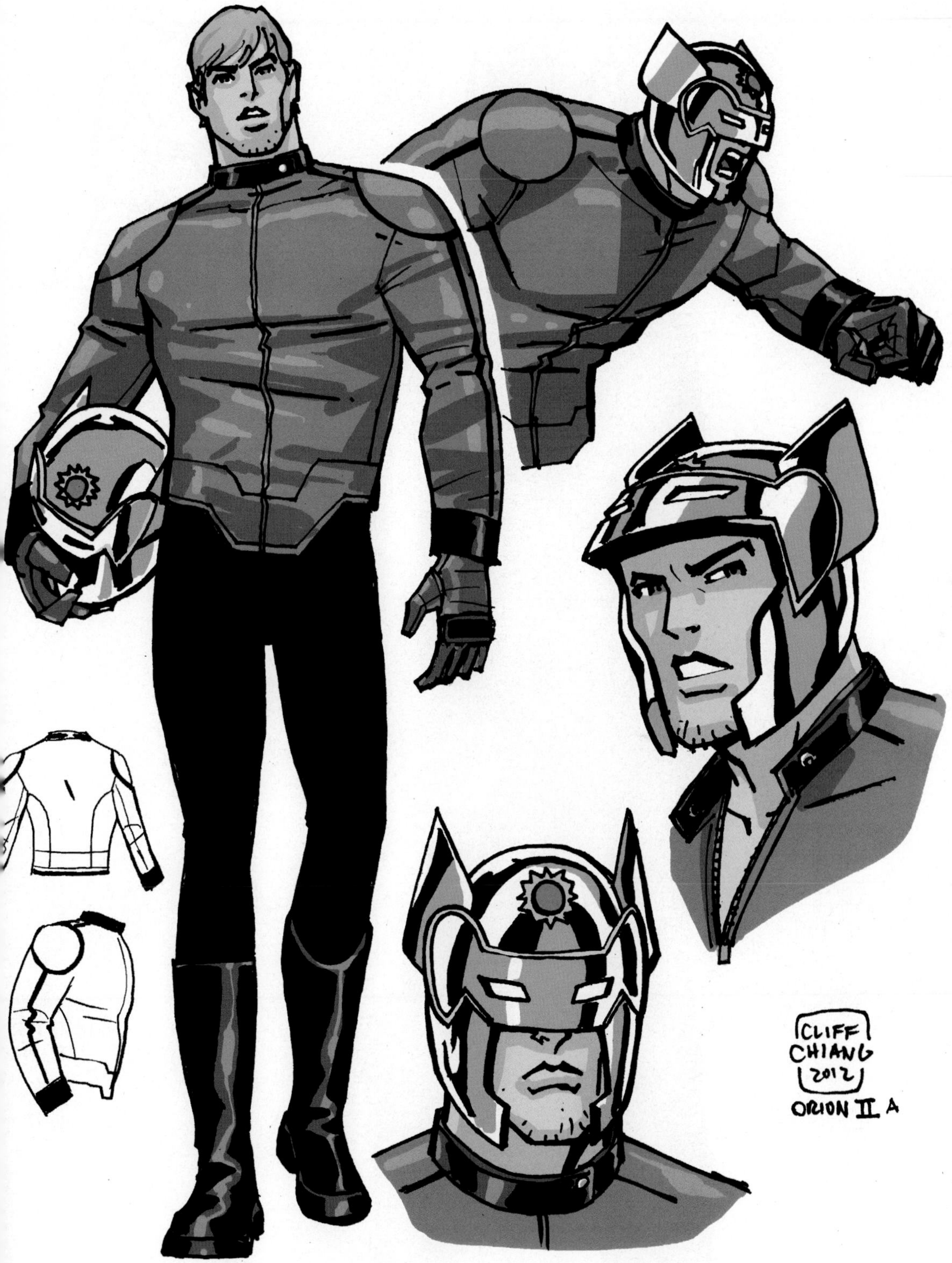
CLIFF
CHIANG
2012
ORION II A

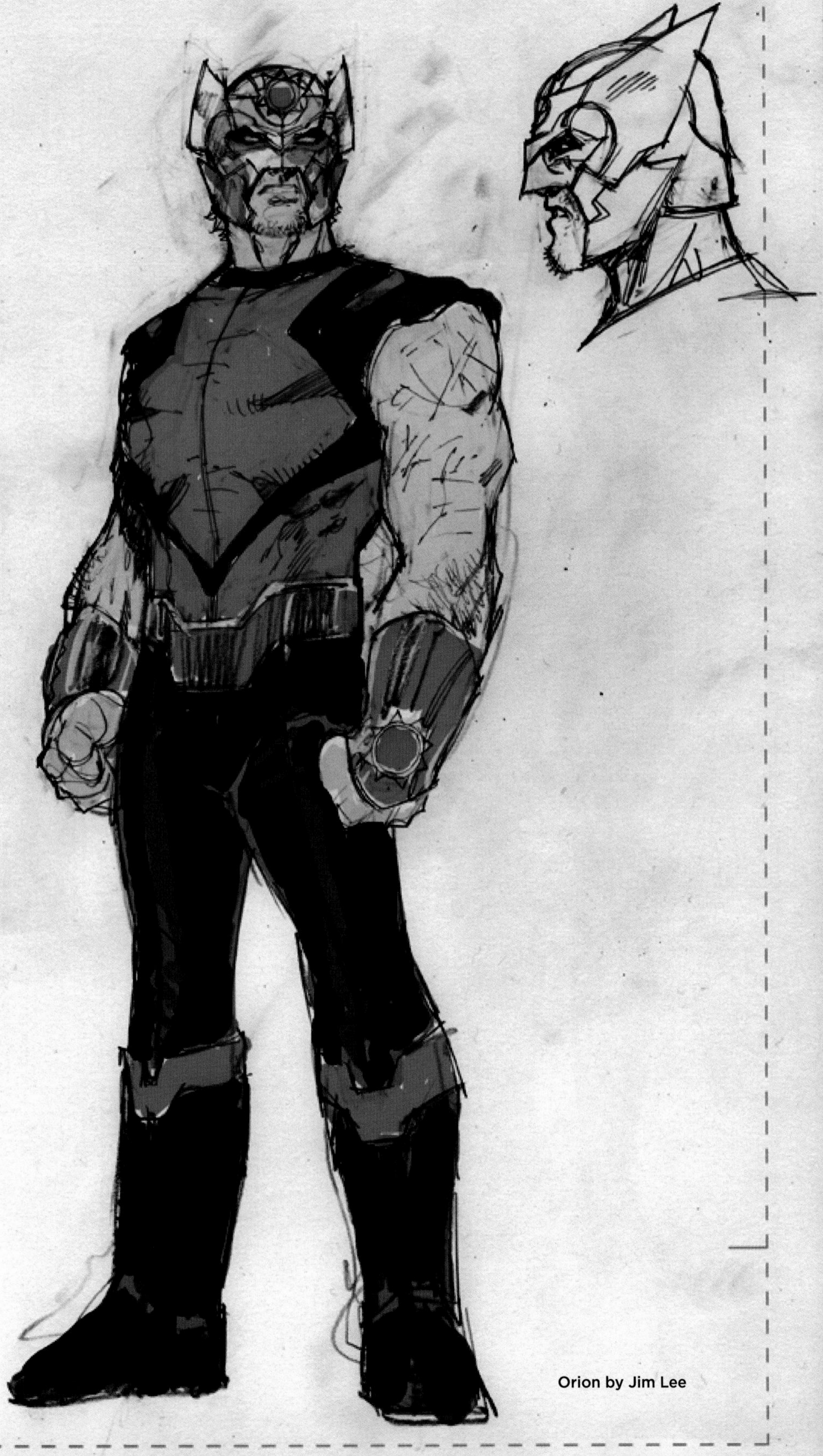

Orion by Jim Lee

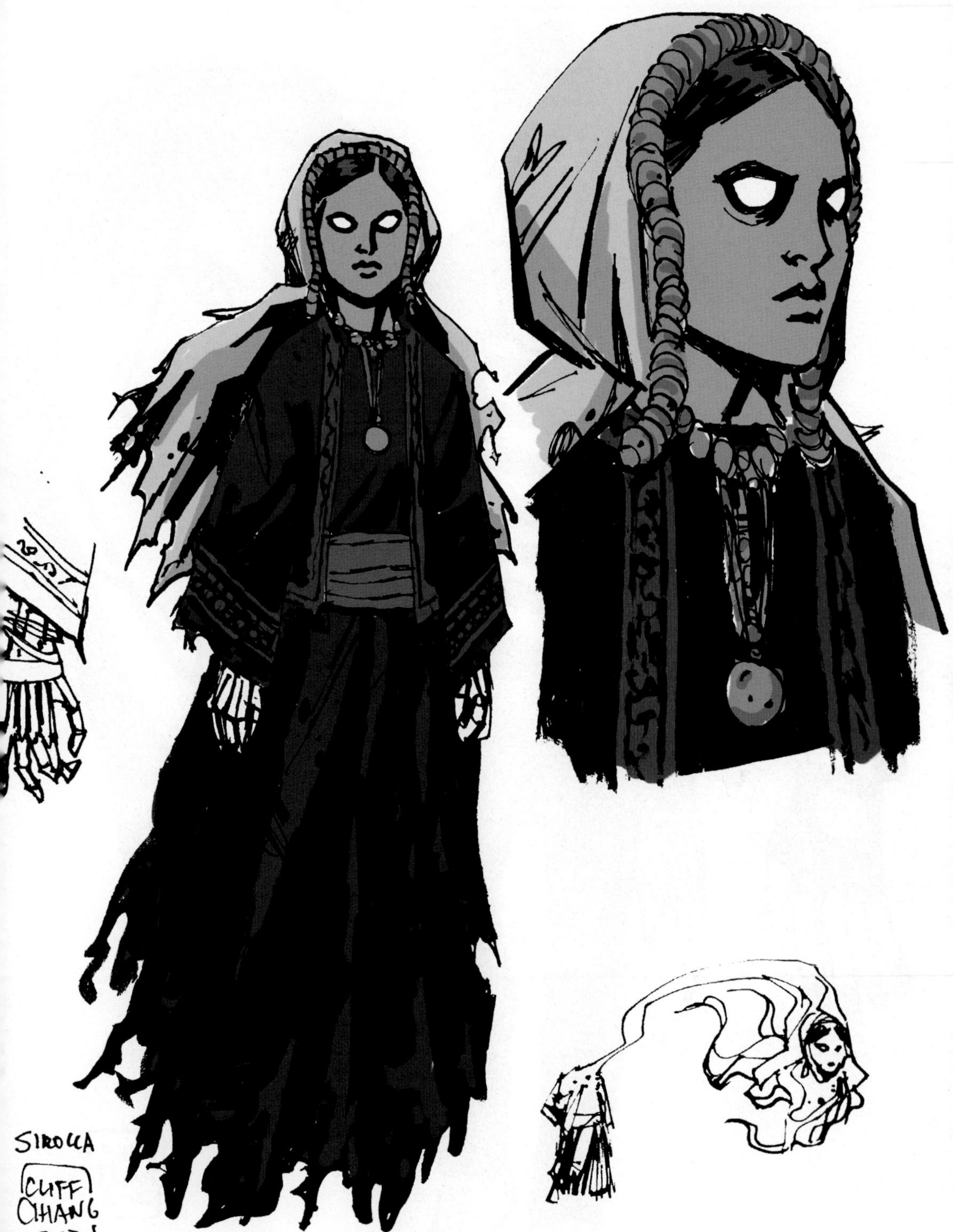
SIROCCA
CLIFF CHIANG 2012

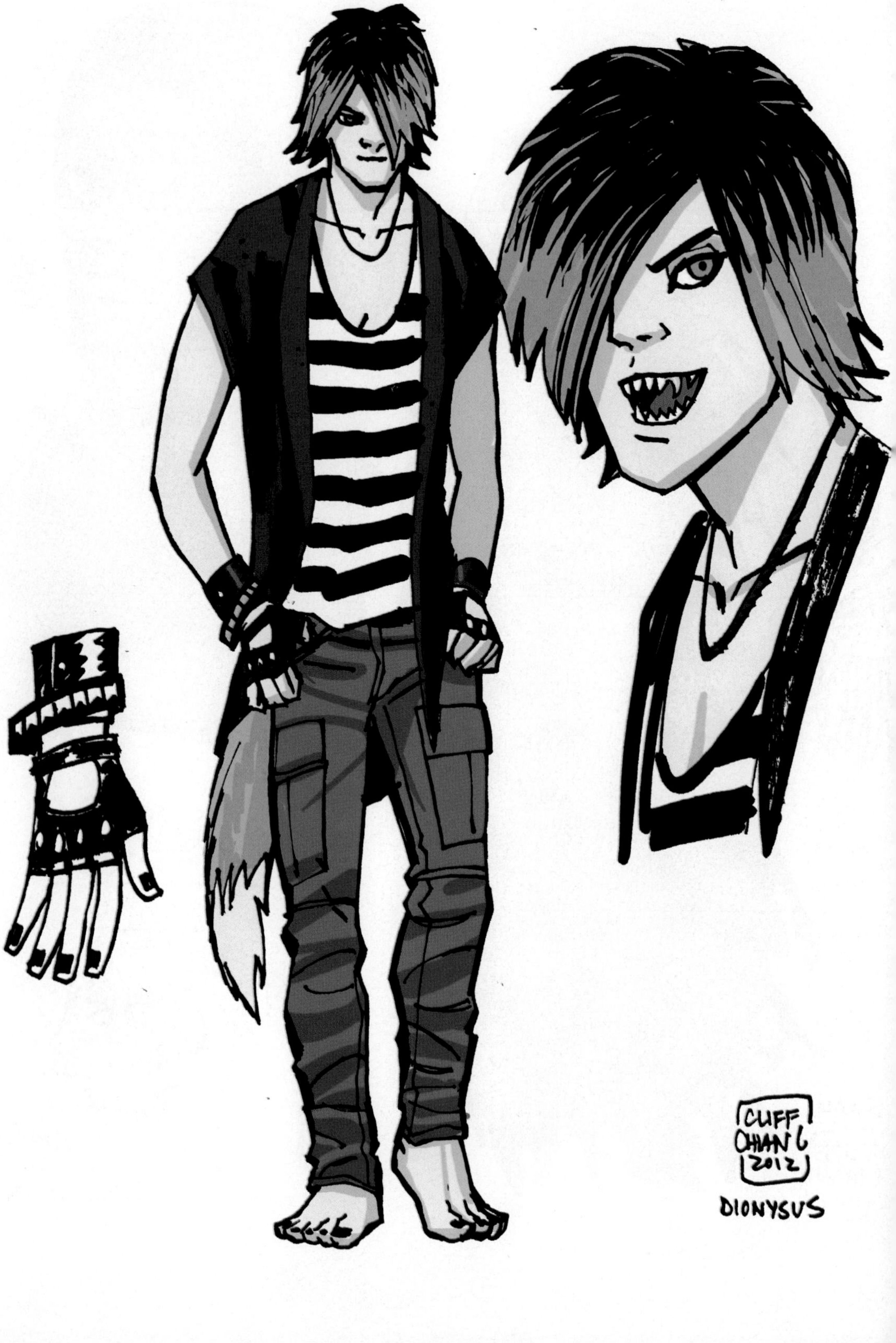
CLIFF CHIANG 2012
DIONYSUS

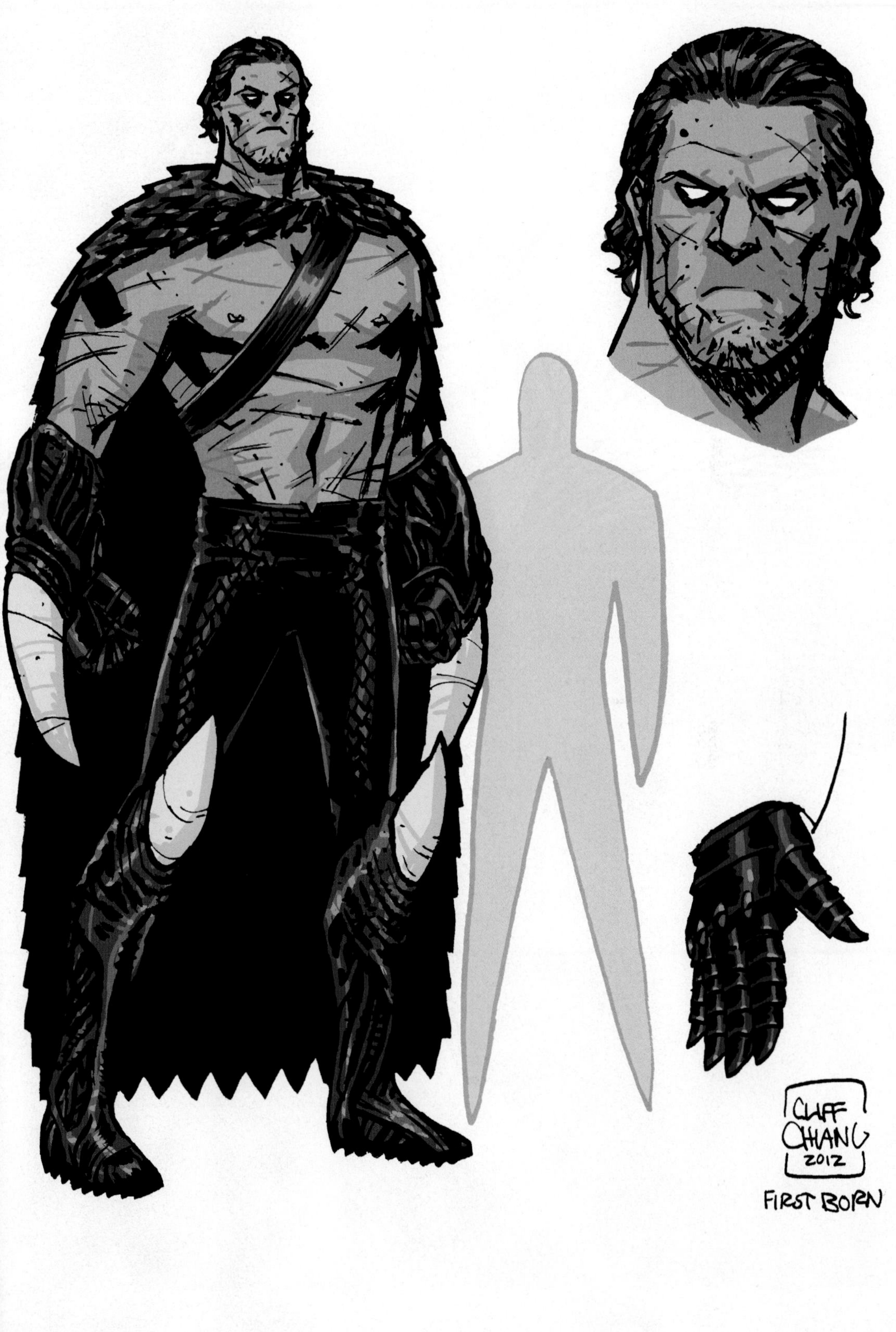
CLIFF CHIANG 2012
FIRST BORN

Issue #0 unused cover by Cliff Chiang

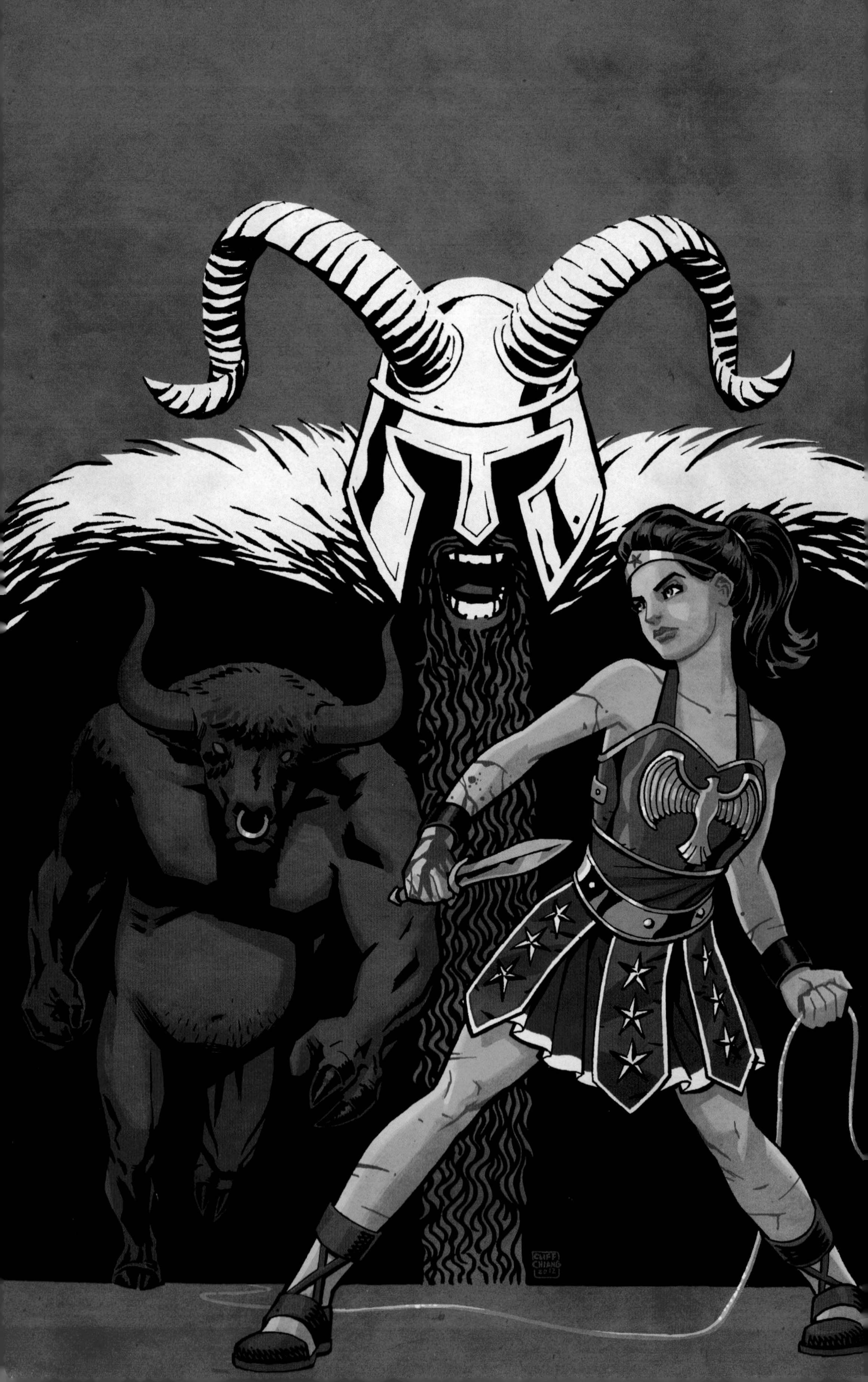
CLIFF CHIANG 2012

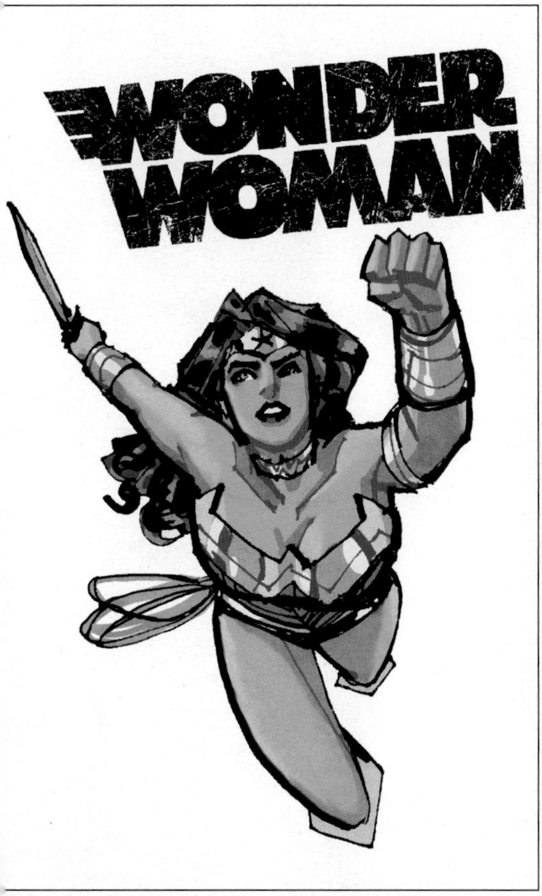
WONDER WOMAN

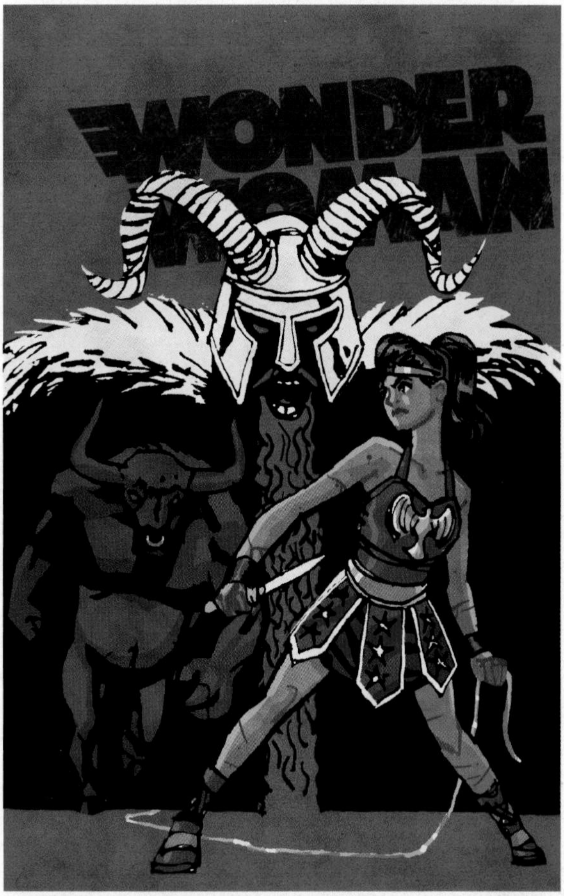
WONDER WOMAN

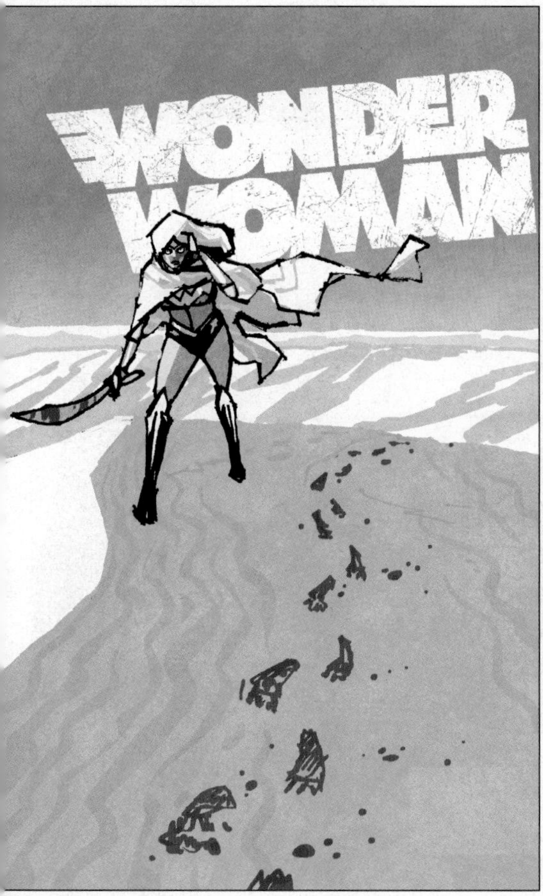
WONDER WOMAN

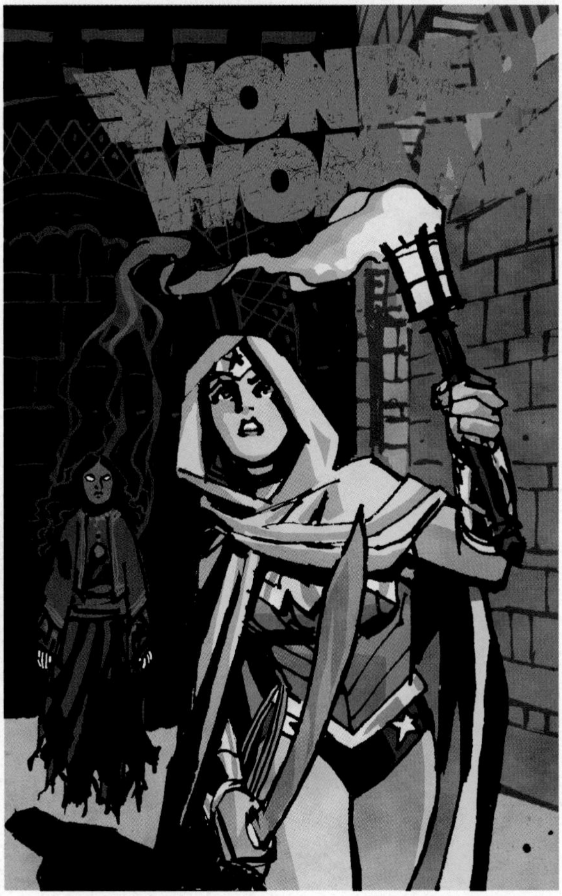
WONDER WOMAN

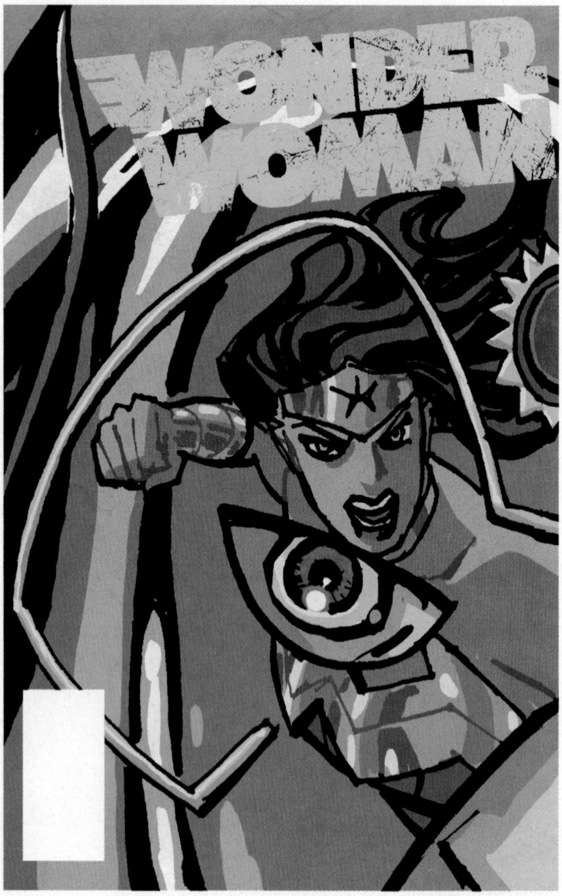
WONDER
WOMAN

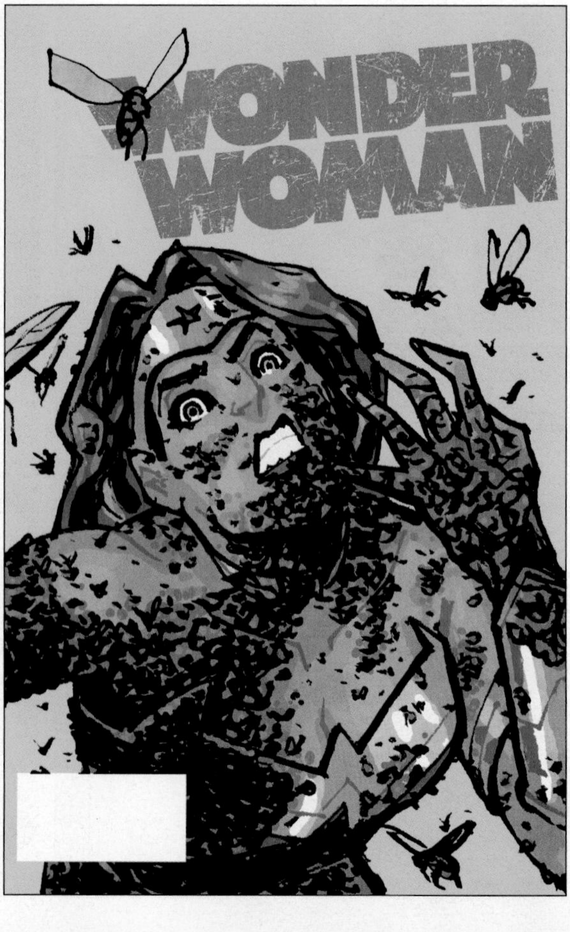
WONDER
WOMAN

WONDER
WOMAN

WONDER
WOMAN

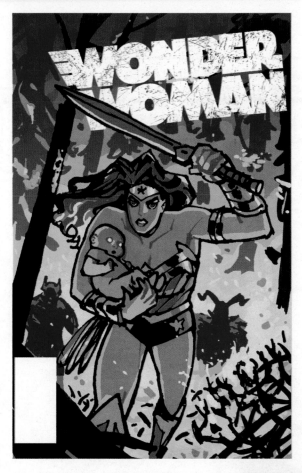

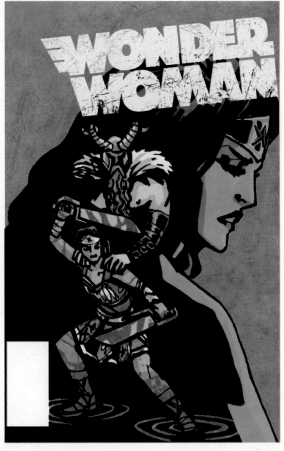

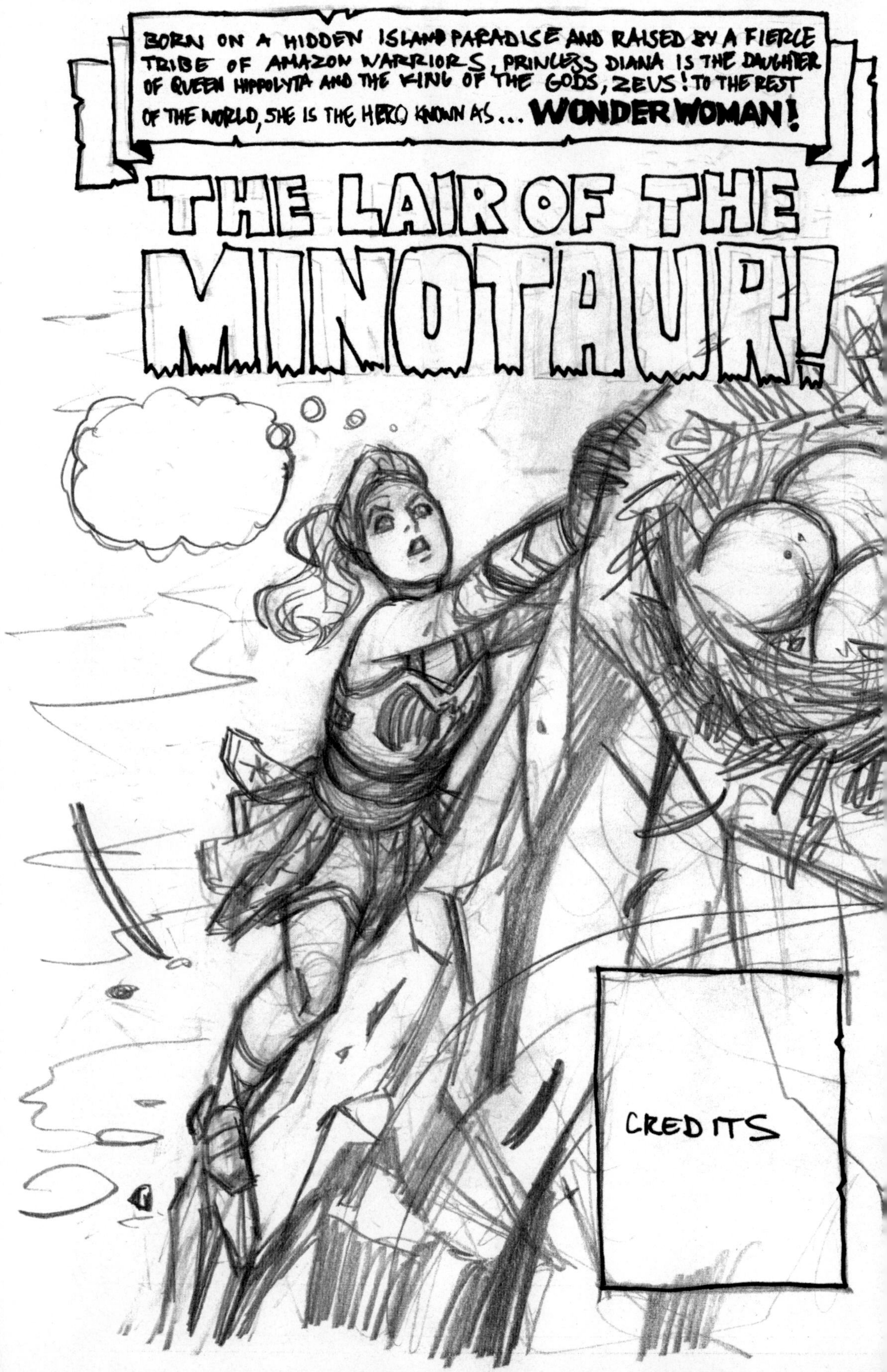
BORN ON A HIDDEN ISLAND PARADISE AND RAISED BY A FIERCE TRIBE OF AMAZON WARRIORS, PRINCESS DIANA IS THE DAUGHTER OF QUEEN HIPPOLYTA AND THE KING OF THE GODS, ZEUS! TO THE REST OF THE WORLD, SHE IS THE HERO KNOWN AS... WONDER WOMAN!
THE LAIR OF THE MINOTAUR!
CREDITS

WONDER WOMAN #0
PLOT BY BRIAN AZZARELLO

WONDER WOMAN #0 - "LAIR OF THE MINOTAUR!"

PAGE 1- Splash, natch.
We open with young Diana scaling a sheer cliff. The wind buffets her. She's climbing towards a nest — one with eggs in it. Below her, the crashing surf. It's daytime.

PAGES 2-3
Reaching the nest, she grabs one of the eggs. Suddenly, a Harpy comes swooping down at her. Holy crap — those are harpy eggs! Diana avoids the sharp talons, then dives off the nest, cradling the egg. She plummets down off the cliff. Just before the harpy can reach her, Diana rolls and hits the water. Under the water, Diana swims towards a cave. Surfacing in the cave, She is met by her mother and a party of Amazon warriors. The cave is lit only by their torches. There is great rejoicing when she presents her mother with the harpy egg — a gift to commemorate her fourteenth birthday. A bottle of mead is raised in Diana's honor; she will make a fine Amazon. In the dark of the cave, Ares watches. This one... she is special.

PAGES 4-5
Later that night, Themyscira celebrates Diana's birthday with jousting games — much like from Issue #2. Of course Diana is taking part. A young Aleka taunts her, calling her Clay. As they joust, Diana is consumed by thoughts; she is not like her sisters, and she wishes she was. She bests Aleka — and almost goes too far, nearly killing her before Hippolyta puts a stop to it. Realizing what she did, Diana runs off into the forest.

PAGE 6

In the forest she again wonders why she must be different. Ares appears, and answers her question. It is a gift to be different, and he offers to show her how. A brave Diana accepts. Ares tells her to meet him here in the forest each full moon, and he will train her to be a warrior. A white owl watches from the trees...

PAGES 7-8

Montage pages, Ares training Diana in combat, showing her the world, taking her to his weapon room, which is loaded with weapons from many eras (including a Mother Box — very important). The moon is always full in the night sky. Also interspersed is her training with other Amazons — and getting the better of them. Both Hippolyta and Ares smile (different panels, or Ares ghostly — they never see each other.) A year goes by.

PAGE 9

Another training page. They are jousting. Ares shows Diana that a clever warrior knows how to use an enemy's weapon against them. When she thrusts at him, he grabs her arm, and turns her blade on herself. She though, turns it on him; she's managed to rope his ankle with her lasso, and pulls his leg out from under him. Very good, little one, very good. I believe next moon, you are ready for a test.

PAGE 10

Okay, how about another Splash? Ares stands behind a cocky and brave Diana, one hand on her shoulder, the other outstretched before them. She holds her dagger and her lasso. Ares tells her that all she's learned will be put to a great test...

PAGE 11

Reverse POV. "Behold, the lair of the Minotaur, the most fearsome beast known to man or God! It is in this maze that you will prove yourself as a warrior." "I will make you proud, War." "I don't doubt you, little one." Diana heads into the maze.

PAGES 12-13

Diana in the maze. Her thoughts are about making Ares proud of her. She comes across human bones, armor, and weapons — the maze is littered with them. She unfurls her lasso, so she can find her way out. The Minotaur stalks her, following her lasso, maybe? Diana hears something behind her. She turns...

PAGES 14-16

The Minotaur comes charging. The battle is on, and it's hard one for Diana. The Minotaur is all brute force, and it's tough for Diana to mount any offense. Luckily, she remembers her last training session with Ares, "Use your enemy's weapon against them." Diana gets some distance between her and the Minotaur, and backs up against a wall. The beast charges her. Just before it hits, she catapults herself out of the way. The Minotaur runs head down into the wall. It's dazed. Using her hand-to-hand combat training, Diana topples the Minotaur.

PAGE 17

As Diana stands over the struggling beast, Ares appears and hands Diana a sword. "Finish the job. Its head will make a fitting tribute to your mother on this, the day that marks your fifteenth season, my warrior." Diana raises the sword... "Do it!" The Minotaur crawls... "Kill him, little one!" She drops the sword. "I won't kill in cold blood."

PAGE 18

Ares is disgusted with Diana, saying she's not a true warrior — she's failed to see that a dangerous enemy must be killed, because it will come back to haunt — maybe even kill her. He goes on, "I was wrong about you. You are no warrior." She runs to him, begging forgiveness. Ares slaps her away. "You are no student of mine." He disappears.

PAGE 19

The Minotaur rises. Diana struggles to her feet. The beast looks at her, then turns back down a tunnel. It proves Ares wrong.

PAGE 20

Diana exits the maze, as the sun rises. She feels good about herself, yet wonders what the future holds. She knows, though, that their paths will cross again.

END

START AT THE BEGINNING!

WONDER WOMAN VOLUME 1: BLOOD

MR. TERRIFIC VOLUME 1: MIND GAMES

BLUE BEETLE VOLUME 1: METAMORPHOSIS

THE FURY OF FIRESTORM: THE NUCLEAR MEN VOLUME 1: GOD PARTICLE

BRIAN **AZZARELLO** CLIFF **CHIANG** TONY **AKINS**